Programming the Perl DBI

Programming the Perl DBI

Alligator Descartes and Tim Bunce

O'REILLY®

Beijing · Cambridge · Farnham · Köln · Paris · Sebastopol · Taipei · Tokyo

Programming the Perl DBI
by Alligator Descartes and Tim Bunce

Copyright © 2000 O'Reilly & Associates, Inc. All rights reserved.
Printed in the United States of America.

Published by O'Reilly & Associates, Inc., 101 Morris Street, Sebastopol, CA 95472.

Editor: Linda Mui

Production Editor: Nicole Arigo

Cover Designer: Hanna Dyer

Printing History:

February 2000:   First Edition.

Library of Congress Cataloging-in-Publication Data

Descartes, Alligator.
  Programming the Perl DBI / Alligator Descartes and Tim Bunce.
    p. cm.
  ISBN 1-56592-699-4

    1. Perl (Computer program language) 2. Database management. I. Bunce, Tim. II. Title.

QA76.73.P22 D47 2000
005.74--dc21

                                                            00-022023

ISBN: 1-56592-699-4   [3/00]

[M]

To Máire.

To Carolyn.

Table of Contents

Preface

The DBI is the standard database interface for the Perl programming language. The DBI is database-independent, which means that it can work with just about any database, such as Oracle, Sybase, Informix, Access, MySQL, etc.

While we assume that readers of this book have some experience with Perl, we don't assume much familiarity with databases themselves. The book starts out slowly, describing different types of databases and introducing the reader to common terminology.

This book is not solely about the DBI—it also concerns the more general subject of storing data in and retrieving data from databases of various forms. As such, this book is split into two related, but standalone, parts. The first part covers techniques for storing and retrieving data without the DBI, and the second, much larger part, covers the use of the DBI and related technologies.

Throughout the book, we assume that you have a basic grounding in programming with Perl and can put together simple scripts without instruction. If you don't have this level of Perl awareness, we suggest that you read some of the Perl books listed in the "Resources" section of this Preface.

Once you're ready to read this book, there are some shortcuts that you can take depending on what you're most interested in reading about. If you are interested solely in the DBI, you can skip Chapter 2 without too much of a problem. On the other hand, if you're a wizard with SQL, then you should probably skip Chapter 3 to avoid the pain of us glossing over many fine details. Chapter 7 is a comparison between the DBI and ODBC and is mainly of interest to database geeks, design aficionados, and those people who have `Win32::ODBC` applications and are desperately trying to port them to DBI.

Here's a rundown of the book, chapter by chapter:

Chapter 1, *Introduction*
> This introduction sets up the general feel for the book.

Chapter 2, *Basic Non-DBI Databases*
> This chapter covers the basics of storing and retrieving data either with core Perl functions through the use of delimited or fixed-width flat-file databases, or via non-DBI modules such as `AnyDBM_File`, `Storable`, `Data::Dumper` and friends. Although the DBI isn't used in this chapter, the way the `Storable` and `Data::Dumper` modules are used to pack Perl data structures into strings can easily be applied to the DBI.

Chapter 3, *SQL and Relational Databases*
> This chapter is a basic overview of SQL and relational databases and how you can write simple but powerful SQL statements to query and manipulate your database. If you already know some SQL, you can skip this chapter. If you don't know SQL, we advise you to read this chapter since the later chapters assume you have a basic knowledge of SQL and relational databases.

Chapter 4, *Programming with the DBI*
> This chapter introduces the DBI to you by discussing the architecture of the DBI and basic DBI operations such as connecting to databases and handling errors. This chapter is essential reading and describes the framework that the DBI provides to let you write simple, powerful, and robust programs.

Chapter 5, *Interacting with the Database*
> This chapter is the meat of the DBI topic and discusses manipulating the data within your database—that is, retrieving data already stored in your database, inserting new data, and deleting and updating existing data. We discuss the various ways in which you can perform these operations from the simple "get it working" stage to more advanced and optimized techniques for manipulating data.

Chapter 6, *Advanced DBI*
> This chapter covers more advanced topics within the sphere of the DBI such as specifying attributes to fine-tune the operation of DBI within your applications, working with LONG/LOB datatypes, statement and database metadata, and finally transaction handling.

Chapter 7, *ODBC and the DBI*
> This chapter discusses the differences in design between DBI and ODBC, the other portable database API. And, of course, this chapter highlights why DBI is easier to program with.

Chapter 8, *DBI Shell and Database Proxying*
> This chapter covers two topics that aren't exactly part of the core DBI, per se, but are extremely useful to know about. First, we discuss the DBI shell, a

command-line tool that allows you to connect to databases and issue arbitrary queries. Second, we discuss the proxy architecture that the DBI can use, which, among other things, allows you to connect scripts on one machine to databases on another machine without needing to install any database networking software. For example, you can connect a script running on a Unix box to a Microsoft Access database running on an Microsoft Windows box.

Appendix A, *DBI Specification*

This appendix contains the DBI specification, which is distributed with `DBI.pm`.

Appendix B, *Driver and Database Characteristics*

This appendix contains useful extra information on each of the commonly used DBDs and their corresponding databases.

Appendix C, *ASLaN Sacred Site Charter*

This appendix contains the charter for the Ancient Sacred Landscape Network, which focuses on preserving sites such as the megalithic sites used for examples in this book.

Resources

To help you navigate some of the topics in this book, here are some resources that you might want to check out before, during, and after reading this book:

http://www.symbolstone.org/technology/perl/DBI

The DBI home page. This site contains lots of useful information about DBI and where to get the various modules from. It also has links to the very active *dbi-users* mailing list and archives.

http://www.perl.com/CPAN

This site includes the Comprehensive Perl Archive Network multiplexer, upon which you find a whole host of useful modules including the DBI.

An Introduction to Database Systems, by C. J. Date

This book is the standard textbook on database systems and is highly recommended reading.

A Guide to the SQL Standard, by C. J. Date and Hugh Darwen

An excellent book that's detailed but small and very readable.

http://w3.one.net/~jhoffman/sqltut.htm
http://www.jcc.com/SQLPages/jccs_sql.htm
http://www.contrib.andrew.cmu.edu/~shadow/sql.html

These web sites contain information, specifications, and links on the SQL query language, of which we present a primer in Chapter 3. Further information can be found by entering "SQL tutorial" or similar expressions into your favorite web search engine.

Learning Perl, by Randal Schwartz and Tom Christiansen

A hands-on tutorial designed to get you writing useful Perl scripts as quickly as possible. Exercises (with complete solutions) accompany each chapter. A lengthy new chapter introduces you to CGI programming, while touching also on the use of library modules, references, and Perl's object-oriented constructs.

Programming Perl, by Larry Wall, Tom Christiansen, and Randal Schwartz

The authoritative guide to Perl version 5, the scripting utility that has established itself as the programming tool of choice for the World Wide Web, Unix system administration, and a vast range of other applications. Version 5 of Perl includes object-oriented programming facilities. The book is coauthored by Larry Wall, the creator of Perl.

The Perl Cookbook, by Tom Christiansen and Nathan Torkington

A comprehensive collection of problems, solutions, and practical examples for anyone programming in Perl. Topics range from beginner questions to techniques that even the most experienced of Perl programmers will learn from. More than just a collection of tips and tricks, *The Perl Cookbook* is the long-awaited companion volume to *Programming Perl*, filled with previously unpublished Perl arcana.

Writing Apache Modules with Perl and C, by Lincoln Stein and Doug MacEachern

This book teaches you how to extend the capabilities of your Apache web server regardless of whether you use Perl or C as your programming language. The book explains the design of Apache, mod_perl, and the Apache API. From a DBI perspective, it discusses the `Apache::DBI` module, which provides advanced DBI functionality in relation to web services such as persistent connection pooling optimized for serving databases over the Web.

Boutell FAQ (http://www.boutell.com/faq/) and others

These links are invaluable to you if you want to deploy DBI-driven web sites. They explain the dos and don'ts of CGI programming in general.

MySQL & mSQL, by Randy Jay Yarger, George Reese, and Tim King

For users of the MySQL and mSQL databases, this is a very useful book. It covers not only the databases themselves but also the DBI drivers and other useful topics like CGI programming.

Typographical Conventions

The following font conventions are used in this book:

`Constant Width`

is used for method names, function names, variables, and attributes. It is also used for code examples.

Italic

　　　is used for filenames, URLs, hostnames, and emphasis.

How to Contact Us

We have tested and verified all the information in this book to the best of our abilities, but you may find that features have changed or that we have let errors slip through the production of the book. Please let us know of any errors that you find, as well as suggestions for future editions, by writing to:

　　　O'Reilly & Associates, Inc.
　　　101 Morris St.
　　　Sebastopol, CA 95472
　　　1-800-998-9938 (in the U.S. or Canada)
　　　1-707-829-0515 (international/local)
　　　1-707-829-0104 (fax)

You can also send messages electronically. To be put on our mailing list or to request a catalog, send email to:

　　　info@oreilly.com

To ask technical questions or to comment on the book, send email to:

　　　bookquestions@oreilly.com

We have a web site for the book, where we'll list examples, errata, and any plans for future editions. You can access this page at:

　　　http://www.oreilly.com/catalog/perldbi/

For more information about this book and others, see the O'Reilly web site:

　　　http://www.oreilly.com

Code Examples

You are invited to copy the code in the book and adapt it for your own needs. Rather than copying by hand, however, we encourage you to download the code from *http://www.oreilly.com/catalog/perldbi/*.

Acknowledgments

Alligator would like to thank his wife, Carolyn, for putting up with his authorial melodramatics and flouncing during the writing of this book. Martin McCarthy should also get his name in lights for proofreading far too many of the early drafts of the book. Phil Kizer also deserves a credit for running the servers that the DBI web site has sat on between 1995 and early 1999. Karin and John Attwood, Andy Burnham, Andy Norfolk, Chris Tweed, and many others on the *stones* mailing list deserve thanks (and beer) for aiding the preservation and presentation of many of the megalithic sites around the UK. Further thanks to the people behind ASLaN for volunteering to do a difficult job, and doing it well.

Linda Mui definitely deserves an O'Reilly bag and pair of old sunglasses for her fabulous editing job, and, last but not least, thanks to Tim for making the book far better than it would have been had I written it alone.

Tim would like to thank his wife, Máire, for being his wife; Larry Wall for giving the world Perl; Ted Lemon for having the idea that was, many years later, to become the DBI, and for running the mailing list for many of those years. Thanks also to Tim O'Reilly for nagging me to write a DBI book, to Alligator for actually starting to do it and then letting me jump on board (and putting up with my pedantic tendencies), and to Linda Mui for being a great editor.

The DBI has a *long* history[*] and countless people have contributed to the discussions and development over the years. First, we'd like to thank the early pioneeers including Kevin Stock, Buzz Moschetti, Kurt Andersen, William Hails, Garth Kennedy, Michael Peppler, Neil Briscoe, David Hughes, Jeff Stander, and Forrest D. Whitcher.

Then, of course, there are the poor souls who have struggled through untold and undocumented obstacles to actually implement DBI drivers. Among their ranks are Jochen Wiedmann, Jonathan Leffler, Jeff Urlwin, Michael Peppler, Henrik Tougaard, Edwin Pratomo, Davide Migliavacca, Jan Pazdziora, Peter Haworth, Edmund Mergl, Steve Williams, Thomas Lowery, and Phlip Plumlee. Without them, the DBI would not be the practical reality it is today.

We would both like to thank the many reviewers to gave us valuable feedback. Special thanks to Matthew Persico, Nathan Torkington, Jeff Rowe, Denis Goddard, Honza Pazdziora, Rich Miller, Niamh Kennedy, Randal Schwartz, and Jeffrey Baker.

---

[*] It all started on September 29, 1992.

1

Introduction

The subject of databases is a large and complex one, spanning many different concepts of structure, form, and expected use. There are also a multitude of different ways to access and manipulate the data stored within these databases.

This book describes and explains an interface called the Perl Database Interface, or DBI, which provides a unified interface for accessing data stored within many of these diverse database systems. The DBI allows you to write Perl code that accesses data without needing to worry about database- or platform-specific issues or proprietary interfaces.

We also take a look at non-DBI ways of storing, retrieving, and manipulating data with Perl, as there are occasions when the use of a database might be considered overkill but some form of structured data storage is required.

To begin, we shall discuss some of the more common uses of database systems in business today and the place that Perl and DBI takes within these frameworks.

From Mainframes to Workstations

In today's computing climate, databases are everywhere. In previous years, they tended to be used almost exclusively in the realm of mainframe-processing environments. Nowadays, with pizza-box sized machines more powerful than room-sized machines of ten years ago, high-performance database processing is available to anyone.

In addition to cheaper and more powerful computer hardware, smaller database packages have become available, such as Microsoft Access and mSQL. These packages give all computer users the ability to use powerful database technology in their everyday lives.

The corporate workplace has also seen a dramatic decentralization in database resources, with radical downsizing operations in some companies leading to their centralized mainframe database systems being replaced with a mixture of smaller databases distributed across workstations and PCs. The result is that developers and users are often responsible for the administration and maintenance of their own databases and datasets.

This trend towards mixing and matching database technology has some important downsides. Having replaced a centralized database with a cluster of workstations and multiple database types, companies are now faced with hiring skilled administration staff or training their existing administration staff for new skills. In addition, administrators now need to learn how to glue different databases together.

It is in this climate that a new order of software engineering has evolved, namely *database-independent* programming interfaces. If you thought administration staff had problems with downsizing database technology, developers may have been hit even harder.

A centralized mainframe environment implies that database software is written in a standard language, perhaps COBOL or C, and runs only on one machine. However, a distributed environment may support multiple databases on different operating systems and processors, with each development team choosing their preferred development environment (such as Visual Basic, PowerBuilder, Oracle Pro*C, Informix E/SQL, C++ code with ODBC—the list is almost endless). Therefore, the task of coordinating and porting software has rapidly gone from being relatively straightforward to extremely difficult.

Database-independent programming interfaces help these poor, beleagured developers by giving them a single, unified interface with which they can program. This shields the developer from having to know which database type they are working with, and allows software written for one database type to be ported far more easily to another database. For example, software originally written for a mainframe database will often run with little modification on Oracle databases. Software written for Informix will generally work on Oracle with little modification. And software written for Microsoft Access will usually run with little modification on Sybase databases.

If you couple this database-independent programming interface with a programming language such as Perl, which is operating-system neutral, you are faced with the prospect of having a single code-base once again. This is just like in the old days, but with one major difference—you are now fully harnessing the power of the distributed database environment.

Database-independent programming interfaces help not only development staff. Administrators can also use them to write database-monitoring and administration software quickly and portably, increasing their own efficiency and the efficiency of the systems and databases they are responsible for monitoring. This process can only result in better-tuned systems with higher availability, freeing up the administration staff to proactively maintain the systems they are responsible for.

Another aspect of today's corporate database lifestyle revolves around the idea of *data warehousing,* that is, creating and building vast repositories of archived infor mation that can be scanned, or *mined,* for information separately from online databases. Powerful high-level languages with database-independent programming interfaces (such as Perl) are becoming more prominent in the construction and maintenance of data warehouses. This is due not only to their ability to transfer data from database to database seamlessly, but also to their ability to scan, order, convert, and process this information efficiently.

In summary, databases are becoming more and more prominent in the corporate landscape, and powerful interfaces are required to stop these resources from flying apart and becoming disparate fragments of localized data. This glueing process can be aided by the use of database-independent programming interfaces, such as the DBI, especially when used in conjunction with efficient high-level data-processing languages such as Perl.

Perl

Perl is a very high-level programming language originally developed in the 1980s by Larry Wall. Perl is now being developed by a group of individuals known as the Perl5-Porters under the watchful eye of Larry. One of Perl's many strengths is its ability to process arbitrary chunks of textual data, known as *strings,* in many powerful ways, including regular-expression string manipulation. This capability makes Perl an excellent choice for database programming, since the majority of information stored within databases is textual in nature. Perl takes the pain of manipulating strings out of programming, unlike C, which is not well-suited for that task. Perl scripts tend to be far smaller than equivalent C programs and are generally portable to other operating systems that run Perl with little or no modification.

Perl also now features the ability to dynamically load external *modules,* which are pieces of software that can be slotted into Perl to extend and enhance its functionality. There are literally hundreds of these modules available now, ranging from mathematical modules to three-dimensional graphics-rendering modules to modules that allow you to interact with networks and network software. The DBI is a set of modules for Perl that allows you to interact with databases.

In recent years, Perl has become a standard within many companies by just being immensely useful for many different applications, the "Swiss army knife of programming languages." It has been heavily used by system administrators who like its flexibility and usefulness for almost any job they can think of. When used in conjunction with DBI, Perl makes loading and dumping databases very straightforward, and its excellent data-manipulation capabilities allow developers to create and manipulate data easily.

Furthermore, Perl has been tacitly accepted as being the de facto language on the World Wide Web for writing CGI programs. What's this got to do with databases? Using Perl and DBI, you can quickly deploy powerful CGI scripts that generate dynamic web pages from the data contained within your databases. For example, online shopping catalogs can be stored within a database and presented to shoppers as a series of dynamically created web pages. The sample code for this book revolves around a database of archaeological sites that you can deploy on the Web.

Bolstered by this proof of concept, and the emergence of new and powerful modules such as the DBI and the rapid GUI development toolkit Tk, major corporations are now looking towards Perl to provide rapid development capabilities for building fast, robust, and portable applications to be deployed within corporate intranets and on the Internet.

DBI in the Real World

DBI is being used in many companies across the world today, including large-scale, mission-critical environments such as NASA and Motorola. Consider the following testimonials by avid DBI users from around the world:

> We developed and support a large scale telephone call logging and analysis system for a major client of ours. The system collects ~1 GB of call data per day from over 1,200,000 monitored phone numbers. ~424 GB has been processed so far (over 6,200,000,000 calls). Data is processed and loaded into Oracle using DBI and DBD::Oracle. The database holds rolling data for around 20 million calls. The system generates over 44,000 PostScript very high quality reports per month (~five pages with eleven color graphs and five tables) generated by using Perl to manipulate FrameMaker templates. [Values correct as of July 1999, and rising steadily.]

> The whole system runs on three dual processor Sun SPARC Ultra 2 machines—one for data acquisition and processing, one for Oracle and the third does most of the report production (which is also distributed across the other two machines). Almost the entire system is implemented in Perl.

> There is only one non-Perl program and that's only because it existed already and isn't specific to this system. The other non-Perl code is a few small libraries linked into Perl using the XS interface.

> A quote from a project summary by a senior manager: "Less than a year later the service went live. This was subsequently celebrated as one of the fastest projects of its size and complexity to go from conception to launch."

Designed, developed, implemented, installed, and supported by the Paul Ingram Group, who received a "Rising to the Challenge" award for their part in the project. Without Perl, the system could not have been developed fast enough to meet the demanding go-live date. And without Perl, the system could not be so easily maintained or so quickly extended to meet changing requirements.

—Tim Bunce, Paul Ingram Group

In 1997 I built a system for NASA's Langley Research Center in Virginia that puts a searchable web front end on a database of about 100,000 NASA-owned equipment items. I used Apache, DBI, Informix, WDB, and mod_perl on a Sparc 20. Ran like a charm. They liked it so much they used it to give demos at meetings on reorganizing the wind tunnels! Thing was, every time they showed it to people, I ended up extending the system to add something new, like tracking equipment that was in for repairs, or displaying GIFs of technical equipment so when they lost the spec sheet, they could look it up online. When it works, success feeds on itself.

—Jeff Rowe

I'm working on a system implemented using Perl, DBI, Apache (mod_perl), hosted using RedHat Linux 5.1 and using a lightweight SQL RDBMS called MySQL. The system is for a major multinational holding company, which owns approximately 50 other companies. They have 30,000 employees world-wide who needed a secure system for getting to web-based resources. This first iteration of the Intranet is specified to handle up to forty requests for web objects per second (approximately 200 concurrent users), and runs on a single processor Intel Pentium-Pro with 512 megs of RAM. We develop in Perl using Object-Oriented techniques everywhere. Over the past couple years, we have developed a large reusable library of Perl code. One of our most useful modules builds an Object-Relational wrapper around DBI to allow our application developers to talk to the database using O-O methods to access or change properties of the record. We have saved countless hours and dollars by building on Perl instead of a more proprietary system.

—Jesse Erlbaum

Motorola Commercial Government and Industrial Systems is using Perl with DBI and DBD Oracle as part of web based reporting for significant portions of the manufacturing and distribution organizations. The use of DBI/DBD-Oracle is part of a movement away from Oracle Forms based reporting to a pure web-based reporting platform. Several moderate-sized applications based on DBI are in use, ranging from simple notification distribution applications, dynamic routing of approvals, and significant business applications. While you need a bit more "patience" to develop the web-based applications, to develop user interfaces that look "good", my experience has been that the time to implement DBI-based applications is somewhat shorter than the alternatives. The time to "repair" the DBI/ DBD based programs also seems to be shorter. The software quality of the DBI/ DBD approach has been better, but that may be due to differences in software development methodology.

—Garth Kennedy, Motorola

A Historical Interlude and Standing Stones

Throughout this book, we intersperse examples on relevant topics under discussion. In order to ensure that the examples do not confuse you any more than you may already be confused, let's discuss in advance the data we'll be storing and manipulating in the examples.

Primarily within the UK, but also within other countries around the world, there are many sites of standing stones or *megaliths.** The stones are arranged into rings, rows, or single or paired stones. No one is exactly sure what the purpose or purposes of these monuments are, but there are certainly a plethora of theories ranging from the noncommittal "ritual" use to the more definitive alien landing-pad theory. The most famous and visited of these monuments is Stonehenge, located on Salisbury Plain in the south of England. However, Stonehenge is a unique and atypical megalithic monument.

Part of the lack of understanding about megaliths stems from the fact that these monuments can be up to 5,000 years old. There are simply no records available to us that describe the monuments' purposes or the ritual or rationale behind their erection. However, there are lots of web sites that explore various theories.

The example code shown within this book, and the sample web application we'll also be providing, uses a database containing information on these sites.

---

* From the Greek, meaning "big stone." This can be a misnomer in the case of many sites as the stones comprising the circle might be no larger than one or two feet tall. However, in many extreme cases, such as Stonehenge and Avebury, the "mega" prefix is more than justified.

2

Basic Non-DBI Databases

There are several ways in which databases organize the data contained within them. The most common of these is the *relational database* methodology. Databases that use a relational model are called *Relational Database Management Systems*, or RDBMSs. The most popular database systems nowadays (such as Oracle, Informix, and Sybase) are all relational in design.

But what does "relational" actually mean? A *relational database* is a database that is perceived by the user as a collection of tables, where a *table* is an unordered collection of rows. (Loosely speaking, a *relation* is a just a mathematical term for such a table.) Each row has a fixed number of fields, and each field can store a predefined type of data value, such as an integer, date, or string.

Another type of methodology that is growing in popularity is the *object-oriented* methodology, or OODBMS. With an object-oriented model, everything within the database is treated as an *object* of a certain *class* that has rules defined within itself for manipulating the data it encapsulates. This methodology closely follows that of object-oriented programming languages such as Smalltalk, C++, and Java. However, the DBI does not support any real OODBMS, so for the moment this methodology will not be discussed further.

Finally, there are several simplistic database packages that exist on various operating systems. These simple database packages generally do not feature the more sophisticated functionality that "real" database engines provide. They are, to all intents, only slightly sophisticated file-handling routines, not actually database packages. However, in their defense, they can be extremely fast, and in certain situations the sophisticated functionality that a "real" database system provides is simply an unnecessary overhead.*

---

* A useful list of a wide range of free databases is available from *ftp://ftp.idiom.com/pub/free-databases*.

In this chapter, we'll be exploring some non-DBI databases, ranging from the very simplest of ASCII data files through to disk-based hash files supporting duplicate keys. Along the way, we'll consider concurrent access and locking issues, and some applications for the rather useful `Storable` and `Data::Dumper` modules. (While none of this is strictly about the DBI, we think it'll be useful for many people, and even DBI veterans may pick up a few handy tricks.)

All of these database technologies, from the most complex to the simplest, share two basic attributes. The first is the very definition of the term: a database is a collection of data stored on a computer with varying layers of abstraction sitting on top of it. Each layer of abstraction generally makes the data stored within easier to both organize and access, by separating the request for particular data from the mechanics of getting that data.

The second basic attribute common to all database systems is that they all use Application Programming Interfaces (APIs) to provide access to the data stored within the database. In the case of the simplest databases, the API is simply the file read/write calls provided by the operating system, accessed via your favorite programming language.

An API allows programmers to interact with a more complex piece of software through access paths defined by the original software creators. A good example of this is the Berkeley Database Manager API. In addition to simply accessing the data, the API allows you to alter the structure of the database and the data stored within the database. The benefit of this higher level of access to a database is that you don't need to worry about *how* the Berkeley Database Manager is managing the data. You are manipulating an abstracted view via the API.

In higher-level layers such as those implemented by an RDBMS, the data access and manipulation API is completely divorced from the structure of the database. This separation of logical model from physical representation allows you to write standard database code (e.g., SQL) that is independent of the database engine that you are using.

Storage Managers and Layers

Modern databases, no matter which methodology they implement, are generally composed of multiple layers of software. Each layer implements a higher level of functionality using the interfaces and services defined by the lower-level layers.

For example, flat-file databases are composed of pools of data with very few layers of abstraction. Databases of this type allow you to manipulate the data stored within the database by directly altering the way in which the data is stored within the data files themselves. This feature gives you a lot of power and flexibility at the expense of being difficult to use, minimal in terms of functionality, and nerve-destroying since you have no safety nets. All manipulation of the data files uses the standard Perl file operations, which in turn use the underlying operating system APIs.

DBM file libraries, like Berkeley DB, are an example of a storage manager layer that sits on top of the raw data files and allows you to manipulate the data stored within the database through a clearly defined API. This storage manager translates your API calls into manipulations of the data files on your behalf, preventing you from directly altering the structure of the data in such a manner that it becomes corrupt or unreadable. Manipulating a database via this storage manager is far easier and safer than doing it yourself.

You could potentially implement a more powerful database system on top of DBM files. This new layer would use the DBM API to implement more powerful features and add another layer of abstraction between you and the actual physical data files containing the data.

There are many benefits to using higher-level storage managers. The levels of abstraction between your code and the underlying database allow the database vendors to transparently add optimizations, alter the structure of the database files, or port the database engine to other platforms without you having to alter a single line of code.

Query Languages and Data Functions

Database operations can be split into those manipulating the database itself (that is, the logical and physical structure of the files comprising the database) and those manipulating the data stored within these files. The former topic is generally database-specific and can be implemented in various ways, but the latter is typically carried out by using a *query language.**

All query languages, from the lowest level of using Perl's string and numerical handling functions to a high-level query language such as SQL, implement four main operations with which you can manipulate the data. These operations are:

Fetching

> The most commonly used database operation is that of retrieving data stored within a database. This operation is known as *fetching*, and returns the appropriate data in a form understood by the API host language being used to query the database. For example, if you were to use Perl to query an Oracle database for data, the data would be requested by using the SQL query language, and the rows returned would be in the form of Perl strings and

---

* We use the term "query language" *very* loosely. We stretch it from verb-based command languages, like SQL, all the way down to hard-coded logic written in a programming language like Perl.

numerics. This operation is also known as *selecting* data, from the SQL
`SELECT` keyword used to fetch data from a database.

Storing

The corollary operation to fetching data is storing data for later retrieval. The
storage manager layers translate values from the programming language into
values understood by the database. The storage managers then store that value
within the data files. This operation is also known as *inserting* data.

Updating

Once data is stored within a database, it is not necessarily immutable. It can
be changed if required. For example, in a database storing information on
products that can be purchased, the pricing information for each product may
change over time. The operation of changing a value of existing data within
the database is known as *updating*. It is important to note that this operation
doesn't add items to or remove items from the database; rather, it just changes
existing items.[*]

Deleting

The final core operation that you generally want to perform on data is to
delete any old or redundant data from your database. This operation will completely remove the items from the database, again using the storage managers
to excise the data from the data files. Once data has been deleted, it cannot be
recovered or replaced except by reinserting the data into the database.[†]

These operations are quite often referred to by the acronym C.R.U.D. (Create, Read,
Update, Delete). This book discusses these topics in a slightly different order primarily because we feel that most readers, at least initially, will be extracting data from
existing databases rather than creating new databases in which to store data.

Standing Stones and the Sample Database

Our small example databases throughout this chapter will contain information on
megalithic sites within the UK. A more complex version of this database is used in
the following chapters.

The main pieces of information that we wish to store about megaliths[‡] are the
name of the site, the location of the site within the UK, a unique map reference for

---

* Logically, that is. Physically, the updates may be implemented as deletes and inserts.

† Unless you are using *transactions* to control your data. More about that in Chapter 6.

‡ Storing anything *on* a megalith is in direct violation of the principles set forth in Appendix C. In case
  you missed it, we introduced megaliths in Chapter 1.

the site, the type of megalithic setting the site is (e.g., a stone circle or standing stone), and a description of what the site looks like.

For example, we might wish to store the following information about Stonehenge in our database:

Name:

Stonehenge

Location:

Wiltshire, England

Map Reference:

SU 123 400

Type:

Stone Circle and Henge

Description:

The most famous megalithic site in the world, comprised of an earthen bank, or *henge*, and several concentric rings of massive standing stones formed into *trilithons.*

With this simple database, we can retrieve all sorts of different pieces of information, such as, "tell me of all the megalithic sites in Wiltshire," or "tell me about all the standing stones in Orkney," and so on.

Now let's discuss the simplest form of database that you might wish to use: the *flat-file database.*

Flat-File Databases

The simplest type of database that we can create and manipulate is the old standby, the *flat-file database.* This database is essentially a file, or group of files, that contains data in a known and standard format that a program scans for the requested information. Modifications to the data are usually done by updating an in-memory copy of the data held in the file, or files, then writing the entire set of data back out to disk. Flat-file databases are typically ASCII text files containing one record of information per line. The line termination serves as the record delimiter.

In this section we'll be examining the two main types of flat-file database: files that separate fields with a delimiter character, and files that allocate a fixed length to each field. We'll discuss the pros and cons of each type of data file and give you some example code for manipulating them.

The most common format used for flat-file databases is probably the *delimited* file in which each field is separated by a delimiting character. And possibly the most common of these delimited formats is the *comma-separated values* (CSV) file, in which fields are separated from one another by commas. This format is understood by many common programs, such as Microsoft Access and spreadsheet programs. As such, it is an excellent base-level and portable format useful for sharing data between applications.[*]

Other popular delimiting characters are the colon (:), the tab, and the pipe symbol (|). The Unix */etc/passwd* file is a good example of a delimited file with each record being separated by a colon. Figure 2-1 shows a single record from an */etc/ passwd* file.

descarte:yaddayadda:444:56:Alligator Descartes:/users/descarte:/bin/zsh

Figure 2-1. The /etc/passwd file record format

Querying Data

Since delimited files are a very low-level form of storage manager, any manipulations that we wish to perform on the data must be done using operating system functions and low-level query logic, such as basic string comparisons. The following program illustrates how we can open a data file containing colon-separated records of megalith data, search for a given site, and return the data if found:

```perl
#!/usr/bin/perl -w
#
# ch02/scanmegadata/scanmegadata: Scans the given megalith data file for
#                                 a given site. Uses colon-separated data.
#

### Check the user has supplied an argument for
###     1) The name of the file containing the data
###     2) The name of the site to search for
die "Usage: scanmegadata <data file> <site name>\n"
    unless @ARGV == 2;

my $megalithFile = $ARGV[0];
my $siteName     = $ARGV[1];

### Open the data file for reading, and die upon failure
open MEGADATA, "<$megalithFile"
    or die "Can't open $megalithFile: $!\n";

### Declare our row field variables
```

---

[*] More excitingly, a DBI driver called DBD::CSV exists that allows you to write SQL code to manipulate a flat file containing CSV data.

```
my ( $name, $location, $mapref, $type, $description );

### Declare our 'record found' flag
my $found;

### Scan through all the entries for the desired site
while ( <MEGADATA> ) {

    ### Remove the newline that acts as a record delimiter
    chop;

    ### Break up the record data into separate fields
    ( $name, $location, $mapref, $type, $description ) =
        split( /:/, $_ );

    ### Test the sitename against the record's name
    if ( $name eq $siteName ) {
        $found = $.;   # $. holds current line number in file
        last;
    }
}

### If we did find the site we wanted, print it out
if ( $found ) {
    print "Located site: $name on line $found\n\n";
    print "Information on $name ( $type )\n";
    print "===============",
        ( "=" x ( length($name) + length($type) + 5 ) ), "\n";
    print "Location:        $location\n";
    print "Map Reference: $mapref\n";
    print "Description:    $description\n";
}

### Close the megalith data file
close MEGADATA;

exit;
```

For example, running that program with a file containing a record in the following format:[*]

```
Stonehenge:Wiltshire:SU 123 400:Stone Circle and Henge:The most famous stone
circle
```

and a search term of **Stonehenge** would return the following information:

```
Located site: Stonehenge on line 1

Information on Stonehenge ( Stone Circle and Henge )
====================================================
Location:       Wiltshire
```

---

[*] In this example, and some others that follow, the single line has been split over two lines just to fit on the printed page.

```
Map Reference: SU 123 400
Description:    The most famous stone circle
```

indicating that our brute-force scan and test for the correct site has worked. As you can clearly see from the example program, we have used Perl's own native file I/O functions for reading in the data file, and Perl's own string handling functions to break up the delimited data and test it for the correct record.

The downside to delimited file formats is that if any piece of data contains the delimiting character, you need to be especially careful not to break up the records in the wrong place. Using the Perl `split()` function with a simple regular expression, as used above, does not take this into account and could produce wrong results. For example, a record containing the following information would cause the `split()` to happen in the wrong place:

```
Stonehenge:Wiltshire:SU 123 400:Stone Circle and Henge:Stonehenge: The most famous
stone circle
```

The easiest quick-fix technique is to translate any delimiter characters in the string into some other character that you're sure won't appear in your data. Don't forget to do the reverse translation when you fetch the records back.

Another common way of storing data within flat files is to use *fixed-length records* in which to store the data. That is, each piece of data fits into an exactly sized space in the data file. In this form of database, no delimiting character is needed between the fields. There's also no need to delimit each record, but we'll continue to use ASCII line termination as a record delimiter in our examples because Perl makes it very easy to work with files line by line.

Using fixed-width fields is similar to the way in which data is organized in more powerful database systems such as an RDBMS. The pre-allocation of space for record data allows the storage manager to make assumptions about the layout of the data on disk and to optimize accordingly. For our megalithic data purposes, we could settle on the data sizes of:[*]

```
Field           Required Bytes
-----           --------------
Name            64
Location        64
Map Reference   16
Type            32
Description     256
```

Storing the data in this format requires slightly different storage manager logic to be used, although the standard Perl file I/O functions are still applicable. To test

---

[*] The fact that these data sizes are all powers of two has no significance other than to indicate that the authors are old enough to remember when powers of two were significant and useful sometimes. They generally aren't anymore.

this data for the correct record, we need to implement a different way of extracting the fields from within each record. For a fixed-length data file, the Perl function unpack() is perfect. The following code shows how the unpack() function replaces the split() used above:

```
### Break up the record data into separate fields
### using the data sizes listed above
( $name, $location, $mapref, $type, $description ) =
    unpack( "A64 A64 A16 A32 A256", $_ );
```

Although fixed-length fields are always the same length, the data that is being put into a particular field may not be as long as the field. In this case, the extra space will be filled with a character not normally encountered in the data or one that can be ignored. Usually, this is a space character (ASCII 32) or a nul (ASCII 0).

In the code above, we know that the data is space-packed, and so we remove any trailing space from the name record so as not to confuse the search. This can be simply done by using the uppercase A format with unpack().

If you need to choose between delimited fields and fixed-length fields, here are a few guidelines:

The main limitations

The main limitation with delimited fields is the need to add special handling to ensure that neither the field delimiter or the record delimiter characters get added into a field value.

The main limitation with fixed-length fields is simply the fixed length. You need to check for field values being too long to fit (or just let them be silently truncated). If you need to increase a field width, then you'll have to write a special utility to rewrite your file in the new format and remember to track down and update every script that manipulates the file directly.

Space

A delimited-field file often uses less space than a fixed-length record file to store the same data, sometimes *very much* less space. It depends on the number and size of any empty or partially filled fields. For example, some field values, like web URLs, are potentially very long but typically very short. Storing them in a long fixed-length field would waste a lot of space.

While delimited-field files often use less space, they do "waste" space due to all the field delimiter characters. If you're storing a large number of very small fields then that might tip the balance in favor of fixed-length records.

Speed

These days, computing power is rising faster than hard disk data transfer rates. In other words, it's often worth using more space-efficient storage even if that means spending more processor time to use it.

Generally, delimited-field files are better for sequential access than fixed-length record files because the reduced size more than makes up for the increase in processing to extract the fields and handle any escaped or translated delimiter characters.

However, fixed-length record files do have a trick up their sleeve: direct access. If you want to fetch record 42,927 of a delimited-field file, you *have* to read the whole file and count records until you get to the one you want. With a fixed-length record file, you can just multiply 42,927 by the total record width and jump directly to the record using seek().

Furthermore, once it's located, the record can be updated *in-place* by overwriting it with new data. Because the new record is the same length as the old, there's no danger of corrupting the following record.

Inserting Data

Inserting data into a flat-file database is very straightforward and usually amounts to simply tacking the new data onto the end of the data file. For example, inserting a new megalith record into a colon-delimited file can be expressed as simply as:

```perl
#!/usr/bin/perl -w
#
# ch02/insertmegadata/insertmegadata: Inserts a new record into the
#                                     given megalith data file as
#                                     colon-separated data
#

### Check the user has supplied an argument to scan for
###     1) The name of the file containing the data
###     2) The name of the site to insert the data for
###     3) The location of the site
###     4) The map reference of the site
###     5) The type of site
###     6) The description of the site
die "Usage: insertmegadata"
    ." <data file> <site name> <location> <map reference> <type> <description>\n"
    unless @ARGV == 6;

my $megalithFile    = $ARGV[0];
my $siteName        = $ARGV[1];
my $siteLocation    = $ARGV[2];
my $siteMapRef      = $ARGV[3];
my $siteType        = $ARGV[4];
my $siteDescription = $ARGV[5];

### Open the data file for concatenation, and die upon failure
open MEGADATA, ">>$megalithFile"
    or die "Can't open $megalithFile for appending: $!\n";

### Create a new record
```

```
my $record = join( ":", $siteName, $siteLocation, $siteMapRef,
                        $siteType, $siteDescription );

### Insert the new record into the file
print MEGADATA "$record\n"
    or die "Error writing to $megalithFile: $!\n";

### Close the megalith data file
close MEGADATA
    or die "Error closing $megalithFile: $!";

print "Inserted record for $siteName\n";

exit;
```

This example simply opens the data file in append mode and writes the new record to the open file. Simple as this process is, there is a potential drawback. This flat-file database does not detect the insertion of multiple items of data with the same search key. That is, if we wanted to insert a new record about Stonehenge into our megalith database, then the software would happily do so, even though a record for Stonehenge already exists.

This may be a problem from a data integrity point of view. A more sophisticated test prior to appending the data might be worth implementing to ensure that duplicate records do not exist. Combining the insert program with the query program above is a straightforward approach.

Another potential (and more important) drawback is that this system will not safely handle occasions in which more than one user attempts to add new data into the database. Since this subject also affects updating and deleting data from the database, we'll cover it more thoroughly in a later section of this chapter.

Inserting new records into a fixed-length data file is also simple. Instead of printing each field to the Perl filehandle separated by the delimiting character, we can use the pack() function to create a fixed-length record out of the data.

Updating Data

Updating data within a flat-file database is where things begin to get a little more tricky. When querying records from the database, we simply scanned sequentially through the database until we found the correct record. Similarly, when inserting data, we simply attached the new data without really knowing what was already stored within the database.

The main problem with updating data is that we need to be able to read in data from the data file, temporarily mess about with it, and write the database back out to the file without losing any records.

One approach is to slurp the entire database into memory, make any updates to the in-memory copy, and dump it all back out again. A second approach is to read the database in record by record, make any alterations to each individual record, and write the record immediately back out to a temporary file. Once all the records have been processed, the temporary file can replace the original data file. Both techniques are viable, but we prefer the latter for performance reasons. Slurping entire large databases into memory can be very resource-hungry.

The following short program implements the latter of these strategies to update the map reference in the database of delimited records:

```perl
#!/usr/bin/perl -w
#
# ch02/updatemegadata/updatemegadata: Updates the given megalith data file
#                                     for a given site. Uses colon-separated
#                                     data and updates the map reference field.
#

### Check the user has supplied an argument to scan for
###      1) The name of the file containing the data
###      2) The name of the site to search for
###      3) The new map reference
die "Usage: updatemegadata <data file> <site name> <new map reference>\n"
    unless @ARGV == 3;

my $megalithFile = $ARGV[0];
my $siteName     = $ARGV[1];
my $siteMapRef   = $ARGV[2];
my $tempFile     = "tmp.$$";

### Open the data file for reading, and die upon failure
open MEGADATA, "<$megalithFile"
    or die "Can't open $megalithFile: $!\n";

### Open the temporary megalith data file for writing
open TMPMEGADATA, ">$tempFile"
    or die "Can't open temporary file $tempFile: $!\n";

### Scan through all the records looking for the desired site
while ( <MEGADATA> ) {

    ### Quick pre-check for maximum performance:
    ### Skip the record if the site name doesn't appear as a field
    next unless m/^\Q$siteName:/;

    ### Break up the record data into separate fields
    ### (we let $description carry the newline for us)
    my ( $name, $location, $mapref, $type, $description ) =
        split( /:/, $_ );

    ### Skip the record if the site name doesn't match. (Redundant after the
    ### reliable pre-check above but kept for consistency with other examples.)
```

```
        next unless $siteName eq $name;

        ### We've found the record to update, so update the map ref value
        $mapref = $siteMapRef;

        ### Construct an updated record
        $_ = join( ":", $name, $location, $mapref, $type, $description );

    }
    continue {

        ### Write the record out to the temporary file
        print TMPMEGADATA $_
            or die "Error writing $tempFile: $!\n";
    }

    ### Close the megalith input data file
    close MEGADATA;

    ### Close the temporary megalith output data file
    close TMPMEGADATA
        or die "Error closing $tempFile: $!\n";

    ### We now "commit" the changes by deleting the old file...
    unlink $megalithFile
        or die "Can't delete old $megalithFile: $!\n";

    ### and renaming the new file to replace the old one.
    rename $tempFile, $megalithFile
        or die "Can't rename '$tempFile' to '$megalithFile': $!\n";

    exit 0;
```

You can see we've flexed our Perl muscles on this example, using a `while` ... `continue` loop to simplify the logic and adding a pretest for increased speed.

An equivalent program that can be applied to a fixed-length file is very similar, except that we use a faster in-place update to change the contents of the field. This principle is similar to the in-place query described previously: we don't need to unpack and repack all the fields stored within each record, but can simply update the appropriate chunk of each record. For example:

```
    ### Scan through all the records looking for the desired site
    while ( <MEGADATA> ) {

        ### Quick pre-check for maximum performance:
        ### Skip the record if the site name doesn't appear at the start
        next unless m/^\Q$siteName/;

        ### Skip the record if the extracted site name field doesn't match
        next unless unpack( "x64 x64 A16", $_ ) eq $siteName;
```

```
                ### Perform in-place substitution to upate map reference field
                substr( $_, 64+64, 16, pack( "A16", $siteMapRef ) );

        }
```

This technique is faster than packing and unpacking each record stored within the file, since it carries out the minimum amount of work needed to change the appropriate field values.

You may notice that the pretest in this example isn't 100% reliable, but it doesn't have to be. It just needs to catch *most* of the cases that won't match in order to pay its way by reducing the number of times the more expensive unpack and field test gets executed. Okay, this might not be a very convincing application of the idea, but we'll revisit it more seriously later in this chapter.

Deleting Data

The final form of data manipulation that you can apply to flat-file databases is the removal, or deletion, of records from the database. We shall process the file a record at a time by passing the data through a temporary file, just as we did for updating, rather than slurping all the data into memory and dumping it at the end.

With this technique, the action of removing a record from the database is more an act of omission than any actual deletion. Each record is read in from the file, tested, and written out to the file. When the record to be deleted is encountered, it is simply *not* written to the temporary file. This effectively removes all trace of it from the database, albeit in a rather unsophisticated way.

The following program can be used to remove the relevant record from the delimited megalithic database when given an argument of the name of the site to delete:

```
#!/usr/bin/perl -w
#
# ch02/deletemegadata/deletemegadata: Deletes the record for the given
#                                     megalithic site. Uses
#                                     colon-separated data
#


### Check the user has supplied an argument to scan for
###     1) The name of the file containing the data
###     2) The name of the site to delete
die "Usage: deletemegadata <data file> <site name>\n"
    unless @ARGV == 2;

my $megalithFile  = $ARGV[0];
my $siteName      = $ARGV[1];
my $tempFile      = "tmp.$$";

### Open the data file for reading, and die upon failure
open MEGADATA, "<$megalithFile"
```

```
    or die "Can't open $megalithFile: $!\n";

### Open the temporary megalith data file for writing
open TMPMEGADATA, ">$tempFile"
    or die "Can't open temporary file $tempFile: $!\n";

### Scan through all the entries for the desired site
while ( <MEGADATA> ) {

    ### Extract the site name (the first field) from the record
    my ( $name ) = split( /:/, $_ );

    ### Test the sitename against the record's name
    if ( $siteName eq $name ) {

        ### We've found the record to delete, so skip it and move to next record
        next;
    }

    ### Write the original record out to the temporary file
    print TMPMEGADATA $_
        or die "Error writing $tempFile: $!\n";
    }

### Close the megalith input data file
close MEGADATA;

### Close the temporary megalith output data file
close TMPMEGADATA
    or die "Error closing $tempFile: $!\n";

### We now "commit" the changes by deleting the old file ...
unlink $megalithFile
    or die "Can't delete old $megalithFile: $!\n";

### and renaming the new file to replace the old one.
rename $tempFile, $megalithFile
    or die "Can't rename '$tempFile' to '$megalithFile': $!\n";

exit 0;
```

The code to remove records from a fixed-length data file is almost identical. The
only change is in the code to extract the field value, as you'd expect:

```
### Extract the site name (the first field) from the record
my ( $name ) = unpack( "A64", $_ );
```

Like updating, deleting data may cause problems if multiple users are attempting
to make simultaneous changes to the data. We'll look at how to deal with this
problem a little later in this chapter.

Putting Complex Data into Flat Files

In our discussions of so-called "flat files" we've so far been storing, retrieving, and manipulating only that most basic of datatypes: the humble string. What can you do if you want to store more complex data, such as lists, hashes, or deeply nested data structures using references?

The answer is to convert whatever it is you want to store *into* a string. Technically that's known as *marshalling* or *serializing* the data. The Perl Module List* has a section that lists several Perl modules that implement data marshalling.

We're going to take a look at two of the most popular modules, `Data::Dumper` and `Storable`, and see how we can use them to put some fizz into our flat files. These techniques are also applicable to storing complex Perl data structures in relational databases using the DBI, so pay attention.

The Perl Data::Dumper Module

The `Data::Dumper` module takes a list of Perl variables and writes their values out *in the form of Perl code,* which will recreate the original values, no matter how complex, when executed.

This module allows you to dump the state of a Perl program in a readable form quickly and easily. It also allows you to restore the program state by simply executing the dumped code using `eval()` or `do()`.

The easiest way to describe what happens is to show you a quick example:

```
#!/usr/bin/perl -w
#
# ch02/marshal/datadumpertest: Creates some Perl variables and dumps them out.
#                              Then, we reset the values of the variables and
#                              eval the dumped ones ...

use Data::Dumper;

### Customise Data::Dumper's output style
### Refer to Data::Dumper documentation for full details
if ($ARGV[0] eq 'flat') {
    $Data::Dumper::Indent = 0;
    $Data::Dumper::Useqq  = 1;
}
$Data::Dumper::Purity = 1;

### Create some Perl variables
my $megalith = 'Stonehenge';
my $districts = [ 'Wiltshire', 'Orkney', 'Dorset' ];
```

---

* The Perl Module List can be found at *http://www.perl.com/CPAN/*.

```
### Print them out
print "Initial Values: \$megalith  = " . $megalith . "\n" .
       "                  \$districts = [ ". join(", ", @$districts) . " ]\n\n";

### Create a new Data::Dumper object from the database
my $dumper = Data::Dumper->new( [   $megalith, $districts ],
                                [ qw( megalith  districts ) ] );

### Dump the Perl values out into a variable
my $dumpedValues = $dumper->Dump();

### Show what Data::Dumper has made of the variables!
print "Perl code produced by Data::Dumper:\n";
print $dumpedValues . "\n";

### Reset the variables to rubbish values
$megalith = 'Blah! Blah!';
$districts = [ 'Alderaan', 'Mordor', 'The Moon' ];

### Print out the rubbish values
print "Rubbish Values: \$megalith  = " . $megalith . "\n" .
       "                  \$districts = [ ". join(", ", @$districts) . " ]\n\n";

### Eval the file to load up the Perl variables
eval $dumpedValues;
die if $@;

### Display the re-loaded values
print "Re-loaded Values: \$megalith  = " . $megalith . "\n" .
       "                  \$districts = [ ". join(", ", @$districts) . " ]\n\n";

exit;
```

This example simply initializes two Perl variables and prints their values. It then creates a `Data::Dumper` object with those values, changes the original values, and prints the new ones just to prove we aren't cheating. Finally, it **eval**s the results of `$dumper->Dump()`, which stuffs the original stored values back into the variables. Again, we print it all out just to doubly convince you there's no sleight-of-hand going on.

```
Initial Values: $megalith  = Stonehenge
                $districts = [ Wiltshire, Orkney, Dorset ]

Perl code produced by Data::Dumper:
$megalith = 'Stonehenge';
$districts = [
             'Wiltshire',
             'Orkney',
             'Dorset'
           ];

Rubbish Values: $megalith  = Blah! Blah!
                $districts = [ Alderaan, Mordor, The Moon ]
```

```
Re-loaded Values: $megalith  = Stonehenge
                  $districts = [ Wiltshire, Orkney, Dorset ]
```

So how do we use `Data::Dumper` to add fizz to our flat files? Well, first of all we have to ask `Data::Dumper` to produce flat output, that is, output with no new-lines. We do that by setting two package global variables:

```
$Data::Dumper::Indent = 0;  # don't use newlines to layout the output
$Data::Dumper::Useqq  = 1;  # use double quoted strings with "\n" escapes
```

In our test program, we can do that by running the program with `flat` as an argument. Here's the relevant part of the output when we do that:

```
$megalith = "Stonehenge";$districts = ["Wiltshire","Orkney","Dorset"];
```

Now we can modify our previous scan (select), insert, update, and delete scripts to use `Data::Dumper` to format the records instead of the `join()` or `pack()` functions we used before. Instead of `split()` or `unpack()`, we now use `eval` to unpack the records.

Here's just the main loop of the update script we used earlier (the rest of the script is unchanged except for the addition of a **use Data::Dumper;** line at the top and setting the `Data::Dumper` variables as described above):

```
### Scan through all the entries for the desired site
while ( <MEGADATA> ) {

    ### Quick pre-check for maximum performance:
    ### Skip the record if the site name doesn't appear
    next unless m/\Q$siteName/;

    ### Evaluate perl record string to set $fields array reference
    my $fields;
    eval $_;
    die if $@;

    ### Break up the record data into separate fields
    my ( $name, $location, $mapref, $type, $description ) = @$fields;

    ### Skip the record if the extracted site name field doesn't match
    next unless $siteName eq $name;

    ### We've found the record to update
    ### Create a new fields array with new map ref value
    $fields = [ $name, $location, $siteMapRef, $type, $description ];

    ### Convert it into a line of perl code encoding our record string
    $_ = Data::Dumper->new( [ $fields ], [ 'fields' ] )->Dump();
    $_ .= "\n";

}
```

So, what have we gained by doing this? We avoid the tedious need to explicitly escape field delimiter characters. `Data::Dumper` does that for us, and there are no fixed-width field length restrictions either.

The big win, though, is the ability to store practically any complex data structure, even object references. There are also some smaller benefits that may be of use to you: undefined (*null*) field values can be saved and restored, and there's no need for every record to have every field defined (variant records).

The downside? There's always a downside. In this case, it's mainly the extra processing time required both to dump the record data into the strings and for Perl to `eval` them back again. There is a version of the `Data::Dumper` module written in C that's much faster, but sadly it doesn't support the `$Useqq` variable yet. To save time processing each record, the example code has a quick precheck that skips any rows that don't at least have the desired site name *somewhere* in them.

There's also the question of security. Because we're using `eval` to evaluate the Perl code embedded in our data file, it's possible that someone could edit the data file and add code that does something else, possibly harmful. Fortunately, there's a simple fix for this. The Perl `ops` pragma can be used to restrict the `eval` to compiling code that contains only simple declarations. For more information on this, see the `ops` documentation installed with Perl:

```
perldoc ops
```

The Storable Module

In addition to `Data::Dumper`, there are other data marshalling modules available that you might wish to investigate, including the fast and efficient `Storable`.

The following code takes the same approach as the example we listed for `Data::Dumper` to show the basic store and retrieve cycle:

```
#!/usr/bin/perl -w
#
# ch02/marshal/storabletest: Create a Perl hash and store it externally. Then,
#                            we reset the hash and reload the saved one.

use Storable qw( freeze thaw );

### Create some values in a hash
my $megalith = {
    'name' => 'Stonehenge',
    'mapref' => 'SU 123 400',
    'location' => 'Wiltshire',
};

### Print them out
print "Initial Values:   megalith = $megalith->{name}\n" .
```

```
        "              mapref   = $megalith->{mapref}\n" .
        "              location = $megalith->{location}\n\n";

    ### Store the values to a string
    my $storedValues = freeze( $megalith );

    ### Reset the variables to rubbish values
    $megalith = {
        'name'     => 'Flibble Flabble',
        'mapref'   => 'XX 000 000',
        'location' => 'Saturn',
    };

    ### Print out the rubbish values
    print "Rubbish Values:   megalith = $megalith->{name}\n" .
        "                  mapref   = $megalith->{mapref}\n" .
        "                  location = $megalith->{location}\n\n";

    ### Retrieve the values from the string
    $megalith = thaw( $storedValues );

    ### Display the re-loaded values
    print "Re-loaded Values: megalith = $megalith->{name}\n" .
        "                  mapref   = $megalith->{mapref}\n" .
        "                  location = $megalith->{location}\n\n";

    exit;
```

This program generates the following output, which illustrates that we are storing data persistently then retrieving it:

```
Initial Values:    megalith = Stonehenge
                   mapref   = SU 123 400
                   location = Wiltshire

Rubbish Values:    megalith = Flibble Flabble
                   mapref   = XX 000 000
                   location = Saturn

Re-loaded Values: megalith = Stonehenge
                   mapref   = SU 123 400
                   location = Wiltshire
```

Storable also has functions to write and read your data structures directly to and from disk files. It can also be used to write to a file cumulatively instead of writing all records in one atomic operation.

So far, all this sounds very similar to Data::Dumper, so what's the difference? In a word, *speed*. Storable is fast, very fast—both for saving data and for getting it back again. It achieves its speed partly by being implemented in C and hooked directly into the Perl internals, and partly by writing the data in its own very compact binary format.

Here's our update program reimplemented yet again, this time to use `Storable`:

```perl
#!/usr/bin/perl -w
#
# ch02/marshal/update_storable: Updates the given megalith data file
#                               for a given site. Uses Storable data
#                               and updates the map reference field.

use Storable qw( nfreeze thaw );

### Check the user has supplied an argument to scan for
###      1) The name of the file containing the data
###      2) The name of the site to search for
###      3) The new map reference
die "Usage: updatemegadata <data file> <site name> <new map reference>\n"
    unless @ARGV == 3;

my $megalithFile = $ARGV[0];
my $siteName     = $ARGV[1];
my $siteMapRef   = $ARGV[2];
my $tempFile     = "tmp.$$";

### Open the data file for reading, and die upon failure
open MEGADATA, "<$megalithFile"
    or die "Can't open $megalithFile: $!\n";

### Open the temporary megalith data file for writing
open TMPMEGADATA, ">$tempFile"
    or die "Can't open temporary file $tempFile: $!\n";

### Scan through all the entries for the desired site
while ( <MEGADATA> ) {

    ### Convert the ASCII encoded string back to binary
    ### (pack ignores the trailing newline record delimiter)
    my $frozen = pack "H*", $_;

    ### Thaw the frozen data structure
    my $fields = thaw( $frozen );

    ### Break up the record data into separate fields
    my ( $name, $location, $mapref, $type, $description ) = @$fields;

    ### Skip the record if the extracted site name field doesn't match
    next unless $siteName eq $name;

    ### We've found the record to update
    ### Create a new fields array with new map ref value
    $fields = [ $name, $location, $siteMapRef, $type, $description ];

    ### Freeze the data structure into a binary string
    $frozen = nfreeze( $fields );

    ### Encode the binary string as readable ASCII and append a newline
```

```perl
        $_ = unpack( "H*", $frozen ) . "\n";

    }
    continue {

        ### Write the record out to the temporary file
        print TMPMEGADATA $_
            or die "Error writing $tempFile: $!\n";
    }

    ### Close the megalith input data file
    close MEGADATA;

    ### Close the temporary megalith output data file
    close TMPMEGADATA
        or die "Error closing $tempFile: $!\n";

    ### We now "commit" the changes by deleting the old file...
    unlink $megalithFile
        or die "Can't delete old $megalithFile: $!\n";

    ### and renaming the new file to replace the old one.
    rename $tempFile, $megalithFile
        or die "Can't rename '$tempFile' to '$megalithFile': $!\n";

    exit 0;
```

Since the `Storable` format is binary, we couldn't simply write it directly to our flat file. It would be possible for our record-delimiter character (`"\n"`) to appear within the binary data, thus corrupting the file. We get around this by encoding the binary data as a string of pairs of hexadecimal digits.

You may have noticed that we've used `nfreeze()` instead of `freeze()`. By default, `Storable` writes numeric data in the fastest, simplest native format. The problem is that some computer systems store numbers in a different way from others. Using `nfreeze()` instead of `freeze()` ensures that numbers are written in a form that's portable to all systems.

You may also be wondering what one of these records looks like. We'll here's the record for the Castlerigg megalithic site:

```
0302000000050a0a436173746c6572696767580a0743756d62726961580a0a4e59203239312032
3336580a0c53746f6e6520436972636c65580aa34f6e65206f6620746865206c6f76656c696573
742073746f6e6520636972636c65732072656d61696e696e6720746f6461792e20546869732073
69746520697320636f6d707269736564206f66206c6172676520726f756e64656420626f756c64
65727320736574742077697468696e2061206e61747572616c20616d706869746865617472652066
6f726d6564206279207375727266f756e64696e672068696c6c732e5858
```

That's all on one line in the data file; we've just split it up here to fit on the page. It doesn't make for thrilling reading. It also doesn't let us do the kind of quick pre-check shortcut that we used with `Data::Dumper` and the previous flat-file update examples. We could apply the pre-check after converting the hex string back to binary, but there's no guarantee that strings appear literally in the `Storable` output. They happen to now, but there's always a risk that this will change.

Although we've been talking about `Storable` in the context of flat files, this technique is also very useful for storing arbitrary chunks of Perl data into a relational database, or any other kind of database for that matter. `Storable` and `Data::Dumper` are great tools to carry in your mental toolkit.

Summary of Flat-File Databases

The main benefit of using flat-file databases for data storage is that they can be fast to implement and fast to use on small and straightforward datasets, such as our megalithic database or a Unix password file.

The code to query, insert, delete, and update information in the database is also extremely simple, with the parsing code potentially shared among the operations. You have total control over the data file formats, so that there are no situations outside your control in which the file format or access API changes. The files are also easy to read in standard text editors (although in the case of the `Storable` example, they won't make very interesting reading).

The downsides of these databases are quite apparent. As we've mentioned already, the lack of concurrent access limits the power of such systems in a multi-user environment. They also suffer from scalability problems due to the sequential nature of the search mechanism. These limitations can be coded around (the concurrent access problem especially so), but there comes a point where you should seriously consider the use of a higher-level storage manager such as DBM files. DBM files also give you access to *indexed* data and allow nonsequential querying.

Before we discuss DBM files in detail, the following sections give you examples of more sophisticated management tools and techniques, as well as a method of handling concurrent users.

Concurrent Database Access and Locking

Before we start looking at DBM file storage management, we should discuss the issues that were flagged earlier regarding concurrent access to flat-file databases, as these problems affect all relatively low-level storage managers.

The basic problem is that concurrent access to files can result in undefined, and generally wrong, data being stored within the data files of a database. For example, if two users each decided to delete a row from the megalith database using the program shown in the previous section, then during the deletion phase, both

users would be operating on the original copy of the database. However, whichever user's deletion finished first would be overwritten as the second user's deletion copied *their* version of the database over the first user's deletion. The first
user's deletion would appear to have been magically restored. This problem is
known as a *race condition* and can be very tricky to detect as the conditions that
cause the problem are difficult to reproduce.

To avoid problems of multiple simultaneous changes, we need to somehow
enforce exclusive access to the database for potentially destructive operations such
as the insertion, updating, and deletion of records. If every program accessing a
database were simply read-only, this problem would not appear, since no data
would be changed. However, if any script were to alter data, the consistency of all
other processes accessing the data for reading or writing could not be guaranteed.

One way in which we can solve this problem is to use the operating system's file-
locking mechanism, accessed by the Perl `flock()` function. `flock()` implements
a cooperative system of locking that must be used by all programs attempting to
access a given file if it is to be effective. This includes read-only scripts, such as
the query script listed previously, which can use `flock()` to test whether or not it
is safe to attempt a read on the database.

The symbolic constants used in the following programs are located within the
`Fcntl` package and can be imported into your scripts for use with `flock()` with
the following line:

```
use Fcntl ':flock';
```

`flock()` allows locking in two modes: *exclusive* and *shared* (also known as *non-
exclusive*). When a script has an exclusive lock, only that script can access the files
of the database. Any other script wishing access to the database will have to wait
until the exclusive lock is released before its lock request is granted. A shared
lock, on the other hand, allows any number of scripts to simultaneously access the
locked files, but any attempts to acquire an exclusive lock will *block.**

For example, the querying script listed in the previous section could be enhanced
to use `flock()` to request a *shared* lock on the database files, in order to avoid
any read-consistency problems if the database was being updated, in the following way:

```
### Open the data file for reading, and die upon failure
open MEGADATA, $ARGV[0] or die "Can't open $ARGV[0]: $!\n";

print "Acquiring a shared lock...";
flock( MEGADATA, LOCK_SH )
```

---

* Users of Perl on Windows 95 may not be surprised to know that the `flock()` function isn't supported
on that system. Sorry. You may be able to use a module like `LockFile::Simple` instead.

```
          or die "Unable to acquire shared lock: $!. Aborting";
    print "Acquired lock. Ready to read database!\n\n";
```

This call to `flock()` will block the script until any exclusive locks have been relinquished on the requested file. When that occurs, the querying script will acquire a shared lock and continue on with its query. The lock will automatically be released when the file is closed.

Similarly, the data insertion script could be enhanced with `flock()` to request an *exclusive* lock on the data file prior to operating on that file. We also need to alter the mode in which the file is to be opened. This is because we must open the file for writing prior to acquiring an exclusive lock.

Therefore, the insert script can be altered to read:

```
### Open the data file for appending, and die upon failure
open MEGADATA, "+>>$ARGV[0]"
    or die "Can't open $ARGV[0] for appending: $!\n";

print "Acquiring an exclusive lock...";
flock( MEGADATA, LOCK_EX )
        or die "Unable to acquire exclusive lock: $!. Aborting";
print "Acquired lock. Ready to update database!\n\n";
```

which ensures that no data alteration operations will take place until an exclusive lock has been acquired on the data file. Similar enhancements should be added to the deletion and update scripts to ensure that no scripts will "cheat" and ignore the locking routines.

This locking system is effective on all storage management systems that require some manipulation of the underlying database files and have no explicit locking mechanism of their own. We will be returning to locking during our discussion of the Berkeley Database Manager system, as it requires a slightly more involved strategy to get a filehandle on which to use `flock()`.

As a caveat, `flock()` might not be available on your particular operating system. For example, it works on Windows NT/2000 systems, but not on Windows 95/98. Most, if not all, Unix systems support `flock()` without any problems.

DBM Files and the Berkeley Database Manager

DBM files are a storage management layer that allows programmers to store information in files as pairs of strings, a key, and a value. DBM files are *binary* files and the key and value strings can also hold binary data.

There are several forms of DBM files, each with its own strengths and weaknesses. Perl supports the *ndbm*, *db*, *gdbm*, *sdbm*, and *odbm* managers via the

NDBM_File, DB_File, GDBM_File, SDBM_File, and ODBM_File extensions.
There's also an AnyDBM_File module that will simply use the best available DBM.
The documentation for the AnyDBM_File module includes a useful table compar-
ing the different DBMs.

These extensions all associate a DBM file on disk with a Perl hash variable (or
associative array) in memory.* The simple *look like a hash* programming interface
lets programmers store data in operating system files without having to consider
how it's done. It just works.

Programmers store and fetch values into and out of the hash, and the underlying
DBM storage management layer will look after getting them on and off the disk.

In this section, we shall discuss the most popular and sophisticated of these stor-
age managers, the Berkeley Database Manager, also known as the Berkeley DB.
This software is accessed from Perl via the DB_File and Berkeley DB extensions.
On Windows systems, it can be installed via the Perl package manager, *ppm*. On
Unix systems, it is built by default when Perl is built *only if* the Berkeley DB
library has already been installed on your system. That's generally the case on
Linux, but on most other systems you may need to fetch and build the Berkeley
DB library first.†

In addition to the standard DBM file features, Berkeley DB and the DB_File module also provide support for several different storage and retrieval algorithms that
can be used in subtly different situations. In newer versions of the software, concurrent access to databases and locking are also supported.

Creating a New Database

Prior to manipulating data within a Berkeley database, either a new database must
be created or an existing database must be opened for reading. This can be done
by using one of the following function calls:

```
tie %hash,   'DB_File', $filename, $flags, $mode, $DB_HASH;
tie %hash,   'DB_File', $filename, $flags, $mode, $DB_BTREE;
tie @array,  'DB_File', $filename, $flags, $mode, $DB_RECNO;
```

The final parameter of this call is the interesting one, as it dictates the way in
which the Berkeley DB will store the data in the database file. The behavior of
these parameters is as follows:

---

* DBM files are implemented by library code that's linked into the Perl extensions. There's no separate
  server process involved.

† Version 1 of Berkeley DB is available from *http://www.perl.com/CPAN/src/misc/db.1.86.tar.gz*. The
  much improved Version 2 (e.g., *db.2.14.tar.gz*) is also available, but isn't needed for our examples and
  is only supported by recent Perl versions. Version 3 is due out soon. See *www.sleepycat.com*.

- DB_HASH is the default behavior for Berkeley DB databases. It stores the data according to a *hash value* computed from the string specified as the key itself. Hashtables are generally extremely fast, in that by simply applying the hash function to any given key value, the data associated with that key can be located in a single operation. This is much faster than sequential scanning. However, hashtables provide no useful ordering of the data by default, and hashtable performance can begin to degrade when several keys have identical hash key values. This results in several items of data being attached to the same hash key value, which results in slower access times.

- With the DB_BTREE format, Berkeley DB files are stored in the form of a balanced binary tree. The B-tree storage technique will sort the keys that you insert into the Berkeley DB, the default being to sort them in lexical order. If you desire, you can override this behavior with your own sorting algorithms.

- The DB_RECNO format allows you to store key/value pairs in both fixed-length and variable-length textual flat files. The key values in this case consist of a line number, i.e., the number of the record within the database.

When initializing a new or existing Berkeley DB database for use with Perl, use the tie mechanism defined within Perl to associate the actual Berkeley DB with either a hash or a standard scalar array. By doing this, we can simply manipulate the Perl variables, which will automatically perform the appropriate operations on the Berkeley DB files instead of us having to manually program the Berkeley DB API ourselves.

For example, to create a simple Berkeley DB, we could use the following Perl script:

```
#!/usr/bin/perl -w
#
# ch02/DBM/createdb: Creates a Berkeley DB

use strict;

use DB_File;

my %database;
tie %database, 'DB_File', "createdb.dat"
    or die "Can't initialize database: $!\n";

untie %database;

exit;
```

If you now look in the directory in which you ran this script, you should hopefully find a new file called *createdb.dat*. This is the disk image of your Berkeley database, i.e., your data stored in the format implemented by the Berkeley DB storage manager. These files are commonly referred to as DBM files.

In the example above, we simply specified the name of the file in which the database is to be stored and then ignored the other arguments. This is a perfectly acceptable thing to do if the defaults are satisfactory. The additional arguments default to the values listed in Table 2-1.

Table 2-1. The Default Argument Values of DB_File

Argument	Default Value
`$filename`	`undef`[a]
`$flags`	`O_CREAT	O_RDWR`
`$mode`	`0666`
`$storage_type`	`$DB_HASH`

[a] If the filename argument is specified as `undef`, the database will be created in-memory only. It still behaves as if written to file, although once the program exits, the database will no longer exist.

The `$flags` argument takes the values that are associated with the standard Perl `sysopen()` function, and the `$mode` argument takes the form of the octal value of the file permissions that you wish the DBM file to be created with. In the case of the default value, `0666`, the corresponding Unix permissions will be:

```
-rw-rw-rw-
```

That is, the file is user, group, and world readable and writeable.[*] You may wish to specify more strict permissions on your DBM files to be sure that unauthorized users won't tamper with them.

Other platforms such as Win32 differ, and do not necessarily use a permission system. On these platforms, the permission mode is simply ignored.

Given that creating a new database is a fairly major operation, it might be worthwhile to implement an exclusive locking mechanism that protects the database files while the database is initially created and loaded. As with flat-file databases, the Perl `flock()` call should be used to perform file-level locking, but there are some differences between locking standard files and DBM files.

Locking Strategies

The issues of safe access to databases that plagued flat-file databases still apply to Berkeley databases. Therefore, it is a good idea to implement a locking strategy that allows safe multi-user access to the databases, if this is required by your applications.

---

[*] We are ignoring any modifications to the permissions that `umask` may make.

The way in which `flock()` is used regarding DBM files is slightly different than that of locking standard Perl filehandles, as there is no direct reference to the underlying filehandle when we create a DBM file within a Perl script.

Fortunately, the `DB_File` module defines a method that can be used to locate the underlying *file descriptor* for a DBM file, allowing us to use `flock()` on it. This can be achieved by invoking the `fd()` method on the object reference returned from the database initialization by `tie()`. For example:

```
### Create the new database ...
$db = tie %database, 'DB_File', "megaliths.dat"
    or die "Can't initialize database: $!\n";

### Acquire the file descriptor for the DBM file
my $fd = $db->fd();

### Do a careful open() of that descriptor to get a Perl filehandle
open DATAFILE, "+<&=$fd" or die "Can't safely open file: $!\n";

### And lock it before we start loading data ...
print "Acquiring an exclusive lock...";
flock( DATAFILE, LOCK_EX )
        or die "Unable to acquire exclusive lock: $!. Aborting";
print "Acquired lock. Ready to update database!\n\n";
```

This code looks a bit gruesome, especially with the additional call to **open()**. It is written in such a way that the original file descriptor being currently used by the DBM file when the database was created is not invalidated. What actually occurs is that the file descriptor is associated with the Perl filehandle in a nondestructive way. This then allows us to `flock()` the filehandle as per usual.

However, after having written this description and all the examples using this standard documented way to lock Berkeley DBM files, it has been discovered that there is a small risk of data corruption during concurrent access. To make a long story short, the DBM code reads some of the file when it first opens it, before you get a chance to lock it. That's the problem.

There is a quick fix if your system supports the O_EXLOCK flag, as FreeBSD does and probably most Linux versions do. Just add the O_EXLOCK flag to the `tie`:

```
use Fcntl;    # import O_EXLOCK, if available
$db = tie %database, 'DB_File', "megaliths.dat", O_EXLOCK;
```

For more information, and a more general workaround, see:

http://www.xray.mpe.mpg.de/mailing-lists/perl5-porters/1999-09/msg00954.html

and the thread of messages that follows it.

Inserting and Retrieving Values

Inserting data into a Berkeley DB using the Perl DB_File module is extremely
simple as a result of using a *tied hash* or *tied array*. The association of a DBM file
and a Perl data structure is created when the database is opened. This allows us to
manipulate the contents of the database simply by altering the contents of the Perl
data structures.

This system makes it very easy to store data within a DBM file and also abstracts
the actual file-related operations for data manipulation away from our scripts.
Thus, the Berkeley DB is a higher-level storage manager than the simple flat-file
databases discussed earlier in this chapter.

The following script demonstrates the insertion and retrieval of data from a DBM
file using a tied hash. This hash has the Perl characteristic of being a key/value
pair. That is, values are stored within the hash table against a unique key. This
affords extremely fast retrieval and an element of indexed data access as opposed
to sequential access. For example:

```
#!/usr/bin/perl -w
#
# ch02/DBM/simpleinsert: Creates a Berkeley DB, inserts some test data
#                        and dumps it out again

use DB_File;
use Fcntl ':flock';

### Initialize the Berkeley DB
my %database;
my $db = tie %database, 'DB_File', "simpleinsert.dat",
        O_CREAT | O_RDWR, 0666
    or die "Can't initialize database: $!\n";

my $fd = $db->fd();
open DATAFILE, "+<&=$fd"
    or die "Can't safely open file: $!\n";
print "Acquiring exclusive lock...";
flock( DATAFILE, LOCK_EX )
    or die "Unable to acquire lock: $!. Aborting";
print "Acquired lock. Ready to update database!\n\n";


### Insert some data rows
$database{'Callanish I'} =
    "This site, commonly known as the "Stonehenge of the North" is in the
form of a buckled Celtic cross.";

$database{'Avebury'} =
    "Avebury is a vast, sprawling site that features, amongst other marvels,
the largest stone circle in Britain. The henge itself is so large,
it almost completely surrounds the village of Avebury.";
```

```
$database{'Lundin Links'} =
    "Lundin Links is a megalithic curiosity, featuring 3 gnarled and
immensely tall monoliths arranged possibly in a 4-poster design.
Each monolith is over 5m tall.";

### Untie the database
undef $db;
untie %database;

### Close the file descriptor to release the lock
close DATAFILE;


### Retie the database to ensure we're reading the stored data
$db = tie %database, 'DB_File', "simpleinsert.dat", O_RDWR, 0444
    or die "Can't initialize database: $!\n";

### Only need to lock in shared mode this time because we're not updating ...
$fd = $db->fd();
open DATAFILE, "+<&=$fd" or die "Can't safely open file: $!\n";
print "Acquiring shared lock...";
flock( DATAFILE, LOCK_SH )
    or die "Unable to acquire lock: $!. Aborting";
print "Acquired lock. Ready to read database!\n\n";

### Dump the database
foreach my $key ( keys %database ) {
    print "$key\n", ( "=" x ( length( $key ) + 1 ) ), "\n\n";
    print "$database{$key}\n\n";
}

### Close the Berkeley DB
undef $db;
untie %database;

### Close the file descriptor to release the lock
close DATAFILE;

exit;
```

When run, this script will generate the following output, indicating that it is indeed retrieving values from a database:

```
Acquiring exclusive lock...Acquired lock. Ready to update database!

Acquiring shared lock...Acquired lock. Ready to read database!

Callanish I
============

This site, commonly known as the "Stonehenge of the North" is in the
form of a buckled Celtic cross.
```

```
Avebury
========

Avebury is a vast, sprawling site that features, amongst other marvels,
the largest stone circle in Britain. The henge itself is so large,
it almost completely surrounds the village of Avebury.

Lundin Links
=============

Lundin Links is a megalithic curiosity, featuring 3 gnarled and
immensely tall monoliths arranged possibly in a 4-poster design.
Each monolith is over 5m tall.
```

You may have noticed that we cheated a little bit in the previous example. We stored only the descriptions of the sites instead of all the information such as the map reference and location. This is the inherent problem with key/value pair databases: you can store only a single value against a given key. You can circumvent this by simply concatenating values into a string and storing that string instead, just like we did using `join()`, `pack()`, `Data::Dumper`, and `Storable` earlier in this chapter.

This particular form of storage jiggery-pokery can be accomplished in at least two ways.* One is to hand-concatenate the data into a string and hand-split it when required. The other is slightly more sophisticated and uses a Perl object encapsulating a megalith to handle, and hide, the packing and unpacking.

Localized storage and retrieval

The first technique—application handling of string joins and splits—is certainly the most self-contained. This leads us into a small digression.

Self-containment can be beneficial, as it tends to concentrate the logic of a script internally, making things slightly more simple to understand. Unfortunately, this localization can also be a real pain. Take our megalithic database as a good example. In the previous section, we wrote four different Perl scripts to handle the four main data manipulation operations. With localized logic, you're essentially implementing the same storing and extraction code in four different places.

Furthermore, if you decide to change the format of the data, you need to keep four different scripts in sync. Given that it's also likely that you'll add more scripts to perform more specific functions (such as generating web pages) with the appropriate megalithic data from the database, that gives your database more points of potential failure and inevitable corruption.

---

* As with all Perl things, There's More Than One Way To Do It (a phrase so common with Perl you'll often see it written as TMTOWTDI). We're outlining these ideas here because they dawned on us first. You might come up with something far more outlandish and obscure, or painfully obvious. Such is Perl.

Getting back to the point, we can fairly simply store complex data in a DBM file by using either `join()`, to create a delimited string, or `pack()`, to make a fixed-length record. `join()` can be used in the following way to produce the desired effect:

```
### Insert some data rows
$database{'Callanish I'} =
    join( ':', 'Callanish I', 'Callanish, Western Isles', 'NB 213 330',
            'Stone Circle', 'Description of Callanish I' );
$database{'Avebury'} =
    join( ':', 'Avebury', 'Wiltshire', 'SU 103 700',
            'Stone Circle and Henge',
            'Description of Avebury' );
$database{'Lundin Links'} =
    join( ':', 'Lundin Links', 'Fife', 'NO 404 027', 'Standing Stones',
            'Description of Lundin Links' );
### Dump the database
foreach my $key ( keys %database ) {
    my ( $name, $location, $mapref, $type, $description ) =
        split( /:/, $database{$key} );
    print "$name\n", ( "=" x length( $name ) ), "\n\n";
    print "Location:       $location\n";
    print "Map Reference: $mapref\n";
    print "Description:    $description\n\n";
}
```

The storage of fixed-length records is equally straightforward, but does gobble up space within the database rather quickly. Furthermore, the main rationale for using fixed-length records is often access speed, but when stored within a DBM file, in-place queries and updates simply do not provide any major speed increase.

The code to insert and dump megalithic data using fixed-length records is shown in the following code segment:

```
### The pack and unpack template.
$PACKFORMAT = 'A64 A64 A16 A32 A256';

### Insert some data rows
$database{'Callanish I'} =
    pack( $PACKFORMAT, 'Callanish I', 'Callanish, Western Isles',
                    'NB 213 330', 'Stone Circle',
                    'Description of Callanish I' );

$database{'Avebury'} =
    pack( $PACKFORMAT, 'Avebury', 'Wiltshire', 'SU 103 700',
                    'Stone Circle and Henge', 'Description of Avebury' );

$database{'Lundin Links'} =
    pack( $PACKFORMAT, 'Lundin Links', 'Fife', 'NO 404 027',
                    'Standing Stones',
                    'Description of Lundin Links' );

### Dump the database
foreach my $key ( keys %database ) {
```

```
    my ( $name, $location, $mapref, $type, $description ) =
        unpack( $PACKFORMAT, $database{$key} );
    print "$name\n", ( "=" x length( $name ) ), "\n\n";
    print "Location:      $location\n";
    print "Map Reference: $mapref\n";
    print "Description:   $description\n\n";
}
```

The actual code to express the storage and retrieval mechanism isn't really much more horrible than the delimited record version, but it does introduce a lot of gibberish in the form of the **pack()** template, which could easily be miskeyed or forgotten about. This also doesn't really solve the problem of localized program logic, and turns maintenance into the aforementioned nightmare.

How can we improve on this?

Packing in Perl objects

One solution to both the localized code problem and the problem of storing multiple data values within a single hash key/value pair is to use a Perl *object* to encapsulate and hide some of the nasty bits.[*]

The following Perl code defines an object of class **Megalith**. We can then reuse this packaged object module in all of our programs without having to rewrite any of them, if we change the way the module works:

```
#!/usr/bin/perl -w
#
# ch02/DBM/Megalith.pm: A perl class encapsulating a megalith

package Megalith;

use strict;
use Carp;

### Creates a new megalith object and initializes the member fields.
sub new {
    my $class = shift;
    my ( $name, $location, $mapref, $type, $description ) = @_;
    my $self = {};
    bless $self => $class;

    ### If we only have one argument, assume we have a string
    ### containing all the field values in $name and unpack it
    if ( @_ == 1 ) {
        $self->unpack( $name );
    }
```

---

[*] This is where people tend to get a little confused about Perl. The use of objects, accessor methods, and data hiding are all very object-oriented. By this design, we get to mix the convenience of non-OO programming with the neat bits of OO programming. Traditional OO programmers have been known to make spluttering noises when Perl programmers discuss this sort of thing in public.

```
        else {
            $self->{name} = $name;
            $self->{location} = $location;
            $self->{mapref} = $mapref;
            $self->{type} = $type;
            $self->{description} = $description;
        }
    return $self;
}


### Packs the current field values into a colon delimited record
### and returns it
sub pack {
    my ( $self ) = @_;

    my $record = join( ':', $self->{name}, $self->{location},
                            $self->{mapref}, $self->{type},
                            $self->{description} );

    ### Simple check that fields don't contain any colons
    croak "Record field contains ':' delimiter character"
        if $record =~ tr/:/:/ != 4;

    return $record;
}


### Unpacks the given string into the member fields
sub unpack {
    my ( $self, $packedString ) = @_;

    ### Naive split...Assumes no inter-field delimiters
    my ( $name, $location, $mapref, $type, $description ) =
        split( ':', $packedString, 5 );

    $self->{name} = $name;
    $self->{location} = $location;
    $self->{mapref} = $mapref;
    $self->{type} = $type;
    $self->{description} = $description;
}


### Displays the megalith data
sub dump {
    my ( $self ) = @_;

    print "$self->{name} ( $self->{type} )\n",
          "=" x ( length( $self->{name} ) +
                  length( $self->{type} ) + 5 ), "\n";
    print "Location:       $self->{location}\n";
    print "Map Reference: $self->{mapref}\n";
    print "Description:    $self->{description}\n\n";
}


1;
```

The record format defined by the module contains the items of data pertaining to each megalithic site that can be queried and manipulated by programs. A new `Megalith` object can be created from Perl via the **new** operator, for example:

```
### Create a new object encapsulating Stonehenge
$stonehenge =
    new Megalith( 'Stonehenge', 'Description of Stonehenge',
                  'Wiltshire', 'SU 123 400' );

### Display the name of the site stored within the object ...
print "Name: $stonehenge->{name}\n";
```

It would be extremely nice if these `Megalith` objects could be stored directly into a DBM file. Let's try a simple piece of code that simply stuffs the object into the hash:

```
### Create a new object encapsulating Stonehenge
$stonehenge =
    new Megalith( 'Stonehenge', 'Description of Stonehenge',
                  'Wiltshire', 'SU 123 400' );

### Store the object within the database hash
$database{'Stonehenge'} = $stonehenge;

### Have a look at the entry within the database
print "Key: $database{'Stonehenge'}\n";
```

This generates some slightly odd results, to say the least:

```
Key: Megalith=HASH(0x80e9aec)
```

What appears to have happened is that the string *describing* the reference to the Perl object has been inserted in the Berkeley DB instead of the object itself!

This result is perhaps not surprising, given that the DBM systems are really designed for storing single string values, and there is no innate understanding of how to compact complex objects into a single value. It simply converts all keys and values into strings.

Fortunately, the problem of storing a Perl object can be routed around by packing, or *marshalling*, all the values of all the `Megalith` object's fields into a single string, and then inserting that string into the database. Similarly, upon extracting the string from the database, a new `Megalith` can be allocated and populated by unpacking the string into the appropriate fields.

By using our conveniently defined `Megalith` class, we can write the following code to do this (note the calling of the **pack()** method):

```
$database{'Callanish I'} =
    new Megalith( 'Callanish I',
                  'Western Isles',
                  'NB 213 330',
```

```
                        'Stone Circle',
                        'Description of Callanish I' )->pack();

### Dump the database
foreach $key ( keys %database ) {

    ### Unpack the record into a new megalith object
    my $megalith = new Megalith( $database{$key} );

    ### And display the record
    $megalith->dump();
}
```

The `Megalith` object has two methods declared within it called `pack()` and `unpack()`. These simply pack all the fields into a single delimited string, and unpack a single string into the appropriate fields of the object as needed. If a `Megalith` object is created with one of these strings as the sole argument, `unpack()` is called internally, shielding the programmer from the internal details of storage management.

Similarly, the actual way in which the data is packed and unpacked is hidden from the module user. This means that if any database structural changes need to be made, they can be made internally without any maintenance on the database manipulation scripts themselves.

If you read the section on putting complex data into flat files earlier in the chapter, then you'll know that there's more than one way to do it.

So although it's a little more work at the outset, it is actually quite straightforward to store Perl objects (and other complex forms of data) within DBM files.

Object accessor methods

A final gloss on the `Megalith` class would be to add *accessor methods* to allow controlled access to the values stored within each object. That is, the example code listed above contains code that explicitly accesses member variables within the object:

```
print "Megalith Name: $megalith->{name}\n";
```

This may cause problems if the internal structure of the `Megalith` object alters in some way. Also, if you write `$megalith->{nme}` by mistake, no errors or warnings will be generated. Defining an accessor method called `getName()`, such as:

```
### Returns the name of the megalith
sub getName {
    my ( $self ) = @_;
    return $self->{name};
}
```

makes the code arguably more readable:

```
print "Megalith Name: " . $megalith->getName() . "\n";
```

and also ensures the correctness of the application code, since the actual logic is migrated, once again, into the object.

Querying limitations of DBM files and hashtables

Even with the functionality of being able to insert complex data into the Berkeley DB file (albeit in a slightly roundabout way), there is still a fundamental limitation of this database software: you can retrieve values via only one key. That is, if you wanted to search our megalithic database, the name, not the map reference or the location, must be used as the search term.

This might be a pretty big problem, given that you might wish to issue a query such as, "tell me about all the sites in Wiltshire," without specifying an exact name. In this case, every record would be tested to see if any fit the bill. This would use a sequential search instead of the indexed access you have when querying against the key.

A solution to this problem is to create secondary *referential hashes* that have key values for the different fields you might wish to query on. The value stored for each key is actually a *reference* to the original hash and not to a separate value. This allows you to update the value in the original hash, and the new value is automatically mirrored within the reference hashes. The following snippet shows some code that could be used to create and dump out a referential hash keyed on the location of a megalithic site:

```
### Build a referential hash based on the location of each monument
$locationDatabase{'Wiltshire'}    = \$database{'Avebury'};
$locationDatabase{'Western Isles'} = \$database{'Callanish I'};
$locationDatabase{'Fife'}         = \$database{'Lundin Links'};

### Dump the location database
foreach $key ( keys %locationDatabase ) {

    ### Unpack the record into a new megalith object
    my $megalith = new Megalith( ${ $locationDatabase{$key} } );

    ### And display the record
    $megalith->dump();
}
```

There are, of course, a few drawbacks to this particular solution. The most apparent is that any data deletion or insertion would require a mirror operation to be performed on each secondary reference hash.

The biggest problem with this approach is that your data might not have unique keys. If we wished to store records for Stonehenge and Avebury, both of those sites have a location of Wiltshire. In this case, the latest inserted record would always overwrite the earlier records inserted into the hash. To solve this general problem, we can use a feature of Berkeley DB files that allows *value chaining*.

Chaining multiple values into a hash

One of the bigger problems when using a DDM file with the storage mechanism of DB_HASH is that the keys against which the data is stored must be unique. For example, if we stored two different values with the key of "Wiltshire," say for Stonehenge and Avebury, generally the last value inserted into the hash would get stored in the database. This is a bit problematic, to say the least.

In a good database design, the *primary key* of any data structure generally should be unique in order to speed up searches. But quick and dirty databases, badly designed ones, or databases with a suboptimal data quality may not be able to enforce this uniqueness. Similarly, using referential hashtables to provide nonprimary key searching of the database also triggers this problem.

A Perl solution to this problem is to push the multiple values onto an array that is stored within the hash element. This technique works fine while the program is running, because the array references are still valid, but when the database is written out and reloaded, the data is invalid.

Therefore, to solve this problem, we need to look at using the different Berkeley DB storage management method of DB_BTREE, which orders its keys prior to insertion. With this mechanism, it is possible to have duplicate keys, because the underlying DBM file is in the form of an array rather than a hashtable. Fortunately, you still reference the DBM file via a Perl hashtable, so DB_BTREE is not any harder to use. The main downside to DB_BTREE storage is a penalty in performance, since a B-Tree is generally slightly slower than a hashtable for data retrieval.

The following short program creates a Berkeley DB using the DB_BTREE storage mechanism and also specifies a flag to indicate that duplicate keys are allowed. A number of rows are inserted with duplicate keys, and finally the database is dumped to show that the keys have been stored:

```
#!/usr/bin/perl -w
#
# ch02/DBM/dupkey1: Creates a Berkeley DB with the DB_BTREE mechanism and
#                   allows for duplicate keys. We then insert some test
#                   object data with duplicate keys and dump the final
#                   database.

use DB_File;
use Fcntl ':flock';
use Megalith;
```

```perl
### Set Berkeley DB BTree mode to handle duplicate keys
$DB_BTREE->{'flags'} = R_DUP;

### Remove any existing database files
unlink 'dupkey2.dat';

### Open the database up
my %database;
my $db = tie %database, 'DB_File', "dupkey2.dat",
                O_CREAT | O_RDWR, 0666, $DB_BTREE
    or die "Can't initialize database: $!\n";

### Exclusively lock the database to ensure no one accesses it
my $fd = $db->fd();
open DATAFILE, "+<&=$fd"
    or die "Can't safely open file: $!\n";
print "Acquiring exclusive lock...";
flock( DATAFILE, LOCK_EX )
    or die "Unable to acquire lock: $!. Aborting";
print "Acquired lock. Ready to update database!\n\n";

### Create, pack and insert some rows with duplicate keys
$database{'Wiltshire'} =
  new Megalith( 'Avebury',
                'Wiltshire',
                'SU 103 700',
                'Stone Circle and Henge',
                'Largest stone circle in Britain' )->pack();

$database{'Wiltshire'} =
  new Megalith( 'Stonehenge',
                'Wiltshire',
                'SU 123 400',
                'Stone Circle and Henge',
                'The most popularly known stone circle in the world' )->pack();

$database{'Wiltshire'} =
  new Megalith( 'The Sanctuary',
                'Wiltshire',
                'SU 118 680',
                'Stone Circle ( destroyed )',
                'No description available' )->pack();

### Dump the database
foreach my $key ( keys %database ) {

    ### Unpack the record into a new megalith object
    my $megalith = new Megalith( $database{$key} );

    ### And display the record
    $megalith->dump();
}

### Close the database
```

```
undef $db;
untie %database;

### Close the filehandle to release the lock
close DATAFILE;

exit;
```

The output you get from running this program is not exactly what we'd hoped for:

```
Acquiring exclusive lock...Acquired lock. Ready to update database!

The Sanctuary ( Stone Circle ( destroyed ) )
==============================================
Location:      Wiltshire
Map Reference: SU 118 680
Description:   No description available

The Sanctuary ( Stone Circle ( destroyed ) )
==============================================
Location:      Wiltshire
Map Reference: SU 118 680
Description:   No description available

The Sanctuary ( Stone Circle ( destroyed ) )
==============================================
Location:      Wiltshire
Map Reference: SU 118 680
Description:   No description available
```

It seems that we've managed to successfully store three copies of the same record instead of three different records!

Fortunately, this isn't actually the case. We have correctly stored the three different records with the same key in the DBM file. The problem lies in the way we've tried to read these records back out of the DBM file. A basic dereference using the hash key obviously doesn't work, since Perl stores only a single value for each key, as we already know.

To get around this limitation, we can use the **seq**() method declared within the `DB_File` module, which is used to traverse *chained* records stored within a single hash element. Figure 2-2 illustrates the principle of chained record traversal within a hash element.

The corrected record dumping chunk is rewritten to use **seq**() in this way:

```
### Dump the database
my ($key, $value, $status) = ('', '', 0);
for ( $status = $db->seq( $key, $value, R_FIRST ) ;
      $status == 0 ;
      $status = $db->seq( $key, $value, R_NEXT ) ) {

    ### Unpack the record into a new megalith object
```

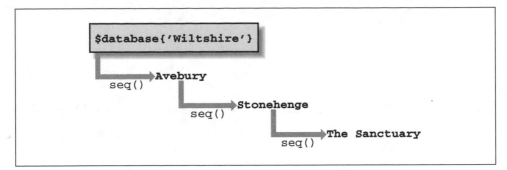

Figure 2-2. Chained record traversal

```
my $megalith = new Megalith( $value );

### And display the record
$megalith->dump();
}
```

Running this corrected version produces the output we expected, i.e., records for three different megalithic sites.

The seq() method is quite simple to use and understand, and it works well when used in conjunction with a for loop, as shown above. The method takes three arguments: the hash key, the hash value, and a flag signifying which element within the chain should be returned. The first two arguments are actually populated with the hash key and the correct hash value, respectively, when seq() is called. Exactly which hash value is returned depends on the value of the third argument:

- R_FIRST returns the first record within the chain of records.

- R_LAST returns the last record stored within the chain of records.

- R_NEXT returns the next record within the chain of records. This is used for forward sequential traversals of the chain.

- R_PREV returns the previous record within the chain of records. This is used for backward sequential traversals of the chain.

- R_CURSOR returns a record in which a *partial match* for the key has been located. This allows a certain element of "fuzzy matching" of keys. This feature is not necessarily accurate and may return the closest match to the desired key rather than an exact match. For example, if you searched for all sites within Wiltshire and asked for a partial match against "wilt", but no exact records matched, you may be returned the entries for the "Western Isles," as these are the closest to the search term.

In the database dumping example shown above, we are simply starting at the beginning of the record chain and traversing through it in a forward direction. We could have performed a backward search by writing:

```
for ( $status = $db->seq( $key, $value, R_LAST ) ;
      $status == 0 ;
      $status = $db->seq( $key, $value, R_PREV ) ) {
    ...
}
```

A quicker and easier utility method for querying duplicate values also exists: get_dup(). This method returns either the number of records with the given key or an array or hash containing the appropriate records. For example, given that we have three records in our database with the key of Wiltshire, we could verify that fact by writing:

```
### Displays the number of records inserted against
### the "Wiltshire" key
my $numRecords = $db->get_dup( 'Wiltshire' );
print "Number of Wiltshire records: $numRecords\n";
```

Deleting Values

Deleting values is the final operation that can be performed on DBM files. Updating is as simple as assigning different values to the appropriate key within the database, and deleting is equally simple. This operation is performed by using the standard Perl delete function on the appropriate key within the database. delete removes it from the hash that represents the database, and because the hash has been tied to the DBM file, it is purged from that also.

The following program inserts three records into a Berkeley DB, and then dumps the database to show that the records are there. Following that process, a single record is deleted and the database is redumped to illustrate the deletion. Here's the program:

```
#!/usr/bin/perl -w
#
# ch02/DBM/delete: Creates a Berkeley DB, inserts some test data then
#                  deletes some of it

use strict;

use DB_File;

### Initialize the Berkeley DB
my %database;
tie %database, 'DB_File', "delete.dat"
    or die "Can't initialize database: $!\n";

### Insert some data rows
```

```
$database{'Callanish I'}  = "Western Isles";
$database{'Avebury'}      = "Wiltshire";
$database{'Lundin Links'} = "Fife";

### Dump the database
print "Dumping the entire database...\n";
foreach my $key ( keys %database ) {
    printf "%15s - %s\n", $key, $database{$key};
}
print "\n";

### Delete a row
delete $database{'Avebury'};

### Re-dump the database
print "Dumping the database after deletions...\n";
foreach my $key ( keys %database ) {
    printf "%15s - %s\n", $key, $database{$key};
}

### Close the Berkeley DB
untie %database;

exit;
```

The output of this program is as expected:

```
Dumping the entire database...
    Callanish I - Western Isles
        Avebury - Wiltshire
    Lundin Links - Fife

Dumping the database after deletions...
    Callanish I - Western Isles
    Lundin Links - Fife
```

That is, the specified row has been permanently removed from the database by deleting the related hash entry.

The MLDBM Module

The MLDBM module is very useful for quickly writing complex Perl data structures to DBM files for persistent storage. The ML in MLDBM stands for *multilevel* and refers to its ability to store complex multilevel data structures. That's something that ordinary hashes, even hashes tied to DBM files, can't do.

The MLDBM module is an excellent example of a layered storage manager. It acts as a thin layer over another DBM module, but intercepts reads and writes to automatically *serialize* (or deserialize) the data using another module.*

---

* We discussed serialization and the Data::Dumper and Storable modules earlier in this chapter.

The module works by automatically serializing the Perl data structures that you wish to store into a single string, which is then stored within a DBM file. The data is recovered by deserializing the data from the stored string back into a valid Perl object. The actual interface for referencing the stored and retrieved data is identical to the API for DBM files. That makes it very easy to "drop in" use of MLDBM instead of your existing DBM module.

The following example shows how we could use DB_File for storage and Data:: Dumper for displaying the restored data:

```perl
#!/usr/bin/perl -w
#
# ch02/mldbmtest: Demonstrates storing complex data structures in a DBM
#                 file using the MLDBM module.

use MLDBM qw( DB_File Data::Dumper );
use Fcntl;

### Remove the test file in case it exists already ...
unlink 'mldbmtest.dat';

tie my %database1, 'MLDBM', 'mldbmtest.dat', O_CREAT | O_RDWR, 0666
    or die "Can't initialize MLDBM file: $!\n";

### Create some megalith records in the database
%database1 = (
    'Avebury' => {
        name => 'Avebury',
        mapref => 'SU 103 700',
        location => 'Wiltshire'
    },
    'Ring of Brodgar' => {
        name => 'Ring of Brodgar',
        mapref => 'HY 294 133',
        location => 'Orkney'
    }
);

### Untie and retie to show data is stored in the file
untie %database1;

tie my %database2, 'MLDBM', 'mldbmtest.dat', O_RDWR, 0666
    or die "Can't initialize MLDBM file: $!\n";

### Dump out via Data::Dumper what's been stored ...
print Data::Dumper->Dump( [ \%database2 ] );

untie %database2;

exit;
```

The results of running this program are:

```
$VAR1 = {
        'Avebury' => {
                         'name' => 'Avebury',
                         'location' => 'Wiltshire',
                         'mapref' => 'SU 103 700'
                     },
        'Ring of Brodgar' => {
                                 'name' => 'Ring of Brodgar',
                                 'location' => 'Orkney',
                                 'mapref' => 'HY 294 133'
                             }
      };
```

This shows that the nested data within the original hash has been restored intact.

Summary

This has been a long chapter, both for you to read and for us to write. We've covered a lot of topics and, hopefully, given you some useful insights into database fundamentals and some new techniques for your mental toolbox.

We're almost ready to discuss the DBI itself, but before we do, we want to introduce you to the joys of SQL.

3

SQL and Relational Databases

The *Structured Query Language*, or *SQL*,* is a language designed for the purpose of manipulating data within databases.

In 1970, E. F. Codd, working for IBM, published a now classic paper, "A Relational Model of Data for Large Shared Data Banks," in which he laid down a set of abstract principles for data management that became known as the *relational model.* The entire field of relational database technology has its roots in that paper.

One of the many research projects sparked by that paper was the design and implementation of a language that could make interacting with relational databases simple. And it didn't make the programmer write horrendously complex sections of code to interact with the database.†

This chapter serves to give the complete database neophyte a very limited overview of what SQL is and how you can do some simple tasks with it. Many of the more complex details of SQL's design and operation have been omitted or greatly simplified to allow the neophyte to learn enough to use the DBI in a simple, but effective, way. The "Resources" section of the Preface lists other books and web sites dedicated to SQL and relational database technologies.

The Relational Database Methodology

The relational database model revolves around data storage units called *tables,* which have a number of attributes associated with them, called *columns.* For

---

* Officially pronounced "ess-que-ell," although "sequel" is also popular. We have also heard the term "squeal," but that's usually only heard when people first see the syntax or when they've just deleted all their data!

† Chapter 2 shows many examples of how long-winded and inflexible database interaction can be!

example, we might wish to store the name of the megalithic site, its location, what sort of site it is, and where it can be found on the map in our `megaliths` table. Each of these items of data would be a separate column.

In most large database systems, tables are created within containing structures known as *schemas*. A schema is a collection of logical data structures, or *schema objects*, such as tables and views. In some databases, a schema corresponds to a user created within the database. In others, it's a more general way of grouping related tables. For example, in our megalithic database, using Oracle, we have created a user called *stones*. Within the *stones* user's schema, the various tables that compose the megalithic database have been created.

Data is stored within a table in the form of *rows*. That is, the data for one site is stored within one row that contains the appropriate values for each column. This sort of data layout corresponds exactly to the row–column metaphor used by spreadsheets, ledgers, or even plain old tabulated lists you might scribble in a notepad.

An example of such a list containing megalithic data is:

```
Site               Location        Type                    Map Reference
----               --------        ----                    -------------
Callanish I        Western Isles   Stone Circle and Rows   NB 213 330
Stonehenge         Wiltshire       Stone Circle and Henge  SU 123 422
Avebury            Wiltshire       Stone Circle and Henge  SU 103 700
Sunhoney           Aberdeenshire   Recumbent Stone Circle  NJ 716 058
Lundin Links       Fife            Four Poster             NO 404 027
```

This system lends itself quite well to a generalized query such as "Give me the names of all the megaliths" or "Give me the map locations of all the megaliths in Wiltshire." To perform these queries, we simply specify the columns we wish to see and the conditions each column in each row must meet to be returned as a valid result.

Similarly, data manipulation operations are easily specified using a similar syntax, such as "Insert a new row into the `megaliths` table with the following values..." or "Delete all the rows containing megaliths in Fife."

The sheer simplicity of SQL belies the fact that it is an extraordinarily powerful syntax for manipulating data stored within databases, and helps enforce a logical structure for your data.

The main thrust of the relational database design is that related information should be stored either in the same place or in a separate place that is related to the original in some meaningful way. It also is designed around the principle that data should not be duplicated within the database.

Using our megalithic database as an example, we have decided to store all information directly related to each megalithic site within the `megaliths` table and all the multimedia clips in a separate table. This is a good example of a relational database, albeit a small one, because if we stored the multimedia clip information in the `megaliths` table, we would duplicate the megalith information many times over—once per clip for that site, in fact. This leads to *redundancy of data*, which is one problem the relational database model is designed to avoid.

We have also split the categorization of a site into a separate table called `site_types` to avoid further redundancy of data.

The process of rationalizing your data into tables to avoid data redundancy is known as *normalization*. The corollary operation is known as *denormalization* and can be desirable in certain situations.

Data stored across multiple normalized tables can be retrieved by making *joins* between the tables that allow queries to retrieve columns from all the tables included in the join. Joins would allow us to fetch the name of the megalithic site and the URL of multimedia clips from the same query, for example. This is an efficient way of storing data and stores exactly enough data necessary to retrieve the desired information.

On the downside, creating multi-table joins on a regular basis can perform badly on databases with large data quantities. Extra disk accesses are required to relate the rows of one table to another, and it can be difficult for the database to work out how best to do it.

This is a major problem in the discipline known as *data warehousing*, in which massive quantities of information are stored to allow users to produce reports and analyses of that data. The typical solution for these situations is to create new wide, *denormalized* tables that contain much information duplicated from other tables. This greatly increases performance at the expense of storage space and, since the information contained within the data warehouses is generally read-only, you don't have to worry about keeping data changes synchronized.

For the purposes of these chapters, a small database containing three tables will be used to demonstrate the various ways in which SQL can be used to query and manipulate data. These tables are named `megaliths`, `media`, and `site_types`. Figure 3-1 illustrates the structure of these three tables.

These tables are designed to contain information on megalithic sites and multimedia clips associated with those sites respectively. In essence, each megalithic site will have zero or more multimedia clips associated with it and will be categorized as exactly one type of site. This small database will form the basis of our examples throughout the remainder of the book.

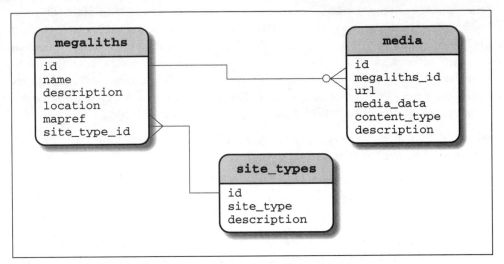

Figure 3-1. Megalith database

Datatypes and NULL Values

One of the most important aspects of the structures defined within a database, such as tables and views, is the *datatype* of each of the columns. Perl is a loosely typed language, whereas SQL is strongly typed. Thus, each field or value is of a given datatype that determines how values and fields are compared. For example, the `mapref` field within the `megaliths` table would not be much use if it could hold only dates!

Therefore, it is important to assign an appropriate datatype to each column. This avoids any potential confusion as to how the values stored within each column are to be interpreted, and also establishes how these values can be compared in query condition clauses.

There are several common datatypes. The most widely used of these can be grouped as follows:

Numeric datatypes

The grouping of numeric datatypes includes types such as integer and floating point (or real) numbers. These types, depending on your database, may include `FLOAT`, `REAL`, `INTEGER`, and `NUMBER`. Numeric datatypes are compared in the obvious way; that is, the actual values are tested.

Character datatypes

Character datatypes are used to store and manipulate textual data. Any characters whatsoever—digits or letters—can be stored within a character datatype.

However, if digits are stored within a character datatype, they will be treated as being a string of characters as opposed to a number. For example, they'll be sorted and ordered as strings and not numbers, so "10" will be less than "9".

Depending on your database system, there can be many different types of character datatypes such as CHAR, VARCHAR, VARCHAR2, and so on. Most databases support at least the most basic of these, CHAR.

When being compared, character datatypes usually apply lexical ordering according to the character set being used by the database.

Date datatypes

Most database systems implement at least one datatype that contains date information, as opposed to a character datatype containing a string representation of a date. This allows you to perform arbitrary arithmetic on date values very easily. For example, you might wish to select rows where the date field corresponds to a Monday.

When comparing dates, a later date is regarded as being greater than an earlier date. datatypes for storing times and timestamps (date plus time) are also common.

Binary object datatypes

Binary object datatypes are a relatively recent addition to database systems and allow you to store massive unstructured chunks of data—typically images, video, or audio clips—within a database. The actual binary object datatypes tend to differ between databases, but usually tend to be called LOBs (large objects) if they do exist. For example, the BLOB datatype stores binary data and CLOB stores large quantities of ASCII character data. Generally, LOB types cannot be compared to one another.

The NULL value

NULL is a special kind of value that actually has no value. It can be contained within columns and signifies that no value is contained within that column for a given row. NULL values are used where the actual value is either not known or not meaningful.

When a table is created, each column can declare to either allow or disallow NULL values, regardless of the datatype of the column.

NULL values should not be confused with the numeric value of zero. They are not the same thing. Zero means zero, whereas NULL means there is no value at all.*

If you attempt to evaluate an expression containing a NULL value, other than with various special NULL handling functions, it will always evaluate to NULL.

---

* Though some databases do treat empty strings as NULL values when inserting data.

Comparing values to NULL should always use `IS NULL` and `IS NOT NULL` instead.* Be careful!

The NULL value plays a part in what are called "three-valued logic" tables that are used when evaluating condition clause truth tables, as discussed later in this chapter. This allows SQL conditional expressions to either be *true, false,* or *NULL.*

Querying Data

The first (and possibly most immediately useful) operation that SQL allows you to perform on data is to select and return rows of data from tables stored within the database. This activity forms the core of exactly what a database represents, a large repository of searchable information.

All SQL queries, no matter how simple or complex, use the `SELECT` keyword to specify the columns to fetch, the tables to fetch them from, and any conditions that must be met for the rows to be retrieved. `SELECT` falls into the group of commands known as *Data Manipulation Language*, or *DML*, commands.

The full syntax for `SELECT` can be intimidating to the new user, primarily because it sports a multitude of different ways in which the query can be customized. For example, you might wish to return only unique data rows, group certain rows together, or even specify how the returned rows should be sorted.

For the moment, we'll just look at the simplest cases.

In our example, we've tended to use capital letters for SQL commands and other reserved words, and lowercase letters for database object names (tables, columns, etc.). In most databases, the SQL commands are not case-sensitive, but the actual database object names may or may not be.

Simple Queries

The simplest SQL query is to ask for certain columns in all rows of a table. The `SELECT` syntax for this form of query can be expressed as simply as:

```
SELECT column, column, ..., column
FROM table
```

or:

```
SELECT *
FROM table
```

which will query and fetch back all the columns within the specified table.

---

* A few databases, such as mSQL, do use = `NULL`.

Therefore, to select some of the rows from some columns in the `megaliths` table, the following SQL statement can be used:

```
SELECT name, location, mapref
FROM megaliths
```

which would return the following information:

```
+--------------------------------------------------------------+
| name          | location                        | mapref     |
+--------------------------------------------------------------+
| Callanish I   | Callanish, Isle of Lewis        | NB 213 330 |
| Lundin Links  | Lundin Links, Fife, Scotland    | NO 404 027 |
| Stonehenge    | Near Amesbury, Wiltshire, England | SU 123 400 |
| Avebury       | Avebury, Wiltshire, England     | SU 103 700 |
| Sunhoney      | Near Insch, Aberdeenshire       | NJ 716 058 |
+--------------------------------------------------------------+
```

So even with the simplest SQL imaginable, the inherent flexibility of the syntax allows us to easily specify exactly which information we want from the database without having to write lots of excruciating lines of code to get it.

Another aspect of the relational database methodology is now visible, in that even though the database contains information on all the columns within a particular table, only a subset of the available columns needs to be retrieved. Therefore, we can extract *exactly* the data we need for a particular query and no more. This is an extremely powerful feature and separates the actual data stored within the database from our desired view of that data.

Queries and Condition Clauses

The previous example relied on retrieving all the rows within a table, whereas the more ordinary, everyday database operations will usually require more accurate targeting of specific rows. For example, "Tell me the names of all the stone circles in Wiltshire" is a more specific query than "Tell me about all the stone circles in the database." To achieve this task, SQL provides the ability to specify conditions that must be met before a row is returned to the user.

SQL's syntax regarding condition clauses is just as straightforward and obvious as that for specifying which columns are of interest. The condition clauses that narrow the query are specified *after* the list of tables from which data is being retrieved, i.e., after the `FROM` clause and table list.

Therefore, a query that retrieves the `name` and `location` columns from rows that contain the string "Wiltshire" in the `location` column, can be written as:

```
SELECT name, location
FROM megaliths
WHERE location LIKE '%Wiltshire%'
```

The information returned from this query would be:

```
+--------------------------------------------------+
| name          | location                         |
+--------------------------------------------------+
| Stonehenge    | Near Amesbury, Wiltshire, England |
| Avebury       | Avebury, Wiltshire, England       |
+--------------------------------------------------+
```

The returned information shows just the columns specified for the sites that have a `location` value containing the string, "Wiltshire." The **WHERE** keyword is the one that specifies the beginning of the list of conditions that must be met for each row to be returned. That is, the condition states that the `location` column value must contain the desired string "Wiltshire."*

The following table lists all of the *comparison operators* used by SQL for testing condition clauses. These conditions are generally Perl-like and should be familiar.

Operator	Purpose

=	This operator tests exact equality between columns and/or literal values. For example, the query:
	```SELECT name, location```
	```FROM megaliths```
	```WHERE location = 'Fife'```
	will return all rows where the location column is equal to the value "Fife".

<>	This operator tests for inequality between columns and/or literal values. For example, the query:
	```SELECT name, location```
	```FROM megaliths```
	```WHERE location <> 'Fife'```
	will return all rows where the location column is *not* equal to the value "Fife". Some databases alternatively use the `!=`, `^=`, or `~=` operators instead of `<>`.

> and <	These two operators represent "greater than" and "less than" tests between columns and/or literal values. For example, the query:
	```SELECT name, location```
	```FROM megaliths```
	```WHERE id < 10```
	```AND id > 5```
	will return the name and location of all megalithic sites whose `id` value is less than 10 and greater than 5. The type of comparison used depends on the datatype of the values involved. So numeric values are compared as numbers, string values are compared as strings, and date values are compared as dates.
	
	On a related note, there also exists the `<=` and `>=` operators that perform "less than or equal to" and "greater than or equal to" tests, respectively.

---

* The % character, in this case, is used as the standard SQL wildcard character to match any number of characters. A few databases use * instead.

Operator	Purpose

IN	This keyword tests equality of a column and/or literal value within a specified set of values. For example, the query:
	`SELECT name, location`
	`FROM megaliths`
	`WHERE location IN ( 'Western Isles', 'Fife' )`
	will compare each member of the set using the equality operator against the specified column. Therefore, in this example, rows with a location column value of either "Western Isles" or "Fife" will be returned.

LIKE	The LIKE operator allows limited wildcard matching of strings against columns and/or literal values. For example, the query:
	`SELECT name, description`
	`FROM megaliths`
	`WHERE description LIKE '%Largest%'`
	will return the name and description columns where the description column contains the string "Largest" at any position in the string.
	
	Wildcard matches for characters in the string may be specified by using either the percent (%) character for multiple-character wildcarding or an underscore (_) for single-character matching.[a]

[a] Some databases use other names instead of LIKE, such as MATCHES or CONTAINS, and may use different wildcard characters such as * or ?.

Over time, the megalithic database might expand and contain information on thousands of sites in the country. Therefore, to quickly locate records, we might need to narrow the search criteria by specifying other condition clauses that must be met for a record to be returned. For example, if you wished to find information on all stone circles in Wiltshire, doing a query simply for all sites in "Wiltshire" could return hundreds of records, which you would have to wade through by hand. We can narrow this search by specifying as an extra condition that the `mapref` column must also begin with the string SU 123:

```
SELECT name, location
FROM megaliths
WHERE location LIKE '%Wiltshire%'
AND mapref LIKE 'SU 123%'
```

In this example, the second condition is simply added to the end of the list of conditions that must be met. The two conditions are joined together by a logical operator, AND. This statement now reads "Give me the name and location of all megalithic sites with a location of Wiltshire that are in the map region SU 123," which would return the **name** and **location** fields for the "Stonehenge" row, but reject the "Avebury" row.

Thus, conditions can be joined together into multiple condition lists, linked by logical boolean operators that control how the truth of the condition is evaluated.

The following table describes the boolean (or logical) operators defined by SQL that can be used to chain your condition clauses together.

Operator	Function			
AND	Returns the logical AND of the two clauses on either side of the keyword. The following truth table can be used to evaluate whether the combined clause is true or not.			
		TRUE	FALSE	NULL
	TRUE	true	false	null
	FALSE	false	false	false
	NULL	null	false	null
OR	Returns the logical OR of the two clauses on either side of the keyword. The following truth table can be used to evaluate whether the combined clause is true or not.			
		TRUE	FALSE	NULL
	TRUE	true	true	true
	FALSE	true	false	null
	NULL	true	null	null
NOT	Negates the logical value of the following expression. The following truth table illustrates this in operation.			
		TRUE	FALSE	NULL
		false	true	null

The truth of the overall condition is determined by combining the truth of each element separately using the AND, OR, and NOT operators.

It is now possible to calculate the effects of multiple condition clauses in a statement. For example, the following condition clauses:

```
WHERE location LIKE '%Wiltshire%'
AND mapref LIKE 'SU 123%'
```

evaluate in the following way for this row:

```
+-----------------------------------------------------------+
| name          | mapref    | location                      |
+-----------------------------------------------------------+
| Avebury       | SU 103 700 | Avebury, Wiltshire, England  |
+-----------------------------------------------------------+

location LIKE '%Wiltshire%'      => TRUE
mapref LIKE 'SU 123%'            => FALSE

TRUE AND FALSE => FALSE
```

thereby returning a false value for that row, causing it to be rejected by the query. However, the following row:

```
+-----------------------------------------------------------+
| name          | mapref    | location                      |
+-----------------------------------------------------------+
| Stonehenge    | SU 123 400 | Near Amesbury, Wiltshire, England |
+-----------------------------------------------------------+
```

evaluates as:

```
location LIKE '%Wiltshire%'     => TRUE
mapref LIKE 'SU 123%'           => TRUE

TRUE AND TRUE => TRUE
```

which ensures that the row is returned by the query.

When combining different logical operators, it is important to consider their *precedence*. The precedence (or priority) of the operators determines which gets combined first. The SQL standard specifies that NOT has the highest precedence, followed by AND, and then OR. Parentheses can be used around groups of operators to change their precedence.

For example, you might wish to select all the megalithic sites in either "Wiltshire" or "Fife" for which the description of the site contains the word "awe-inspiring."

This query could be wrongly expressed as:

```
SELECT name, location
FROM megaliths
WHERE location LIKE '%Wiltshire%' OR location LIKE '%Fife%'
AND description LIKE '%awe-inspiring%'
```

While this query looks correct at first, it does not take into account the order in which the condition clauses are combined. It would, in fact, select the awe-inspiring sites in Fife, but it would also select *all* the sites in Wiltshire regardless of their type.

This happens because the AND operator has a higher precedence than the OR operator and so is evaluated first. Therefore, our SQL statement evaluates by AND combining `location LIKE %Fife%` and `description LIKE %awe-inspiring%`. It then OR combines the result of the AND operation with `location LIKE %Wiltshire%`. This isn't quite what we had in mind.

This query can be more correctly written by using parentheses to logically group operators within the statement.

For example:

```
SELECT name, location
FROM megaliths
WHERE ( location LIKE '%Wiltshire%' OR location LIKE '%Fife%' )
AND description LIKE '%awe-inspiring%'
```

This changes the way in which the condition clauses are evaluated by evaluating the grouped clauses into a single truth value for the entire group. This is then used instead of truth values for each individual clause within the group.

Finally, there is another even more complex way of specifying condition clauses that is used quite frequently. This technique is to supply the values with which we are doing a comparison from a subquery.* For example:

```
SELECT name, description
FROM megaliths
WHERE name IN
    ( SELECT tourist_sitename
      FROM wiltshire_tourist_sites )
```

If we knew in advance that the subquery would return only a single row of information, then the = operator could be used instead of IN.

Queries over Multiple Tables

The previous section covered the structure of SQL statements in general, and how SQL may be used to query data from single tables in the database. However, from the discussion on relational database theory earlier in this chapter, you should remember that the power and flexibility of relational database design lies in the ability to join tables together—that is, to link disparate records of data that are held in separate tables to reduce data duplication. This linking of records is a key part of working with relational databases.

To illustrate this concept, it is time to reintroduce the other tables we shall be using in our examples, namely the media table and site_types table.

The media table contains information on where multimedia clips for given sites can be located, allowing an external application to view or listen to these clips while the user is reading the textual information on the site stored in the megaliths table.

Similarly, the site_types table contains a lookup table of the different categorizations of megalithic sites described within the database.

To specify a SELECT statement from two or more tables in the database, we simply add the table names after the FROM keyword. Therefore, a sample query to fetch all the rows in two of the tables should theoretically look something like:

```
SELECT name, description, location, url, content_type
FROM megaliths, media
```

However, the output from this query will look somewhat scrambled. For each and every row in the first table, *all* the rows in the second table will be selected!† This

---

* Support for this functionality is not necessarily present in all database systems supported by the DBI and its drivers.

† This is known as a "Cartesian Product." If there were 100 rows in each, you'd get 10,000 rows returned. If there were 1,000,000 rows in each, you'd get 1,000,000,000,000 rows returned. To avoid this, you should ensure that if you have *n* tables, you have at least *n* - *1* join conditions.

means that the media records for "Lundin Links" may be returned at the same time as the site information for "Avebury."

How do you make sure that the values in the fields from the second table related to the values from the first—that is, that the media clips for "Stonehenge" are only returned with the "Stonehenge" site information?

In our `megaliths` table, we have already defined a column called `id` that contains a unique identifier for each and every row stored within the table. Similarly, the `media` table has a column called `id` that performs the same purpose. Furthermore, the `media` table also contains a column called `megaliths_id`. When a row is inserted into the `megaliths` or `media` tables, a unique identifier is inserted into the `id` columns. Also, when a row is inserted into the `media` table, the `megaliths_id` column is populated with the unique identifier of the megalithic site to which the media clip relates.

This relationship of a link field is generally termed a *primary key* and *foreign key* relationship. The primary key is the unique value stored within the "master" table. The foreign key is that same value stored within multiple rows of the other "detail" table.

We can now write a query to fetch the appropriate information back from the database by *joining* the two tables on their *related* fields. This ensures that the media clips are associated with the correct site:

```
SELECT name, description, url, content_type
FROM megaliths, media
WHERE megaliths.id = megaliths_id
```

This illustrates another aspect of SQL conditions: instead of testing arbitrary values against columns in a table, it is possible to test against the value of another column. In the above case, we test to see if the primary and foreign keys of the two tables match, and, if so, the aggregated row created from the columns of both tables is returned.

Also note how we qualified the `id` field name in the condition clause by prepending it with the table name and a dot. Without that, the database would not have known if we were referring to the `id` field in the `megaliths` table or the `media` table and would fail with an error.

Similarly, if we wished to select the `id` fields of both tables, the following statement would simply confuse the database, and we'd get another error:

```
SELECT id, id, megaliths_id
FROM megaliths, media
WHERE id = megaliths_id
```

Therefore, it is good practice to explicitly specify the table name that the field belongs to, in cases where it may be ambiguous. For example:

```
SELECT megaliths.name, megaliths.description,
       media.url, media.content_type
FROM megaliths, media
WHERE megaliths.id = media.megaliths_id
```

Of course, the downside to this process is that it takes forever to type. A saner alternative is to *alias* the table names. To do this, simply add the alias after its name in the FROM clause. For example:

```
SELECT mega.name, mega.description, med.url, med.content_type
FROM megaliths mega, media med
WHERE mega.id = med.megaliths_id
```

It is more common just to use the initial character of the table name provided the aliases are unique.

This theory of table joins is extensible to any number of tables.[*] In fact, it is not uncommon for some tables within a database to contain nothing but columns containing foreign keys that can be used to make multi-table joins more effective. The main point to remember here is that all tables involved in the query must be joined to another table on some column. Otherwise, a large quantity of very strange results may be returned from the database!

For example, fetching both the media associated with a site and the site type information can be expressed with the following query:

```
SELECT mega.name, mega.description, st.site_type,
       med.url, med.description
FROM megaliths mega, media med, site_types st
WHERE mega.id = med.megaliths_id
AND mega.site_type_id = st.id
```

Another type of join also possible with SQL is the *outer join*. In addition to the results returned by a simple join, an outer join also returns the rows from one table for which no rows from the other table satisfy the join condition. This is achieved by returning NULL values for all rows in the second table that have no matching values in the first table.

For example, we might wish to retrieve information on all of the sites located within Wiltshire and, if any exist, the URLs of any multimedia clips associated with them. Using a simple join such as:

```
SELECT mega.name, mega.location, med.url
FROM megaliths mega, media med
WHERE mega.id = med.megaliths_id
AND mega.location LIKE '%Wiltshire%'
```

---

[*] In practice, databases that support joins often have some upper limit on the number of tables.

would return only those sites in Wiltshire that had media clips associated with them. It would exclude those sites that had no media clips. An *outer join* is the way to solve this problem.

The official standard way to express an outer join is by using the phrase LEFT OUTER JOIN or RIGHT OUTER JOIN between the tables to be joined, instead of a comma, and adding an ON condition_expression clause.[*]

For example, the standard query to retrieve the information we desired can be written as:

```
SELECT mega.name, mega.location, med.url
FROM megaliths mega
     LEFT OUTER JOIN media med ON mega.id = med.megaliths_id
WHERE mega.location LIKE '%Wiltshire%'
```

In this example, we have made a left outer join on the id and megaliths_id columns because for any sites without media clips, there are no corresponding records in the media table. The left outer join will ensure that even if no media clip records exist, at least the name and location of each and every site in Wiltshire will be returned. A right outer join in this query would have returned the values where no entries in the megaliths table existed.

Finally, it is worth mentioning some ways to make efficient table joins. In our examples, we added additional columns to our tables to make a join between them. We could have simply added a column to the media table that contained the name of the megalithic site.

There are a few good reasons why we didn't do that:

1. If the name of the megalithic site was updated for some reason—for example, if a spelling mistake needed correcting—the name contained within the media table would be out of date and incorrect. This would break the join between the two tables for that particular row.

2. Integer keys use much less space than strings when building indexes on a table. Less space means more index entries per block of disk space, and therefore fewer disk reads. The smaller index and fewer disk reads make up for the slightly increased size of the master data table, and usually give you both speed and space gains.

3. It is slower to test strings than to test numbers, especially integers. As such, in a well-designed database, integers are often used for primary and foreign keys because they are faster to test against with comparison operators. A string, on

---

[*] Many database systems either don't fully support outer joins or use different syntax for it. Oracle 7 outer joins, for example, look just like inner joins but have the three characters (+) appended to one side of the join condition.

the other hand, requires testing of every character within each string, which can be time-consuming.

Therefore, to help maximize speed on queries, you can design your database to perform joins using integer columns. It is also often worth building an index on the foreign key columns of the "detail" tables, if your database supports such functionality.

Grouping and Ordering Data

Often you'll desire a little more control over how your selected data is retrieved. The two most common ways of organizing your data are to order the retrieved rows by one or more columns, or to group the retrieved rows and apply functions to the groups instead of to individual rows.

Perl is well-suited to these tasks within your program, but performing ordering and grouping *via* SQL will offload the task onto the database server and also will save you writing, or using, potentially suboptimal techniques for organizing the data. Therefore, generally, use SQL rather than your own application-level code.

Ordering data

Ordering the data retrieved by a **SELECT** statement is easy and can be achieved simply by an **ORDER BY** clause. This clause is always found at the end of your queries, after all the join conditions have been specified.

The **ORDER BY** clause is specified as a comma-separated list of columns that should be used to order the data. For example, an **ORDER BY** clause of:

```
ORDER BY name, location
```

would order the rows by name and, if the names of the sites are identical, the location column would be used as a secondary ordering. You can change the direction of the ordering from the default "ascending" order (which goes from A to Z) to a "descending" order by appending the **DESC** keyword to any field names in the **ORDER BY** clause.

Grouping data

The ability to group items of data is very useful when attempting to make summarized reports. SQL features a clause called **GROUP BY** that allows you to group rows that share a common set of values and apply *group functions* to them.

A good example of this operation is where you want to total the values contained within a column in a table. In this instance, you would use the **sum()** grouping function in the following way to calculate the total value of orders taken on a given date:

```
SELECT order_date, sum( net ), sum( vat ), sum( total )
FROM sales
GROUP BY order_date
```

As with ORDER BY, groupings can be chained together in a comma-separated list to create complex subgroupings of columns.

Modifying Data Within Tables

Read-only databases (that is, databases that only allow you to SELECT data from them) are very useful. *Data warehouses* are typically massive read-only databases populated with archived data mangled into a form suitable for reporting. However, in the cut-and-thrust world of transaction-processing databases, the ability to *modify* data within the database quickly and efficiently is of paramount importance.

There are several core operations that comprise the broader definition of data modification, namely:

- *Inserting* new data into the database
- *Deleting* data from the database
- *Updating*, or modifying, existing data within the database

Each of these operations falls into the grouping of Data Manipulation Language commands, or DMLs, alongside SELECT.

We shall discuss each of these tasks in turn and apply the theory to our example database.

Inserting Data

Before a database can be really of any use, data must be inserted into it by some means, either by manual data entry or with an automated batch loading program. The action of inserting data only applies to cases in which you wish to load a completely new record of information into the database. If the record already exists and merely requires modification of a column value, the *update* operation should be used instead.

Data inserts in the relational database model are done on a row-by-row basis: each record or item of information that you load into the database corresponds to a brand-new row within a given existing table. As each inserted record corresponds to a new row in one table, multitable inserts are not possible.*

---

* Well, this is not strictly true these days, as database servers get smarter. Oracle, for example, allows inserts into equi-join views and also supports "INSTEAD OF" triggers that make just about anything possible.

The SQL INSERT keyword provides a simple mechanism for inserting new rows of data into the database. For example, assuming the megaliths table is already present in the database and and contains the six columns shown earlier in Figure 3-1, a single row of data can be inserted into it using the following SQL statement:

```
INSERT INTO megaliths VALUES ( 0, 'Callanish I',
                               '"Stonehenge of the North"',
                               'Western Isles',
                               'NB 213 330', 1 )
```

If you then SELECT back all the rows in the table, you should be able to see the row that has just been inserted.

Just as the SELECT statement could specify which columns from a table should be returned in the query, it is also possible (and good practice) to specify into which columns of the table the values should be inserted. The unspecified columns will take the default value, typically NULL. For example, if you wished to specify only the id and name columns of the table, allowing description and location to be NULL, the SQL statement would be:

```
INSERT INTO megaliths ( id, name ) VALUES ( 0, 'Callanish I' )
```

There must be an exact mapping between the number of columns and column values specified in the SQL statement. It is also essential to make sure that the datatypes of the supplied values and the corresponding columns match.

Using INSERT for data transfers

One of the more sneaky uses for the INSERT keyword is to transfer data from one table or column to another in one easy operation. This seems to fly in the face of our previous assertion that only one row can be inserted with each INSERT statement, but in fact, follows the rules correctly (in an underhand manner).

For example, if we wanted to make a quick copy of the megaliths table into a new table called megaliths_copy, the following SQL statement can be used:

```
INSERT INTO megaliths_copy
    SELECT *
    FROM megaliths
```

This process inserts each row returned from the SELECT statement into the new table, row by row, until an exact copy is created. This feature of INSERT is extremely useful for making quick copies of tables if you need to do some destructive maintenance work on the original, such as pruning redundant data. For this SQL to work, the original table and destination table must have an identical structure.

You can further refine this operation by specifying conditions that the rows to be transferred must meet before being inserted. For example, to copy across only the rows of data for megaliths located in Wiltshire:

```
INSERT INTO megaliths_copy
    SELECT *
    FROM megaliths
    WHERE location LIKE '%Wiltshire%'
```

Furthermore, you can make *extracts* of data from tables into new tables by explicitly specifying the targeted columns in the new table. This is useful when building large denormalized tables for use within a data warehouse. Therefore, if we had a table called **megalocations** that contained two columns called **name** and **location**, we could populate this new table from the **megaliths** table in the following way:

```
INSERT INTO megalocations
    SELECT name, location
    FROM megaliths
```

Or, we can even select data from multiple tables for inserting. A denormalized table containing the rows coalesced from the **megaliths** and **media** tables might contain two columns, **name** and **url**. Populating this table with an **INSERT** statement is easy:

```
INSERT INTO megamedia
    SELECT name, url
    FROM megaliths, media
    WHERE megaliths.id = media.megaliths_id
```

However, in general, table population via **INSERT** statements is usually performed by batch-loading programs that generate suitable SQL statements and execute them within the database, such as Oracle's SQL*Loader. Of course, Perl is a good example of a programming language that makes loading data from a file remarkably easy via the DBI.

Deleting Data

Now that you have spent copious amounts of time loading data into your tables to play with, the next thing you'll want to do is tidy it up and remove redundant or unwanted data.

The **DELETE** keyword defined within SQL is exactly what you are looking for, providing a simple syntax for permanently removing rows of data from tables. As with the **INSERT** statement, deleting rows applies only to a single table at a time; therefore, if you want to remove rows that are referred to by records in other tables, you should first delete those associated *foreign key* records from the secondary tables. This preserves the *referential integrity* of your database and is known as *delete cascading.*[*] Some databases support cascading delete mechanisms that automate these extra deletes.

For example, a cascading delete applied to rows in the `megaliths` table would also need to remove the appropriate rows in the `media` table where the following join condition is true:

```
megaliths.id = media.megaliths_id
```

However, `DELETE` statements do not have the same "single row at a time" restriction that `INSERT` statements suffer from. `DELETE` can purge a table entirely in one statement. For example, to remove all the rows within the `megaliths` table, we could simply write:

```
DELETE FROM megaliths
```

Of course, we may not wish to remove *all* the rows from a table, but only certain rows. This can be done in a familiar manner by specifying a list of conditions that the data within a row must meet for it to be removed. Therefore, if we wanted to delete all the rows of data within the `megaliths` table that contain sites located in "Wiltshire," then the following statement would work nicely:

```
DELETE FROM megaliths
WHERE location LIKE '%Wiltshire%'
```

To remove all the rows relating to stone circles, we could narrow the criterion that a row must meet by saying that the type of the site must be equal to "Stone Circle." The tighter query would read:

```
DELETE FROM megaliths
WHERE location LIKE '%Wiltshire%'
AND site_type_id IN = (SELECT id FROM site_types
                        WHERE site_type = 'Stone Circle')
```

It should be noted that deleting all the rows from a table does not actually remove the table from the database. The table will be left in place, but it will have no rows in it.[†]

A more powerful way to determine which rows of data to delete can be expressed by using a subquery to return the target rows. A good example of this sort of behavior is deleting the foreign keys from a table when the primary keys are being deleted. This can be broken up into two separate `DELETE` statements, the first removing the foreign key rows, the second removing the primary key rows. The

---

[*] An analogy for this process is removing a file on a Unix system that has several symbolic links associated with it. It is good housekeeping to remove the stale symbolic links when the target file has been removed. This also applies to Windows and Macintosh systems with shortcuts to documents.

[†] Some databases feature a faster and more efficient way of removing all the rows from a table with the `TRUNCATE TABLE` keyword. But beware! In some databases, that keyword removes all indices as well.

following examples remove the rows relating to megalithic sites in "Wiltshire" from both the **media** and **megaliths** tables:

```
DELETE FROM media
WHERE megaliths_id IN (
    SELECT id
    FROM megaliths
    WHERE location LIKE '%Wiltshire%'
  )

DELETE FROM megaliths
WHERE location LIKE '%Wiltshire%'
```

To sum up, removing data from tables is made extremely simple (perhaps too simple!) by use of the **DELETE** keyword. Later in this chapter, we'll discuss the database's perspective of the deletion process in more detail, including the all-important possibility of undoing deletions that go wrong.

Updating Data

The final way in which modifications can be performed on data stored within tables in a database is to make in-place modifications of existing data by updating the values of particular columns in particular rows. With an **UPDATE** statement, rows are neither inserted nor deleted, and the structure of the table itself is not altered.

UPDATE statements are extremely powerful, in that it is possible to update multiple rows of data in one statement. If desired, the new values may be supplied by the returned values from a **SELECT** statement following the syntax of the **INSERT** command.

The most simple and useful **UPDATE** is to update a column of a single row within a table to a new value. For example, if you wanted to update the location of the "Avebury" row within the **megaliths** table, the following SQL statement would work.

```
UPDATE megaliths
SET location = 'Near Devizes, Wiltshire'
WHERE name = 'Avebury'
```

You should notice the condition clause specified in this statement. If the statement did not check for the exact name of the site, *every* row within the table would have had the **UPDATE** statement performed against it, causing a potentially disastrous data corruption. Condition clauses may be specified in exactly the same way as used in other SQL commands such as **DELETE** and **SELECT**.

UPDATE statements may also update more than one column in a single statement, by simply listing the columns we wish to update in a comma-separated list. For example, to update both the `name` and `description` fields within the `megaliths` table, you can write the following SQL statement:

```
UPDATE megaliths
SET location = 'Callanish, Isle of Lewis',
    description = 'Complex site shaped as a buckled Celtic cross'
WHERE name = 'Callanish I'
```

In some database systems, it is also possible to update multiple columns simultaneously by using a subquery to return a list of values from another table. Those values are then used as the new values for the specified columns. For example, if we wanted to synchronize our megalithic database with the Wiltshire Tourist Board Database to use the same names and locations, we could use the following SQL statement:

```
UPDATE megaliths
SET ( name, location ) =
    ( SELECT tourist_site_name, tourist_site_location
      FROM tourist_sites
      WHERE tourist_site_name LIKE '%Avebury%'
      AND tourist_site_type = 'Stone Circle' )
WHERE name = 'Avebury'
```

This statement would update the `name` and `location` fields within the `megaliths` table with values returned by a query running against another table. An important note about this technique is that the subquery must return only a single row of data, otherwise the `UPDATE` will fail with an error.

Committing and Rolling Back Modifications

So, what happens if you make a horrible mistake when you are modifying the data within your database? Is the only course of action to resign? Fear not! Some database engines have a capability known as *transaction rollback* that will save not only your neck, but your data as well.

The principle of rollback is quite a simple one. For each modification to rows of data within the database, a copy of the row prior to modification is written into a log that records all the modifications made. Once you have decided that these changes are indeed correct, you can opt to *commit* the changes to the database. If the committed changes are actually wrong, then you're in trouble: you can clear out your desk and dust off your resume.

However, if by some sheer luck you check the modified rows and see that they are wrong before you commit the changes, you can rollback the modifications you have made, returning the rows to the values they held before you started modifying them. Your job is safe.

Even better, the changes you made within the transaction were not visible to anyone else looking at the database at that time. So no one need know of your mistake, and your reputation is safe.

Most databases automatically commit data upon disconnection from the database unless a rollback is explicitly issued. Therefore, if the software that is being run is not performing suitable error checking on the modifications it is making, it may disconnect and inadvertently commit wrong data to the database. There is a moral in this—*always check for errors!*

Some database systems don't have a feature as sophisticated as rollback or undo. In these cases, it is even more important that before unleashing dramatic data manipulation SQL on your database, you make a backup. Backups are always a good idea, even in databases that do support transactions.

Creating and Destroying Tables

The previous section discusses the operations SQL can perform to manipulate data stored as rows within tables in the database. However, there is a separate set of statements that covers the manipulation of the tables (and other objects) within the database themselves. These statements are known as *Data Definition Language* commands, or *DDLs*.

The operations that can be performed on tables are fairly basic, since they are quite far-reaching in their consequences. The two simplest operations available are:

Creating a new table

This is done via the **CREATE TABLE** command, the syntax of which varies depending on the database platform being used. However, this statement generally specifies the name of the table to be created and the definition of all the columns of the table (both names and datatypes).

For example, the SQL we used to create the megaliths table within our database was:

```
CREATE TABLE megaliths (
    id              INTEGER NOT NULL,
    name            VARCHAR(64),
    location        VARCHAR(64),
    description     VARCHAR(256),
    site_type_id    INTEGER,
    mapref          VARCHAR(16)
)
```

CREATETABLE will create a brand-new table with the given definition, which will be completely empty until you insert rows into it.

Deleting, or dropping, an existing table

This action is as drastic as data modification can get. The actual table structure within the database is completely removed, as are any rows of data currently stored within that table. This operation cannot usually be rolled back from. Once the fatal statement is typed, the specified table has gone forever (unless you have made a backup).

The syntax for dropping tables is fairly standard across databases and is extremely straightforward.* To completely get rid of our `megaliths` table, we can issue the SQL statement of:

```
DROP TABLE megaliths
```

There are other ways in which table definitions can be manipulated, and also other database structures that can be created (such as views and indexes). But these are beyond the scope of this book. You should consult your database documentation for more information.

---

* Something so deadly should have a far more complicated syntax!

4

Programming with the DBI

In this chapter, we'll discuss in detail the actual programming interface defined by the DBI module. We'll start with the very architecture of DBI, continue with explaining how to use the handles that DBI provides to interact with databases, then cover simple tasks such as connecting and disconnecting from databases. Finally, we'll discuss the important topic of error handling and describe some of the DBI's utility methods and functions. Future chapters will discuss how to manipulate data within your databases, as well as other advanced functionality.

DBI Architecture

The DBI architecture is split into two main groups of software: the DBI itself, and the *drivers*. The DBI defines the actual DBI programming interface, routes method calls to the appropriate drivers, and provides various support services to them. Specific drivers are implemented for each different type of database and actually perform the operations on the databases. Figure 4-1 illustrates this architecture.

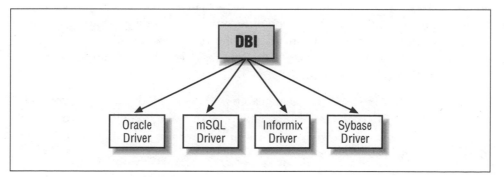

Figure 4-1. The DBI architecture

Therefore, if you are authoring software using the DBI programming interface, the method you use is defined within the DBI module. From there, the DBI module works out which driver should handle the execution of the method and passes the method to the appropriate driver for actual execution. This is more obvious when you recognize that the DBI module does not perform any database work itself, nor does it even know about any types of databases whatsoever. Figure 4-2 shows the flow of data from a Perl script through to the database.

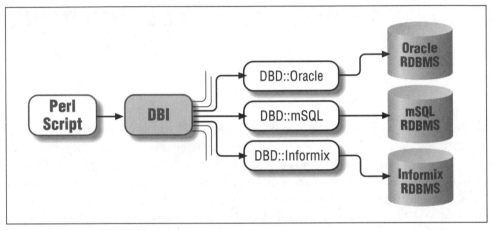

Figure 4-2. Data flow through DBI

Under this architecture, it is relatively straightforward to implement a driver for any type of database. All that is required is to implement the methods defined in the DBI specification,* as supported by the DBI module, in a way that is meaningful for that database. The data returned from this module is passed back into the DBI module, and from there it is returned to the Perl program. All the information that passes between the DBI and its drivers is standard Perl datatypes, thereby preserving the isolation of the DBI module from any knowledge of databases.

The separation of the drivers from the DBI itself makes the DBI a powerful programming interface that can be extended to support almost any database available today. Drivers currently exist for many popular databases including Oracle, Informix, mSQL, MySQL, Ingres, Sybase, DB2, Empress, SearchServer, and PostgreSQL. There are even drivers for XBase and CSV files.

These drivers can be used interchangeably with little modification to your programs. Couple this database-level portability with the portability of Perl scripts across multiple operating systems, and you truly have a rapid application development tool worthy of notice.

---

* Few methods actually need to be implemented since the DBI provides suitable defaults for most of them. The DBI::DBD module contains documentation for any intrepid driver writers.

Drivers are also called database drivers, or DBDs, after the namespace in which they are declared. For example, Oracle uses `DBD::Oracle`, Informix uses `DBD::Informix`, and so on. A useful tip in remembering the DBI architecture is that DBI can stand for *DataBase Independent* and DBD can stand for *DataBase Dependent*.

Because DBI uses Perl's object-orientation features, it is extremely simple to initialize DBI for use within your programs. This can be achieved by adding the line:

```
use DBI;
```

to the top of your programs. This line locates and loads the core DBI module. Individual database driver modules are loaded as required, and should generally not be explicitly loaded.

Handles

The DBI defines three main types of objects that you may use to interact with databases. These objects are known as *handles*. There are handles for drivers, which the DBI uses to create handles for database connections, which, in turn, can be used to create handles for individual database commands, known as *statements*. Figure 4-3 illustrates the overall structure of the way in which handles are related, and their meanings are described in the following sections.

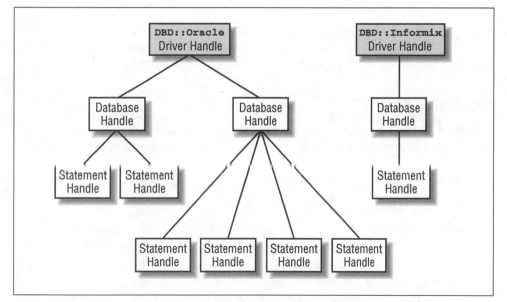

Figure 4-3. DBI handles

Driver Handles

Driver handles represent loaded drivers and are created when the driver is loaded and initialized by the DBI. There is exactly one driver handle per loaded driver. Initially, the driver handle is the only contact the DBI has with the driver, and at this stage, no contact has been made with any database through that driver.

The only two significant methods available through the driver handle are `data_sources()`, to enumerate what can be connected to, and `connect()`, to actually make a connection. These methods are more commonly invoked as DBI class methods, however, which we will discuss in more detail later in this chapter.

Since a driver handle completely encapsulates a driver, there's no reason why multiple drivers can't be simultaneously loaded. This is part of what makes the DBI such a powerful interface.

For example, if a programmer is tasked with the job of transferring data from an Oracle database to an Informix database, it is possible to write a single DBI program that connects simultaneously to both databases and simply passes the data backwards and forwards as needed. In this case, two driver handles would be created, one for Oracle and one for Informix. No problems arise from this situation, since each driver handle is a completely separate Perl object.

Within the DBI specification, a driver handle is usually referred to as `$drh`.

Driver handles should not normally be referenced within your programs. The actual instantiation of driver handles happens "under the hood" of DBI, typically when `DBI->connect()` is called.

Database Handles

Database handles are the first step towards actually doing work with the database, in that they encapsulate a single connection to a particular database. Prior to executing SQL statements within a database, we must actually *connect* to the database. This is usually achieved through the DBI's `connect()` method:

```
$dbh = DBI->connect( $data_source, ... );
```

The majority of databases nowadays tend to operate in a multiuser mode, allowing many simultaneous connections, and database handles are designed accordingly. An example might be if you wanted to write a stock-monitoring program that simultaneously monitored data in tables within different user accounts in the database. A DBI script could make multiple connections to the database, one for each user account, and execute SQL statements on each. Database handles are completely encapsulated objects, meaning that transactions from one database handle cannot "cross-over" or "leak" into another.

Database handles are *children* of their corresponding driver handle, which supports the notion that we could also make multiple simultaneous connections to multiple database types, as well as multiple simultaneous connections to databases of the same type. For example, a more complicated DBI script could make two connections to each of an Oracle and an Informix database to perform the above-mentioned monitoring. Figure 4-3, shown earlier, illustrates the capability of having multiple database handles connecting through a driver handle to an Oracle database.

Keep in mind that had the monitoring program been written in C, two copies of code would be required, one for Oracle's programming interface and one for Informix's. DBI levels the playing field.

Within the DBI specification and sample code, database handles are usually referred to as $dbh.

Statement Handles

Statement handles are the final type of object that DBI defines for database interaction and manipulation. These handles actually encapsulate individual SQL statements to be executed within the database.

Statement handles are *children* of their corresponding database handle. Since statement handles are objects in their own right, data within one statement is protected from tampering or modification by other statement handles.

For a given database handle, there is no practical limit to the number of statement handles that can be created and executed.* Multiple statements can be created and executed within one script, and the data can be processed as it returns. A good example of this might be a data-mining robot that connects to a database, then executes a large number of queries that return all sorts of different types of information. Instead of attempting to write convoluted SQL to correlate the information within the database, the Perl script fetches all the data being returned from the many statements and performs analysis there, using the fully featured text and data manipulation routines that Perl has to offer.

Within the DBI specification and sample code, statement handles are generally referred to as $sth.

Data Source Names

When connecting to a database via the DBI, you need to tell the DBI where to find the database to connect to. For example, the database driver might require a

---

* In reality, the number of concurrent statement handles is dependent on the underlying database. For information on how many concurrent statement handles your database can support, see Appendix B.

database name, or a physical machine name upon which the database resides. This information is termed a *data source name,* and of all the aspects of DBI, this is possibly the most difficult to standardize due to the sheer number and diversity of connection syntaxes.

The DBI requires the data source name to start with the characters `dbi:`, much like a URL begins with `http:`, and then the name of the driver, followed by another colon—for example, `dbi:Oracle:`. Any text that follows is passed to the driver's own `connect()` method to interpret as it sees fit. Most drivers expect either a simple database name or, more often, a set of one or more name/value pairs separated with semicolons. Some common examples are listed later in this section.

For example, mSQL requires the hostname, database name, and potentially, the TCP/IP port number for connecting to the database server. However, Oracle may require only a single word that is an alias to a more complicated connection identifier that is stored in separate Oracle configuration files.

DBI offers two useful methods for querying which data sources are available to you for each driver you have installed on your system.

Firstly, you can get a list of all the available drivers installed on your machine by using the `DBI->available_drivers()` method. This returns a list with each element containing the data source prefix of an installed driver,* such as `dbi:Informix:`.

Secondly, you can invoke the `DBI->data_sources()` method against one or more of the drivers returned by the `DBI->available_drivers()` method to enumerate which data sources are known to the driver.† Calling the `data_sources()` method will actually load the specified driver and validate that it is completely and correctly installed. Because DBI dies if it can't load and initialize a driver, this method should be called inside an `eval{} block` if you need to catch that error.

The following script lists all the drivers and data sources for each driver on your system:

```
#!/usr/bin/perl -w
#
# ch04/listdsns: Enumerates all data sources and all installed drivers
#
```

---

* The actual definition of "installed driver" is a little loose. The DBI simply searches the directories in @INC looking for any DBD subdirectories that contain *.pm* files. Those are assumed to be drivers. It does not verify that the modules are completely and correctly installed. In practice, this process is fast and works well.

† Note that not necessarily every data source that is reachable via the driver is returned. Similarly, the inclusion of a data source does not imply that it is actually currently available for connection.

```
use DBI;

### Probe DBI for the installed drivers
my @drivers = DBI->available_drivers();

die "No drivers found!\n" unless @drivers; # should never happen

### Iterate through the drivers and list the data sources for each one
foreach my $driver ( @drivers ) {
    print "Driver: $driver\n";
    my @dataSources = DBI->data_sources( $driver );
    foreach my $dataSource ( @dataSources ) {
        print "\tData Source is $dataSource\n";
    }
    print "\n";
}

exit;
```

The output from this script on my machine looks like:

```
Driver: ADO

Driver: CSV
    Data source is DBI:CSV:f_dir=megaliths
    Data source is DBI:CSV:f_dir=pictish_stones

Driver: ExampleP
    Data Source is dbi:ExampleP:dir=.

Driver: File
    Data Source is DBI:File:f_dir=megaliths
    Data Source is DBI:File:f_dir=pictish_stones

Driver: ODBC

Driver: Proxy

Driver: XBase
    Data Source is dbi:XBase:.
```

which tells us that we have the standard drivers DBD::Proxy, DBD::ADO, DBD::
File, and DBD::ExampleP installed, as well as DBD::ODBC, DBD::XBase, and
DBD::CSV.

While this may be interesting in theory, in practice you rarely need to use these
methods. Most applications are written to use one data source name, either hard-
coded into the application or passed in as a parameter in some way.

When specifying a data source name for a database, the text following the driver
prefix should be of the form that is appropriate for the particular database that you

wish to connect to. This is very database-specific, but the following table shows some examples.[*]

Database	Example Connection Syntax

mSQL	`dbi:mSQL:hostname:database:port_number`
	
	For example, to connect to a database called *archaeo* located on a machine called *fowliswester.arcana.co.uk* running on port number 1114, the following `$data_source` argument would be used:
	    `dbi:mSQL:fowliswester.arcana.co.uk:archaeo:1114`

Oracle	`dbi:Oracle:connection_descriptor`
	
	Oracle has a slightly less cut-and-dried way of specifying connection identifiers due to the many different ways in which the Oracle database software can actually handle connections.
	To break this nightmarish topic down into bite-sized chunks, Oracle may use two different types of connection. For local connections, Oracle uses a single item of information as the connection descriptor, either the name of the database or an alias to the database as specified in the Oracle configuration files. For a network-based connection, Oracle usually needs to know the alias of the connection descriptor as specified in the Oracle configuration files, or, if you are feeling suitably masochistic, you can specify the whole connection descriptor ... but, believe me, it isn't pretty.
	
	For example, a simple Oracle `$data_source` value might be:
	    `dbi:Oracle:archaeo`

CSV	`dbi:CSV:f_dir=/datafiles` The `DBD::CSV` module treats a group of comma-separated value files in a common directory as a database. The data source for this driver can contain a parameter `f_dir` that specifies the directory in which the files are located.

In the case of the `$data_source` argument, an empty or undefined value will result in the environment variable `DBI_DSN` being checked for a valid value. If this environment variable is not defined, or does not contain a valid value, the DBI will call `die()`.

Connection and Disconnection

The main activity in database programming usually involves the execution of SQL statements within a database. However, to accomplish this task, a *connection* to a database must be established first. Furthermore, after all the work has been done, it is good manners to *disconnect* from the database to free up both your local machine resources and, more importantly, valuable database resources.

---

[*] An excellent example of an application that figures out data source names at runtime is `dbish`, discussed more fully in Chapter 8.

Connection

In the case of simple databases, such as flat-file or Berkeley DB files, "connecting" is usually as simple as opening the files for reading or using the tie mechanism. However, in larger database systems, connecting may be considerably more complicated.

A relatively simple RDBMS is mSQL, which has a simple method of connection: to connect, a program connects to a TCP/IP port on the computer running the database. This establishes a live connection within the database. However, more complex systems, such as Oracle, have a lot more internal security and housekeeping work that must be performed at connection time. They also have more data that needs to be specified by the program, such as the username and password that you wish to connect with.

By looking at a broad spectrum of database systems, the information required to connect can be boiled down to:

1. The *data source name*, a string containing information specifying the driver to use, what database you wish to connect to, and possibly its whereabouts. This argument takes the format discussed in the previous section and is highly database-specific.

2. The *username* that you wish to connect to the database as. To elaborate on the concept of usernames a little further, some databases partition the database into separate areas, called schemas, in which different users may create tables and manipulate data. Users cannot affect tables and data created by other users. This setup is similar to accounts on a multiuser computer system, in that users may create their own files, which can be manipulated by them, but not necessarily by other users. In fact, users may decide to disallow all access to their files, or tables, from all other users, or allow access to a select group or all users.*

   Most major database systems enforce a similar security policy, usually with an administrator having access to an account that allows them to read, modify, and delete any user's tables and data. All other users must connect as themselves. On these systems, your database username may be the same as your system login username, but it doesn't have to be.

   More minimal database systems may not have any concept of username-based authentication, but you still need to supply the username and password arguments, typically as empty strings.

3. The *password* associated with the supplied username.

---

* In general, this is true. However, some database systems, such as MySQL, support different users but only one schema.

In light of these common arguments, the syntax for connecting to databases using DBI is to use the **connect()** call, defined as follows:

```
$dbh = DBI->connect( $data_source, $username, $password, \%attr );
```

The final argument, **\%attr**, is optional and may be omitted. **\%attr** is a reference to a hash that contains handle attributes to be applied to this connection. One of the most important items of the information supplied in this hash is whether or not automatic error handling should be supplied by DBI. We will discuss this in further detail in the following section, but the two common attributes are called **RaiseError** and **PrintError**, which cause the DBI to die or print a warning automatically when a database error is detected.

This method, when invoked, returns a database handle if the connection has been successfully made to the database. Upon failure, the value **undef** is returned.

To illustrate the **DBI->connect()** method, assume that we have an Oracle database called **archaeo**. To connect to this database, we might use the following code:

```
#!/usr/bin/perl -w
#
# ch04/connect/ex1: Connects to an Oracle database.

use DBI;              # Load the DBI module

### Perform the connection using the Oracle driver
my $dbh = DBI->connect( "dbi:Oracle:archaeo", "username", "password" )
    or die "Can't connect to Oracle database: $DBI::errstr\n";

exit;
```

This simple example illustrates the use of the **DBI->connect()** method to make one connection to the database. We also perform error checking on the call to ensure that the connection occurs; upon failure, the error message will be printed along with the database-specific reason for the failure, which will be contained within the variable **$DBI::errstr.**[*]

A more complicated example might be to connect twice to the same database from within the one script:

```
#!/usr/bin/perl -w
#
# ch04/connect/ex2: Connects to two Oracle databases simultaneously
#                   with identical arguments. This is to illustrate
#                   that all database handles, even if identical
#                   argument-wise, are completely separate from
```

---

* Actually, the error message will be displayed twice for reasons that will be explained in the "Error Handling" section later in this chapter.

```
#                       one another.

use DBI;                # Load the DBI module

### Perform the connection using the Oracle driver
my $dbh1 = DBI->connect( "dbi:Oracle:archaeo", "username", "password" )
    or die "Can't make 1st database connect: $DBI::errstr\n";

my $dbh2 = DBI->connect( "dbi:Oracle:archaeo", "username", "password" )
    or die "Can't make 2nd database connect: $DBI::errstr\n";

exit;
```

or to connect simultaneously to two different databases. For example:

```
#!/usr/bin/perl -w
#
# ch04/connect/ex3: Connects to two Oracle databases simultaneously.

use DBI;                # Load the DBI module

### Perform the connection using the Oracle driver
my $dbh1 = DBI->connect( "dbi:Oracle:archaeo", "username", "password" )
    or die "Can't connect to 1st Oracle database: $DBI::errstr\n";

my $dbh2 = DBI->connect( "dbi:Oracle:seconddb", "username", "password" )
    or die "Can't connect to 2nd Oracle database: $DBI::errstr\n";

exit;
```

This former example is quite interesting, because even though we have used identical arguments to DBI->connect(), the two database handles created are completely separate and do not share any information.

A final example of using DBI->connect() is to connect to two different databases (one Oracle, one mSQL) within the same script. In this case, DBI's automatic error reporting mechanism will be disabled in the mSQL database by passing an attribute hash to the connect() call, as shown here:

```
#!/usr/bin/perl -w
#
# ch04/connect/ex4: Connects to two database, one Oracle, one mSQL
#                   simultaneously. The mSQL database handle has
#                   auto-error-reporting disabled.

use DBI;                # Load the DBI module

### Perform the connection using the Oracle driver
my $dbh1 = DBI->connect( "dbi:Oracle:archaeo", "username", "password" )
    or die "Can't connect to Oracle database: $DBI::errstr\n";

my $dbh2 = DBI->connect( "dbi:mSQL:seconddb", "username", "password" , {
        PrintError => 0
    } )
```

```
    or die "Can't connect to mSQL database: $DBI::errstr\n";

exit;
```

The $username and $password arguments should be specified but may be empty
(' ') if not required. As discussed previously, the $data_source argument can
also be undefined and the value of the environment variable DBI_DSN will be
used instead, if it has been set.

Disconnection

Explicit disconnection from the database is not strictly necessary if you are exiting
from your program after you have performed all the work, but it is a good idea.
We strongly recommend that you get into the habit of disconnecting explicitly.

DBI provides a method through which programmers may disconnect a given database handle from its database. This is good practice, especially in programs in
which you have performed multiple connections or will be carrying out multiple
sequential connections.

The method for performing disconnections is:

```
    $rc = $dbh->disconnect();
```

According to this definition, disconnect() is invoked against a specific database
handle. This preserves the notion that database handles are completely discrete.
With multiple database handles active at any given time, each one must explictly
be disconnected.

An example of using disconnect() might look like:

```
    #!/usr/bin/perl -w
    #
    # ch04/disconnect/ex1: Connects to an Oracle database
    #                      with auto-error-reporting disabled
    #                      then performs an explicit disconnection.

    use DBI;            # Load the DBI module

    ### Perform the connection using the Oracle driver
    my $dbh = DBI->connect( "dbi:Oracle:archaeo", "username", "password" , {
            PrintError => 0
        } )
        or die "Can't connect to Oracle database: $DBI::errstr\n";

    ### Now, disconnect from the database
    $dbh->disconnect
        or warn "Disconnection failed: $DBI::errstr\n";

    exit;
```

Upon successful disconnection, the return value will be true. Otherwise, it will be false. In practice, failure to disconnect usually means that the connection has already been lost for some reason. After disconnecting the database handle can't be used for anything worthwhile.

What happens if you don't explicitly disconnect? Since DBI handles are references to Perl objects, Perl's own garbage collector will move in and sweep up any object trash you leave lying around. It does that by calling the object's `DESTROY` method when there are no longer any references to the object held by your script, or when Perl is exiting.

The `DESTROY` method for a database handle will call `disconnect()` for you, if you've left the handle connected, in order to disconnect cleanly from the database. But it will complain about having to do so by issuing a warning:

```
Database handle destroyed without explicit disconnect.
```

A major caveat with the `disconnect()` method regards its behavior towards automatically committing transactions at disconnection. For example, if a program has updated data but has not called `commit()` or `rollback()` before calling `disconnect()`, the action taken by different database systems varies. Oracle will automatically commit the modifications, whereas Informix may not. To deal with this, the `DESTROY` method has to call `rollback()` before `disconnect()` if `AutoCommit` is not enabled. In Chapter 6, we'll discuss the effect of `disconnect()` and `DESTROY` on transactions in more detail.

Error Handling

The handling of errors within programs, or the lack thereof, is one of the more common causes of questions concerning programming with DBI. Someone will ask "Why doesn't my program work?" and the answer generally runs along the lines of "Why aren't you performing error checking?" Sure enough, nine out of ten times when error checking is added, the exact error message appears and the cause for error is obvious.

Automatic Versus Manual Error Checking

Early versions of the DBI required programmers to perform their own error checking, in a traditional way similar to the examples listed earlier for connecting to a database. Each method that returned some sort of status indicator as to its success or failure should have been followed by an error condition checking statement. This is an excellent, slightly C-esque way of programming, but it quickly gets to be tiresome, and the temptation to skip the error checking grows.

The DBI now has a far more straightforward error-handling capability in the style of *exceptions*. That is, when DBI internally detects that an error has occurred after a DBI method call, it can automatically either `warn()` or `die()` with an appropriate message. This shifts the onus of error checking away from the programmer and onto DBI itself, which does the job in the reliable and tireless way that you'd expect.

Manual error checking still has a place in some applications where failures are expected and common. For example, should a database connection attempt fail, your program can detect the error, sleep for five minutes, and automatically re-attempt a connection. With automatic error checking, your program will exit, telling you only that the connection attempt failed.

DBI allows mixing and matching of error-checking styles by allowing you to selectively enable and disable automatic error checking on a per-handle basis.

Manual error checking

Of course, the DBI still allows you to manually error check your programs and the execution of DBI methods. This form of error checking is more akin to classic C and Perl programming, where each important statement is checked to ensure that it has executed successfully, allowing the program to take evasive action upon failure.

DBI, by default, performs basic automatic error reporting for you by enabling the `PrintError` attribute. To disable this feature, simply set the value to 0 either via the handle itself after instantiation, or, in the case of database handles, via the attribute hash of the `connect()` method.

For example:

```
### Attributes to pass to DBI->connect()
%attr = (
    PrintError => 0,
    RaiseError => 0
);

### Connect...
my $dbh = DBI->connect( "dbi:Oracle:archaeo", "username", "password" , \%attr );

### Re-enable warning-level automatic error reporting...
$dbh->{PrintError} = 1;
```

Most DBI methods will return a false status value, usually `undef`, when execution fails. This is easily tested by Perl in the following way:

```
### Try connecting to a database
my $dbh = DBI->connect( ... )
    or die "Can't connect to database: $DBI::errstr!\";
```

The following program disables automatic error handling, with our own tests to check for errors. This example also moves the attributes into the `connect()` method call itself, a clean style that's commonly used:

```
#!/usr/bin/perl -w
#
# ch04/error/ex1: Small example using manual error checking.

use DBI;                # Load the DBI module

### Perform the connection using the Oracle driver
my $dbh = DBI->connect( undef, "stones", "stones", {
    PrintError => 0,
    RaiseError => 0
} ) or die "Can't connect to the database: $DBI::errstr\n";

### Prepare a SQL statement for execution
my $sth = $dbh->prepare( "SELECT * FROM megaliths" )
    or die "Can't prepare SQL statement: $DBI::errstr\n";

### Execute the statement in the database
$sth->execute
    or die "Can't execute SQL statement: $DBI::errstr\n";

### Retrieve the returned rows of data
my @row;
while ( @row = $sth->fetchrow_array() ) {
    print "Row: @row\n";
}
warn "Data fetching terminated early by error: $DBI::errstr\n"
    if $DBI::err;

### Disconnect from the database
$dbh->disconnect
    or warn "Error disconnecting: $DBI::errstr\n";

exit;
```

As can be seen from the example, the code to check the errors that may have arisen in a DBI method is actually longer than the code to perform the operations themselves. Similarly, it is entirely possible that you may just genuinely forget to add a check after a statement, which may result in extremely bizarre program execution and error reporting, not to mention hours of wasted debugging time!

Automatic error checking

The automatic error checking capabilities of the DBI operates on two levels. The `PrintError` handle attribute tells DBI to call the Perl `warn()` function (which typically results in errors being printed to the screen when encountered) and the `RaiseError` handle attribute (which tells DBI to call the Perl `die()` function upon error, typically causing the script to immediately abort).

Because the standard Perl functions of `warn()` and `die()` are used, you can change the effects of `PrintError` and `RaiseError` with the `$SIG{__WARN__}` and `$SIG{__DIE__}` signal handlers. Similarly, a `die()` from `RaiseError` can be caught via `eval {...}`.

These different levels of automatic error checking can be turned on for any handle, although database handles are usually the most common and useful. To enable the style of automatic error checking you want, you may set the value of either of the following two attributes:

```
$h->{PrintError} = 1;
$h->{RaiseError} = 1;
```

Similarly, to disable automatic error checking, simply set the value of these attributes to 0.

If both `RaiseError` and `PrintError` are enabled, an error will cause `warn()` and `die()` to be executed sequentially. If no `$SIG{__DIE__}` handle has been defined, `warn()` is skipped to avoid the error message being printed twice.*

A more common way in which these attributes are used is to specify them in the optional attribute hash supplied to `DBI->connect()` when connecting to a database. Automatic error checking is the recommended style in which to write DBI code, so `PrintError` is enabled by default in `DBI->connect()`. You can think of this as training wheels for novices and grease for quick-and-dirty script writers. Authors of more significant works usually either enable `RaiseError` or disable `PrintError` and do their own error checking.

The following short example illustrates the use of `RaiseError` instead of manual error checking is:

```
#!/usr/bin/perl -w
#
# ch04/error/ex2: Small example using automatic error handling with
#                 RaiseError, i.e., the program will abort upon detection
#                 of any errors.

use DBI;              # Load the DBI module

my ($dbh, $sth, @row);

### Perform the connection using the Oracle driver
$dbh = DBI->connect( "dbi:Oracle:archaeo", "username", "password" , {
    PrintError => 0,    ### Don't report errors via warn()
    RaiseError => 1     ### Do report errors via die()
} );
```

---

* The exact behavior when both attributes are set may change in future versions. This is something to consider if the code is inside an `eval`.

```
### Prepare a SQL statement for execution
$sth = $dbh->prepare( "SELECT * FROM megaliths" );

### Execute the statement in the database
$sth->execute();

### Retrieve the returned rows of data
while ( @row = $sth->fetchrow_array() ) {
    print "Row: @row\n";
}

### Disconnect from the database
$dbh->disconnect();

exit;
```

This example is both shorter and more readable than the manual error checking shown in a following example. The actual program logic is clearer. The most obvious additional benefit is that we can forget to handle error checking manually after a DBI operation, since the DBI will check for errors for us.

Mixed error checking

You can mix error checking styles within a single program, since automatic error checking can be easily enabled and disabled on a per-handle basis. There are plenty of occasions where mixed error checking is useful. For example, you might have a program that runs continuously, such as one that polls a database for recently added stock market quotes every couple of minutes.

Disaster occurs! The database crashes! The ideal situation here is that the next time the program tries connecting to the database and fails, it'll wait a few minutes before retrying rather than aborting the program altogether. Once we've connected to the database, the error checking should now simply warn when a statement fails and not die.

This mixed style of error checking can be broken down into two areas: manual error checking for the `DBI->connect()` call, and automatic error checking via `PrintError` for all other statements. This is illustrated in the following example program:

```
#!/usr/bin/perl -w
#
# ch04/error/mixed1: Example showing mixed error checking modes.

use DBI;            # Load the DBI module

### Attributes to pass to DBI->connect() to disable automatic
### error checking
my %attr = (
    PrintError => 0,
```

```
        RaiseError => 0,
);


### The program runs forever and ever and ever and ever ...
while ( 1 ) {
    my $dbh;

    ### Attempt to connect to the database. If the connection
    ### fails, sleep and retry until it succeeds ...
    until (
        $dbh = DBI->connect( "dbi:Oracle:archaeo", "username", "password" ,
            \%attr )
    ) {
        warn "Can't connect: $DBI::errstr. Pausing before retrying.\n";
        sleep( 5 * 60 );
    }

    eval {       ### Catch _any_ kind of failures from the code within

        ### Enable auto-error checking on the database handle
        $dbh->{RaiseError} = 1;

        ### Prepare a SQL statement for execution
        my $sth = $dbh->prepare( "SELECT stock, value FROM current_values" );

        while (1) {

            ### Execute the statement in the database
            $sth->execute();

            ### Retrieve the returned rows of data
            while ( my @row = $sth->fetchrow_array() ) {
                print "Row: @row\n";
            }

            ### Pause for the stock market values to move
            sleep 60;
        }

    };
    warn "Monitoring aborted by error: $@\n" if $@;

    ### Short sleep here to avoid thrashing the database
    sleep 5;
}

exit;
```

This program demonstrates that with DBI, you can easily write explicit error checking and recovery code alongside automatic error checking.

Error Diagnostics

The ability to trap errors within the DBI is very useful, with either manual or automatic error checking, but this information is only marginally useful on its own. To be truly useful, it is necessary to discern exactly what the error was in order to track it down and debug it.

To this end, DBI defines several error diagnostic methods that can be invoked against any valid handle, driver, database, or statement. These methods will inform the programmer of the error code and report the verbose information from the last DBI method called. These are:

```
$rv  = $h->err();
$str = $h->errstr();
$str = $h->state();
```

These various methods return the following items of information that can be used for more accurate debugging of errors:

- $h->err() returns the error number that is associated with the current error flagged against the handle $h. The values returned will be completely dependent on the values produced by the underlying database system. Some systems may not support particularly meaningful information; for example, mSQL errors always have the error number of -1. Oracle is slightly more helpful: a connection failure may flag an ORA-12154 error message upon connection failure, which would return the value of 12154 by invoking $h->err(). Although this value is usually a number, you should not rely on that.

- $h->errstr() is a slightly more useful method, in that it returns a string containing a description of the error, as provided by the underlying database. This string should correspond to the error number returned in $h->err().

  For example, mSQL returns -1 as the error number for all errors, which is not particularly useful. However, invoking $h->errstr() provides far more useful information. In the case of connection failure, the error:

  ```
  ERROR : Can't connect to local MSQL server
  ```

  might be generated and returned by $h->errstr(). Under Oracle, a connection failure returning the error number of 12154 will return the following string as its descriptive error message:

  ```
  ORA-12154: TNS:could not resolve service name (DBD ERROR: OCIServerAttach)
  ```

- $h->state() returns a string in the format of the standard SQLSTATE five-character error string. Many drivers do not fully support this method, and upon invoking it to discern the SQLSTATE code, the value:

  ```
  S1000
  ```

  will be returned. The specific general success code 00000 is translated to 0, so that if no error has been flagged, this method will return a **false** value.

The error information for a handle is reset by the DBI before most DBI method calls. Therefore, it's important to check for errors from one method call before calling the next method on the same handle. If you need to refer to error information later you'll need to save it somewhere else yourself.

A rewriting of the previous example to illustrate using the specific handle methods to report on errors can be seen in the following code:

```
#!/usr/bin/perl -w
#
# ch04/error/ex3: Small example using manual error checking which also uses
#                 handle-specific methods for reporting on the errors.

use DBI;                 # Load the DBI module

### Attributes to pass to DBI->connect() to disable automatic
### error checking
my %attr = (
    PrintError => 0,
    RaiseError => 0,
);

### Perform the connection using the Oracle driver
my $dbh = DBI->connect( "dbi:Oracle:archaeo", "username", "password" , \%attr )
    or die "Can't connect to database: ", $DBI::errstr, "\n";

### Prepare a SQL statement for execution
my $sth = $dbh->prepare( "SELECT * FROM megaliths" )
    or die "Can't prepare SQL statement: ", $dbh->errstr(), "\n";

### Execute the statement in the database
$sth->execute
    or die "Can't execute SQL statement: ", $sth->errstr(), "\n";

### Retrieve the returned rows of data
while ( my @row = $sth->fetchrow_array() ) {
    print "Row: @row\n";
}
warn "Problem in fetchrow_array(): ", $sth->errstr(), "\n"
    if $sth->err();

### Disconnect from the database
$dbh->disconnect
    or warn "Failed to disconnect: ", $dbh->errstr(), "\n";

exit;
```

As you can see, it's even more long-winded than using the $DBI::errstr variable, which can at least be interpolated directly into the error messages.

In addition to these three methods, which allow finely grained error checking at a handle level, there are three corresponding variables that will contain the same information, but at a DBI class level:

```
$DBI::err
$DBI::errstr
$DBI::state
```

Use of these variables is essentially the same as that of `$h->err()` and friends, but the values referred to are for the *last handle used* within DBI. They are particularly handy for interpolating into strings for error messages.

Since these variables are associated with the last handle used within the DBI, they have an even shorter lifespan than the handle error methods, and should be used only immediately after the method call that failed. Otherwise, it is highly likely they will contain misleading error information.

The one case where the variables are very useful is for connection errors. When these errors occur, there's no new handle returned in which to hold error information. Since scripts don't use the internal driver handles, the `$DBI::errstr` variable provides a very simple and effective way to get the error message from a `connect()` failure.

In summary, for most applications, automatic error checking using `RaiseError` and/or `PrintError` is recommended. Otherwise, manual checking can be used and `$DBI::errstr` can easily be interpolated into messages. The handle methods are available for more complex applications.

Utility Methods and Functions

To round off our basic introduction to DBI, we'll tell you about some useful utility methods and functions that will make your life that little bit easier. These include the very useful *quote escaping* method, DBI execution tracing, and various functions to tidy up your data.

Database-Specific Quote Handling

By far the most important utility method is `quote()`, which correctly quotes and escapes SQL statements in a way that is suitable for a given database engine. This feature is important if you have a Perl string that you wish to insert into a database, as the data will be required, in most cases, to have quotation marks around it.

To confuse matters, database engines tend to have a different format for specifying these surrounding quotation marks. DBI circumvents this problem by declaring the `quote()` method to be executed against a database handle, which ensures that the correct quotation rules are applied.

This method, when executed against a database handle, converts the string given as an argument according to defined rules, and returns the correctly escaped string for use against the database.

For example:

```
#!/usr/bin/perl -w
#
# ch04/util/quote1: Demonstrates the use of the $dbh->quote() method

use DBI;

### The string to quote
my $string = "Don't view in monochrome (it looks 'fuzzy')!";

### Connect to the database
my $dbh = DBI->connect( "dbi:Oracle:archaeo", "username", "password" , {
    RaiseError => 1
} );

### Escape the string quotes ...
my $quotedString = $dbh->quote( $string );

### Use quoted string as a string literal in a SQL statement
my $sth = $dbh->prepare( "
    SELECT *
    FROM media
    WHERE description = $quotedString
  " );
$sth->execute();

exit;
```

For example, if you quoted the Perl string of Do it! via an Oracle database handle, you would be returned the value of 'Do it!'. However, the quote()
method also takes care of cases such as Don't do it! which needs to be translated to 'Don''t do it!' for most databases. The simplistic addition of surrounding quotes would have produced 'Don't do it!' which is not a valid SQL string
literal.

Some databases require a more complex quote() method, and some drivers
(though not all) have a quote() method that can cope with multiline strings and
even binary data.

As a special case, if the argument is undef, the quote() method returns the string
NULL, without quotes. This corresponds to the DBI's use of undef to represent
NULL values, and to how NULL values are used in SQL.

Tracing DBI Execution

DBI sports an extremely useful ability to generate runtime tracing information of
what it's doing, which can be a huge time-saver when trying to track down strange
problems in your DBI programs.

At the highest level, you can call the DBI->trace() method, which enables tracing on all DBI operations from that point onwards. There are several valid tracing levels:

0   Disables tracing.

1   Traces DBI method execution showing returned values and errors.

2   As for 1, but also includes method entry with parameters.

3   As for 2, but also includes more internal driver trace information.

4   Levels 4, and above can include more detail than is helpful.

The trace() method can be used with two argument forms, either specifying only the trace level or specifying both the trace level and a file to which the trace information is appended. The following example shows the use of DBI->trace():

```perl
#!/usr/bin/perl -w
#
# ch04/util/trace1: Demonstrates the use of DBI tracing.

use DBI;

### Remove any old trace files
unlink 'dbitrace.log' if -e 'dbitrace.log';

### Connect to a database
my $dbh = DBI->connect( "dbi:Oracle:archaeo", "username", "password" );

### Set the tracing level to 1 and prepare()
DBI->trace( 1 );
doPrepare();

### Set trace output to a file at level 2 and prepare()
DBI->trace( 2, 'dbitrace.log' );
doPrepare();

### Set the trace output back to STDERR at level 2 and prepare()
DBI->trace( 2, undef );
doPrepare();

exit;

### prepare a statement (invalid to demonstrate tracing)
sub doPrepare {
    print "Preparing and executing statement\n";
    my $sth = $dbh->prepare( "
        SELECT * FROM megalith
    " );
    $sth->execute();
    return;
}

exit;
```

This program generates quite a bit of trace information, of which we'll show just a small fragment:

```
-> prepare for DBD::Oracle::db (DBI::db=HASH(0xcd45c)~0xcd4a4 '
   SELECT * FROM megalith
') thr0
<- prepare= DBI::st=HASH(0xcd648) at trace1 line 30.
-> execute for DBD::Oracle::st (DBI::st=HASH(0xcd648)~0x16afec) thr0
dbd_st_execute SELECT (out0, lob0)...
!! ERROR: 942 'ORA-00942: table or view does not exist (DBD ERROR:
   OCIStmtExecute)'
<- execute= undef at trace1 line 33.
DBD::Oracle::st execute failed: ORA-00942: table or view does not exist (DBD
ERROR: OCIStmtExecute) at trace1 line 33.
```

This trace information was generated with a setting of level 2, and shows the operations that DBI undertook when trying to prepare and execute a statement. Lines prepended with -> are written when the method is being entered, and lines prepended with <- are written when the method is returning. These lines also show the information being returned from the method call. The DBI trace output is indented by four spaces to make it easier to distinguish the trace output from any other program output.

You can see the **prepare()** method being called along with its parameters: a database handle and the SQL statement to prepare.* The next line shows the **prepare()** returning a statement handle. It also shows the file and line number that **prepare()** was called from. Following that, we see **execute()** being called, a trace line from the driver itself, and the method returning after logging an error. Finally we see the warning generated by the DBI due to the **PrintError** attribute, which is on by default.

The trace information generated at level 1 is similar. The main difference is that the method entry lines (->) are not shown.

The one drawback to this form of tracing is that if your program uses a lot of handles, then the volume of tracing information could be quite vast. Similarly, you might have tracked your problem down to a specific database operation that you'd like to trace individually.

The **trace()** method is also available at a handle level, allowing you to individually trace any database and statement handle operations. Therefore, you could trace operations on a given database handle to level 1 and a single statement handle to level 2. For example:

---

* If the Perl you are using was built with threading enabled, then each method entry line also shows the thread number, e.g., thr0. The DBI implements a per-driver mutex so that each DBD driver may only be entered by one thread at a time. Trace levels 4 and above show this in action.

```
### Connect to a database...
my $dbh = DBI->connect( "dbi:Oracle:archaeo", "username", "password" );

### Trace the database handle to level 1 to the screen
$dbh->trace( 1 );

### Create a new statement
my $sth = ...;

### Trace the statement to level 2 to the file 'trace.lis'
$sth->trace( 2, 'trace.lis' );
```

Note that if a filename is specified when calling **trace**(), then currently, trace output from *all* handles is redirected to that file.

If your programs are exhibiting odd behavior or are generating errors on a regular basis, you should consider using the built-in tracing features of DBI to help you resolve your problems. This tool is extremely useful, as you will be able to see exactly what data is being passed to the database, allowing you to ensure that it's in the correct format.

Finally, tracing can also be controlled via the use of an environment variable called **DBI_TRACE**, which acts in a similar manner to the **DBI->trace**() method. That is, it traces all handles used within the program. This environment variable can be used in three ways that are summarized in the following table.

DBI_TRACE Value	Effect on DBI
1	DBI->trace(1);
dbitrace.log	DBI->trace(2, 'dbitrace.log');
4=dbitrace.log	DBI->trace(4, 'dbitrace.log');

If the trace level isn't specified in the **DBI_TRACE** environment variable, it will default to 2, as shown in the table above.

Neat and Tidy Formatting

The DBI features a couple of utility functions that can be used to tidy up strings into a form suitable for easy reading. These two functions are **neat**() and **neat_list**(), the former operating on a single scalar value, the latter operating on a list of scalar values.

For example, to use **neat**() to tidy up some strings, you could write:

```
#!/usr/bin/perl -w
#
# ch04/util/neat1: Tests out the DBI::neat() utility function.
#
```

```
use DBI;

### Declare some strings to neatify
my $str1 = "Alligator's an extremely neat() and tidy person";
my $str2 = "Oh no\nhe's not!";

### Neatify this first string to a maxlen of 40
print "String: " . DBI::neat( $str1, 40 ) . "\n";

### Neatify the second string to a default maxlen of 400
print "String: " . DBI::neat( $str2 ) . "\n";

### Neatify a number
print "Number: " . DBI::neat( 42 * 9 ) . "\n";

### Neatify an undef
print "Undef: " . DBI::neat( undef ) . "\n";

exit;
```

which generates the output of:

```
String: 'Alligator's an extremely neat() and...'
String: 'Oh no
he's not!'
Number: 378
Undef:  undef
```

demonstrating that string values are quoted,* whereas values known to be numeric
are not. The first string has been truncated to the desired length with ... added.
Undefined values are recognized and returned as the string undef without quotes.

While the neat() function is handy for single values, the neat_list() function
is handy for lists. It simply calls neat() on each element of the referenced list
before joining the list of values together with the desired separator string. For
example:

```
#!/usr/bin/perl -w
#
# ch04/util/neat2: Tests out the DBI::neat_list() utility function

use DBI qw( neat_list );

### Declare some strings to neatify
my @list = ( 'String-a-string-a-string-a-string-a-string', 42, 0, '', undef );

### Neatify the strings into an array
print neat_list( \@list, 40, ", " ), "\n";

exit;
```

---

* Note that internal quotes are not escaped. That's because neat() is designed to produce output for
human readers, and to do so quickly since it's used by the internal trace mechanisms. If you wish quote
escaping to occur, you could use the quote() method instead.

which generates the output of:

```
'String-a-string-a-string-a-string-a...', 42, 0, '', undef
```

This example also shows that the utility functions can be imported into your package so you can drop the `DBI::` prefix.

DBI uses `neat()` and `neat_list()` internally to format the output generated by tracing. That's important to know if you're wondering why the trace output is truncating your huge SQL statements down to 400 characters.[*]

Numeric Testing

The final utility function supplied by DBI that we'll look at is quite a curious one called `looks_like_number()`. This function quite simply tells you whether or not a value looks like a number or not.

`looks_like_number()` operates by taking a list of values as an argument and returns a new array signifying whether or not the corresponding value within the original array was a number, not a number, or undefined.

This may seem rather a curious thing to want to do, but in the case of handling large quantities of data, it's useful for working out which values might need to have their quotes escaped via the `quote()` method.

The returned array will contain the same number of values as the original data array, with the elements containing one of three values signifying the following:

true	The original value is a number.
false	The original value is not a number.
undef	The original value is empty or undefined.

The following example illustrates how this process works:

```
#!/usr/bin/perl -w
#
# ch04/util/lookslike: Tests out the DBI::looks_like_number() function
#

use DBI;

### Declare a list of values
my @values = ( 333, 'Choronzon', 'Tim', undef, 'Alligator', 1234.34,
               'Linda', 0x0F, '0x0F', 'Larry Wall' );

### Check to see which are numbers!
my @areNumbers = DBI::looks_like_number( @values );
```

---

[*] 400 characters is the default value for the `$DBI::neat_maxlen` variable, which defines the default maximum length for the `neat()` function.

```
for (my $i = 0; $i < @values; ++$i ) {

    my $value = (defined $values[$i]) ? $values[$i] : "undef";

    print "values[$i] -> $value ";

    if ( defined $areNumbers[$i] ) {
        if ( $areNumbers[$i] ) {
            print "is a number!\n";
        }
        else {
            print "is utterly unlike a number and should be quoted!\n";
        }
    }
    else {
        print "is undefined!\n";
    }
}

exit;
```

The results from this program illustrate how the values are treated and shows that hexadecimal values are not treated as numbers:

```
values[0] -> 333 is a number!
values[1] -> Choronzon is utterly unlike a number and should be quoted!
values[2] -> Tim is utterly unlike a number and should be quoted!
values[3] -> undef is undefined!
values[4] -> Alligator is utterly unlike a number and should be quoted!
values[5] -> 1234.34 is a number!
values[6] -> Linda is utterly unlike a number and should be quoted!
values[7] -> 15 is a number!
values[8] -> 0x0F is utterly unlike a number and should be quoted!
values[9] -> Larry Wall is utterly unlike a number and should be quoted!
```

The first `0x0F` in the list of values is reported as looking like a number because Perl converted it into one (15) when the script was compiled. The second is not reported as looking like a number because the `looks_like_number()` function only looks for integers and floating-point numbers.

And that brings us to the end of the introduction to DBI and its architecture. We'll be talking more on how to actually *do* stuff with DBI in the next chapter.

5

Interacting with the Database

In our journey through the DBI so far, we have discussed ways in which you can connect and disconnect from databases of various types within Perl programs. We have also discussed ways in which you can detect and rectify errors when calling DBI methods.

What we haven't discussed yet is how to manipulate data within your databases: that is, retrieving, updating, and deleting information (amongst other activities). This chapter discusses how to perform these activities with the DBI and how to use Perl's powerful data manipulation functionality to efficiently manipulate your data.

Recall the discussion in Chapter 4 about the architecture of DBI—specifically, the topic of *statement handles*. These handles, and the methods associated with them, provide the functionality to manipulate data within your databases.

Issuing Simple Queries

The most common interaction between a program and a database is retrieving or fetching data. In standard SQL, this process is performed with the SELECT keyword. With Perl and the DBI, we have far more control over the way in which data is retrieved from the database. We also have far more control over how to post-process the fetched data.

Retrieving data from a database using DBI is essentially a four-stage cycle:

1. The *prepare* stage parses an SQL statement, validates that statement, and returns a statement handle representing that statement within the database.

2. Providing the prepare stage has returned a valid statement handle, the next stage is to *execute* that statement within the database. This actually performs

the query and begins to populate data structures within the database with the queried data. At this stage, however, your Perl program does not have access to the queried data.

3. The third stage is known as the *fetch* stage, in which the actual data is fetched from the database using the statement handle. The fetch stage pulls the queried data, row by row, into Perl data structures, such as scalars or hashes, which can then be manipulated and post-processed by your program.

   The fetch stage ends once all the data has been fetched, or it can be terminated early using the finish() method.

   If you'll need to re-execute() your query later, possibly with different parameters, then you can just keep your statement handle, re-execute() it, and so jump back to stage 2.

4. The final stage in the data retrieval cycle is the *deallocation* stage. This is essentially an automatic internal cleanup exercise in which the DBI and driver deallocate the statement handle and associated information. For some drivers, that process may also involve talking to the database to tell it to deallocate any information it may hold related to the statement.

   All this is done for you automatically, triggered by Perl's own *garbage collection* mechanism.

This cycle occurs for every SQL SELECT statement executed. For other SQL statements, such as INSERT, UPDATE, and DELETE, the fetch is skipped and only the prepare, execute, and deallocation stages apply (as we'll discuss later in this chapter).

To understand how this four-stage data fetch cycle fits into your programs, we'll take a closer look at each stage individually.

Preparing SQL Statements

The first stage of the cycle to retrieve data from your database is to *prepare* the statement handle from an SQL statement. This stage generally corresponds to the *parse* stage that occurs internally within your database engine.

What typically occurs is that the SQL statement is sent as a string of characters via a valid database handle to the database. This string is then parsed by the database itself to ensure that it is valid SQL, both in terms of syntax and also in terms of entities referred to within the database (e.g., to make sure you aren't referring to tables that don't exist and that you have permission to refer to those that do).

Provided that the database swallows this statement without any complaints, it will return some sort of database-specific data structure that encapsulates that parsed statement. It is this database-specific data structure that the DBI further encapsulates as a *statement handle*. Figure 5-1 shows this process more clearly.

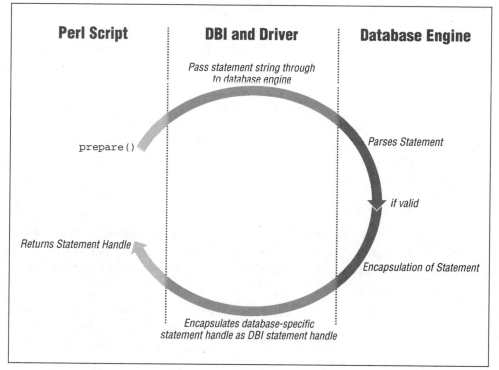

Figure 5-1. Statement preparation data flow via DBI

It is through this DBI statement handle that you perform the remainder of the data-fetching cycle.

In DBI terms, the way to prepare a statement is to use the **prepare()** method, which is executed via a database handle. For example, a simple DBI program that creates a statement handle can be written as follows:

```
#./usr/bin/perl   w
#
# ch05/prepare/ex1: Simply creates a database handle and a statement handle

use DBI;

### The database handle
my $dbh = DBI->connect( "dbi:Oracle:archaeo", "username", "password" );

### The statement handle
my $sth = $dbh->prepare( "SELECT id, name FROM megaliths" );

exit;
```

This, of course, assumes that all goes well with the parsing of the statement. It is possible that you made a mistake when typing in your SQL statement, or that the database failed to parse the statement for any number of other reasons. If this occurs, a value of `undef` is returned from the `prepare()` call, signifying that the parse has failed.

In addition to this return value, the DBI would also print out an error message because the `PrintError` attribute is enabled by default on database handles from `DBI->connect()`. See Chapter 4 for more about `PrintError`.

Finally, there's an important twist to preparing statements, in that drivers are allowed to defer actually *doing* the prepare stage of the cycle until `execute()` is called. That's because some databases don't provide any other way of doing it. So everything that's been said about `prepare()`—what it does and why it may fail— may actually not apply until `execute()` is called.

Constructing "on-the-fly" statements

It is also possible to construct "on-the-fly" SQL statements using Perl's built-in string handling capabilities, which can then be passed to `prepare()`. A good example of this functionality can be demonstrated using DBI to integrate databases and web sites.

Suppose you had your megalith database available on the Web for easy online browsing. When a user types in the name of a site, it gets passed into a CGI script in the form of a string. This string is then used in an SQL statement to retrieve the appropriate information on the site from the database.

Therefore, to be able to accomplish this sort of interactivity, you need to be able to custom-build SQL statements, and using Perl's string handling is one way to do it.* The following code illustrates the principle:

```
### This variable is populated from the online form, somehow...
my $siteNameToQuery = $CGI->param( "SITE_NAME" );

### Take care to correctly quote it for use in an SQL statement
my $siteNameToQuery_quoted = $dbh->quote( $siteNameToQuery );

### Now interpolate the variable into the double-quoted SQL statement
$sth = $dbh->prepare( "
        SELECT meg.name, st.site_type, meg.location, meg.mapref
        FROM megaliths meg, site_types st
        WHERE name = $siteNameToQuery_quoted
        AND meg.site_type_id = st.id
    " );
$sth->execute();
@row = $sth->fetchrow_array();
...
```

Furthermore, *any* part of this query can be constructed on the fly since the SQL statement is, at this stage, simply a Perl string. Another neat trick is to adaptively

---

* A frequently better way is to use *bind values*, which we'll discuss later in this chapter.

query columns from the database depending on which fields the online browser wants to display. Figure 5-2 shows the web page from which the user selects his or her desired columns.

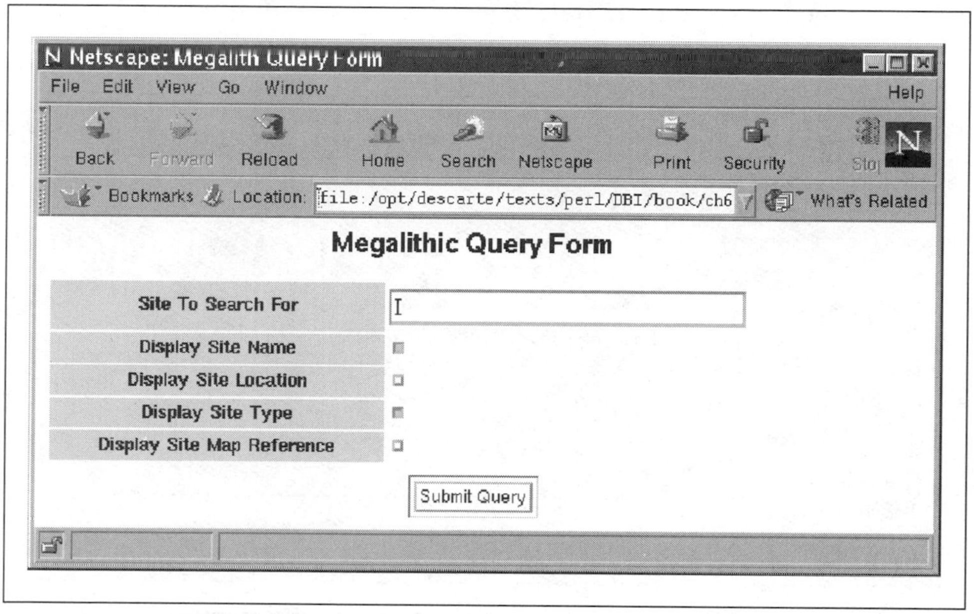

Figure 5-2. Megalithic query form

The code required to drive this form of SQL generation can be written neatly as:

```
### Collect the selected field names
@fields = ();

### Work out which checkboxes have been selected
push @fields, "name"     if $nameCheckbox     eq "CHECKED";
push @fields, "location" if $locationCheckbox eq "CHECKED";
push @fields, "type"     if $typeCheckbox     eq "CHECKED";
push @fields, "mapref"   if $maprefCheckbox   eq "CHECKED";

### Sanity-check that *something* was selected
die "No fields were selected for querying!\n"
    unless @fields;

### Now build the SQL statement
$statement = sprintf "SELECT %s FROM megaliths WHERE name = %s",
    join(", ", @fields), $dbh->quote($siteNameToQuery);

### Perform the query
$sth = $dbh->prepare( $statement );
$sth->execute();
@row = $sth->fetchrow_array();
...
```

That is, the entire SQL query, from the columns to fetch to the conditions under which the data is fetched, has been constructed dynamically and passed to the database for processing.

The web page that was displayed on the user's browser after executing this query can be seen in Figure 5-3.

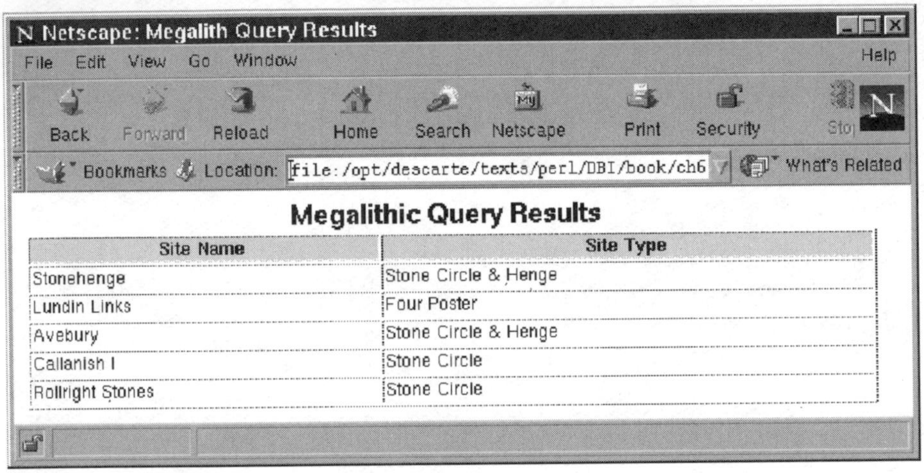

Figure 5-3. Megalithic query results

Therefore, by using Perl's string handling to build SQL statements based on input from the user, DBI can be used to drive quite complex web forms in a very simple and flexible manner.

Executing Select Statements

The second stage of the data fetch cycle is to inform the database to go ahead and *execute* the SQL statement that you have prepared. This execution stage will actually tell the database to perform the query and begin to collect the result set of data.

Performing the execution of the SQL statement occurs via a valid statement handle created when the **prepare()** method successfully completes. For example, execution of an SQL statement can be expressed as simply as:

```
### Create the statement handle
my $sth = $dbh->prepare( "SELECT id, name FROM megaliths" );

### Execute the statement handle
$sth->execute();
```

Assuming that all goes well with the execution of your statement, a `true` value will be returned from the `execute()` call. Otherwise, a value of `undef` is returned, signifying that the execution has failed.

As with most DBI methods, if `PrintError` is enabled, then an error message will be generated via `warn()`. Alternatively, if `RaiseError` is enabled, an exception will be generated via `die()`. However you choose to do it, it is always a good idea to check for errors.*

After `execute()` returns successfully, the database has not necessarily completed the execution of the `SELECT` statement; it may have only just started. Imagine that megaliths are very common, and our megaliths table has ten million rows. In response to the `execute()` earlier, the database may do no more than set a pointer, known as a *cursor*, to just above the first row of the table.

So, after successful execution, the database and driver are ready to return the results, but those results will not have been returned to your Perl program yet. This is an important point to remember. To extract the results data from the database, you need to explicitly *fetch* them. This is the third stage in the cycle.

Fetching Data

Fetching data is the main object of issuing queries to the database. It's fine to exercise a database by executing queries, but unless you actually retrieve that data, your program will never be able to make use of it.

The data retrieved by your SQL query is known as a *result set* (so called because of the mathematical *set theory* on which relational databases are based). The result set is fetched into your Perl program by iterating through each record, or row, in the set and bringing the values for that row into your program. This form of fetching result set data on a row-by-row basis is generally termed a *cursor*.

Cursors are used for sequential fetching operations: records are fetched in the order in which they are stored within the result set. Currently, records cannot be skipped over or randomly accessed. Furthermore, once a row addressed by a cursor has been fetched, it is "forgotten" by the cursor. That is, cursors cannot step backwards through a result set.

Therefore, the general way in which we fetch data from the database's result set is to loop through the records returned via the statement handle, processing each row until no rows are left to fetch. This can be expressed by the following pseudo-code.

---

* We sometimes don't explicitly check for errors in the fragments of code we use as examples. In these cases, you can safely assume that we're strapped into our `RaiseError` ejector seat.

```
while ( records to fetch from $sth ) {
    ### Fetch the current row from the cursor
    @columns = get the column values;
    ### Print it out...
    print "Fetched Row: @columns\n";
}
```

The DBI simplifies this process even further by combining the check for more data and the fetching of that data into a single method call.

There are several ways in which rows can be retrieved from the result set using different Perl datatypes. For example, you can fetch a row in the form of a simple list of values, a reference to an array of values, or a reference to a hash of field-name/value pairs. All essentially retrieve the current row from the cursor, but return the data to your Perl program in different formats.

The simplest form of data fetching is to use the `fetchrow_array()` method, which returns an array, or rather a list, containing the fields of the row. Let's say that we wanted to fetch the name of a megalithic site and what sort of site it is from our megaliths database. Therefore, to fetch this data from the table, we would write:

```
### Prepare the SQL statement ( assuming $dbh exists )
$sth = $dbh->prepare( "
            SELECT meg.name, st.site_type
            FROM megaliths meg, site_types st
            WHERE meg.site_type_id = st.id
        " );

### Execute the SQL statement and generate a result set
$sth->execute();

### Fetch each row of result data from the database as a list
while ( ( $name, $type ) = $sth->fetchrow_array ) {
    ### Print out a wee message....
    print "Megalithic site $name is a $type\n";
}
```

You could also fetch the data via `fetchrow_array()` into an array variable instead of a list of scalar variables by writing:

```
while ( @row = $sth->fetchrow_array ) {
    ### Print out a wee message
    print "Megalith site $row[0] is a $row[1]\n";
}
```

which is functionally identical.

The fundamentally important thing to remember is that the fields in the result set are in the order in which you asked for the columns in the SQL statement. Therefore, in the example code listed above, the **name** field was requested before the **site_type** field. This ensured that the first element of the array or scalar list was the value of the **name** field, followed by the values of the **site_type** field.

The **while** loop keeps looping until the expression in parentheses evaluates to **false**. Naturally, we want to stop looping when there's no more data to fetch, and the **fetchrow_array()** method arranges that for us. It returns an empty list when there's no more data. Perl treats that as a **false** value, thus stopping the loop.

An important point to remember about fetch loops is that the fetch methods return the same value for both the no-more-data condition and an error condition. So an error during fetching will cause the loop to exit as if all the data had been fetched. When not using **RaiseError**, it's therefore good practice to check for the occurrence of errors immediately after every loop exits. The example below demonstrates this.[*]

Another way in which you can fetch the data from the database is to use the **fetchrow_arrayref()** method, which returns a reference to an array rather than an array itself. This method has a performance benefit over **fetchrow_array()**, as the returned data is not copied into a new array for each row fetched. For example:

```
### Fetch the rows of result data from the database
### as an array ref....
while ( $array_ref = $sth->fetchrow_arrayref ) {
    ### Print out a wee message....
    print "Megalithic site $arrayref->[0] is a $array_ref->[1]\n";
}
die "Fetch failed due to $DBI::errstr" if $DBI::err;
```

An important thing to watch out for is that currently the same array reference is used for all rows fetched from the database for the current statement handle. This is of utmost importance if you are storing the row data somewhere for future reference. For example, the following code was written to stash the returned megalith data in a persistent store for future reference after fetching:

```
### The stash for rows...
my @stash;

### Fetch the row references and stash 'em!
while ( $array_ref = $sth->fetchrow_arrayref ) {
    push @stash, $array_ref;        # XXX WRONG!
}

### Dump the stash contents!
foreach $array_ref ( @stash ) {
    print "Row: @$array_ref\n";
}
```

---

[*] Other fetch loop examples in the book assume that **RaiseError** is enabled.

Something very strange happens here. All the rows printed out from the stash are identical instead of being different. This is because you've stored the *reference* to the row data instead of the row data itself, and since DBI reuses the same reference for each row, you don't quite get the results you expect. Be sure to store a copy of the values that the array reference points to rather than the reference itself, as this example shows:

```
### The stash for rows...
my @stash;

### Fetch the row references and stash 'em!
while ( $array_ref = $sth->fetchrow_arrayref ) {
    push @stash, [ @$array_ref ];  # Copy the array contents
}

### Dump the stash contents!
foreach $array_ref ( @stash ) {
    print "Row: @$array_ref\n";
}
```

The `fetchrow_arrayref()` method is used especially in conjunction with *column binding*, which we shall discuss later in this chapter.

The final cursor-based way to fetch the rows of your result set data from the database is to grab it as a hash reference. This functionality is implemented via the `fetchrow_hashref()` method, which is used in the same way as `fetchrow_arrayref()`. For example:

```
### Fetch the current row into a hash reference
while ( $hash_ref = $sth->fetchrow_hashref ) {
    ...
```

The hash pointed to by the reference has the names of the fetched fields as the keys to the hash, and the values of those fields are stored as the hash values. Thus, if we fetched the `name` and `site_type` fields from the database, we could address the hash elements like this:

```
### Fetch rows into a hash reference
while ( $hash_ref = $sth->fetchrow_hashref ) {
    print "Megalithic site $hash_ref->{name} is a $hash_ref->{site_type}\n";
}
```

There are, as you might expect, a few caveats to using this particular method. The most important thing to watch out for is the actual name of the field that you've fetched. Some databases will do strange things to the field name, such as convert it to all uppercase or all lowercase characters, which could cause you to access the wrong hash key. You can avoid this problem by telling `fetchrow_hashref()` the name of the *attribute* to use to supply the field names. That is, you could use `NAME` as the default; `NAME_uc` to force field names to be uppercase; and `NAME_lc` to force them to be lowercase. For example, a portable way to use hash references can be written as:

```
### Fetch rows into a hash reference with uppercase field names
while ( $hash_ref = $sth->fetchrow_hashref('NAME_lc') {
    print "Megalithic site $hash_ref->{name} is a $hash_ref->{site_type}\n";
}
```

Specifying `NAME_uc` or `NAME_lc` is recommended, and doesn't have any impact on performance.

There are a couple more caveats with `fetchrow_hashref()` that we should discuss. If your `SELECT` statement uses a fully qualified field name, such as:

```
SELECT megaliths.id, ...
```

then most databases will still return only the string `id` as the name of the field. That's not usually a problem but can trip you up if you have selected more than one field with the same name, for example:

```
SELECT megaliths.id, media.id ...
```

Since the hash returned by `fetchrow_hashref()` can have only one `id` key, you can't get values for both fields. You can't even be sure which of the two `id` field values you've got. Your only options here are to either use a different method to fetch the rows or to *alias* the column names. Aliasing the columns is similar to aliasing the table names, which we discussed in Chapter 3. You can put an alias name after the column expression:

```
SELECT megaliths.id meg_id, media.id med_id ...
```

though some databases require the slightly more verbose form:

```
SELECT megaliths.id AS meg_id, media.id AS med_id ...
```

This alias technique is also very handy when selecting expressions such as:

```
SELECT megaliths.id + 1 ...
```

because databases differ in how they name columns containing expressions. Using aliases not only makes it easier to refer to the columns but also makes your application more portable.

When discussing `fetchrow_arrayref()`, we pointed out that it currently returns the same array reference for each row. Well, `fetchrow_hashref()` currently doesn't return the same hash reference for each row but definitely will in a future release. (This change will also make it faster, as it's a little slower than we'd like at the moment.)

There are other techniques for fetching data from the database, but these deal with either *batch fetching* or *atomic fetching* and are discussed later in this chapter.

A quick way to fetch and print

The DBI supports a utility method called `dump_results()` for fetching all of the rows in a statement handle's result set and printing them out. This method is invoked via a prepared and executed statement handle, and proceeds to fetch and print all the rows in the result set from the database. As each line is fetched, it is formatted according either to default rules or to rules specified by you in your program. Once `dump_results()` has finished executing, it prints the number of rows fetched from the database and any error message. It then returns with the number of rows fetched.

For example, to quickly display the results of a query, you can write:

```
$sth = $dbh->prepare( "
            SELECT name, mapref, location
            FROM megaliths
        " );
$sth->execute();
$rows = $sth->dump_results();
```

which would display the following results:

```
'Balbirnie', 'NO 285 029', 'Balbirnie Park, Markinch, Fife'
'Castlerigg', 'NY 291 236', 'Near Keswick, Cumbria, England'
'Sunhoney', 'NJ 716 058', 'Near Insch, Aberdeenshire'
'Avebury', 'SU 103 700', 'Avebury, Wiltshire, England'
4 rows
```

You can customize the way in which this output is formatted by specifying the maximum length of each field within the row, the characters separating each field within the row, and the characters separating each row. You can also supply a Perl filehandle to which the output is written.

The default settings for these parameters are:

```
1:  Maximum Field Length  -    35
2:  Line Separator        -    "\n"
3:  Field Separator       -    ","
4:  Output file handle    -    STDOUT
```

Therefore, to generate output with 80 character fields separated by colons to a file, you can write:

```
### Prepare and execute the query
$sth = $dbh->prepare( "
            SELECT name, location, mapref
            FROM megaliths
        " );
$sth->execute();

### Open the output file
open FILE, ">results.lis" or die "Can't open results.lis: $!";
```

```
### Dump the formatted results to the file
$rows = $sth->dump_results( 80, '\n', ':', \*FILE );

### Close the output file
close FILE or die "Error closing result file: $!\n";
```

`dump_results()` internally uses the `neat_list()` utility function (described in the previous chapter) for the actual formatting operation. Because of this, you should not use the output of `dump_results()` for any data transfer or data processing activity. It's only meant for human consumption.

Finishing a Data Fetch Early

When a statement handle for a `SELECT` statement has been successfully executed, it is said to be *active*. There's even a boolean statement handle attribute called `Active` that you can read. Being active simply means that there's something actively going on within the database server on behalf of this handle.

When you call a fetch method again, after fetching the last row of data, the driver automatically finishes whatever is actively going on within the database server on behalf of this `execute()` and resets the `Active` attribute. Most drivers don't actually have to do anything in this particular case because the server knows that the driver has fetched the last row. So the server has automatically freed up any resources it was using to store that result set.

Since this finishing-up is done automatically when a fetch method returns an end-of-data status, there's usually no need to be aware of it. However, there are two types of situations where it's appropriate to take matters into your own hands by calling the `finish()` method on the statement handle. (Keep in mind that `finish()` doesn't "finish" the statement handle itself—it finishes only the current *execution* of it. You can still call `execute()` on the handle again later.)

The first situation is a little obscure and relates to being a good database-citizen. If the database server is using a significant amount of temporary disk space to hold your result set, *and* you haven't fetched all the records, *and* you won't be destroying or re-executing the statement handle soon, *then* it's appropriate to call `finish()`. That way, the server can free up the temporary disk space it's holding for your results.*

The second type of situation is less obscure, mainly because the DBI nags you about it by issuing warnings like this one from `disconnect()`:

```
disconnect invalidates 1 active statement handle
(either destroy statement handles or call finish on them before disconnecting)
```

---

* A classic example is `SELECT dialled_number, count(*) FROM calls WHERE subscriber = ?` GROUP BY `dialled_number` ORDER BY `count(*)` DESC when you only want to fetch the first few rows out of the thousands that the database has stored in temporary buffer space and sorted for you.

What's happening here is that the DBI is warning you that an active statement handle, that may still have data to be fetched from it, is being invalidated (i.e., made unusable) by disconnecting from the database.

Why does the DBI bother to warn you? The idea is to help you spot cases where you have not caught and dealt with an error from a fetch method that has terminated a fetch loop before all the data has been retrieved. Some row fetch errors, such as a transaction being aborted, mean that it's not possible for more rows to be fetched from that statement handle. In those cases, the driver resets the `Active` flag. For others though, such as a divide-by-zero in a column expression, or a long field value being truncated, further rows can be fetched, so the driver leaves the `Active` flag set.

In practice, there are other situations apart from fetch loops that can leave you with active statement handles both in the normal flow of events and due to exceptional circumstances.

The most humble is the common desire to fetch only n rows because you know there are only n rows to be fetched. Most drivers can't tell that you've fetched the last row, so they can't reset the `Active` flag. This is similar to the "good database-citizen" situation we discussed earlier. The following example shows the `finish()` method being called after fetching the one and only row of interest:

```
sub select_one_row {
    my $sth = shift;
    $sth->execute(@_) or return;
    my @row = $sth->fetchrow_array();
    $sth->finish();
    return @row;
}
```

A more exceptional situation is often related to using `RaiseError`. When an exception is thrown, such as when the DBI detects an error on a handle with `RaiseError` set, or when any other code calls `die()`, then the flow of control within your script takes a sudden leap from where it was up to the nearest enclosing `eval` block. It's quite possible that this process may leave handles with unfinished data.

The warning from `disconnect()`, and most other DBI warnings, can be silenced for a given handle by resetting the `Warn` attribute of that handle. This practice is generally frowned upon, but if you must, you can.

Remember that calling `finish()` is never essential, does not destroy the Perl statement handle object itself, is not required to avoid leaks, and does not stop `execute()` being called again on the handle. All of those are common misconceptions, often perpetuated in other books. We'll discuss how statement handles actually do get destroyed in the next section.

Deallocating Statement Handles

When a statement is prepared, the returned statement handle is associated with allocated memory resources within both your Perl script and the database server you're connected to. When you no longer need a statement handle, you should destroy it. That sounds drastic, but all it really means is letting go.

Statement handles are actually represented by Perl objects and, as such, are subject to the machinations of Perl's garbage collector. This implies that when no references to a statement handle remain (for example, the handle variable has gone out of scope or has been overwritten with a new value), Perl itself will destroy the object and reclaim the resources used by it.

Here's an example of a short-lived statement handle:

```
if ($fetch_new_data) {
    my $sth = $dbh->prepare( ... );
    $sth->execute();
    $data = $sth->fetchall_arrayref();
}
```

Notice that we don't have to make any explicit steps to free or deallocate the statement handle. Perl is doing that for us. The `my` `$sth` variable holds the only reference to that particular statement handle object. When the `$sth` variable ceases to exist at the end of the block, the last reference is removed and Perl's garbage collector swings into action. Similarly, when the script exits, all global variables cease to exist and any objects they refer to are deallocated in the same way.

Here's a slightly different example:

```
### Issue SQL statements to select sites by type
foreach ( 'Stone Circle', 'Monolith', 'Henge' ) {
    my $sth = $dbh->prepare( ... $_ ... );
    $sth->execute();
    $sth->dump_results();
}
```

The second and subsequent itterations of the loop assign a new statement handle reference to the `$sth` variable, which deletes the reference it previously held. So once again, since that was the only reference to the handle and it's now been deleted, the handle gets deallocated.

You might have an application that prepares, uses, and discards thousands (or hundreds of thousands) of statement handles throughout its lifetime. If the database resources for the statements were not freed until the database connection was closed, you could easily exhaust the database resources in a short amount of time.

In practice, the only time that you might overload the database is when you're storing the statement handles in arrays or hashes. If you're not careful to delete or overwrite old values, then handles can accumulate.

To keep track of how many statement handles are allocated for a database handle (for example, to help spot leaks), you can use the `Kids` and `ActiveKids` database handle attributes. Both of these will return integer counts. The first counts all statement handles; the second counts only those that have their `Active` attribute set.

Executing Non-SELECT Statements

We discussed in Chapter 3 the various data manipulation techniques that you might wish to use on your data. So far in this chapter, we have discussed the most commonly used data manipulation operation, fetching. But what about inserting, deleting, and updating data?

These operations are treated somewhat differently than querying, as they do not use the notion of a cursor to iterate through a result set. They simply affect rows of data stored within tables without returning any rows to your programs. As such, the full prepare–execute–fetch–deallocate cycle is not as appropriate for these operations. The fetch stage simply doesn't apply.

Since you're usually going to invoke these statements only once, it would be very tiresome to have to call `prepare()` to get a statement handle and then call `execute()` on that statement handle to actually invoke it, only to immediately discard that statement handle.

Fortunately, the DBI defines a shortcut for carrying out these operations—the `do()` method, invoked against a valid database handle. Using `do()` is extremely easy. For example, if you wished to delete some rows of data from the `megaliths` table, the following code is all that's required:

```
### Assuming a valid database handle exists....
### Delete the rows for Stonehenge!
$rows = $dbh->do( "
        DELETE FROM megaliths
        WHERE name = 'Stonehenge'
    " );
```

To signify whether or not the SQL statement has been successful, a value is returned from the call signifying either the number of rows affected by the SQL statement, or `undef` if an error occurred.

Some databases and some statements will not be able to return the number of rows affected by some statements; `-1` will be returned in these cases.

As a special case, a row count of zero is returned as the string `0E0`, which is just a fancy mathematical way of saying zero. Returning `0E0` instead of `0` means that the `do()` method still returns a value that Perl interprets as `true`, even when no rows have been affected.* The `do()` method returns a **false** value only on an error.

A good DBI method to remember is `quote()`—especially when building SQL statements, and especially when inserting new data into the database via `do()`. This method correctly quotes values as literal strings within your SQL statement before it is issued to the database. We discussed this method in Chapter 4.

Binding Parameters to Statements

One topic we have mentioned in our discussion of the preparation of statement handles is *bind values*. You may also have come across the phrases *placeholders*, *parameters*, and *binding*. What are these things?

A bind value is a value that can be bound to a placeholder declared within an SQL statement. This is similar to creating an on-the-fly SQL statement such as:

```
$sth = $dbh->prepare( "
        SELECT name, location
        FROM megaliths
        WHERE name = " . $dbh->quote( $siteName ) . "
    " );
```

but instead of interpolating the generated value into the SQL statement, you specify a placeholder and then bind the generated value to that. For example:

```
$sth = $dbh->prepare( "
        SELECT name, location
        FROM megaliths
        WHERE name = ?
    " );
$sth->bind_param( 1, $siteName );
```

The `bind_param()` method is the call that actually associates the supplied value with the given placeholder. The underlying database will correctly parse the placeholder and reserve a space for it which is "filled in" when `bind_param()` is called. It is important to remember that `bind_param()` must be called *before* `execute()`; otherwise, the missing value will not have been filled in and the statement execution will fail.

It's equally simple to specify multiple bind values within one statement, since `bind_param()` takes the index, starting from 1, of the parameter to bind the given value to. For example:

```
$sth = $dbh->prepare( "
        SELECT name, location
```

---

* Perl actually has special logic to allow the string 0 but true to be used for this kind of purpose. The DBI doesn't use that because people are bound to write messages like `print Deleted $rows rows\n` and `Deleted 0E0 rows` reads slightly better than `Deleted 0 but true rows`.

```
            FROM megaliths
            WHERE name = ?
            AND mapref = ?
            AND type LIKE ?
    " );
$sth->bind_param( 1, "Avebury" );
$sth->bind_param( 2, $mapreference );
$sth->bind_param( 3, "%Stone Circle%" );
```

You may have noticed that we haven't called the **quote()** method on the values. Bind values are passed to the database separately from the SQL statement,* so there's no need to "wrap up" the value in SQL quoting rules.

Some database drivers can accept placeholders in the form of :1, :2, and so on, or even :name or :somevalue, but this is not guaranteed to be portable between databases. The only guaranteed portable placeholder form is a single question mark, ?. Of course, if the underlying database in question doesn't support binding, the driver may fail to parse the statement completely.

Bind Values Versus Interpolated Statements

So, why use bind values? What's the real differences between these and interpolated on-the-fly SQL statements?

On the face of it, there's no obvious difference. Interpolated statement creation uses Perl's string-handling functionality to create a complete SQL statement to send to the database. The bind values are sent to the database after the SQL statement, but just before it's executed. In both cases, the same result is achieved.

The actual difference lies in the way that databases handle bind values, assuming that they do. For example, most large database systems feature a data structure known as the "Shared SQL Cache," into which SQL statements are stored along with additional related information such as a *query execution plan*.

The general idea here is that if the statement already exists within the Shared SQL Cache, the database doesn't need to reprocess that statement before returning a handle to the statement. It can simply reuse the information stored in the cache. This process can increase performance quite dramatically in cases where the same SQL is executed over and over again.†

---

* This is not strictly true, since some drivers emulate placeholders by doing a textual replacement of the placeholders with bind values before passing the SQL to the database. Such drivers use Perl's internal information to guess whether each value needs quoting or not. Refer to the driver documentation for more information.

† I've known a case where the database spent over a minute just trying to work out a "good enough" query execution plan for a complex SQL query. In cases like this, reuse of the processed statement handle makes for a very large improvement in performance.

For example, say we wished to fetch the general information for 100 megalithic sites, using the name as the search field. We can write the following SQL to do so:

```
SELECT name, location, mapref
FROM megaliths
WHERE name = <search_term>
```

By using interpolated SQL, we would actually issue 100 different SQL statements to the database. Even though they are almost identical, they are different enough for the database to re-parse the statement and not use the cached information. By using a bind value, the same piece of SQL and the same "execution plan" will be reused over and over again, even though a different bind value is supplied for each query.

Therefore, for databases that support it, using bind values with prepared statement handles can quite dramatically increase the performance of your applications and the efficiency of your database. This is especially significant when trying to insert many records.

That said, there are good reasons to use interpolated SQL statements instead of bind values. One of these reasons could be simply that your database doesn't support bind values! A more complex reason is that your database may have restrictive rules about what parts of an SQL statement may use placeholders.

In the examples listed above, we've illustrated the use of bind values to supply conditions for the query. For the sake of badness, say we wanted to iterate through a list of database tables and return the row count from each one. The following piece of code illustrates the idea using an interpolated SQL statement:

```
foreach $tableName ( qw( megaliths, media, site_types ) ) {
    $sth = $dbh->prepare( "
            SELECT count(*)
            FROM $tableName
        " );
    $sth->execute();
    my $count = $sth->selectrow_array();
    print "Table $tableName has $count rows\n";
}
```

By using an interpolated statement, this code would actually execute correctly and produce the desired results, albeit at the cost of parsing and executing four different SQL statements within the database. We could rewrite the code to use bind values, which would be more efficient (theoretically):

```
$sth = $dbh->prepare( "
        SELECT count(*)
        FROM ?
    " );
$sth->bind_param( 1, $tableName );
...
```

On most databases, this statement would actually fail to parse at the **prepare()**
call, because placeholders can generally be used only for literal values. This is
because the database needs enough information to create the query execution
plan, and it can't do that with incomplete information (e.g., if it doesn't know the
name of the table).

Additionally, the following code will fail, since you are binding more than just literal values:

```
$sth = $dbh->prepare( "
          SELECT count(*)
          FROM megaliths
          ?
" );
$sth->bind_param( 1, "WHERE name = 'Avebury'" );
...
```

Of course, your driver might just support this sort of thing, but don't rely on it
working on other database systems!

Bind Values and Data Typing

Perl is a loosely typed language, in that you have strings and you have numbers.
Numbers can be strings and strings can, on occasion, be numbers. You can perform arithmetic on strings. It can all be very confusing for us, so you can imagine
how the driver feels when confronted with bind values.

To help the driver work out what sort of data is being supplied in a bind value,
you can supply an additional argument that specifies the datatype. For example,
the following code will bind the appropriately typed bind values to the statement
for execution in the database:

```
use DBI qw(:sql_types);

$sth = $dbh->prepare( "
          SELECT meg.name, meg.location, st.site_type, meg.mapref
          FROM megaliths meg, site_types st
          WHERE name = ?
          AND id = ?
          AND mapref = ?
          AND meg.site_type_id = st.id
        " );
### No need for a datatype for this value. It's a string.
$sth->bind_param( 1, "Avebury" );

### This one is obviously a number, so no type again
$sth->bind_param( 2, 21 );

### However, this one is a string but looks like a number
$sth->bind_param( 3, 123500, { TYPE => SQL_VARCHAR } );
```

```
### Alternative shorthand form of the previous statement
$sth->bind_param( 3, 123500, SQL_VARCHAR );

### All placeholders now have values bound, so we can execute
$sth->execute();
```

The use DBI qw(:sql_types); statement asks for the standard SQL types to be imported as names, actually subroutines, that return the corresponding standard SQL integer type value. SQL_VARCHAR, for example, returns 12. If you don't want to import the SQL type names, you can add a DBI:: prefix, so that SQL_VARCHAR would be DBI::SQL_VARCHAR. However, that's not recommended because you lose the significant benefits of compile-time checking by use strict;.

If a type is specified, the driver should take that as a strong hint about what to do. But it is just a hint. Some drivers don't pay any attention to the specified type. Of those that do, most only use it to differentiate between strings, numbers, and LONG/LOB types. This is a relatively new area for the DBI and drivers, and one that's advancing slowly.

In general, databases tend to support a far wider range of datatypes than numbers and strings. Date types are very common and have widely varying formats. The DBI currently copes with these quite happily, by ducking the issue and expecting you to supply strings containing the data, formatted in the form expected by the database for the appropriate datatype.[*]

Binding Input and Output Parameters

There is a counterpart method to the bind_param() method called bind_param_ inout(), which can be used to sneakily return values from the statement. Typically, this is only useful with stored procedures that take input parameters and return values. Furthermore, few databases, and even fewer drivers, support this functionality, so beware.

bind_param_inout() behaves in a similar way to bind_param(), but uses a *reference* to a bind value instead of the value itself. This allows the bind value to be updated with the return value from the statement.

An additional argument stating the maximum length of the value to be returned must also be specified. If the returned value exceeds this value, the execute() call will fail. Therefore, if you aren't sure how large the return value might be, you should be pessimistic and supply a large value for this parameter. The only cost of doing so is using more memory than you need to.

A final, optional, argument that can be supplied is that of the datatype of the bind value. This behavior is identical to datatype specification in bind_param().

---

[*] Future versions may acquire ODBC-style escape functions.

See the previous section for more details on how to supply values for this argument.

An Oracle-specific example showing how `bind_param_inout()` works revolves around the following stored procedure, which returns the nearest integer values to a given input value:

```
-- Example stored procedure written in Oracle PL/SQL
PROCEDURE ceiling_floor (value IN NUMBER, c OUT NUMBER, f OUT NUMBER) IS
BEGIN
    c := CEIL(value);
    f := FLOOR(value);
END;
```

The DBI code to get these return values out of this procedure can be written as follows:

```
### The variables to be populated as return values...
my $ceiling;
my $floor;

$sth = $dbh->prepare( "BEGIN ceiling_floor( ?, ?, ? ); END;" );
$sth->bind_param( 1, 42.3 );
$sth->bind_param_inout( 2, \$ceiling, 50 );
$sth->bind_param_inout( 3, \$floor, 50 );
$sth->execute();

print "Stored procedure returned $ceiling, $floor\n";
```

You can use both `bind_param()` and `bind_param_inout()` on the same statement handle quite happily. Of course, if you use `bind_param()` when a return value is expected, that return value will be lost.

There is one quite subtle difference between `bind_param()` and `bind_param_inout()` that's worth pointing out. When you call `bind_param()`, the bind value you supply is copied and can't be changed without calling `bind_param()` again. However, when you call `bind_param_inout()`, it is the *reference* that's copied. The actual value that the reference points to is not read until `execute()` is called.

Binding Values Without bind_param()

Calling `bind_param()` for each placeholder can be rather long-winded and tedious when you have many placeholders, so the DBI provides a simpler way to do it via the `execute()` method. When you call `execute()`, you can simply give it a list of values, and `execute()` will call `bind_param()` on each one for you.

Furthermore, the `do()` method described above, and the `selectrow_array()` and `selectall_arrayref()` methods, which we'll discuss shortly, all call `execute()` one way or another, and also accept a list of bind values.

The following code illustrates passing a bind value to the **execute()** method:

```
$sth = $dbh->prepare( "
        SELECT name, location, mapref
        FROM megaliths
        WHERE name = ? OR description LIKE ?
        " );
$sth->execute( "Avebury", "%largest stone circle%" );
...
```

When specifying bind values in this manner, explicit data typing of the supplied values is not possible. In some cases, the underlying driver will correctly guess the type, but in most cases all values are passed to the database as **SQL_VARCHAR** values. However, if you have previously called **bind_param()** or **bind_param_inout()** for some or all placeholders with an explicitly specified datatype, that datatype will be used instead. For example:

```
$sth->prepare( "
        SELECT name, location, mapref
        FROM megaliths
        WHERE id = ?
        " );
$sth->bind_param( 1, 42, SQL_INTEGER );
$sth->execute( 123456 );
...
```

will result in the value of **123456** being supplied to the database as the bind value with the type of **SQL_INTEGER** instead of **SQL_VARCHAR**.

Binding Output Columns

In the examples of fetching data that we've seen so far, a **fetch()** method has been called that returns values we've copied into Perl variables. For example:

```
while( ( $foo, $bar ) = $sth->fetchrow_array ) { ... }
```

This syntax is fine, but it can get messy if many fields are being returned. It also involves extra copying of data, which can get expensive if many large strings are being fetched.

DBI supports a feature that simplifies the fetching of data and avoids the extra copying. This has the desired effect of making fetches very fast. It's known as *binding columns*, and it works by nominating a Perl variable to be used directly for storing values of a particular column as they are fetched. This has the basic effect that when data is fetched from the database via a **fetch()** method,* the Perl variables associated with each column are automatically updated with the fetched values.

---

* **fetch()** is just a handy short alias for **fetchrow_arrayref()**.

The best way to illustrate this process is by an example:

```
### Perl variables to store the field data in
my ( $name, $location, $type );

### Prepare and execute the SQL statement
$sth = $dbh->prepare( "
          SELECT meg.name, meg.location, st.site_type
          FROM megaliths meg, site_types st
          WHERE meg.site_type_id = st.id
        " );
$sth->execute();

### Associate Perl variables with each output column
$sth->bind_col( 1, \$name );
$sth->bind_col( 2, \$location );
$sth->bind_col( 3, \$type );

### Fetch the data from the result set
while ( $sth->fetch ) {
    print "$name is a $type located in $location\n";
}
```

The method we have used to explicitly associate the Perl variables to the output columns is `bind_col()`, which takes the index of the column to associate, starting from 1, and a reference to the Perl variable to associate it with. Thus, when the `fetch()` call completes, the associated Perl variables will be automatically updated without having to explicitly assign the fetched values. This is an extremely efficient way of fetching data from the database, both from a programming perspective and also from a performance point of view. `bind_col()` uses references to Perl variables, and, as such, there is no additional object or memory allocation when using bound output columns.

To ensure maximum portability, `bind_col()` should be called against an executed statement handle. For example, if your database does not return any real information from the `prepare()` call, `bind_col()` will not have sufficient information to succesfully associate the output columns with the Perl variables. This might lead to extremely peculiar results.

Using `bind_col()` to explicitly bind each column individually can get a bit tiresome, especially if many output columns are used. Fortunately, DBI defines an additional method called `bind_columns()` that can be used to quickly specify column bindings for multiple columns in one call.

`bind_columns()` works in an almost identical way to `bind_col()` except that instead of explicitly specifying the column index to bind a Perl variable to, you simply specify the Perl variables and the column assignation occurs automatically. For example, the code from earlier can be rewritten in the following way to use `bind_columns()`:

```
### Perl variables to store the field data in
my ( $name, $location, $type );

### Prepare and execute the SQL statement
$sth = $dbh->prepare( "
            SELECT meg.name, meg.location, st.site_type
            FROM megaliths meg, site_types st
            WHERE meg.site_type_id = st.id
          " );
$sth->execute();

### Associate Perl variables with each output column
$sth->bind_columns( undef, \$name, \$location, \$type );

### Fetch the data from the result set
while ( $sth->fetch ) {
    print "$name is a $type located in $location\n";
}
```

It is important to know that the number of columns specified in the SQL statement and the number of Perl variables specified in `bind_columns()` must match exactly. You cannot pick and choose which columns to fetch the data from as you can with `bind_col()`.[*]

Since `bind_columns()` uses `bind_col()` internally, the rules for using these two methods are the same.

Finally, we should mention that bind values specified with a SQL statement are completely unrelated to the ability to bind Perl variables to output columns of an SQL statement. They are separate operations. Bind values operate at a database input level, whereas output column bindings operate purely at a Perl output level.

do() Versus prepare()

As we mentioned in a previous section, the `do()` method supplied by the DBI makes executing non-SELECT statements much simpler than repeatedly preparing and executing statements. This is achieved by simply wrapping the prepare and execute stages into one composite method.

There is a drawback to doing this, however: performance. If you invoked `do()` repeatedly to insert a huge number of rows into a table, you could be preparing a statement handle many times more than is required, especially if the statement contained placeholder variables. For example, the following script inserts some rows into the `megaliths` table:

```
### Iterate through the various bits of data...
foreach $item ( qw( Stonehenge Avebury Castlerigg Sunhoney ) ) {
```

---

[*] The first argument to `bind_columns()` is an `undef`, due to historical reasons. It's no longer required if you are using DBI 1.08 or later.

```
### ... and insert them into the table
$dbh->do( "INSERT INTO megaliths ( name ) VALUES ( ? )",
        undef, $name );
}
```

Internally, what happens is that for each row being inserted, a new statement handle is created, and the statement is prepared, executed, and finally destroyed. Therefore, this loop has four prepare calls, four executes, and four destroys. However, since we're using a bind value for each loop, the database will likely need to parse the statement only once and use that statement again from the Shared SQL Cache. Therefore, in essence, our program is "wasting" three prepares of that statement.

This is a rather inefficient process. In this case, it would be better to hand-prepare and re-execute the statement handle for each iteration of the loop. For example:

```
### Setup the statement for repeated execution
$sth = $dbh->prepare( "INSERT INTO megaliths ( name ) VALUES ( ? )" );

### Iterate through the various bits of data...
foreach $item ( qw( Stonehenge Avebury Castlerigg Sunhoney ) ) {
    ### ... and insert them into the table
    $sth->execute( $name );
}
```

This code prepares the statement only once and executes it four times, once per row to be inserted. This is slightly less convenient to write, but typically significantly faster to execute.

While we're on the subject of insertion speed, it's important to point out that there may be a faster way. Using a Perl script with the DBI is unlikely ever to be as fast for bulk loading of records as the database vendors' own specially optimized tools such as Oracle's SQL*Loader or Sybase's BCP. But don't lose heart; Perl is the ideal tool to create and manipulate the data files that these loaders use.

Atomic and Batch Fetching

Atomic and *batch* fetching are two slightly more interesting ways of getting data out of your database. The two procedures are somewhat related to each other, in that they potentially make life a lot easier for you, but they do it in radically different ways.

Atomic Fetching

When you want to fetch only one row, atomic fetching allows you to compress the four-stage data fetching cycle (as described earlier) into a single method. The two methods you can use for atomic fetching are **selectrow_array()** and **select-**

`row_arrayref()`. They behave in a similar fashion to their row-oriented cousins, `fetchrow_array()` and `fetchrow_arrayref()`, the major differences being that the two atomic methods do not require a prepared and executed statement handle to work, and, more importantly, that they will return only one row of data.

Because neither method requires a statement handle to be used, they are actually invoked via a database handle. For example, to select the `name` and `type` fields from any arbitrary row in our `megaliths` database, we can write the following code:

```
### Assuming a valid $dbh exists...
( $name, $mapref ) =
    $dbh->selectrow_array( "SELECT name, mapref
                                FROM megaliths" );
print "Megalith $name is located at $mapref\n";
```

This is far more convenient than using the **prepare()** and **execute()** then the `fetchrow_array()` or `fetchrow_arrayref()` methods for single rows.

Finally, bind values can be supplied, which again helps with the reuse of database resources.

Batch Fetching

Batch fetching is the ability to fetch the entire result set from an SQL query in one call, as opposed to iterating through the result set using row-oriented methods such as `fetchrow_array()`, etc.

The DBI defines several methods for this purpose, including `fetchall_arrayref()` and `selectall_arrayref()`, which basically retrieve the entire result set into a Perl data structure for you to manipulate. They are invoked against a prepared and executed statement handle.

`fetchall_arrayref()` operates in three different modes depending on what arguments have been passed to it. It can be called with no arguments, with a reference to an array slice as an argument, and with a reference to a hash slice as an argument. We'll discuss these modes in the following sections.

No arguments

When `fetchall_arrayref()` is invoked with no arguments, it returns a reference to an array containing references to each row in the result set. Each of those references refers to an array containing the field values for that row. Figure 5-4 illustrates the data structure returned.

This looks pretty convoluted, but it is, in fact, extremely simple to access the data stored within the data structure. For example, the following code shows how to

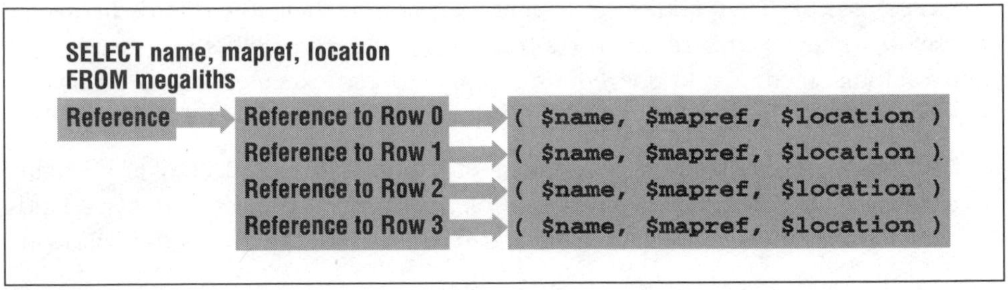

Figure 5-4. fetchall_arrayref( ) data structure

dereference the data structure returned by `fetchall_arrayref()` when run with
no arguments:

```
#!/usr/bin/perl -w
#
# ch05/fetchall_arrayref/ex1: Complete example that connects to a database,
#                             executes a SQL statement, then fetches all the
#                             data rows out into a data structure. This
#                             structure is then traversed and printed.

use DBI;

### The database handle
my $dbh = DBI->connect( "dbi:Oracle:archaeo", "username", "password" , {
    RaiseError => 1
});

### The statement handle
my $sth = $dbh->prepare( " SELECT name, location, mapref FROM megaliths " );

### Execute the statement
$sth->execute();

### Fetch all the data into a Perl data structure
my $array_ref = $sth->fetchall_arrayref();

### Traverse the data structure and dump each piece of data out
###
### For each row in the returned array reference ...
foreach my $row (@$array_ref) {
    ### Split the row up and print each field ...
    my ( $name, $type, $location ) = @$row;
    print "\tMegalithic site $name, found in $location, is a $type\n";
}

exit;
```

Therefore, if you want to fetch all of the result set from your database, `fetchall_`
`arrayref()` is an efficient and easy way of doing it. This is doubly true if you
were planning on building an in-memory data structure containing the returned

rows for post-processing. Instead of doing it yourself, you can simply use what `fetchall_arrayref()` returned instead.

Slice array reference argument

It is also possible to use `fetchall_arrayref()` to return a data structure containing only certain columns from each row returned in the result set. For example, we might issue an SQL statement selecting the `name`, `site_type`, `location`, and `mapref` fields, but only wish to build an in-memory data structure for the rows `name` and `location`.

This cannot be done by the standard no-argument version of `fetchall_arrayref()`, but is easily achieved by specifying an array slice as an argument to `fetchall_arrayref()`.

Therefore, if our original SQL statement was:

```
SELECT meg.name, st.site_type, meg.location, meg.mapref
FROM megaliths meg, site_types st
WHERE meg.site_type_id = st.id
```

then the array indices for each returned row would map as follows:

```
name        -> 0
site_type   -> 1
location    -> 2
mapref      -> 3
```

By knowing these array indices for the columns, we can simply write:

```
### Retrieve the name and location fields...
$array_ref = $sth->fetchall_arrayref( [ 0, 2 ] );
```

The array indices are specified in the form standard to Perl itself, so you can quite easily use ranges and negative indices for special cases. For example:

```
### Retrieve the second last and last columns
$array_ref = $sth->fetchall_arrayref( [ -2, -1 ] );

### Fetch the first to third columns
$array_ref = $sth->fetchall_arrayref( [ 0 .. 2 ] );
```

The actual data structure created when `fetchall_arrayref()` is used like this is identical in form to the structure created by `fetchall_arrayref()` when invoked with no arguments.

Slice hash reference argument

The final way that `fetchall_arrayref()` can be used is to selectively store columns into an array reference by passing a hash reference argument containing the columns to store. This is similar to the `fetchrow_hashref()` method but returns a reference to an array containing hash references for all rows in the result set.

If we wished to selectively store the `name` and `location` columns from an SQL statement declared as:

```
SELECT name, location, mapref
FROM megaliths
```

we can instruct `fetchall_arrayref()` to store the appropriate fields by passing an anonymous hash as an argument. This hash should be initialized to contain the names of the columns to store.

For example, storing the `name` and `location` columns can be written easily as:

```
### Store the name and location columns
$array_ref = $sth->fetchall_arrayref( { name => 1, location => 1 } );
```

The data structure created by `fetchall_arrayref()` running in this mode is a reference to an array of hash references, with each hash reference keyed by the column names and populated with the column values for the row in question. Traversing this data structure is quite straightforward. The following code illustrates a technique to do it:

```
#!/usr/bin/perl -w
#
# ch05/fetchall_arrayref/ex3: Complete example that connects to a database,
#                             executes a SQL statement, then fetches all the
#                             data rows out into a data structure. This
#                             structure is then traversed and printed.

use DBI;

### The database handle
my $dbh = DBI->connect( "dbi:Oracle:archaeo", "username", "password" , {
    RaiseError => 1,
} );

### The statement handle
my $sth = $dbh->prepare( " SELECT name, location, mapref FROM megaliths " );

### Execute the statement
$sth->execute();

### Fetch all the data into an array reference of hash references!
my $array_ref = $sth->fetchall_arrayref( { name => 1, location => 1 } );

### Traverse the data structure and dump each piece of data out
###
### For each row in the returned array reference.....
foreach my $row (@$array_ref) {
    ### Get the appropriate fields out the hashref and print...
    print "\tMegalithic site $row->{name}, found in $row->{location}\n";
}

exit;
```

There are a couple of important points to be noted with this form of result set fetching:

- If you have issued a SQL statement with multiple columns with the same name, the returned hash references will have only a single entry for all the columns. That is, earlier entries will be overwritten and lost. The same condition applies to `fetchrow_hashref()`, since this method is what `fetchall_arrayref()` calls internally when given a hash slice.

  An example piece of SQL that would cause problems is:

  ```
  SELECT m.name, c.name
  FROM megaliths m, countries c
  WHERE m.country_id = c.id
  ```

  In this case, the returned hash reference for the rows would contain either the country column values, or the `megalith` column values, but not both.

- The second point regarding this use of `fetchall_arrayref()` is that the column names stored in the returned hash are always lowercase. The case that the database uses and the case used in the parameter to `fetchall_arrayref()` are ignored.

To sum up, batch value fetching is a convenient way to retrieve all the data in the result set into Perl data structures for future processing. Do keep in mind, though, that large results sets will eat large amounts of memory. If you try to fetch too large a data set, you will run out of memory before the method returns to you. Your system administrator may not be amused.

6

Advanced DBI

This chapter covers some of the more advanced topics of using DBI, including the ability to alter the way in which the database and statement handles function on-the-fly, as well as how to use explicit transaction handling within your database. These topics are not strictly necessary for basic DBI usage, but they contain useful information that will allows you to maximize the potential of your DBI programs.

Handle Attributes and Metadata

In addition to methods associated with database and statement handles, the DBI also defines *attributes* for these handles that allow the developer to examine or fine-tune the environment in which the handles operate. Some attributes are unique to either database or statement handles, and some are common to both.

The attribute values of a handle can be thought of as a hash of key/value pairs, and can be manipulated in the same way as you would manipulate an ordinary hash via a reference. Here are a few examples using the `AutoCommit` attribute:

```
### Set the database handle attribute "AutoCommit" to 1 (e.g., on)
$dbh->{AutoCommit} = 1;

### Fetch the current value of "AutoCommit" from the handle
$foo = $dbh->{AutoCommit};
```

Fetching attributes as hash values, rather than as method calls, has the added bonus that the hash lookup can be *interpolated* inside double-quoted strings:

```
### Print the current value of "AutoCommit" from the handle
print "AutoCommit: $dbh->{AutoCommit}\n";
```

With AutoCommit enabled, that would print:

```
AutoCommit: 1
```

as you might expect. Actually, since `AutoCommit` is a *boolean* attribute, it would print 1 after any value that Perl considers *true* had been assigned to it.

After a *false* value was assigned, you may reasonably expect a 0 to be printed, but you might be surprised to see:

```
AutoCommit.
```

That's because Perl uses an internal representation of `false` that is both a numeric zero and an empty string at the same time. When used in a string context, the empty string is printed. In a numeric context, the zero is used.

When getting or setting an attribute value, the DBI automatically checks that the attribute name you are using and generates an error if it's not known.[*] Similarly, any attempts to set a read-only attribute will result in an error. Be aware, however, that these errors are reported using `die()` regardless of the setting of the `RaiseError` attribute, and are thus potentially fatal. That's another good reason to use `eval {...}` blocks, as we discussed in Chapter 4, *Programming with the DBI.*

A statement handle is known as a child, or kid, of its parent database handle. Similarly, database handles are themselves children of their parent driver handle. Child handles inherit some attribute values from parent handles. The rules for this behavior are defined in a common-sense manner and are as follows:

- A statement handle will inherit (copy) the current values of certain attributes from its parent database handle.

- If that new statement handle then has its attribute values altered, this affects neither the parent database handle nor any other statement handles. The changes are contained entirely within the altered statement handle.

- Changes to attributes within a database handle do not affect any of its existing child statement handles. The database handle attribute changes only affect future statement handles created from that database handle.

The DBI specification in Appendix A should be consulted for complete information on which attributes are inherited.

Passing Attributes to DBI Methods

Handles carry with them their set of current attribute values that methods often use to control how they behave. Many methods are defined to also accept an optional reference to a hash of attribute values.

---

[*] Driver-specific attributes, e.g., those that start with a lowercase letter, are a special case. Any get or set of a driver-specific attribute that hasn't been handled by the driver is handled by the DBI without error. That makes life easier for driver developers. On the other hand, you need to take extra care with the spelling.

This is primarily an escape mechanism for driver developers and their users, and so does not always work in the way you might think. For example, you might expect this code:

```
$dbh->{RaiseError} = 1;
...
$dbh->do( $sql_statement, undef, { RaiseError => 0 } );  # WRONG
```

to turn off `RaiseError` for the `do()` method call. But it doesn't! Attribute parameters are *ignored* by the DBI on *all* database handle and statement handle method calls. You don't even get a warning that the attribute has been ignored.

If they're ignored, then what's the point in having them? Well, the DBI itself ignores them, but the DBD driver that processed the method call may not. Or then again, it may! Attribute hash parameters to methods are *hints* to the driver and typically only usefully hold driver-specific attributes.*

That doesn't apply to the `DBI->connect()` method call because it's not a driver method, it's a DBI method. Its attribute hash parameter, `\%attr`, *is* used to set the attributes of the newly created database handle. We gave some examples using `RaiseError` in Chapter 4, and we give more in the following section.

Connecting with Attributes

One of Perl's many catch phrases is "there's more than one way to do it," and the DBI is no exception. In addition to being able to set attributes on a handle by simple assignment and by the attribute parameter of the `connect()` method (as shown earlier), the DBI provides another way.

You can include attribute assignments in the data source name parameter of the `connect()` method. For example:

```
$dbh = DBI->connect( "dbi:Oracle:archaeo", "username", "password" , {
    RaiseError => 1
});
```

can also be expressed as:

```
$dbh = DBI->connect( "dbi:Oracle(RaiseError=>1):archaeo", '', '');
```

You can't have any space before the opening parenthesis or after the closing one before the colon, but you can have spaces within the parentheses. You can also use just = instead of => if you prefer. If you want to set more than one attribute then use a comma to separate each one.

The attribute settings in the data source name parameter take precedence over those in the attribute parameter. This can be very handy when you want to

---

* It's possible that a future version of the DBI may look for certain non-driver-specific attributes, such as `RaiseError`.

override a hardcoded attribute setting, such as `PrintError`. For example, this code will leave `PrintError` on:

```
$dbh = DBI->connect( "dbi:Oracle(PrintError=>1):archaeo", '', '', {
    PrintError => 0
});
```

But what's the point of just hardcoding the attribute setting in two different places? This example is not very useful as it stands, but we could let the application accept the data source name parameter from the command line as an option, or leave it empty and use the `DBI_DSN` environment variable. That makes the application much more flexible.

The Significance of Case

You may have noticed that some attribute names use all uppercase letters, like `NUM_OF_FIELDS`, while others use mixed case letters, like `RaiseError`. If you've seen any descriptions of individual database drivers you may have also noticed some attribute names that use all lowercase letters, like `ado_conn` and `ora_type`.

There is a serious method behind the apparently inconsistent madness. The letter case used for attribute names is significant and plays an important part in the portability of DBI scripts and the extensibility of the DBI itself. The letter case of the attribute name is used to signify *who* defined the meaning of that name and its values, as follows:

UPPER_CASE

Attribute names that use only uppercase letters and underscores are defined by external standards, such as ISO SQL or ODBC.

The statement handle `TYPE` attribute is a good example here. It's an uppercase attribute because the values it returns are the standard portable datatype numbers defined by ISO SQL and ODBC, and not the nonportable native database datatype numbers.

MixedCase

Attribute names that start with an uppercase letter but include lowercase letters are defined by the DBI specification.

lower_case

Attribute names that start with a lowercase letters are defined by individual database drivers. These are known as driver-specific attributes.

Because the meanings are assigned by driver authors without any central control, it's important that two driver authors don't pick the same name for attributes with different behaviors. To ensure this, driver-specific attributes all begin with a prefix that identifies the particular driver. For example, `DBD::ADO` attributes all begin with `ado_`, `DBD::Informix` attributes begin with `ix_`, etc.

For example, most drivers provide a driver-specific version of the statement handle `TYPE` attribute that returns the native database datatype numbers instead of the standard ones. `DBD::Oracle` calls it `ora_type`, `DBD::Ingres` calls it `ing_ingtype`, and `DBD::mysql` calls it `mysql_type`. The prefix also makes it easier to find driver-specific code in applications when maintaining them.

Driver-specific attributes play an important role in the DBI. They are an escape valve. They let drivers expose more of the special functionality and information that they have available without having to fit it inside the fairly narrow DBI straitjacket.

Common Attributes

Common attributes are those that can be queried and set within both database and statement handles. This section discusses some of the most commonly used attributes, including:

PrintError

The `PrintError` attribute, when enabled, will cause the DBI to issue a warning when a DBI method returns with an error status. This functionality is extremely useful for rapid debugging of your programs, as you may not have written explicit return value checking code after every DBI statement.

The printed error string lists the class of the database driver through which the DBI method was dispatched, the method that caused the error to occur, and the value of `$DBI::errstr`. The following message was generated when the `prepare()` method did not successfully execute against an Oracle7 database using the `DBD::Oracle` driver:

```
DBD::Oracle::db prepare failed: ORA-00904:
    invalid column name (DBD: error possibly near <*> indicator at char 8 in '
            SELECT <*>nname, location, mapref
            FROM megaliths
        ') at /opt/WWW/apache/cgi-bin/megalith/megadump line 79.
```

`PrintError` uses the standard Perl function called `warn()` to render the error message. Therefore, you could use a `$SIG{__WARN__}` error handler or an error handling module such as `CGI::ErrorWrap` to re-route the error messages from `PrintError`.

This attribute is enabled by default.

RaiseError

The `RaiseError` attribute is similar in style to its `PrintError` cousin, but differs slightly in operation. Whereas `PrintError` simply displayed a message when the DBI detected an error had occurred, `RaiseError` usually kills the program stone-dead.

RaiseError uses the standard Perl function die() to throw the exception and exit. This means you can use eval to catch the exception and deal with it yourself.* This is an important and valuable error handling strategy for larger applications and is highly recommended when using transactions.

The format of the error message printed by RaiseError is identical to that of PrintError. It both PrintError and RaiseError are defined, PrintError will be skipped if no $SIG{__DIE__} handler is installed.†

RaiseError is disabled by default.

ChopBlanks

This attribute regulates the behavior of the underlying database driver regarding the CHAR datatype in fixed-width and blank-padded character columns. By setting this attribute to a true value, any CHAR columns returned by a SELECT statement will have any trailing blanks chopped off. No other datatypes are affected even when trailing blanks are present.

Setting ChopBlanks usually occurs when you simply want to remove trailing spaces from data without having to write some explicit truncation code either in the original SQL statement or in Perl.

This can be a very handy mechanism when dealing with old databases that tend to use fixed-width, blank-padded CHAR types more often than VARCHAR types. The blank padding added by the database tends to get in the way.

This attribute is currently disabled by default.

LongReadLen and LongTruncOk

Many databases support BLOB (binary large object), LONG, or similar datatypes for holding very long strings or large amounts of binary data in a single field. Some databases support variable-length long values over 2,000,000,000 bytes in length.

Since values of that size can't usually be held in memory, and because databases can't usually know in advance the length of the longest LONG that will be returned from a SELECT statement (unlike other datatypes), some special handling is required. In this situation, the value of the LongReadLen attribute is used to determine how much buffer space to allocate when fetching such fields.

LongReadLen typically defaults to 0 or a small value like 80, which means that little or no LONG data will be fetched at all. If you plan to fetch any LONG

---

* It also allows you to define a $SIG{__DIE__} handler, which handles the die() call instead of the Perl default behavior.

† A future release may also skip PrintError if RaiseError is set and the current code is executing within an eval.

datatypes, you should set `LongReadLen` within your application to slightly more than the length of the longest long column you expect to fetch. Setting it too high just wastes memory.[*]

The `LongTruncOk` attribute is used to determine how to behave if a fetched value turns out to be larger than the buffer size defined by `LongReadLen`. For example, if `LongTruncOk` is set to a true value, (e.g., "truncation is okay") the over-long value will be silently truncated to the length specified by `Long-ReadLen`, without an error.

On the other hand, if `LongTruncOk` is false then fetching a LONG data value larger than `LongReadLen` is treated as an error. If `RaiseError` is not enabled then the fetch call retrieving the data will appear to *fail* in the usual way, which looks like the end of data has been reached.

`LongTruncOk` is set to false by default, which causes overly long data fetches to fail. Be sure to enable `RaiseError` or check for errors after your fetch loops.

We'll discuss handling LONG data in more detail in later in this chapter.

The DBI specification in Appendix A provides a complete list of all the common attributes defined within the DBI.

Database Handle Attributes

Database handle attributes are specific to database handles and are not valid for other types of handles. They include:

AutoCommit

The `AutoCommit` database handle attribute can be used to allow your programs to use fine-grained transaction behavior (as opposed to the default "commit everything" behavior).

The functionality of this attribute is closely tied into the way in which DBI defines transaction control. Therefore, a complete description of this parameter can be found later in this chapter.

Name

The `Name` database handle attribute holds the "name" of the database. Usually the same as the "`dbi:DriverName:...`" string used to connect to the database, but with the leading "`dbi:DriverName:`" removed.

---

[*] Using a value which is a power of two, such as 64 KB, 512 KB, 8 MB etc., can actually cause twice that amount to be taken on systems that have poor memory allocators. That's because a few extra bytes are needed for housekeeping information and, because the dumb allocator only works with powers of two, it has to double the allocation to make room for it.

The DBI Specification in Appendix A provides a complete list of all the database handle attributes defined within the DBI. We'll discuss statement handle attributes in a moment, but first we'll explore database metadata.

Database Metadata

Database metadata is high-level information, or "data about data," stored within a database describing that database. This information is extremely useful for dynamically building SQL statements or even generating dynamic views of the database contents.

The metadata stored by a database, and the way in which it's stored, varies widely between different database systems. Most major systems provide a *system catalog*, consisting of a set of tables and views that can be queried to get information about all the entities in the database, including tables and views. There are two common problems with trying to query the system catalog directly: they can be complex and difficult to query, and the queries are not portable to other types of database.

The DBI should provide a range of handy methods to access this information in a portable way, and one day it will. However, currently it only provides two methods that can be executed against a valid database handle to extract entity metadata from the database.

The first of these methods is called `tables()`, and simply returns an array containing the names of tables and views within the database defined by the relevant database handle. The following code illustrates the use of this method:

```
### Connect to the database
my $dbh = DBI->connect( 'dbi:Oracle:archaeo', 'stones', 'stones' );

### Get a list of tables and views
my @tables = $dbh->tables();

### Print 'em out
foreach my $table ( @tables ) {
    print "Table: $table\n";
}
```

Connecting to a MySQL database would generate:

```
Table: megaliths
Table: media
Table: site_types
```

However, connecting to an Oracle database would generate:

```
Table: STONES.MEGALITHS
Table: STONES.MEDIA
Table: STONES.SITE_TYPES
```

In both cases, if the database contains other tables, they'd be included in the output.

Oracle stores all names in uppercase by default, so that explains one of the differences, but what about the "STONES." that's been prefixed to each table name?

Oracle, like most other big database systems, supports the concept of *schemas.* A schema is a way of grouping together related tables and other database objects into a named collection. In Oracle each user gets their own schema with the same name as the user. (Not all databases that support schemas take this approach.)

If an Oracle user other than *stones* wanted to refer to the media table then, by default, they would need to *fully qualify* the table name by adding the *stones* schema name, e.g., stones.media. If they didn't then the database would think they were refering to a media table in their own schema.

So, the leading STONES in the output is the name of the schema that the tables are defined in. Returning the fully qualified table names is important because the tables() method will return the names of all the tables owned by all the users that it can discover.

The other method used to retrieve database metadata is called table_info(), and returns more detailed information about the tables and views stored within the database.

When invoked, table_info() returns a prepared and executed statement handle that can be used to fetch information on the tables and views in the database. Each row fetched from this statement handle contains *at least* the following fields in the order listed:[*]

TABLE_QUALIFIER
> This field contains the table qualifier identifier. In most cases this will be undef (NULL).

TABLE_OWNER
> This field contains the name of the owner of the table. If your database does not support multiple schema or table owners, this field will contain undef (NULL).

TABLE_NAME
> This field contains the name of the table and should *never* be undef.

TABLE_TYPE
> This field contains the "type" of entity signified by this row. The possible values include TABLE, VIEW, SYSTEM TABLE, GLOBAL TEMPORARY, LOCAL TEMPORARY, ALIAS, SYNONYM, or some database driver-specific identifier.

---

[*] Database drivers are free to include additional columns of information in the result data.

REMARKS

This field contains a description or comment about the table. This field may be undef (NULL).

Therefore, if we wished to list some basic information on the tables contained within the current schema or database, we can write the following program that uses table_info() to retrieve all the table information, then formats the output:

```
#!/usr/bin/perl -w
#
# ch06/dbhdump: Dumps information about a SQL statement.

use DBI;

### Connect to the database
my $dbh = DBI->connect( "dbi:Oracle:archaeo", "username", "password" , {
    RaiseError => 1
} );

### Create a new statement handle to fetch table information
my $tabsth = $dbh->table_info();

### Print the header
print "Qualifier  Owner     Table Name                        Type   Remarks\n";
print "=========  ========  ==============================    =====  =======\n\n";

### Iterate through all the tables...
while ( my ( $qual, $owner, $name, $type, $remarks ) =
        $tabsth->fetchrow_array() ) {

    ### Tidy up NULL fields
    foreach ($qual, $owner, $name, $type, $remarks) {
        $_ = "N/A" unless defined $_;
    }

    ### Print out the table metadata...
    printf "%-9s  %-9s %-32s %-6s %s\n", $qual, $owner, $name, $type, $remarks;
}

exit;
```

Running this program against our megalithic database on an Oracle database produces the following output:

```
Qualifier  Owner     Table Name                        Type   Remarks
=========  ========  ==============================    =====  =======

N/A        STONES    MEDIA                             TABLE  N/A
N/A        STONES    MEGALITHS                         TABLE  N/A
N/A        STONES    SITE_TYPES                        TABLE  N/A
```

This form of metadata is not tremendously useful, as it lists only metadata about the objects within the database, and not the structure of the objects themselves (such as table column names). Extracting the structure of each table or view within the database requires us to look to a different type of metadata, which is available via statement handles.

Statement Handle Attributes or Statement Metadata

Statement handle attributes are specific to statement handles, and inherit any inheritable attributes from their parent database handle. Many statement handle attributes are defined as being read-only because they simply describe the prepared statement or its results.

In theoretical terms, these attributes should be defined when the statement handle is prepared, but in practical terms, you should only rely on the attribute values after the statement handle has been both prepared *and executed.* Similarly, with a few drivers, fetching all the data from a SELECT statement or explicitly invoking the finish() method against a statement handle may cause the values of the statement handle attributes to be no longer available.

The DBI specification in Appendix A provides a complete list of all the statement handle attributes defined within the DBI.

Statement

> This attribute contains the statement string passed to the prepare() method.

NUM_OF_FIELDS

> This attribute is set to contain the number of columns that will be returned by a SELECT statement. For example:

```
$sth = $dbh->prepare( "
            SELECT name, location, mapref
            FROM megaliths
        " );
$sth->execute();
print "SQL statement contains $sth->{NUM_OF_FIELDS} columns\n";
```

> Non-SELECT statements will contain the attribute value of zero. This allows you to quickly determine whether or not the statement is a SELECT statement.

NAME

NAME_uc

NAME_lc

> The NAME attribute contains the names of the selected columns within the statement. The attribute value is actually a reference to an array, with length equal to the number of fields in the original statement.

> For example, you can list all the column names of a table like this:

```
$sth = $dbh->prepare( "SELECT * FROM megaliths" );
$sth->execute();
```

```
for ( $i = 1 ; $i <= $sth->{NUM_OF_FIELDS} ; $i++ ) {
    print "Column $i is called $sth->{NAME}->[$i-1]\n";
}
```

The names contained within the attribute array are the column names returned by the underlying database.

There are two additional attributes relating to the column names. NAME_uc contains the same column names as the NAME attribute, but with any lower-case characters converted to uppercase. Similarly the NAME_1c attribute has any uppercase characters converted to lowercase. Generally these attributes should be used in preference to NAME.

TYPE

The TYPE attribute contains a reference to an array of integer values representing the international standard values for the respective datatypes. The array of integers has a length equal to the number of columns selected within the original statement, and can be referenced in a similar way to the NAME attribute example shown earlier.

The standard values for common types are:

```
SQL_CHAR              1
SQL_NUMERIC           2
SQL_DECIMAL           3
SQL_INTEGER           4
SQL_SMALLINT          5
SQL_FLOAT             6
SQL_REAL              7
SQL_DOUBLE            8
SQL_DATE              9
SQL_TIME             10
SQL_TIMESTAMP        11
SQL_VARCHAR          12
SQL_LONGVARCHAR      -1
SQL_BINARY           -2
SQL_VARBINARY        -3
SQL_LONGVARBINARY    -4
SQL_BIGINT           -5
SQL_TINYINT          -6
SQL_BIT              -7
SQL_WCHAR            -8
SQL_WVARCHAR         -9
SQL_WLONGVARCHAR    -10
```

While these numbers are fairly standard,[*] the way drivers map their native types to these standard types varies greatly. Native types that don't correspond

---

[*] Some are ISO standard, others are Microsoft ODBC de facto standard. See *ftp://jerry.ece.umassd.edu/ isowg3/dbl/SQL_Registry* and search for "SQL Data Types," or the types names of interest, on *http:// search.microsoft.com/us/dev/* and browse the results.

well to one of these types may be mapped into the range officially reserved for use by the Perl DBI: –9999 to –9000.

PRECISION

The `PRECISION` attribute contains a reference to an array of integer values that represent the defined length or size of the columns in the SQL statement.

There are two general ways in which the precision of a column is calculated. String datatypes, such as `CHAR` and `VARCHAR`, return the maximum length of the column. For example, a column defined within a table as:

```
location        VARCHAR2(1000)
```

would return a precision value of 1000.

Numeric datatypes are treated slightly differently in that the number of *significant digits* is returned. This may have no direct relationship with the space used to store the number. Oracle, for example, stores numbers with 38 digits of precision but uses a variable length internal format of between 1 and 21 bytes.

For floating-point types such as `REAL`, `FLOAT`, and `DOUBLE`, the maximum "display size" can be up to seven characters greater than the precision due to concatenated sign, decimal point, the letter "E," a sign, and two or three exponent digits.

SCALE

The `SCALE` attribute contains a reference to an array of integer values that represents the number of decimal places in the column. This is obviously only of any real use with floating-point numbers. Integers and non-numeric datatypes will return zero.

NULLABLE

The `NULLABLE` attribute contains a reference to an array of integer values that tells us whether or not a column may contain a NULL value. The elements of the attribute array each contain one of three values:

0   The column cannot contain a NULL value.

1   The column can contain a NULL value.

2   It is unknown if the column can contain a null value.

NUM_OF_PARAMS

The `NUM_OF_PARAMS` attribute contains the number of parameters (placeholders) specified within the statement.

Common uses for these statement handle attributes are to format and display data fetched from queries dynamically and to find out information about the tables stored within the database.

The following script performs the latter operation by first creating a statement handle that fetches information on all tables, as discussed in the "Database Metadata" section earlier, and then iterating through each table listing the table structure via the statement metadata:

```perl
#!/usr/bin/perl -w
#
# ch06/tabledump: Dumps information about all the tables.

use DBI;

### Connect to the database
my $dbh = DBI->connect( "dbi:Oracle:archaeo", "username", "password" , {
    RaiseError => 1
});

### Create a new statement handle to fetch table information
my $tabsth = $dbh->table_info();

### Iterate through all the tables...
while ( my ( $qual, $owner, $name, $type ) = $tabsth->fetchrow_array() ) {

    ### The table to fetch data for
    my $table = $name;

    ### Build the full table name with quoting if required
    $table = qq{"$owner"."$table"} if defined $owner;

    ### The SQL statement to fetch the table metadata
    my $statement = "SELECT * FROM $table";

    print "\n";
    print "Table Information\n";
    print "=================\n\n";
    print "Statement:     $statement\n";

    ### Prepare and execute the SQL statement
    my $sth = $dbh->prepare( $statement );
    $sth->execute();

    my $fields = $sth->{NUM_OF_FIELDS};
    print "NUM_OF_FIELDS: $fields\n\n";

    print "Column Name                      Type  Precision  Scale  Nullable?\n";
    print "----------------------------     ----  ---------  -----  ---------\n\n";

    ### Iterate through all the fields and dump the field information
    for ( my $i = 0 ; $i < $fields ; $i++ ) {

        my $name = $sth->{NAME}->[$i];

        ### Describe the NULLABLE value
        my $nullable = ("No", "Yes", "Unknown")[ $sth->{NULLABLE}->[$i] ];
```

```
        ### Tidy the other values, which some drivers don't provide
        my $scale = $sth->{SCALE}->[$i];
        my $prec  = $sth->{PRECISION}->[$i];
        my $type  = $sth->{TYPE}->[$i];

        ### Display the field information
        printf "%-30s %5d      %4d    %4d    %s\n",
               $name, $type, $prec, $scale, $nullable;
    }

    ### Explicitly deallocate the statement resources
    ### because we didn't fetch all the data
    $sth->finish();
}

exit;
```

When executed against our megalithic database, the following output is displayed:

```
Table Information
=================

Statement: SELECT * FROM STONES.MEDIA
NUM_OF_FIELDS: 5

Column Name                     Type  Precision  Scale  Nullable?
-----------------------------   ----  ---------  -----  ---------

ID                               3        38       0   No
MEGALITH_ID                      3        38       0   Yes
URL                             12      1024       0   Yes
CONTENT_TYPE                    12        64       0   Yes
DESCRIPTION                     12      1024       0   Yes

Table Information
=================

Statement: SELECT * FROM STONES.MEGALITHS
NUM_OF_FIELDS: 6

Column Name                     Type  Precision  Scale  Nullable?
-----------------------------   ----  ---------  -----  ---------

ID                               3        38       0   No
NAME                            12       512       0   Yes
DESCRIPTION                     12      2048       0   Yes
LOCATION                        12      2048       0   Yes
MAPREF                          12        16       0   Yes
SITE_TYPE_ID                     3        38       0   Yes

Table Information
=================

Statement: SELECT * FROM STONES.SITE_TYPES
NUM_OF_FIELDS: 3
```

```
Column Name                     Type  Precision  Scale  Nullable?
-----------------------------   ----  ---------  -----  ---------

ID                                3        38      0    No
SITE_TYPE                        12       512      0    Yes
DESCRIPTION                      12      2048      0    Yes
```

This output shows the structural information of entities within our database. We could have achieved the same effect by querying our database's underlying system tables. This would give us more information, but would not be portable.

Handling LONG/LOB Data

The DBI requires some additional information to allow you to query back LONG/LOB (long/large object) datatypes from a database. As we discussed earlier in the section on the LongReadLen and LongTruncLen attributes, the DBI is unable to determine how large a buffer to allocate when fetching columns containing LOB data. Therefore, we cannot simply issue a **SELECT** statement and expect it to work.

Selecting LOB data is straightforward and essentially identical to selecting any other column of another datatype, with the important exception that you should set at least the LongReadLen attribute value prior to preparing the statement that will return the LOB. For example:

```
### We're not expecting binary data of more than 512 KB...
$dbh->{LongReadLen} = 512 * 1024;

### Select the raw media data from the database
$sth = $dbh->prepare( "
        SELECT mega.name, med.media_data
        FROM megaliths mega, media med
        WHERE mega.id = med.megaliths_id
    " );
$sth->execute();
while ( ($name, $data) = $sth->fetchrow_array ) {
    ...
}
```

Without the all-important setting of LongReadLen, the fetchrow_array() call would likely fail when fetching the first row, because the default value for LongReadLen is very small—typically 80 or less.

What happens if there's a rogue column in the database that is longer than LongReadLen? How would the code in the previous example cope? What would happen?

When the length of the fetched LOB data exceeds the value of LongReadLen, an error occurs *unless* you have set the LongTruncOk attribute to a true value. The DBI defaults LongTruncOk to false to ensure that accidental truncation is an error.

But there's a potential problem here if `RaiseError` is not enabled. How does the snippet of code above behave if it tries to fetch a row with a LOB field that exceeds the value of `LongReadLen`? The `fetchrow_array()` returns an empty list if there's an error when trying to fetch a row. But `fetchrow_array()` also returns an empty list when there's no more data to fetch. The `while` loop will simply end and any code following it will be executed. If the loop should have fetched 50 records it might stop after 45 if the 46th record was too big. Without error checking, you may never realize that you're missing some rows! The same applies to loops using other `fetchrow` methods such as `fetchrow_hashref()`.

Few people remember to check for errors after fetch loops and that's a common cause of problems with code that handles LONG/LOB fields. Even when not handling special datatypes it's *always* a good idea to check for errors after fetch loops, or let the DBI do it for you by enabling `RaiseError`, as we discussed in Chapter 4.

Getting back to our little snippet of code, let's assume that we *are* happy for values longer than `LongReadLen` to be silently truncated without causing an error. The following code stub would correctly handle this eventuality:

```
### We are interested in the first 512 KB of data
$dbh->{LongReadLen} = 512 * 1024;
$dbh->{LongTruncOk} = 1;     ### We're happy to truncate any excess

### Select the raw media data from the database
$sth = $dbh->prepare( "
            SELECT mega.name, med.media_data
            FROM megaliths mega, media med
            WHERE mega.id = med.megaliths_id
        " );
$sth->execute();
while ( ($name, $data) = $sth->fetchrow_arrayref ) {
    ...
}
```

The only change, apart from comments, is the addition of a line setting the `LongTruncOk` attribute to a true value.

The ability to truncate LOB data when overly large is quite useful for text and some forms of binary data, but not for others. Storing streaming media that is interpreted on a temporal basis doesn't unduly suffer from being truncated, as you will be able to view or listen to the stream up until the point of truncation. However, binary files such as ZIP files that store a checksum at the very end will be rendered useless when truncated. With this sort of data, it's not recommended that `LongTruncOk` be enabled, as it will allow truncated, and hence corrupted, data to be returned with no indication that there's a problem. In that situation, you won't be able to determine whether or not the column contains corrupted data, or if the column has been chopped by DBI. Caveat emptor!

One thing to be aware of when writing portable code to fetch LOB data from a database is that the format of that data may vary on a per-database and datatype basis. For example, in Oracle, a column with a LONG RAW datatype, rather than a simple LONG type, is passed to and from the database encoded as a pair of hexadecimal digits for each byte. So after fetching the hex string, you'd need to decode it using `unpack("H*", ...)` to get the original binary value. For historical reasons, for these datatypes, the `LongReadLen` attribute refers to the length of the binary data, so hex-encoded strings up to twice that length may be fetched.

The DBI currently defines no way to fetch LONG/LOB values *piece-wise*, in other words, piece-by-piece. That means you're limited to fetching values that will fit into your available memory. It also means you can't *stream* the data out while still fetching it from the database. Some drivers do implement an unofficial `blob_ read()` method, so take a look at your driver documentation if you need piece-wise fetches.

Inserting and Updating LONG/LOB Columns

Some databases let you insert into LONG/LOB columns using SQL statements with literal strings, like this:

```
INSERT INTO table_name (key_num, long_description) VALUES (42, '...')
```

Ignoring portability for the moment, that's fine for simple short textual strings, but soon runs into problems for anything else. Firstly, most databases have a limit on the maximum length of an SQL statement, and it's usually far shorter than the maximum length of a LONG/LOB column. Secondly, most databases have limits on which characters can be included in literal strings. The DBD driver's `quote()` method will do its best, but it's often not possible to put all possible binary data values into a string. Finally, coming back to portability, many databases are strict about data typing and just don't let you assign literal strings to LONG/LOB columns.

So how do we avoid these problems? Here's where *placeholders* come to our aid once again. We discussed placeholders in some detail in Chapter 5 so we'll only cover LONG/LOB issues here.

To use placeholders, we'd implement the statement above using the DBI as:

```
use DBI qw(:sql_types);

$sth = $dbh->prepare( "
    INSERT INTO table_name (key_num, long_description) VALUES (?, ?)
" );
$sth->bind_param( 1, 42 );
$sth->bind_param( 2, $long_description, SQL_LONGVARCHAR);
$sth->execute();
```

Passing SQL_LONGVARCHAR as the optional TYPE parameter to bind_param() gives the driver a strong hint that you're binding a LONG/LOB type. Some drivers don't need the hint but it's always a good idea to include it.

The DBI currently defines no way to insert or update LONG/LOB values *piece-wise*, in other words, piece by piece. That means you're limited to handling values that will fit into your available memory.

Transactions, Locking, and Isolation

The final topic in this chapter deals with the important (and hair-raising!) topic of *transaction handling.*

Transaction handling is a feature of the more powerful database systems in which SQL statements can be grouped into logical chunks. Each chunk is known as a *transaction,* and the operations it performs are guaranteed to be atomic for the purposes of recovery. According to the ANSI/ISO SQL standard, a transaction begins with the first executable SQL statement and ends when it is explicitly committed or rolled back.

The process of committing data writes it into the database tables and make it visible to other concurrent users. Rolling back discards any changes that have been made to any tables since the beginning of the current transaction.

The standard example to explain transactions is a bank transfer in which a customer transfers $1000 from one bank account to another. The bank transfer consists of three distinct stages:

1. Decrease the source account by the required amount.
2. Increase the target account by the required amount.
3. Write a journal entry recording the transfer.

When viewed as three separate stages, the possibility of disaster is quite obvious. Suppose there's a power outage between stages 1 and 2. The hapless customer is now $1000 poorer, as the money has neither reached the target account nor been logged in the transfer journal. The bank is now $1000 richer.*

Of course, if the power outage occurred between stages 2 and 3, the customer would have the correct amount of money in the correct accounts, but the bank would have no record of the transactions. This would lead to all sorts of book-keeping problems.

---

* No wonder the money is decremented first.

The answer is to treat the three separate stages as one logical unit, or transaction. Thus, when stage 1 starts executing, the transaction is started automatically. The same transaction continues until stage 3 is completed, after which point the transaction can be terminated with all the changes either being committed to the database or rolled back and discarded. Therefore, if a power outage happens at any point during the transaction, the entire transaction can be automatically rolled back when the database restarts and no permanent changes to the data will have been made.

A transaction is an all-or-nothing situation. Either it all works, or it all fails—which is great news for our luckless bank customer.

Transactions are also sometimes described as having A.C.I.D. properties:

Atomic

A transaction's changes to the database are atomic: either all happen or none happen.

Consistent

A transaction is a correct transformation of the state. The actions taken as a group do not violate any of the integrity constraints associated with the state.

Isolated

Even though transactions can execute concurrently, it appears to each transaction that others executed either before or after it.

Durable

Once a transaction completes successfully (e.g., `commit()` returns success), then its changes to the state of the database survive any later failures.

Implementing ACID transaction handling within a database requires the use of a journal log file, along with some sophisticated techniques and much careful coding. That's why it's rare to find ACID transactions supported on free databases (with the notable exception of PostgreSQL), and why it carries a performance penalty when it is supported.

On the upside, full transaction handling brings with it far greater safety from power failures, client failures, database failures, and other popular forms of disaster. Simple explicit locking mechanisms do not afford the same level of safety and recoverability, as we shall discuss later.

Since not all database systems support transaction processing, you may not have the luxury of being able to roll back from inadvertent data corruptions or be saved from power outage. But if your database does support transactions, the DBI makes it easy to manage them in a portable manner.

Automatic Transaction Handling

The ISO standard for SQL defines a particular model for transactions. It says that a database connection is always *in* a transaction. Each and every transaction will end with either a commit or a rollback, and every new transaction will begin with the next statement executed. Most systems also define an *auto-commit* mechanism that acts as if `commit()` is automatically called after each statement.

The DBI standard tries to find a way to let all drivers for all databases appear to offer the same facilities, as much as possible. It does this by relying on the fact that there's little practical difference between a database that supports transactions but has auto-commit enabled, versus a database that doesn't support transactions at all.

The DBI standard also tries to ensure that an application written to require transactions can't accidentally be run against a database that doesn't support them. It does this by treating an attempt to disable auto-commit as a fatal error for such a database.

Given that the ability to enable and disable auto-commit is important, the DBI defines a database handle attribute called `AutoCommit` that regulates whether or not DBI should *appear to* automatically force a data commit after every statement.

For example, if you issue a statement like `$dbh->do()` that deletes some data within your database, and `AutoCommit` is set to a true value, you cannot roll back your change even if the database supports transactions.

The DBI defaults to having `AutoCommit` enabled, making this potentially dangerous behavior automatic unless explicitly disabled. This is due to the precedent set by ODBC and JDBC. It was probably a mistake for the DBI to put standards compliance above safety in this case. A future version may issue a warning if `AutoCommit` is not specified as an attribute to `DBI->connect()`, so it's worth getting used to adding it now.

The behavior of changing this attribute depends on which type of transaction handling your database supports. There are three possibilities:

No transaction support

> Databases that have no transaction support are treated as always having `AutoCommit` enabled. Attempting to disable `AutoCommit` will result in a fatal error.

Always active transaction support

> This group of databases includes mainstream commercial RDBMS products, such as Oracle, that support the ANSI/ISO standard for transaction behavior.

If `AutoCommit` is switched from being enabled to disabled, no immediate actions should occur. Any future statements that you issue become part of a new transaction that must be committed or rolled back.

If `AutoCommit` is switched from being disabled to enabled, any outstanding database changes will be automatically committed.

Explicit transaction support

Some databases, such as Informix, support the idea that transactions are optional and must be explicitly started by applications when required.

The DBI attempts to treat these systems as systems that have always active transactions. To accomplish this, the DBI requires the driver to automatically begin a transaction when `AutoCommit` is switched from enabled to disabled. Once a transaction has been committed or rolled back, the driver will automatically start a new transaction.

Therefore, despite its database independence, the DBI offers both simple automatic transaction committing and powerful manual transaction processing modes.

Forcing a Commit

The DBI defines a method called `commit()` for explicitly committing any uncommitted data within the current transaction. This method is executed against a valid database handle:

```
$dbh->commit();
```

If `commit()` is invoked while `AutoCommit` is enabled, a warning will be displayed similar to:

```
commit ineffective with AutoCommit
```

which merely tells you that the database changes have already been committed. This warning will also be displayed when `commit()` is invoked against a database that has no transaction support because, by definition, `AutoCommit` will be enabled.

Rolling Back Changes

The corollary operation to committing data to the database is to roll it back. The DBI defines a method called `rollback()`, which can be used to roll back the most recent uncommitted database changes.

Like `commit()`, the `rollback()` method is executed against a database handle:

```
$dbh->rollback();
```

Similarly, if `rollback()` is invoked while `AutoCommit` is enabled, a warning will be displayed similar to:

```
rollback ineffective with AutoCommit
```

signifying that the database changes have already been committed. This warning will also be displayed when `rollback()` is invoked against a database that has no transaction support because, by definition, `AutoCommit` will be enabled.

Disconnecting, One Way or Another

The transaction effect of explicitly disconnecting from a database while `AutoCommit` is disabled is, sadly, undefined. Some database systems, such as Oracle and Ingres, will automatically commit any outstanding changes. However, other database systems, such as Informix, will roll back any outstanding changes. Because of this, applications not using `AutoCommit` should *always* explicitly call `commit()` or `rollback()` before calling `disconnect()`.

So what happens if you don't explicitly call `disconnect()`, or don't have the chance to because the program exits after a `die`? Well, because DBI handles are object references, we can be sure that Perl itself will call the `DESTROY` method for us on each handle if the program exits, the handle goes out of scope, or the only copy of a handle is overwritten by another value.

The actual implementation of the `DESTROY` method is in the hands of the driver author. If the database handle is still connected then it *should* automatically call `rollback()` (unless `AutoCommit` is enabled) before calling `disconnect()`. Calling `rollback()` in `DESTROY` is critical. If the driver doesn't, then a program aborting due to a `die` part way though a transaction may actually "accidentally" commit the incomplete transaction! Fortunately, all the drivers that we're aware of that support transactions do the right thing.

As an extra sanity check, if you disconnect from a database while you still have active statement handles, you will get a warning. We discussed active statement handles and related topics in Chapter 5.

Combining Automatic Error Handling with Transactions

Transactions, as you've probably realized by now, are closely related to error handling. This is especially true when you have to clean up after an error by putting everything in the database back to the way it was before the transaction started.

In Chapter 4, we discussed error handling in some detail and sang the praises of using the `RaiseError` attribute for automatic error detection.

Imagine combining the automatic error *detection* of the DBI's `RaiseError` attribute and the error *trapping* of Perl's `eval { ... }` and the error *handling* properties of transactions. The result is a simple yet powerful way to write robust applications in Perl.

There is a fairly common structure to these kind of applications, so to help us discuss the issues, we've included the following example.

This outline example processes CSV files containing sales data from one country, it fetches currency exchange rate information from a web site and adds that to the data, it then performs a series of inserts, selects, updates and more inserts of the data to update the database. That processing is repeated for a series of countries.

Here's the code:

```
### Connect to the database with transactions and error handing enabled
my $dbh = DBI->connect( "dbi:Oracle:archaeo", "username", "password" , {
    AutoCommit => 0,
    RaiseError => 1,
} );

### Keep a count of failures. Used for program exit status
my @failed;

foreach my $country_code ( qw(US CA GB IE FR) ) {

    print "Processing $country_code\n";

    ### Do all the work for one country inside an eval
    eval {

        ### Read, parse and sanity check the data file (e.g., using DBD::CSV)
        my $data = load_sales_data_file( "$country_file.csv" );

        ### Add data from the Web (e.g., using the LWP modules)
        add_exchange_rates( $data, $country_code,
                            "http://exchange-rate-service.com" );

        ### Perform database loading steps (e.g., using DBD::Oracle)
        insert_sales_data( $dbh, $data );
        update_country_summary_data( $dbh, $data );
        insert_processed_files( $dbh, $country_code );

        ### Everything done okay for this file, so commit the database changes
        $dbh->commit();

    };

    ### If something went wrong...
    if ($@) {

        ### Tell the user that something went wrong, and what went wrong
        warn "Unable to process $country_code: $@\n";
```

```
        ### Undo any database changes made before the error occured
        $dbh->rollback();

        ### Keep track of failures
        push @failed, $country_code;

    }
}
$dbh->disconnect();

### Exit with useful status value for caller
exit @failed ? 1 : 0;
```

In the following list, we make some observations about how and why the code is structured the way it is and discuss a few related issues:

Unit of work

A key design issue is what the "unit of work" should be. In other words, how much work should we do before committing and thus how much would be undone by a rollback on error? The smallest unit should correspond to the smallest logically complete change to the database. In our example, that corresponds to the complete processing of one country file, and that's what we've chosen as the unit of work here.

We could have opted for a larger unit of work. Processing all the files as one unit would be another obvious choice. In that case, we'd simply need to move the `foreach` loop to inside the `eval`. You should be aware that most databases have limits on the amount of database changes you can make without committing. It's usually large, and always configurable, but you need to be aware that there are limits that may bite you if you try to do too much.

Where to commit

It's important to have the `commit()` inside the `eval`. The commit call is the most critical part of the transaction. Don't assume that the `commit()` will succeed just because the previous statements didn't return an error. Databases are free to defer much of the real work till commit is called.

The `commit()` call should be the very last thing before the end of the `eval` block. Sometimes it's more tricky. Imagine that the requirements changed and you were asked to make the script delete the files as it processed them. Where would you put the `unlink()` call? Before or after the `commit()`? Think about that for a moment. Remember that there's always the risk that either the `commit()` or the `unlink()` could fail. You need to weigh up both the risks and the after effects of either case.

Here's how it applies in our example: if you commit first and the unlink fails, then you'll process the file again the next time the script is run. If you unlink first and the commit fails, then you've lost the data. In this case, the lesser of the two evils is clearly to commit first and risk double processing, especially as double processing is probably easy to avoid by checking the data in the file against what's already in the database.

In the real world, things can be rather more complex. However, there are plenty of creative ways to address this *two system commit* problem. The most important thing to remember is that there *is* a problem to address whenever some change outside the database has to be *committed* at the same time that the database changes are committed.

When things go wrong

The first thing to do in your `if ($@) {...}` block is to print an error message. The error message code helps document what the error handling block is dealing with. And doing it first avoids the risk that another fatal error will happen before your message is printed, thus masking the underlying problem.

Please do yourself and your users a favor by *always* including as much useful information in your error messages as possible. It sounds simple, but over and over again we see code like:

```
$dbh->commit() or die "commit failed!"; # DUMB!
```

Using `RaiseError` helps here because it generates a message (or Perl `$@` variable value) that includes the underlying error from the driver, and the driver and method names.[*]

So, if you catch an error using `eval`, remember to print the contents of `$@`. But don't stop at that. In most applications, there are variables that indicate what's being processed at the time. Including one or more of those, like `$country_code` in our example, adds valuable context to the error message.

As a general guide, every `die` or `warn` should have at least one variable interpolated into it, not counting `$!` or `$@`.

Consider protecting the rollback

So things have gone wrong, you've printed your error message, now it's time to `rollback()`. Pause for a moment. Remember that the database handle you're using has `RaiseError` set. That means that if the rollback itself fails then a new exception will be "thrown" and the script will immediately exit or jump into the arms of an enclosing `eval`.

Ask yourself if you're happy for a rollback error to trigger another exception. If not, then wrap it in an `eval` like this:

```
eval { $dbh->rollback };
```

---

[*] It also includes the filename and line number of the code where the error happened, but you can strip that off using a regular expression if you like.

Likely reasons for `rollback()` failing include database server shutdown or network communications failure, either of which may have been the cause of the error you're handling now. A rollback failure generally means that the database server is having a problem, and it's not worth trying to continue, so the default behavior is often what you want.

Exit status

Returning a reliable success/fail exit status from your scripts, even if you don't think you'll need it, is just good design. We recommend good design.

Death by misadventure

One of the important things to remember with transactions is that *any* calls made within an `eval` block can cause the program to die, and many of these calls may be totally unrelated to DBI. Therefore, by using an `eval` to trap *any* sort of problem whatsoever, you guarantee that you can cleanly roll back any incomplete transactions.

ODBC and the DBI

Open Database Connectivity, commonly known as *ODBC*, defines a database-independent API. The *ODBC Driver Manager* supports the API and manages one or more plug-in drivers for talking to different types of databases. The architecture is shown in Figure 7-1.

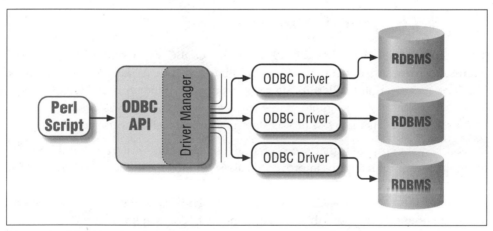

Figure 7-1. The ODBC architecture

Doesn't this all sound rather familiar? The ODBC driver manager and drivers are doing just what the DBI and its drivers are doing: defining and implementing a database-independent, application-programming interface.

This leads us to a whole bunch of questions: What's the difference? Why not just use ODBC and not the DBI? Can the DBI and ODBC work together? What advantages does one have over the other?

Before we try to answer those questions, let's get some perspective by looking into the history and goals of ODBC and the DBI, and take a look at the `Win32::ODBC` module, which implements a direct interface to ODBC for Perl.

ODBC—Embraced and Extended

In the early 1990s, a consortium of vendors formed the SQL Access Group to support SQL interoperability across disparate systems. In October 1992 and October 1993, a major part of that work was published as a draft standard entitled "Call Level Interface," or CLI, which is another name for an Application Programing Interface, or API. However, the SQL Access Group CLI standard never really took off. At least, not in that form.

Microsoft needed to implement a similar concept, to avoid having to release multiple versions of any product that needed to talk to multiple databases. They saw the SQL Access Group CLI standard and "embraced and extended" it, radically. The result was the Open Database Connectivity interface, which rapidly became a de facto standard. In fairness, Microsoft turned an incomplete paper standard into a fully featured practical reality.

DBI—Thrashed and Mutated

Meanwhile, since September 29, 1992, before ODBC even existed, a group of interested parties had been working on thrashing out a database-independent interface specification for Perl 4. After approximately eighteen months, DBperl (as it was then known) was quite stable, and implementation was about to start.[*] However, at this time, Larry Wall was starting to release alpha versions of Perl 5.

It soon became apparent that the object-oriented features of Perl 5 could be used to implement a dramatically improved database interface. So the work on the DBI took a new direction and, at the same time, started to be loosely modeled as a superset of the SQL Access Group CLI standard. Thus, at a high-level, the DBI has much in common with both that standard and ODBC as we know it today.

The Nuts and Bolts of ODBC

We'll now take a look at the main features of ODBC that set it apart from the DBI and that enable it to work well as a database-independent interface. The four main features are:

---

[*] Archaeologists can find the specification of this very old version at *http://www.perl.com/CPAN/modules/ dbperl/DBI/dbispec.v05*.

- A standard SQL syntax

- Standard error codes

- Rich metadata

- Many attributes and options

A Standard SQL Syntax

Standardized SQL syntax is something of a Holy Grail. ODBC drivers generally do a good job of implementing it, whereas the DBI just ducks the issue entirely! The problem is that while SQL may be a standardized language in theory, in practice it's far enough from the standard on most vendors' databases to cause portability problems.

For example, even a simple task like concatenating two database fields needs to be written like this (for databases conforming to the SQL-92 standard):

```
SELECT first_name || ' ' || last_name FROM table
```

Other databases require one of these forms:

```
SELECT first_name + ' ' + last_name FROM table
SELECT CONCAT(first_name, ' ', last_name) FROM table
SELECT CONCAT(CONCAT(first_name, ' ') last_name) FROM table
SELECT first_name CONCAT  ' ' CONCAT last_name FROM table
```

The SQL dialect used by different database systems is riddled with such inconsistencies, not to mention endless "extensions" to the standard. This is a major headache for developers wishing to write an application that will work with any of a number of databases.

The ODBC approach to this problem is rather elegant. It allows portability when using standard SQL, but doesn't prevent access to database-specific features. When an application passes an SQL statement to the driver, the driver parses it as an SQL-92 statement, and then rewrites it to match the actual syntax of the database being used.

If the parse fails because the SQL doesn't conform to the standard, then the original SQL is passed to the database unaltered. That way, database-specific features can be accessed, and the ODBC parsing doesn't get in the way.

The DBI ducked this whole issue because it would require drivers to be far more complicated than they are now. Parsing and rewriting SQL is not a trivial activity; therefore, the DBI does not try to offer SQL-level portability. In practice, that hasn't been a big problem for people. Perl makes it very easy for applications to build SQL statements as needed for the database being used, as we discussed in Chapter 5.

Standard Error Codes

If an INSERT statement fails, how can you tell whether it was because the table already has a record with the same primary key? With ODBC, you'd check the SQLSTATE error indicator to see if it was "23000", regardless of the database being used. With DBI, you're on your own.

ODBC defines a large number of standard error codes that you can use to determine in reasonable detail what went wrong. They're not often needed, but when they are, they're very useful. Having said that, this idyllic picture is tarnished by the fact that many of the codes change depending on the version of the ODBC driver being used. For example, while an ODBC 2.x driver returns "S0011" when a CREATE INDEX statement names an index that already exists, an ODBC 3.x driver returns "42S11". So much for standards!

The DBI leaves you with having to check for different $DBI::err values or $DBI::errstr strings, depending on the database driver being used. The DBI does provide a $DBI::state variable and $h->state() method that drivers can use to provide the standard error codes, but few do at the moment.

Rich Metadata

ODBC defines a wide range of metadata functions that provide information both about the structure of the data in the database and the datatypes supported by the database. The following table lists the functions and shows which are supported by the Win32::ODBC and DBI modules.

ODBC Function	Win32::ODBC	DBI
Tables	✓	✓
TablePrivileges		
Columns	✓	
ColumnPrivileges		
SpecialColumns	✓	
Statistics	✓	
PrimaryKeys	✓	
ForeignKeys	✓	
Procedures		
ProcedureColumns		
GetTypeInfo	✓	✓

As you can see, the DBI lags behind the Win32::ODBC module. By the time you read this book, the DBI may have defined interfaces for some of the functions, but how quickly the drivers actually implement the functions is harder to guess. The DBD::ODBC and DBD::Oracle modules will probably lead the way.

Many Attributes and Options

In trying to be a comprehensive interface to a very wide variety of real-world data sources, ODBC provides a way to tell the application about every minute detail of the driver and data source it's connected to. There are so many details available via the `GetInfo()` function—over 200 at the last count—that we're not going to waste paper listing any of them.

Though some books include the list as a great way of adding impressive bulk, we'll just direct you to the online version at Microsoft:

> *http://msdn.microsoft.com/library/sdkdoc/dasdk/odch_5fu7.htm*

If that URL ceases to work, then use the MSDN search facility at:

> *http://msdn.microsoft.com/us/dev/*

and search for `SQLGetInfo returns` using the exact phrase option. The link you want will probably just be called `SQLGetInfo`.*

ODBC also provides for a great many knobs and buttons that you can use to tailor the fine details of driver behavior to suit your application. These can be accessed via the following functions:

```
GetEnvAttr       SetEnvAttr        --  4 attributes
GetConnectAttr   SetConnectAttr    -- 16 attributes
GetStmtAttr      SetStmtAttr       -- 33 attributes
```

Prior to ODBC 3.x, there was an older set of functions with names that end in `Option` instead of `Attr`. These functions are almost identical to those above, but accept a smaller range of attributes. To find details of all these functions, you can use the Microsoft MSDN search procedure described earlier in this section.

The `Win32::ODBC` module provides access to the `GetInfo()`, `Get/SetConnect-Option()`, and `Get/SetStmtOption()` functions. The DBI defines only a very limited subset of this functionality via an assortment of DBI handle attributes.

ODBC from Perl

So we've established that the ODBC standard is a rather good thing, but how can you use it?

To use ODBC from Perl, there are only two practical options: the `Win32::ODBC` module and the DBI with the `DBD::ODBC` module. We'll describe `DBD::ODBC` first and then take a deeper look at `Win32::ODBC`.

---

* Microsoft ODBC functions all have an SQL prefix.

DBD::ODBC

The DBD::ODBC module was written by Tim Bunce and Jeff Urlwin, based on original code by Thomas K. Wenrich. It's a Perl extension written in C and is not tied
to Microsoft Win32 platforms. That makes it a good option for directly using
ODBC on Unix, VMS, and other non-Windows systems.

Being a DBI driver, the main goal of the DBD::ODBC module is to implement the
functionality required by the DBI, not simply to give access to ODBC from Perl.

The DBD::ODBC driver is described in more detail in Appendix B, *Driver and
Database Characteristics.*

Win32::ODBC

The Win32::ODBC module was written by Dave Roth, based on original code by
Dan DeMaggio. It's a Perl extension written in C++ and is closely associated with
the Win32 platform.

The main goal of the Win32::ODBC module is to provide direct access to the
ODBC functions. From that point of view, Win32::ODBC provides a fairly thin,
low-level interface.

Here's a sample of Win32::ODBC code:

```
use Win32::ODBC;

### Connect to a data source
$db = new Win32::ODBC("DSN=MyDataDSN;UID=me;PWD=secret")
    or die Win32::ODBC::Error();

### Prepare and Execute a statement
if ($db->Sql("SELECT item, price FROM table")) {
    print "SQL Error: " . $db->Error() . "\n";
    $db->Close();
    exit;
}

### Fetch row from data source
while ($db->FetchRow) {
    my ($item, $price) = $db->Data();   ### Get data values from the row
    print "Item $item = $price\n";
}

### Disconnect
$db->Close();
```

The most significant disadvantages of Win32::ODBC compared to DBD::ODBC are:

There is no separate statement handle
    The database connection handle is used to store the details of the current
    statement. There is no separate statement handle, so only one statement can

execute per database handle. But that's not as bad as it may seem, because it's possible to clone database handles so that more than one handle can share the same underlying ODBC database connection.

There are no separate prepare and execute steps

You cannot prepare a statement for execution later. The `Sql()` method, like the DBI `do()` method, combines both.

Placeholders and bind parameters are not supported

This is perhaps the most significant disadvantage of `Win32::ODBC`. All values must be passed as literal text values within the SQL statements.

The lack of support for placeholders, especially when coupled with the inability to prepare statements, means that nontrivial applications based on `Win32::ODBC` tend to place a greater burden on database servers and thus run more slowly.

It also causes problems when trying to insert binary data such as images.

Fetching rows is a two-step process

The `FetchRow()` method doesn't actually return any data to the script. To get the row of data values, you need to call either the `Data()` method to get a simple list (like `fetchrow_array()`), or the `DataHash()` method to get a hash (like `fetchrow_hashref()`).

This is more of a nuisance than a significant disadvantage. It's also another reason why `Win32::ODBC` is a little slower than using DBI.

There is no automatic error handling

In ODBC, there is no equivalent to the DBI's `RaiseError` and `PrintError` mechanism. You need to explicitly test the return status of all `Win32::ODBC` method calls if you want to write a robust application.

The lack of automatic error handling makes `Win32::ODBC` less suitable for nontrivial applications when application reliability is important. This is especially true where transactions are being used.

Win32::ODBC is slightly slower than DBD::ODBC

Even for simple queries, `Win32::ODBC` tends to be slightly slower than `DBD::ODBC` for the same platform and database. As always with benchmarks, your mileage may vary, so test it yourself if this is an issue for you.

There are plans to address some of these disadvantages in a later release. The most significant advantages of `Win32::ODBC` compared to `DBD::ODBC` are:

Most of the ODBC API is available to use

This is currently the biggest advantage that `Win32::ODBC` has over `DBD::ODBC`.

The remaining items in this list are really significant ODBC features rather than features of the `Win32::ODBC` module itself, but until `DBD::ODBC` supports them, they still count as advantages of `Win32::ODBC`.

Attributes, options, and metadata are available

These are described in the previous section. A wide range of metadata functions is available, along with functions for controlling many attributes and options.

Scrolling cursors are supported

Scrolling cursors let you read the rows of data returned by a query in any order. You can jump to the last row and read backwards. You can jump to any row either by absolute row number or relative to the current row. That's very handy for interactive browsing applications.

The Marriage of DBI and ODBC

The DBI has been strongly influenced by ODBC and the international standards that lie behind it (X/Open SQL CLI and ISO/IEC 9075-3:1995 SQL/CLI). The development of the `DBD::ODBC` module has given the DBI a more solid footing in the world of ODBC.

The DBI specification naturally evolves over time. The ODBC standard gives it a standards-based framework to build around. So, for example, if a method to return information about the datatypes supported by a database needs to be added, then following the proven standard function that makes much more sense than defining a new way. Thus, the DBI `type_info` method is modeled very closely on the `GetTypeInfo` ODBC function.

As the DBI and `DBD::ODBC` modules evolve, they'll naturally move closer together. As there are two excellent portable Open Source driver managers available,* the `DBD::ODBC` module should become as portable as DBI itself. At that point, it may well make sense to combine the two.

Questions and Choices

Hopefully by now we've answered all your questions about using ODBC from Perl, except one. If you need to choose between `Win32::ODBC` and `DBD::ODBC`, which do you choose?

It's actually a reasonably straightforward choice. If you need to use more of the ODBC API than is available through `DBD::ODBC`, then use `Win32::ODBC`. Otherwise the DBI plus `DBD::ODBC` combination is probably your best bet.

---

* It's available from the FreeODBC project at: *http://users.ids.net/~bjepson/FreeODBC/*.

Moving Between Win32::ODBC and the DBI

Let's say that you've already written an application that uses `Win32::ODBC`, but you now need to run it on a non-Windows machine, or just want to use the DBI for some other reason.

The best technical approach would be to rewrite the application, but the real world doesn't often give us that kind of luxury. A more practical solution would be to use some kind of emulation of `Win32::ODBC` that uses the DBI "under the hood". The `Win32::DBIODBC` module bundled with the DBI does just that.

The `Win32::DBIODBC` module implements enough of the `Win32::ODBC` API for many simple applications to be ported with only a one-line change. Instead of saying:

```
use Win32::ODBC;
```

you just say:

```
use Win32::DBIODBC;
```

In the rest of your code, you still refer to the `Win32::ODBC` module. There is also an easy way to test your applications without having to change them at all. Just load `Win32::DBIODBC` from the command line:

```
perl -MWin32::DBIODBC your_script_name
```

`Win32::DBIODBC` fools Perl into thinking that `Win32::ODBC` has been loaded, so the `use Win32::ODBC;` line in your script won't have any effect.

Once you're using the emulation, you have the option to start rewriting the application to use the DBI directly at your own pace.

And What About ADO?

ADO (ActiveX Data Objects) is Microsoft's latest flavor of proprietary Win32-only data access API. They say "ADO is Microsoft's strategic, high-level interface to all kinds of data."

If it helps, you can think of ADO as a layer of gloss over ODBC, though in fact it's built on Microsoft's OLE DB API. ADO provides access to ODBC databases and also to many new data sources not previously available via ODBC. It's object-oriented and designed to be easy to use, in theory.

You can use ADO from Perl via the Win32::OLE module. Here's an example:

```
use Win32::OLE;
$conn = Win32::OLE->new("ADODB.Connection");
$conn->Open("DSN=MyDSN;UID=MyUID;PWD=MyPwd");
```

```
$RS = $conn->Execute("SELECT isbn, title FROM books");
if (!$RS) {
    $Errors = $conn->Errors();
    die "Errors:\n", map { "$_->{Description}\n" } keys %$Errors;
}

while ( !$RS->EOF ) {
    my ($isbn, $title) = (
        $RS->Fields('isbn')->Value,
        $RS->Fields('title')->Value,
    );
    print "$isbn : $title\n";
    $RS->MoveNext();
}
$RS->Close();
$conn->Close();
```

To save you from having to learn yet another data access API, the DBI comes to
your rescue with DBD::ADO. The DBD::ADO driver lets you connect to any ADO
data source and fetch data from it using portable DBI Perl code. There's no need
to learn a new API, and you'll have a far easier life if you need to port applications to or from ADO.

DBI Shell and Database Proxying

This chapter takes a look at two essential additions to the Perl DBI armory: a command-line shell for databases, and the proxying drivers that provide network access to remote database drivers.

dbish—The DBI Shell

The DBI Shell, or dbish, is a command-line tool that allows you to run arbitrary SQL statements and diagnostics against databases without needing to write a complete Perl program.

For example, let's say we wanted to get a quick list of all the megaliths in Wiltshire. We could write a complete Perl program that connects to the database, prepares and executes the appropriate SQL statement, fetches the data back, formats it, and disconnects from the database.

With the DBI, this process is easy, but it's a bit tedious if you just want some quick information.

This is where the dbish comes into play. dbish allows you to connect to a data source and type an SQL statement straight into it. dbish handles all the underlying connecting, preparing, and executing, and also gives you the results right away.

Starting Up dbish

dbish is an executable program bundled with the DBI. You should be able to start it up by typing:

```
dbish
```

which will return a prompt in the following manner:

```
DBI::Shell 10.5 using DBI 1.14

WARNING: The DBI::Shell interface and functionality are
======= very likely to change in subsequent versions!

Available DBI drivers:
 1: dbi:ADO
 2: dbi:ExampleP
 3: dbi:Oracle
 4: dbi:Proxy
Enter driver name or number, or full 'dbi:...:...' DSN:
```

Some drivers require real username and password authentication to connect to databases. To support this requirement, you can supply additional arguments to **dbish** in the form of:

```
dbish <data_source> [username] [password]
```

For example:

```
dbish '' stones stones
```

or:

```
dbish dbi: stones stones
```

In this case, we haven't specified a driver, and so we'll choose one interactively through the menus. We can also bypass the menus by putting in the data source name for the desired database:

```
dbish dbi:Oracle:archaeo stones stones
```

If you don't specify a driver on the command line, the displayed menus allow you to select a type of database by listing the various drivers available. For example, if an Oracle database contained the megalithic database, you would select the **dbi: Oracle** data source by typing 3. This will result in that specific database driver being queried for available data sources. For example:

```
Enter data source to connect to:
 1: dbi:Oracle:archaeo
 2: dbi:Oracle:sales
Enter data source or number, or full 'dbi:...:...' DSN:
```

This example shows that the underlying Oracle database driver is aware of two locally configured Oracle databases. Our megalithic database is stored in the **archaeo** database, so type 1.

At this stage, **dbish** will attempt to connect to the database. Once you have connected successfully to a data source, you will see a prompt such as:

```
stones@dbi:Oracle:archaeo>
```

telling you that you are connected to the data source `dbi:Oracle:archaeo` as the user `stones`, and that `dbish` is ready for you to issue commands to it.

You can make a connection to another database from within `dbish` by using the `/connect` command. For example:

```
stones@dbi:Oracle:archaeo> /connect dbi:Oracle:sales dbusername
Disconnecting from dbi:Oracle:archaeo.
Connecting to 'dbi:Oracle:sales' as 'dbusername'...
Password for 'dbusername' (not echoed to screen): ......
stones@dbi:Oracle:sales>
```

Unfortunately, connecting to multiple databases simultaneously is not yet supported by `dbish`.

Handling Statements

In general, the most common reason for using `dbish` is to issue ad-hoc SQL statements to a database, either to check that the statement works before including it in a Perl program, or just to get some quick answers. This task is exactly what `dbish` was designed for.

`dbish` commands are entered as a forward slash (/) followed by a command name and optionally some extra arguments. For example:

```
/help
```

Anything entered that doesn't start with a forward slash is considered to be part of an SQL statement and is appended to a "statement buffer." Once the SQL statement is complete, you can execute it, and the results, if any, will be returned to your screen.

For example, to query the names of all sites in the megalithic database, type:

```
stones@dbi:Oracle:archaeo> SELECT name FROM megaliths
Current statement buffer (enter '/' to execute or '/help' for help):
SELECT name FROM megaliths

stones@dbi:Oracle:archaeo> /
'Avebury'
'Stonehenge'
'Lundin Links'
...
[132 rows of 1 fields returned]
stones@dbi:Oracle:archaeo>
```

Note that a forward slash by itself can be used to execute statements. After executing a statement, the statement buffer is cleared. But suppose we start typing in a new query and then change our minds about what we want to return:

```
stones@dbi:Oracle:archaeo> SELECT name FROM megaliths
Current statement buffer (enter '/' to execute or '/help' for help):
SELECT name FROM megaliths
```

```
stones@dbi:Oracle:archaeo> SELECT name, mapref FROM megaliths
Current statement buffer (enter '/' to execute or '/help' for help):
SELECT name FROM megaliths
SELECT name, mapref FROM megaliths

stones@dbi:Oracle:archaeo>
```

This is totally wrong! Fortunately, you can clear the statement buffer of old statements and start new ones afresh with the /clear command. Statements that have been executed are automatically cleared from the statement buffer, but can be recalled with the /history command. You can even use the /edit command to start up an external editor for editing your SQL.

The way in which results of **SELECT** statements are displayed is also configurable using the /format command. The two options currently available are /format neat and /format box. The default option is neat, which uses the DBI::neat_ list() function to format the data. For example, the statement:

```
stones@dbi:Oracle:archaeo> SELECT name, mapref FROM megaliths /
```

has the following output:

```
'Avebury', 'SU 102 699'
'Stonehenge' 'SU 123 422',
'Lundin Links', 'NO 404 027'
...
[132 rows of 1 fields returned]
```

The **box** option is prettier:

```
+--------------+------------+
| name         | mapref     |
+--------------+------------+
| Avebury      | SU 102 699 |
+--------------+------------+
| Stonehenge   | SU 123 422 |
+--------------+------------+
| Lundin Links | NO 404 027 |
+--------------+------------+
```

It's also possible to issue non-**SELECT** statements from **dbish** with the / command. Want to delete all the rows from a table? Simply type:

```
stones@dbi:Oracle:archaeo> delete from megaliths /
[132 rows affected]
stones@dbi:Oracle:archaeo>
```

Quick, easy, and very deadly! Any non-**SELECT** statement can be issued in this way, including **CREATE TABLE** statements or even stored procedure calls, if your database supports them.*

---

* There's a /do command that forces the do() method to be used instead of a prepare() followed by an execute(). In practice, it's rarely needed.

Some Miscellaneous dbish Commands

As dbish is a fairly fully featured command-line shell,* it has some convenient commands defined within it that allow you to commit and roll back database changes, recall statements and commands that you'd executed in the past, and even execute arbitrary Perl statements!

One of the most useful of the miscellaneous statements is /table_info, which lists the tables in the database that you are currently connected to. This statement is indispensable when you're trying to remember exactly what that pesky table name is!

A full list of these commands can be seen by typing the all-important /help command.

dbish is currently a handy tool for performing quick tasks on a database. It should continue to evolve over time into an indispensable part of the database administrator's and database developer's armory, much like proprietary tools such as Oracle's SQL*Plus utility.

Database Proxying

Database proxying is the ability to forward database queries to a database, using an intermediate piece of software, the proxy, and return the results from those queries without the client program having any database drivers installed.

For example, a common use for a database proxy is for a client program located on a Unix machine to query a Microsoft Access database located on a Windows machine. Suppose the Unix machine has no ODBC software or drivers installed and thus doesn't know anything about ODBC. This means that it needs to forward any queries to a proxy server that does know about ODBC and the Access database. The proxy server then issues the query and gathers the results, which it then passes back to the client program for processing.

This functionality is extremely powerful, as it allows us to access databases on virtually any operating system from any other operating system, provided that they are both running Perl and the DBI. There is an additional benefit in terms of software distribution: if client PCs used Perl scripts to access an Oracle database located on a central Unix server, you don't have to undergo a potentially complex Oracle client software installation. DBI proxy capabilities make this client software unnecessary.

---

* dbish's powerful command-line editing functionality comes courtesy of the Term::Readline and Term::Readline::Gnu modules. You don't need to install them to use dbish, but it helps.

Furthermore, you can automatically add "network awareness" to types of databases that could never otherwise support such a thing. For example, with the DBI proxy capabilities, you could run a Perl script on a Windows machine that queries data from a CSV file over the network.

Finally, the DBI proxy architecture allows for on-the-fly compression of query and result data, and also encryption of that data. These two facilities make DBI a powerful tool for pulling large results sets of data over slow network links such as a modem. It also makes DBI a secure tool for querying sensitive data. We shall discuss these two topics in greater detail in a later section.

The Database Proxy Architecture

The DBI supports database proxying through two modules, `DBD::Proxy` and `DBI::ProxyServer`. `DBD::Proxy` is used by client programs to talk to a proxy server that is implemented with the `DBI::ProxyServer` module. Figure 8-1 illustrates the architecture.

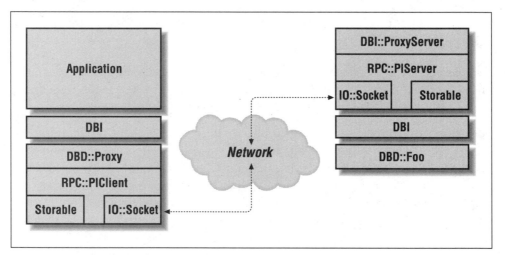

Figure 8-1. DBI proxy architecture

Because the `DBI::ProxyServer` module uses the underlying database drivers to actually interface with the databases, any type of database can be queried and manipulated via proxy, including CSV files and XBase (DBF) files. The DBI proxy architecture does not restrict you to using high-end databases such as Oracle or Informix.

So how do we use this proxy server? Let's look at the common example of a Perl program running on a Unix box that wants to query a Microsoft Access database running on a Windows machine.

Setting up a proxy server

The DBI proxy server is simply a layer on top of the DBI; it can only be a server for the data sources that the underlying DBI is able to connect to. So, before we get involved in setting up the proxy server to accept proxy client connections, we must install any database drivers that its clients may need. For our example of connecting to an Access database, we'll need to install the `DBD::ODBC` module.[*]

You will also need to configure your ODBC data source within the Windows ODBC Control Panel. For our megalithic database, let's call the ODBC data source `archaeo`.

We can test that this data source is correctly configured using the DBI Shell `dbish` locally on the Windows machine:

```
dbish dbi:ODBC:archaeo
```

or via a short script that can be run on your Windows machine:

```
use DBI;
$dbh = DBI->connect( "dbi:ODBC:archaeo", "username", "password" );
$dbh->disconnect();
```

If `dbish` connects, or if no errors occur when executing the script, it looks like everything's installed and configured correctly.

The easiest way to set up a DBI proxy server is to use the script called `dbiproxy`, which is distributed with the core DBI module. The `DBI::ProxyServer` module, used by `dbiproxy`, has a few prerequisite modules that must be installed in order for it to work: `PlRPC` and `Net::Daemon`. These can be downloaded and installed from CPAN using:

```
perl -MCPAN -e 'install Bundle::DBI'
```

Or, if you are running the ActiveState Perl for Windows, you can install these modules separately via PPM (since PPM currently does not currently support bundles).

The crucial information required by `dbiproxy` is the port number to which the proxy server should listen for incoming proxy client connections. If the port number is `3333`, we can run the proxy server with the following command:

```
dbiproxy --localport 3333
```

This will start up the server; it's now waiting for connections. If you want to verify that the server is indeed up and running, you can run it with the `--debug` flag and the optional `--logfile` flag to specify where the debug output will go.

---

[*] If you have a compiler, you can get the source from CPAN and build it yourself, or, on Windows, just fetch and install a pre-built version using the PPM tool supplied with ActiveState Perl.

For example:

```
dbiproxy --localport 3333 --debug
```

will produce debug output either in the command prompt window on a Windows machine, and or via **syslog(1)** on a Unix machine. On Unix workstations, you can redirect the output to the current terminal with:

```
dbiproxy --localport 3333 --debug --logfile /dev/tty
```

This should behave correctly under most modern Unix platforms.

Connecting to the proxy server

Now that we have configured our proxy server to sit and wait on port 3333 on our Windows machine, we need to tell the client Perl program on the Unix machine to use that proxy server instead of attempting to make a direct database connection itself.

For example, the ODBC test script above connects directly via the **DBD::ODBC** module with the following **DBI->connect()** call:

```
$dbh = DBI->connect( "dbi:ODBC:archaeo", "username", "password" );
```

This is fine for local connections, but how do we translate that into something the proxy server can use?

DBD::Proxy makes liberal use of the optional arguments that can be added to a DSN when specifying which database to connect to. **DBD::Proxy** allows you to specify the hostname of the machine upon which the proxy server is running, the port number that the proxy server is listening to, and the data source of the database that you wish the proxy server to connect to.

Therefore, to connect to the ODBC database called **archaeo** on the Windows machine **fowliswester** with a proxy server running on port 3333, you should use the following **DBI->connect()** syntax:

```
$dsn   = "dbi:ODBC:archaeo";
$proxy = "hostname=fowliswester;port=3333";
$dbh = DBI->connect( "dbi:Proxy:$proxy;dsn=$dsn", '', '' );
```

This looks quite long-winded, but it's a very compact and portable way to make a pass-through connection to a remote database by proxy.

Once you have connected to the proxy server and it connects to the desired data source, a valid database handle will be returned, allowing you to issue queries exactly as if you had connected directly to that database. Therefore, when using a proxy server, only the **DBI->connect()** call will vary—which is exactly the same behavior as changing from one database to another.

Having said that, it's even possible to use the proxy without editing your programs at all. You just need to set the DBI_AUTOPROXY environment variable and the DBI will do the rest. For the example above, you can leave the connect() statement referring to dbi:ODBC:archaeo and just set the DBI_AUTOPROXY environment variable to:

```
dbi:Proxy:hostname=fowliswester;port=3333
```

The value contained within the DBI_AUTOPROXY value has the DSN specified in the DBI->connect() call concatenated to it to produce the correct proxy DSN. For example:

```
$ENV{DBI_AUTOPROXY} = 'dbi:Proxy:hostname=fowliswester;port=3333';
$dbh = DBI->connect( "dbi:ODBC:archaeo", "username", "password" );
```

would result in the script attempting a connection to the DSN of:

```
dbi:Proxy:hostname=fowliswester;port=3333;dsn=dbi:ODBC:archaeo
```

The other important point to stress regarding the client is that you do not need to install any database drivers whatsoever. The database drivers are used only by the proxy server.

Advanced Topics

The DBI proxy architecture is implemented on top of a couple of lower-level Perl networking modules such as PlRPC and, in the case of DBI::ProxyServer, Net::Daemon. As such, these modules have a lot of features that are inherited into the DBI proxy architecture, such as powerful access-list configuration and on-the-fly compression and ciphering.

We shall look at each of these topics in more detail and explain how they can be used effectively in your software.

Access configuration

The Net::Daemon, RPC::PlServer, and DBI::ProxyServer modules share a common configuration filesystem because of the ways that RPC::PlServer inherits from Net::Daemon and DBI::ProxyServer inherits from RPC::PlServer.*

The configuration files for these modules are expressed as Perl scripts in which various options are set. The most useful options are those that allow you to specify access lists. Access lists allow you to control which machines may connect to the proxy server, and the mode that the network transport between these machines and the proxy server operates in.

---

* All these modules, including DBD::Proxy were designed and implemented by a single author, Jochen Wiedmann. Thank you, Jochen.

For example, if you had a secure corporate LAN containing a database server and client PCs, you might say that the client PCs could connect to the central database via a proxy server without any authentication or encryption. That is, a PC connected to the LAN is *trusted*.

However, computers in employees' houses that need access to the database are not trusted, as the data flowing across the phone line might be somehow intercepted by competitors. Therefore, the network transport between these machines and the central database server is encrypted.

A sample configuration file for the proxy server might look like:

```
{
    facility => 'daemon',
    pidfile  => '/var/dbiproxy/dbiproxy.pid',
    user  => 'nobody',
    group => 'nobody',
    localport => '3333',
    mode      => 'fork',

    # Access control
    clients => [
        # Accept the local LAN ( 192.168.1.* )
        {
            mask   => '^192\.168\.1\.\d+$',
            accept => 1
        },
        # Accept our off-site machines ( 192.168.2.* ) but with a cipher
        {
            mask   => '^192\.168\.2\.\d+$',
            accept => 1,
            # We'll discuss secure encryption ciphers shortly
            cipher => Crypt::IDEA->new( 'be39893df23f98a2' )
        },
        # Deny everything else
        {
            mask   => '.*',
            accept => 0
        }
    ]
}
```

The **dbiproxy** script can be started with this custom configuration file in the following way:

```
dbiproxy --configfile <filename>
```

For example, if we had saved the above configuration file as **proxy.config**, we could start up **dbiproxy** with the command:

```
dbiproxy  -configfile proxy.config
```

Furthermore, the `DBI::ProxyServer` configuration file also allows us to apply access lists to individual types of statements. For example, you might want the workstations of sales operators to be able to query data, but not change it in any way. This can be done using the following configuration options:

```
# Only allow the given SELECT queries from sales
# workstations ( 192.168.3.* )
clients => [
    {
        mask    => '^192\.168\.3\.\d+$',
        accept => 1,
        sql     => {
            select => 'SELECT name, mapref FROM megaliths WHERE name = ?'
        }
    },
]
```

The other statement restriction keys that you can use are `insert`, `update`, and `delete`. For example, if you wished to allow only particular `DELETE` statements to be executed, you could write the following access control:

```
sql => {
    delete => 'DELETE FROM megaliths WHERE id = ?'
}
```

This control would refuse any `DELETE` statements that did not conform to the given control mask, such as someone maliciously executing `DELETE FROM megaliths`.

Therefore, the access control functionality inherent in `DBI::ProxyServer` and its parent modules can be used to build complex (yet flexible) networked database systems quickly and easily.

Compression

In the previous example, we discussed the possibility of a user querying the database via a modem link and proxy server. Suppose the user executes a query that returns 100,000 rows of data, each row being around 1 KB. That's a lot of information to pull across a slow network connection.

To speed things up, you could configure the proxy server to use on-the-fly compression (via the `Compress::Zlib` module) to clients querying the database over dial-up connection. This will radically reduce the quantity of data being transferred across the modem link. You can do this by running the `dbiproxy` script with the additional arguments of:

```
--compression gzip
```

which specifies that the GNU `gzip` compression method should be used.

In order for your client to be able to send and receive compressed data from the DBI proxy server, you also must tell the proxy driver to use a compressed data stream. This is done by specifying the additional DSN key/value pair of `compression=gzip` when connecting to the database. For example:

```
$proxyloc = 'hostname=fowliswester;port=3333';
$compression = 'compression=gzip';
$dsn = 'dbi:ODBC:archaeo';
$dbh = DBI->connect( "dbi:Proxy:$proxyloc;$compression;dsn=$dsn",
                     "username", "password" );
```

The trade-off is the cost in CPU time for the proxy server and proxy client to compress and decompress the data, respectively. From a client perspective, this is probably not an issue, but the proxy server might be affected, especially if several large queries are being executed simultaneously, with each requiring compression.

However, compression is a useful and transparent feature that can increase the efficiency of your networks and databases when using DBI proxying.

Ciphers

The final configuration topic that we will cover for the DBI proxy architecture is that of on-the-fly encryption of data.

This functionality is useful if you are implementing a secure networked database environment where database operations might be occurring over nonsecure network links, such as a phone line through a public ISP. For example, an employee at home might use his or her own ISP to access a secure company database. Or you might wish to make an e-commerce transaction between two participating financial institutions.

Both of these examples are prime candidates for using the cipher mechanism in `DBI::ProxyServer`. Ciphering is implemented within the `RPC::PlClient` and `RPC::PlServer` modules. This allows `DBD::Proxy` and `DBI::ProxyServer` to use those mechanisms by means of inheritance. The actual ciphering mechanism uses external modules such as `Crypt::IDEA` or `Crypt::DES` for key generation and comparison.*

The very basic premise of an encrypted data stream is that the client and server generate *keys*, which are then sent to each other. When the client wishes to transmit data to the server, it encrypts the data with the server's key. Similarly, if the server wishes to send data to the client, it uses the client's key to encrypt it first. This system allows the client and server to decode the incoming data safely. Since the data is encrypted before transmission and decoded after receipt, anyone snooping on the network will see only encrypted data.

---

* The technical differences and ins and outs of these algorithms are way beyond the scope of this book. You should consult the documentation for these modules for pointers to texts discussing the various cryptographic algorithms.

Therefore, to support encryption via DBI proxying, we need to configure both the client connecting to the proxy server to use encryption and also configure the server to use the same encryption.

The configuration of the client is trivial and is simply a case of specifying additional arguments to the DBI->connect() call. For example, to use Crypt::IDEA as the underlying ciphering method, we can write:

```
use Crypt::IDEA;

### The key is a random, but long, hexadecimal number!
$key = 'b3a6d83ef3187ac4';

### Connect to the proxy server
$dbh = DBI->connect( "dbi:Proxy:cipher=IDEA;key=$key;...", '', '' );
```

The actual key creation occurs by instantiating a new object of the given cipher type (in this case Crypt::IDEA) with the given key value. This cipher object is then passed to the proxy server. We could have used the Crypt::DES module to provide the underlying encryption services by simply changing cipher=IDEA to cipher=DES.* This demonstrates the configurability of the DBI proxy encryption mechanisms.

For example, if we were transmitting sensitive but not confidential data from our internal database to someone's home PC, we might wish to use the relatively low-grade encryption offered by Crypt::DES. However, if more confidential data was being transmitted, we might wish to switch over to using the stronger but slower encryption of Crypt::IDEA.

Configuring the proxy server is equally straightforward and is achieved by specifying the encryption rules within the proxy server configuration file. For example, a simple proxy server configuration that encrypts all traffic with Crypt::IDEA can be written as:

```
require Crypt::IDEA;

### The key to encrypt data with
$key = 'b3a6d83ef3187ac4';

{
    clients => [ {
        'accept' => 1,
        'cipher' => IDEA->new( pack( "H*", $key ) )
      } ]
}
```

---

* We would also need to change the use Crypt::IDEA; line accordingly.

The important aspect of this configuration file is that the key being used to create the `Crypt::IDEA` object matches that used by the client programs connecting to this proxy server. If the keys do not match, no connection will be made, as the client and server will not be able to decode data flowing over the network connection.

DBI Specification

This appendix is a slightly edited version of the DBI specification, a "living document" that evolves at a slow but steady pace as new versions of the DBI are released. This document is based on the DBI specification for DBI version 1.14.

Although we know that it will be slightly out of date by the time you read it, we have included this specification in the book because it is important reference material, and we believe the book would be incomplete without it. For up-to-date information, consult the online documentation for the version of the DBI you have installed. You can usually access the online documentation with the `perldoc DBI` command. The *Changes* file supplied with the DBI distribution contains detailed change information.

Note that whenever the DBI changes, the drivers take some time to catch up. Recent versions of the DBI have added new features (marked *NEW* in the text) that may not yet be supported by the drivers you use. Talk to the authors of those drivers if you need support for new features.

Synopsis

```
use DBI;

@driver_names = DBI->available_drivers;
@data_sources = DBI->data_sources($driver_name);

$dbh = DBI->connect($data_source, $username, $auth, \%attr);

$rv  = $dbh->do($statement);
$rv  = $dbh->do($statement, \%attr);
$rv  = $dbh->do($statement, \%attr, @bind_values);

$ary_ref = $dbh->selectall_arrayref($statement);
```

```
@row_ary = $dbh->selectrow_array($statement);
$ary_ref = $dbh->selectcol_arrayref($statement);

$sth = $dbh->prepare($statement);
$sth = $dbh->prepare_cached($statement);

$rv = $sth->bind_param($p_num, $bind_value);
$rv = $sth->bind_param($p_num, $bind_value, $bind_type);
$rv = $sth->bind_param($p_num, $bind_value, \%attr);

$rv = $sth->execute;
$rv = $sth->execute(@bind_values);

$rc = $sth->bind_col($col_num, \$col_variable);
$rc = $sth->bind_columns(@list_of_refs_to_vars_to_bind);

@row_ary  = $sth->fetchrow_array;
$ary_ref  = $sth->fetchrow_arrayref;
$hash_ref = $sth->fetchrow_hashref;

$ary_ref  = $sth->fetchall_arrayref;

$rv  = $sth->rows;

$rc  = $dbh->commit;
$rc  = $dbh->rollback;

$sql = $dbh->quote($string);

$rc  = $h->err;
$str = $h->errstr;
$rv  = $h->state;

$rc  = $dbh->disconnect;
```

Getting Help

If you have questions about DBI, you can get help from the *dbi-users@isc.org* mailing list. You can subscribe to the list by visiting:

> *http://www.isc.org/dbi-lists.html*

Also worth a visit is the DBI home page at:

> *http://www.symbolstone.org/technology/perl/DBI*

Before asking any questions, reread this document, consult the archives, and read the DBI FAQ. The archives are listed at the end of this document. The FAQ is installed as a `DBI::FAQ` module, so you can read it by executing `perldoc` `DBI::FAQ`.

Please note that Tim Bunce does not maintain the mailing lists or the web page (generous volunteers do that). So please don't send mail directly to him; he just doesn't have the time to answer questions personally. The *dbi-users* mailing list has lots of experienced people who should be able to help you if you need it.

Description

The DBI is a database access module for the Perl programming language. It defines a set of methods, variables, and conventions that provide a consistent database interface, independent of the actual database being used.

It is important to remember that the DBI is just an interface. The DBI is a layer of "glue" between an application and one or more database *driver* modules. It is the driver modules that do most of the real work. The DBI provides a standard interface and framework for the drivers to operate within.

Architecture of a DBI Application

The API, or Application Programming Interface, defines the call interface and variables to Perl scripts to use. The API is implemented by the Perl DBI extension (see Figure A-1).

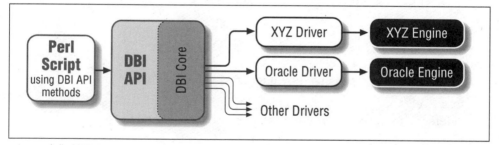

Figure A-1 DBI application architecture

The DBI "dispatches" the method calls to the appropriate driver for actual execution. The DBI is also responsible for the dynamic loading of drivers, error checking and handling, providing default implementations for methods, and many other non-database–specific duties.

Each driver contains implementations of the DBI methods using the private interface functions of the corresponding database engine. Only authors of sophisticated/multi-database applications or generic library functions need to be concerned with drivers.

Notation and Conventions

The following conventions are used in this document:

`$dbh`
> Database handle object

`$sth`
> Statement handle object

`$drh`
> Driver handle object (rarely seen or used in applications)

`$h`
> Any of the handle types above (`$dbh`, `$sth`, or `$drh`)

`$rc`
> General return code (boolean: `true`=ok, `false`=error)

`$rv`
> General Return Value (typically an integer)

`@ary`
> List of values returned from the database, typically a row of data

`$rows`
> Number of rows processed (if available, else –1)

`$fh`
> A filehandle

`undef`
> NULL values are represented by undefined values in Perl

`\%attr`
> Reference to a hash of attribute values passed to methods

Note that Perl will automatically destroy database and statement handle objects if all references to them are deleted.

Outline Usage

To use DBI, first you need to load the DBI module:

```
use DBI;
use strict;
```

(The `use strict;` isn't required but is strongly recommended.)

Then you need to *connect* to your data source and get a *handle* for the connection:

```
$dbh = DBI->connect($dsn, $user, $password,
                    { RaiseError => 1, AutoCommit => 0 });
```

Since connecting can be expensive, you generally just connect at the start of your program and disconnect at the end.

Explicitly defining the required `AutoCommit` behavior is strongly recommended and may become mandatory in a later version. This determines if changes are automatically committed to the database when executed, or if they need to be explicitly committed later.

The DBI allows an application to "prepare" statements for later execution. A prepared statement is identified by a statement handle held in a Perl variable. We'll call the Perl variable `$sth` in our examples.

The typical method call sequence for a **SELECT** statement is:

```
prepare,
   execute, fetch, fetch, ...
   execute, fetch, fetch, ...
   execute, fetch, fetch, ...
```

For example:

```
$sth = $dbh->prepare("SELECT foo, bar FROM table WHERE baz=?");

$sth->execute( $baz );

while ( @row = $sth->fetchrow_array ) {
  print "@row\n";
}
```

The typical method call sequence for a *non*-**SELECT** statement is:

```
prepare,
  execute,
  execute,
  execute.
```

For example:

```
$sth = $dbh->prepare("INSERT INTO table(foo,bar,baz) VALUES (?,?,?)");

while(<CSV>) {
  chop;
  my ($foo,$bar,$baz) = split /,/;
      $sth->execute( $foo, $bar, $baz );
}
```

The `do()` method can be used for non-repeated, *non*-**SELECT** statements (or with drivers that don't support placeholders):

```
$rows_affected = $dbh->do("UPDATE your_table SET foo = foo + 1");
```

To commit your changes to the database (when `AutoCommit` is off):

```
$dbh->commit;  # or call $dbh->rollback; to undo changes
```

Finally, when you have finished working with the data source, you should disconnect from it:

```
$dbh->disconnect;
```

General Interface Rules and Caveats

The DBI does not have a concept of a "current session." Every session has a handle object (i.e., a $dbh) returned from the **connect** method. That handle object is used to invoke database-related methods.

Most data is returned to the Perl script as strings. (Null values are returned as **undef**.) This allows arbitrary precision numeric data to be handled without loss of accuracy. Beware that Perl may not preserve the same accuracy when the string is used as a number.

Dates and times are returned as character strings in the native format of the corresponding database engine. Time zone effects are database/driver-dependent.

Perl supports binary data in Perl strings, and the DBI will pass binary data to and from the driver without change. It is up to the driver implementors to decide how they wish to handle such binary data.

Most databases that understand multiple character sets have a default global charset. Text stored in the database is, or should be, stored in that charset; if not, then that's the fault of either the database or the application that inserted the data. When text is fetched, it should be automatically converted to the charset of the client, presumably based on the locale. If a driver needs to set a flag to get that behavior, then it should do so; it should not require the application to do that.

Multiple SQL statements may not be combined in a single statement handle ($sth), although some databases and drivers do support this feature (notably Sybase and SQL Server).

Non-sequential record reads are not supported in this version of the DBI. In other words, records can be fetched only in the order that the database returned them, and once fetched they are forgotten.

Positioned updates and deletes are not directly supported by the DBI. See the description of the **CursorName** attribute for an alternative.

Individual driver implementors are free to provide any private functions and/or handle attributes that they feel are useful. Private driver functions can be invoked using the DBI **func()** method. Private driver attributes are accessed just like standard attributes.

Many methods have an optional **\%attr** parameter which can be used to pass information to the driver implementing the method. Except where specifically documented, the \%attr parameter can be used only to pass driver-specific hints. In general, you can ignore \%attr parameters or pass it as undef.

Naming Conventions and Name Space

The DBI package and all packages below it (DBI::*) are reserved for use by the DBI. Extensions and related modules use the DBIx:: namespace (see *http://www. perl.com/CPAN/modules/by-module/DBIx/*). Package names beginning with DBD:: are reserved for use by DBI database drivers. All environment variables used by the DBI or by individual DBDs begin with DBI_ or DBD_.

The letter case used for attribute names is significant and plays an important part in the portability of DBI scripts. The case of the attribute name is used to signify who defined the meaning of that name and its values, as the following table shows.

Case of Name	Has a Meaning Defined By
UPPER_CASE	Standards, e.g., X/Open, ISO SQL92, etc. (portable)
MixedCase	DBI API (portable), underscores are not used
lower_case	Driver or database engine specific (non-portable)

It is of the utmost importance that driver developers use only lowercase attribute names when defining private attributes. Private attribute names must be prefixed with the driver name or suitable abbreviation (e.g., ora_ for Oracle, ing_ for Ingres, etc.).

Here's a sample of the Driver Specific Prefix Registry:

```
ado_      DBD::ADO
best_     DBD::BestWins
csv_      DBD::CSV
db2_      DBD::DB2
f_        DBD::File
file_     DBD::TextFile
ib_       DBD::InterBase
ing_      DBD::Ingres
ix_       DBD::Informix
msql_     DBD::mSQL
mysql_    DBD::mysql
odbc_     DBD::ODBC
ora_      DBD::Oracle
proxy_    DBD::Proxy
solid_    DBD::Solid
syb_      DBD::Sybase
tuber_    DBD::Tuber
xbase_    DBD::XBase
```

SQL—A Query Language

Most DBI drivers require applications to use a dialect of SQL (Structured Query Language) to interact with the database engine. The following URLs provide useful information and further links about SQL:

http://www.altavista.com/query?q=sql+tutorial
http://www.jcc.com/sql_stnd.html
http://www.contrib.andrew.cmu.edu/~shadow/sql.html

The DBI itself does not mandate or require any particular language to be used; it is language-independent. In ODBC terms, the DBI is in "pass-thru" mode, although individual drivers might not be. The only requirement is that queries and other statements must be expressed as a single string of characters passed as the first argument to the **prepare** or **do** methods.

For an interesting diversion on the *real* history of RDBMS and SQL, from the people who made it happen, see:

http://ftp.digital.com/pub/DEC/SRC/technical-notes/SRC-1997-018-html/sqlr95.html

Follow the "And the rest" and "Intergalactic dataspeak" links for the SQL history.

Placeholders and Bind Values

Some drivers support placeholders and bind values. *Placeholders*, also called parameter markers, are used to indicate values in a database statement that will be supplied later, before the prepared statement is executed. For example, an application might use the following to insert a row of data into the **sales** table:

```
INSERT INTO sales (product_code, qty, price) VALUES (?, ?, ?)
```

or the following, to select the description for a product:

```
SELECT description FROM products WHERE product_code = ?
```

The ? characters are the placeholders. The association of actual values with placeholders is known as *binding*, and the values are referred to as *bind values*.

When using placeholders with the SQL **LIKE** qualifier, you must remember that the placeholder substitutes for the whole string. So you should use "... **LIKE** ? ..." and include any wildcard characters in the value that you bind to the placeholder.

Null values

Undefined values, or **undef**, can be used to indicate null values. However, care must be taken in the particular case of trying to use null values to qualify a **SELECT** statement.

For example:

```
SELECT description FROM products WHERE product_code = ?
```

Binding an **undef** (NULL) to the placeholder will *not* select rows that have a NULL **product_code**. (Refer to the SQL manual for your database engine or any SQL book for the reasons for this.) To explicitly select NULLs, you have to say "**WHERE product_code IS NULL**" and to make that general, you have to say:

```
... WHERE (product_code = ? OR (? IS NULL AND product_code IS NULL))
```

and bind the same value to both placeholders.

Performance

Without using placeholders, the insert statement shown previously would have to contain the literal values to be inserted and would have to be re-prepared and re-executed for each row. With placeholders, the insert statement needs to be prepared only once. The bind values for each row can be given to the **execute** method each time it's called. By avoiding the need to re-prepare the statement for each row, the application typically runs many times faster.

Here's an example:

```
my $sth = $dbh->prepare(q{
    INSERT INTO sales (product_code, qty, price) VALUES (?, ?, ?)
}) || die $dbh->errstr;
while (<>) {
    chop;
    my ($product_code, $qty, $price) = split /,/;
    $sth->execute($product_code, $qty, $price) || die $dbh->errstr;
}
$dbh->commit || die $dbh->errstr;
```

See **execute** and **bind_param** for more details.

The q{...} style quoting used in this example avoids clashing with quotes that may be used in the SQL statement. Use the double-quote like the qq{...} operator if you want to interpolate variables into the string. See the section on "Quote and Quote-Like Operators" in the *perlop* manpage for more details.

See also the **bind_column** method, which is used to associate Perl variables with the output columns of a SELECT statement.

The DBI Class

In this section, we cover the DBI class methods, utility functions, and the dynamic attributes associated with generic DBI handles.

DBI Class Methods

The following methods are provided by the DBI class:

connect

```
$dbh = DBI->connect($data_source, $username, $password)
        || die $DBI::errstr;
$dbh = DBI->connect($data_source, $username, $password, \%attr)
        || die $DBI::errstr;
```

connect establishes a database connection, or session, to the requested $data_source. Returns a database handle object if the connection succeeds. Use $dbh->disconnect to terminate the connection.

If the connect fails (see below), it returns undef and sets both $DBI::err and $DBI::errstr. (It does *not* set $!, etc.) You should generally test the return status of connect and print $DBI::errstr if it has failed.

Multiple simultaneous connections to multiple databases through multiple drivers can be made via the DBI. Simply make one connect call for each database and keep a copy of each returned database handle.

The $data_source value should begin with dbi:*driver_name*:. The *driver_name* specifies the driver that will be used to make the connection. (Letter case is significant.)

As a convenience, if the $data_source parameter is undefined or empty, the DBI will substitute the value of the environment variable DBI_DSN. If just the *driver_name* part is empty (i.e., the $data_source prefix is dbi::), the environment variable DBI_DRIVER is used. If neither variable is set, then connect dies.

Examples of $data_source values are:

```
dbi:DriverName:database_name
dbi:DriverName:database_name@hostname:port
dbi:DriverName:database=database_name;host=hostname;port=port
```

There is *no standard* for the text following the driver name. Each driver is free to use whatever syntax it wants. The only requirement the DBI makes is that all the information is supplied in a single string. You must consult the documentation for the drivers you are using for a description of the syntax they require. (Where a driver author needs to define a syntax for the $data_source, it is recommended that he or she follow the ODBC style, shown in the last example above.)

If the environment variable DBI_AUTOPROXY is defined (and the driver in $data_source is not Proxy) then the connect request will automatically be changed to:

```
dbi:Proxy:$ENV{DBI_AUTOPROXY};dsn=$data_source
```

and passed to the DBD::Proxy module. DBI_AUTOPROXY is typically set as "hostname=...;port=...". See the DBD::Proxy documentation for more details.

If $username or $password are undefined (rather than just empty), then the DBI will substitute the values of the DBI_USER and DBI_PASS environment variables, respectively. The DBI will warn if the environment variables are not defined. However, the everyday use of these environment variables is not recommended for security reasons. The mechanism is primarily intended to simplify testing.

DBI->connect automatically installs the driver if it has not been installed yet. Driver installation either returns a valid driver handle, or it *dies* with an error message that includes the string install_driver and the underlying problem. So DBI->connect will die on a driver installation failure and will only return undef on a connect failure, in which case $DBI::errstr will hold the error message.

The $data_source argument (with the "dbi:...:" prefix removed) and the $username and $password arguments are then passed to the driver for processing. The DBI does not define any interpretation for the contents of these fields. The driver is free to interpret the $data_source, $username, and $password fields in any way, and supply whatever defaults are appropriate for the engine being accessed. (Oracle, for example, uses the ORACLE_SID and TWO_TASK environment variables if no $data_source is specified.)

The AutoCommit and PrintError attributes for each connection default to "on." (See AutoCommit and PrintError for more information.) However, it is strongly recommended that you explicitly define AutoCommit rather than rely on the default. Future versions of the DBI may issue a warning if AutoCommit is not explicitly defined.

The \%attr parameter can be used to alter the default settings of PrintError, RaiseError, AutoCommit, and other attributes. For example:

```
$dbh = DBI->connect($data_source, $user, $pass, {
    PrintError => 0,
    AutoCommit => 0
});
```

You can also define connection attribute values within the $data_source parameter. For example:

```
dbi:DriverName(PrintError=>0,Taint=>1):...
```

Individual attribute values specified in this way take precedence over any conflicting values specified via the \%attr parameter to connect.

Where possible, each session ($dbh) is independent from the transactions in other sessions. This is useful when you need to hold cursors open across transactions—

for example, if you use one session for your long lifespan cursors (typically read-only) and another for your short update transactions.

For compatibility with old DBI scripts, the driver can be specified by passing its name as the fourth argument to connect (instead of \%attr):

```
$dbh = DBI->connect($data_source, $user, $pass, $driver);
```

In this "old-style" form of connect, the $data_source should not start with dbi:*driver_name*:. (If it does, the embedded *driver_name* will be ignored). Also note that in this older form of connect, the $dbh->{AutoCommit} attribute is *undefined*, the $dbh->{PrintError} attribute is off, and the old DBI_DBNAME environment variable is checked if DBI_DSN is not defined. Beware that this "old-style" connect will be withdrawn in a future version of DBI.

connect_cached (NEW)

```
$dbh = DBI->connect_cached($data_source, $username, $password)
        || die $DBI::errstr;
$dbh = DBI->connect_cached($data_source, $username, $password, \%attr)
        || die $DBI::errstr;
```

connect_cached is like *connect*, except that the database handle returned is also stored in a hash associated with the given parameters. If another call is made to connect_cached with the same parameter values, then the corresponding cached $dbh will be returned if it is still valid. The cached database handle is replaced with a new connection if it has been disconnected or if the ping method fails.

Note that the behavior of this method differs in several respects from the behavior of persistent connections implemented by Apache::DBI.

Caching can be useful in some applications, but it can also cause problems and should be used with care. The exact behavior of this method is liable to change, so if you intend to use it in any production applications you should discuss your needs on the *dbi-users* mailing list.

The cache can be accessed (and cleared) via the CachedKids attribute.

available_drivers

```
@ary = DBI->available_drivers;
@ary = DBI->available_drivers($quiet);
```

Returns a list of all available drivers by searching for DBD::* modules through the directories in @INC. By default, a warning is given if some drivers are hidden by others of the same name in earlier directories. Passing a true value for $quiet will inhibit the warning.

data_sources

```
@ary = DBI->data_sources($driver);
@ary = DBI->data_sources($driver, \%attr);
```

Returns a list of all data sources (databases) available via the named driver. The driver will be loaded if it hasn't been already. If $driver is empty or undef, then the value of the DBI_DRIVER environment variable is used.

Data sources are returned in a form suitable for passing to the connect method (that is, they will include the dbi:$driver: prefix).

Note that many drivers have no way of knowing what data sources might be available. These drivers return an empty or incomplete list.

trace

```
DBI->trace($trace_level)
DBI->trace($trace_level, $trace_filename)
```

DBI trace information can be enabled for all handles using the trace DBI class method. To enable trace information for a specific handle, use the similar $h-> trace method described elsewhere.

Trace levels are as follows:

0   Trace disabled.

1   Trace DBI method calls returning with results or errors.

2   Trace method entry with parameters and returning with results.

3   As above, adding some high-level information from the driver and some internal information from the DBI.

4   As above, adding more detailed information from the driver. Also includes DBI mutex information when using threaded Perl.

5 and above
As above, but with more and more obscure information.

Trace level 1 is best for a simple overview of what's happening. Trace level 2 is a good choice for general purpose tracing. Levels 3 and above (up to 9) are best reserved for investigating a specific problem, when you need to see "inside" the driver and DBI.

The trace output is detailed and typically very useful. Much of the trace output is formatted using the neat function, so strings may be edited and truncated.

Initially, trace output is written to STDERR. If $trace_filename is specified, the file is opened in append mode and all trace output (including that from other handles) is redirected to that file. Further calls to trace without a $trace_filename do not alter where the trace output is sent. If `$trace_filename` is undefined, then trace output is sent to `STDERR` and the previous trace file is closed.

See also the `$h->trace` and `$h->trace_msg` methods for information about the `DBI_TRACE` environment variable.

DBI Utility Functions

In addition to the methods listed in the previous section, the DBI package also provides the following utility functions:

neat

```
$str = DBI::neat($value, $maxlen);
```

Returns a string containing a neat (and tidy) representation of the supplied value.

Strings will be quoted, although internal quotes will *not* be escaped. Values known to be numeric will be unquoted. Undefined (NULL) values will be shown as `undef` (without quotes). Unprintable characters will be replaced by a dot (.).

For result strings longer than `$maxlen`, the result string will be truncated to `$maxlen-4`, and "`...'`" will be appended. If `$maxlen` is 0 or `undef`, it defaults to `$DBI::neat_maxlen`, which, in turn, defaults to 400.

This function is designed to format values for human consumption. It is used internally by the DBI for `trace` output. It should typically *not* be used for formatting values for database use. (See also `quote`.)

neat_list

```
$str = DBI::neat_list(\@listref, $maxlen, $field_sep);
```

Calls `DBI::neat` on each element of the list and returns a string containing the results joined with `$field_sep`. `$field_sep` defaults to "`, `".

looks_like_number

```
@bool = DBI::looks_like_number(@array);
```

Returns true for each element that looks like a number. Returns false for each element that does not look like a number. Returns `undef` for each element that is undefined or empty.

DBI Dynamic Attributes

Dynamic attributes are always associated with the *last handle used* (that handle is represented by `$h` in the descriptions below).

Where an attribute is equivalent to a method call, refer to the method call for all related documentation.

Warning: these attributes are provided as a convenience, but they do have limitations. Specifically, they have a short lifespan: because they are associated with the last handle used, they should be used only *immediately* after calling the method that "sets" them. If in any doubt, use the corresponding method call.

`$DBI::err`
> Equivalent to $h->err.

`$DBI::errstr`
> Equivalent to $h->errstr.

`$DBI::state`
> Equivalent to $h->state.

`$DBI::rows`
> Equivalent to $h->rows. Please refer to the documentation for the **rows** method.

Methods Common to All Handles

The following methods can be used by all types of DBI handles:

err

```
$rv = $h->err;
```

Returns the *native* database engine error code from the last driver method called. The code is typically an integer, but you should not assume that.

The DBI resets $h->err to **undef** before most DBI method calls, so the value has only a short lifespan. Also, most drivers share the same error variables across all their handles, so calling a method on one handle will typically reset the error on all the other handles that are children of that driver.

If you need to test for individual errors *and* have your program be portable to different database engines, then you'll need to determine what the corresponding error codes are for all those engines, and test for all of them.

errstr

```
$str = $h->errstr;
```

Returns the native database engine error message from the last driver method called. This has the same lifespan issues as the **err** method described above.

state

```
$str = $h->state;
```

Returns an error code in the standard SQLSTATE five-character format. Note that the specific success code 00000 is translated to 0 (false). If the driver does not support SQLSTATE (and most don't), then state will return S1000 (General Error) for all errors.

trace

```
$h->trace($trace_level);
$h->trace($trace_level, $trace_filename);
```

DBI trace information can be enabled for a specific handle (and any future children of that handle) by setting the trace level using the **trace** method.

Trace level 1 is best for a simple overview of what's happening. Trace level 2 is a good choice for general-purpose tracing. Levels 3 and above (up to 9) are best reserved for investigating a specific problem, when you need to see "inside" the driver and DBI. Set $trace_level to 0 to disable the trace.

The trace output is detailed and typically very useful. Much of the trace output is formatted using the **neat** function, so strings may be edited and truncated.

Initially, trace output is written to STDERR. If $trace_filename is specified, then the file is opened in append mode and *all* trace output (including that from other handles) is redirected to that file. Further calls to **trace** without a $trace_filename do not alter where the trace output is sent. If $trace_filename is undefined, then trace output is sent to STDERR and the previous trace file is closed.

See also the DBI->**trace** method for information about the DBI_TRACE environment variable.

trace_msg

```
$h->trace_msg($message_text);
$h->trace_msg($message_text, $min_level);
```

Writes $message_text to the trace file if **trace** is enabled for $h or for the DBI as a whole. Can also be called as DBI->trace_msg($msg). See **trace**.

If $min_level is defined, then the message is output only if the trace level is equal to or greater than that level. $min_level defaults to 1.

func

```
$h->func(@func_arguments, $func_name);
```

The `func` method can be used to call private non-standard and non-portable methods implemented by the driver. Note that the function name is given as the last argument.

This method is not directly related to calling stored procedures. Calling stored procedures is currently not defined by the DBI. Some drivers, such as `DBD::Oracle`, support it in non-portable ways.

See driver documentation for more details.

Attributes Common to All Handles

These attributes are common to all types of DBI handles.

Some attributes are inherited by child handles. That is, the value of an inherited attribute in a newly created statement handle is the same as the value in the parent database handle. Changes to attributes in the new statement handle do not affect the parent database handle and changes to the database handle do not affect existing statement handles, only future ones.

Attempting to set or get the value of an unknown attribute is fatal, except for private driver-specific attributes (which all have names starting with a lowercase letter).

For example:

```
$h->{AttributeName} = ...;     # set/write
... = $h->{AttributeName};     # get/read
```

Warn (boolean, inherited)

Enables useful warnings for certain bad practices. Enabled by default. Some emulation layers, especially those for Perl 4 interfaces, disable warnings. Since warnings are generated using the Perl `warn` function, they can be intercepted using the Perl `$SIG{__WARN__}` hook.

Active (boolean, read-only)

True if the handle object is "active." This is rarely used in applications. The exact meaning of active is somewhat vague at the moment. For a database handle, it typically means that the handle is connected to a database (`$dbh->disconnect` sets `Active` off). For a statement handle, it typically means that the handle is a `SELECT` that may have more data to fetch. (Fetching all the data or calling `$sth->finish` sets `Active` off.)

Kids (integer, read-only)

For a driver handle, Kids is the number of currently existing database handles that were created from that driver handle. For a database handle, Kids is the number of currently existing statement handles that were created from that database handle.

ActiveKids (integer, read-only)

Like Kids, but only counting those that are Active (as above).

CachedKids (hash ref)

For a database handle, returns a reference to the cache (hash) of statement handles created by the prepare_cached method. For a driver handle, returns a reference to the cache (hash) of database handles created by the connect_cached method.

CompatMode (boolean, inherited)

Used by emulation layers (such as Oraperl) to enable compatible behavior in the underlying driver (e.g., DBD::Oracle) for this handle. Not normally set by application code.

InactiveDestroy (boolean)

This attribute can be used to disable the *database engine* related effect of destroying a handle (which would normally close a prepared statement or disconnect from the database, etc.).

For a database handle, this attribute does not disable an *explicit* call to the disconnect method, only the implicit call from DESTROY.

This attribute is specifically designed for use in Unix applications that "fork" child processes. Either the parent or the child process, but not both, should set InactiveDestroy on all their shared handles.

PrintError (boolean, inherited)

This attribute can be used to force errors to generate warnings (using warn) in addition to returning error codes in the normal way. When set "on," any method that results in an error occurring will cause the DBI to effectively do a warn("$class $method failed: $DBI::errstr") where $class is the driver class, and $method is the name of the method which failed.

For example:

```
DBD::Oracle::db prepare failed: ... error text here ...
```

By default, `DBI->connect` sets `PrintError` to "on."

If desired, the warnings can be caught and processed using a `$SIG{__WARN__}` handler or modules like `CGI::Carp` and `CGI::ErrorWrap`.

RaiseError (boolean, inherited)

This attribute can be used to force errors to raise exceptions rather than simply return error codes in the normal way. It is "off" by default. When set to "on", any method that results in an error will cause the DBI to effectively do a `die("$class $method failed: $DBI::errstr")`, where `$class` is the driver class, and `$method` is the name of the method that failed. For example:

```
DBD::Oracle::db prepare failed: ... error text here ...
```

If `PrintError` is also on, then the `PrintError` is done before the `RaiseError` unless no `__DIE__` handler has been defined, in which case `PrintError` is skipped, since the `die` will print the message.

If you want to temporarily turn `RaiseError` off (inside a library function that is likely to fail, for example), the recommended way is like this:

```
{
    local $h->{RaiseError}; # localize and turn off for this block
    ...
}
```

The original value will automatically and reliably be restored by Perl, regardless of how the block is exited. The same logic applies to other attributes, including `PrintError`.

Sadly, this doesn't work for Perl versions up to and including 5.004_04. For backwards compatibility, you could just use `eval { ... }` instead.

ChopBlanks (boolean, inherited)

This attribute can be used to control the trimming of trailing space characters from fixed-width character (CHAR) fields. No other field types are affected, even where field values have trailing spaces.

The default is false (although it is possible that the default may change). Applications that need specific behavior should set the attribute as needed. Emulation interfaces should set the attribute to match the behavior of the interface they are emulating.

Drivers are not required to support this attribute, but any driver that does not support it must arrange to return undef as the attribute value.

LongReadLen (unsigned integer, inherited)

This attribute may be used to control the maximum length of long fields ("blob," "memo," etc.), which the driver will read from the database automatically when it fetches each row of data. The LongReadLen attribute relates only to fetching and reading long values; it is not involved in inserting or updating them.

A value of 0 means not to automatically fetch any long data. (fetch should return undef for long fields when LongReadLen is 0.)

The default is typically 0 (zero) bytes but may vary between drivers. Applications fetching long fields should set this value to slightly larger than the longest long field value to be fetched.

Some databases return some long types encoded as pairs of hex digits. For these types, LongReadLen relates to the underlying data length and not the doubled-up length of the encoded string.

Changing the value of LongReadLen for a statement handle after it has been prepare'd will typically have no effect, so it's common to set LongReadLen on the $dbh before calling prepare.

Note that the value used here has a direct effect on the memory used by the application, so don't be too generous.

See LongTruncOk for more information on truncation behavior.

LongTruncOk (boolean, inherited)

This attribute may be used to control the effect of fetching a long field value that has been truncated (typically because it's longer than the value of the LongRead-Len attribute).

By default, LongTruncOk is false, and so fetching a long value that needs to be truncated will cause the fetch to fail. (Applications should always be sure to check for errors after a fetch loop in case an error, such as a divide by zero or long field truncation, caused the fetch to terminate prematurely.)

If a fetch fails due to a long field truncation when LongTruncOk is false, many drivers will allow you to continue fetching further rows.

See also LongReadLen.

Taint (boolean, inherited)

If this attribute is set to a true value *and* Perl is running in taint mode (e.g., started with the –T option), then all data fetched from the database is tainted, and the arguments to most DBI method calls are checked for being tainted. *This may change.*

The attribute defaults to off, even if Perl is in taint mode. See the *perlsec* manpage for more about taint mode. If Perl is not running in taint mode, this attribute has no effect.

When fetching data that you can trust, you can turn off the taint attribute for that statement handle, for the duration of the fetch loop.

Currently only fetched data is tainted. It is possible that the results of other DBI method calls, and the value of fetched attributes, may also be tainted in future versions. That change may well break your applications unless you take great care now. If you use DBI taint mode, please report your experience and any suggestions for changes.

private_*

The DBI provides a way to store extra information in a DBI handle as "private" attributes. The DBI will allow you to store and retrieve any attribute that has a name starting with private_. It is strongly recommended that you use just *one* private attribute (e.g., use a hash ref) and give it a long and unambiguous name that includes the module or application name that the attribute relates to (e.g., private_YourFullModuleName_thingy).

DBI Database Handle Objects

This section covers the methods and attributes associated with database handles.

Database Handle Methods

The following methods are specified for DBI database handles:

do

```
$rc = $dbh->do($statement)              || die $dbh->errstr;
$rc = $dbh->do($statement, \%attr)      || die $dbh->errstr;
$rv = $dbh->do($statement, \%attr, @bind_values) || ...
```

Prepares and executes a single statement. Returns the number of rows affected or **undef** on error. A return value of –1 means the number of rows is not known or is not available.

This method is typically most useful for *non*-SELECT statements that either cannot be prepared in advance (due to a limitation of the driver) or do not need to be executed repeatedly. It should not be used for SELECT statements because it does not return a statement handle (so you can't fetch any data).

The default do method is logically similar to:

```
sub do {
    my($dbh, $statement, $attr, @bind_values) = @_;
    my $sth = $dbh->prepare($statement, $attr) or return undef;
    $sth->execute(@bind_values) or return undef;
    my $rows = $sth->rows;
    ($rows == 0) ? "0E0" : $rows; # always return true if no error
}
```

For example:

```
my $rows_deleted = $dbh->do(q{
    DELETE FROM table
    WHERE status = ?
}, undef, 'DONE') || die $dbh->errstr;
```

Using placeholders and @bind_values with the do method can be useful because it avoids the need to correctly quote any variables in the $statement. But if you'll be executing the statement many times, then it's more efficient to prepare it once and call execute many times instead.

The q{...} style quoting used in this example avoids clashing with quotes that may be used in the SQL statement. Use the double-quote-like qq{...} operator if you want to interpolate variables into the string. See the section on "Quote and Quote-Like Operators" in the *perlop* manpage for more details.

selectrow_array

```
@row_ary = $dbh->selectrow_array($statement);
@row_ary = $dbh->selectrow_array($statement, \%attr);
@row_ary = $dbh->selectrow_array($statement, \%attr, @bind_values);
```

This utility method combines prepare, execute, and fetchrow_array into a single call. If called in a list context, it returns the first row of data from the statement. If called in a scalar context, it returns the first field of the first row. The $statement parameter can be a previously prepared statement handle, in which case the prepare is skipped.

If any method fails, and RaiseError is not set, selectrow_array will return an empty list.

In a scalar context, selectrow_array returns the value of the first field. An undef is returned if there are no matching rows or if an error occurred. Since that undef can't be distinguished from an undef returned because the first field value was NULL, calling `selectrow_array` in a scalar context should be used with caution.

selectall_arrayref

```
$ary_ref = $dbh->selectall_arrayref($statement);
$ary_ref = $dbh->selectall_arrayref($statement, \%attr);
$ary_ref = $dbh->selectall_arrayref($statement, \%attr, @bind_values);
```

This utility method combines **prepare**, **execute**, and **fetchall_arrayref** into a single call. It returns a reference to an array containing a reference to an array for each row of data fetched.

The `$statement` parameter can be a previously prepared statement handle, in which case the **prepare** is skipped. This is recommended if the statement is going to be executed many times.

If any method except `fetch` fails, and `RaiseError` is not set, `selectall_arrayref` will return `undef`. If `fetch` fails, and `RaiseError` is not set, then it will return with whatever data it has fetched thus far.

selectcol_arrayref

```
$ary_ref = $dbh->selectcol_arrayref($statement);
$ary_ref = $dbh->selectcol_arrayref($statement, \%attr);
$ary_ref = $dbh->selectcol_arrayref($statement, \%attr, @bind_values);
```

This utility method combines **prepare**, **execute**, and fetching one column from all the rows, into a single call. It returns a reference to an array containing the values of the first column from each row.

The `$statement` parameter can be a previously prepared statement handle, in which case the **prepare** is skipped. This is recommended if the statement is going to be executed many times.

If any method except `fetch` fails, and `RaiseError` is not set, `selectcol_arrayref` will return `undef`. If `fetch` fails and `RaiseError` is not set, then it will return with whatever data it has fetched thus far.

prepare

```
$sth = $dbh->prepare($statement)          || die $dbh->errstr;
$sth = $dbh->prepare($statement, \%attr)  || die $dbh->errstr;
```

Prepares a single statement for later execution by the database engine and returns a reference to a statement handle object.

The returned statement handle can be used to get attributes of the statement and invoke the **execute** method. See "Statement Handle Methods."

Drivers for engines without the concept of preparing a statement will typically just
store the statement in the returned handle and process it when $sth->execute is
called. Such drivers are unlikely to give much useful information about the statement, such as $sth->{NUM_OF_FIELDS}, until after $sth->execute has been
called. Portable applications should take this into account.

In general, DBI drivers do not parse the contents of the statement (other than simply counting any *placeholders*). The statement is passed directly to the database
engine, sometimes known as pass-thru mode. This has advantages and disadvantages. On the plus side, you can access all the functionality of the engine being
used. On the downside, you're limited if you're using a simple engine, and you
need to take extra care if you're writing applications intended to be portable
between engines.

Portable applications should not assume that a new statement can be prepared
and/or executed while still fetching results from a previous statement.

Some command-line SQL tools use statement terminators, like a semicolon, to indicate the end of a statement. Such terminators should not normally be used with
the DBI.

prepare_cached

```
$sth = $dbh->prepare_cached($statement)
$sth = $dbh->prepare_cached($statement, \%attr)
$sth = $dbh->prepare_cached($statement, \%attr, $allow_active)
```

Like **prepare** except that the statement handle returned will be stored in a hash
associated with the $dbh. If another call is made to **prepare_cached** with the
same $statement and %attr values, then the corresponding cached $sth will be
returned without contacting the database server.

This caching can be useful in some applications, but it can also cause problems
and should be used with care. A warning will be generated if the cached $sth
being returned is active (i.e., it is a SELECT that may still have data to be fetched).
This warning can be suppressed by setting $allow_active to true. The cache can
be accessed (and cleared) via the CachedKids attribute.

Here's an example of one possible use of **prepare_cached**:

```
while ( ($field, $value) = each %search_fields ) {
    push @sql,    "$field = ?";
    push @values, $value;
}
$qualifier = "";
$qualifier = "where ".join(" and ", @sql) if @sql;
$sth = $dbh->prepare_cached("SELECT * FROM table $qualifier");
$sth->execute(@values);
```

commit

```
$rc  = $dbh->commit      || die $dbh->errstr;
```

Commits (makes permanent) the most recent series of database changes if the database supports transactions and `AutoCommit` is off.

If AutoCommit is on, then calling commit will issue a "commit ineffective with AutoCommit" warning.

rollback

```
$rc  = $dbh->rollback    || die $dbh->errstr;
```

Rolls back (undoes) the most recent series of uncommitted database changes if the database supports transactions and `AutoCommit` is off.

If `AutoCommit` is on, then calling `rollback` will issue a "rollback ineffective with AutoCommit" warning.

disconnect

```
$rc = $dbh->disconnect   || warn $dbh->errstr;
```

Disconnects the database from the database handle. `disconnect` is typically used only before exiting the program. The handle is of little use after disconnecting.

The transaction behavior of the `disconnect` method is, sadly, undefined. Some database systems (such as Oracle and Ingres) will automatically commit any outstanding changes, but others (such as Informix) will roll back any outstanding changes. Applications not using `AutoCommit` should explicitly call `commit` or `rollback` before calling `disconnect`.

The database is automatically disconnected by the `DESTROY` method if still connected when there are no longer any references to the handle. The `DESTROY` method for each driver should implicitly call `rollback` to undo any uncommitted changes. This is vital behavior to ensure that incomplete transactions don't get committed simply because Perl calls `DESTROY` on every object before exiting. Also, do not rely on the order of object destruction during "global destruction," as it is undefined.

Generally, if you want your changes to be commited or rolled back when you disconnect, then you should explicitly call `commit` or `rollback` before disconnecting.

If you disconnect from a database while you still have active statement handles, you will get a warning. The statement handles should either be cleared (destroyed) before disconnecting, or the `finish` method should be called on each one.

ping

```
$rc = $dbh->ping;
```

Attempts to determine, in a reasonably efficient way, if the database server is still running and the connection to it is still working. Individual drivers should implement this function in the most suitable manner for their database engine.

The current *default* implementation always returns true without actually doing anything. Actually, it returns "0 but true", which is true but zero. That way you can tell if the return value is genuine or just the default. Drivers should override this method with one that does the right thing for their type of database.

Few applications would have use for this method. See the specialized Apache::DBI module for one example usage.

table_info *(NEW)*

```
$sth = $dbh->table_info;
```

Warning: This method is experimental and may change.

Returns an active statement handle that can be used to fetch information about tables and views that exist in the database.

The handle has at least the following fields in the order show below. Other fields, after these, may also be present.

TABLE_CAT
Table catalog identifier. This field is NULL (undef) if not applicable to the data source, which is usually the case. This field is empty if not applicable to the table.

TABLE_SCHEM
The name of the schema containing the TABLE_NAME value. This field is NULL (undef) if not applicable to data source, and empty if not applicable to the table.

TABLE_NAME
Name of the table (or view, synonym, etc.).

TABLE_TYPE
One of the following: "TABLE," "VIEW," "SYSTEM TABLE," "GLOBAL TEMPORARY," "LOCAL TEMPORARY," "ALIAS," "SYNONYM," or a type identifier that is specific to the data source.

REMARKS
A description of the table. May be NULL (undef).

Note that `table_info` might not return records for all tables. Applications can use any valid table regardless of whether it's returned by `table_info`. See also `tables`.

For more detailed information about the fields and their meanings, refer to:

> *http://msdn.microsoft.com/library/psdk/dasdk/odch6wyb.htm*

If that URL ceases to work, then use the MSDN search facility at:

> *http://search.microsoft.com/us/dev/*

and search for `SQLTables returns` using the exact phrase option. The link you want will probably just be called `SQLTables` and will be part of the Data Access SDK.

tables (NEW)

```
@names = $dbh->tables;
```

Warning: This method is experimental and may change.

Returns a list of table and view names, possibly including a schema prefix. This list should include all tables that can be used in a **SELECT** statement without further qualification.

Note that `table_info` might not return records for all tables. Applications can use any valid table regardless of whether it's returned by tables. See also `table_info`.

type_info_all (NEW)

```
$type_info_all = $dbh->type_info_all;
```

Warning: This method is experimental and may change.

Returns a reference to an array that holds information about each datatype variant supported by the database and driver. The array and its contents should be treated as read-only.

The first item is a reference to a hash of **Name => Index** pairs. The following items are references to arrays, one per supported datatype variant. The leading hash defines the names and order of the fields within the following list of arrays. For example:

```
$type_info_all = [
  {   TYPE_NAME        => 0,
      DATA_TYPE        => 1,
      COLUMN_SIZE      => 2,      # was PRECISION originally
      LITERAL_PREFIX   => 3,
      LITERAL_SUFFIX   => 4,
      CREATE_PARAMS    => 5,
```

```
        NULLABLE            => 6,
        CASE_SENSITIVE      => 7,
        SEARCHABLE          => 8,
        UNSIGNED_ATTRIBUTE=> 9,
        FIXED_PREC_SCALE    => 10,     # was MONEY originally
        AUTO_UNIQUE_VALUE   => 11,     # was AUTO_INCREMENT originally
        LOCAL_TYPE_NAME     => 12,
        MINIMUM_SCALE       => 13,
        MAXIMUM_SCALE       => 14,
        NUM_PREC_RADIX      => 15,
    },
    [ 'VARCHAR', SQL_VARCHAR,
        undef, "'","'", undef,0, 1,1,0,0,0,undef,1,255, undef
    ],
    [ 'INTEGER', SQL_INTEGER,
        undef, "", "", undef,0, 0,1,0,0,0,undef,0,  0, 10
    ],
];
```

Note that more than one row may have the same value in the DATA_TYPE field if there are different ways to spell the type name and/or there are variants of the type with different attributes (e.g., with and without AUTO_UNIQUE_VALUE set, with and without UNSIGNED_ATTRIBUTE, etc.).

The rows are ordered by DATA_TYPE first and then by how closely each type maps to the corresponding ODBC SQL datatype, closest first.

The meaning of the fields is described in the documentation for the type_info method. The index values shown above (e.g., NULLABLE => 6) are for illustration only. Drivers may define the fields with a different order.

This method is not normally used directly. The type_info method provides a more useful interface to the data.

type_info (NEW)

```
@type_info = $dbh->type_info($data_type);
```

Warning: This method is experimental and may change.

Returns a list of hash references holding information about one or more variants of $data_type. The list is ordered by DATA_TYPE first and then by how closely each type maps to the corresponding ODBC SQL datatype, closest first. If called in a scalar context then only the first (best) element is returned.

If $data_type is undefined or SQL_ALL_TYPES, then the list will contain hashes for all datatype variants supported by the database and driver.

If $data_type is an array reference, then type_info returns the information for the *first* type in the array that has any matches.

The keys of the hash follow the same letter case conventions as the rest of the DBI (see "Naming Conventions and Name Space"). The following items should exist:

TYPE_NAME (string)

Datatype name for use in `CREATE TABLE` statements, etc.

DATA_TYPE (integer)

SQL datatype number.

COLUMN_SIZE (integer)

For numeric types, this is either the total number of digits (if the `NUM_PREC_RADIX` value is 10) or the total number of bits allowed in the column (if `NUM_PREC_RADIX` is 2).

For string types, this is the maximum size of the string in bytes.

For date and interval types, this is the maximum number of characters needed to display the value.

LITERAL_PREFIX (string)

Characters used to prefix a literal. A typical prefix is "'" for characters, or possibly "0x" for binary values passed as hexadecimal. NULL (`undef`) is returned for datatypes for which this is not applicable.

LITERAL_SUFFIX (string)

Characters used to suffix a literal. Typically "'" for characters. NULL (`undef`) is returned for datatypes where this is not applicable.

CREATE_PARAMS (string)

Parameters for a datatype definition. For example, `CREATE_PARAMS` for a `DECIMAL` would be "`precision,scale`" if the `DECIMAL` type should be declared as `DECIMAL(precision,scale)` where *precision* and *scale* are integer values. For a `VARCHAR` it would be "`max length`". NULL (`undef`) is returned for datatypes for which this is not applicable.

NULLABLE (integer)

Indicates whether the datatype accepts a NULL value: 0 = no, 1 = yes, 2 = unknown.

CASE_SENSITIVE (boolean)

Indicates whether the datatype is case-sensitive in collations and comparisons.

SEARCHABLE (integer)

Indicates how the datatype can be used in a `WHERE` clause, as follows:

0   Cannot be used in a `WHERE` clause

1   Only with a `LIKE` predicate

2   All comparison operators except `LIKE`

3   Can be used in a `WHERE` clause with any comparison operator

UNSIGNED_ATTRIBUTE (boolean)

Indicates whether the datatype is unsigned. NULL (`undef`) is returned for datatypes for which this is not applicable.

FIXED_PREC_SCALE (boolean)

Indicates whether the datatype always has the same precision and scale (such as a money type). NULL (`undef`) is returned for datatypes for which this is not applicable.

AUTO_UNIQUE_VALUE (boolean)

Indicates whether a column of this datatype is automatically set to a unique value whenever a new row is inserted. NULL (`undef`) is returned for datatypes for which this is not applicable.

LOCAL_TYPE_NAME (string)

Localized version of the `TYPE_NAME` for use in dialog with users. NULL (`undef`) is returned if a localized name is not available (in which case `TYPE_NAME` should be used).

MINIMUM_SCALE (integer)

The minimum scale of the datatype. If a datatype has a fixed scale, then `MAXIMUM_SCALE` holds the same value. NULL (`undef`) is returned for datatypes for which this is not applicable.

MAXIMUM_SCALE (integer)

The maximum scale of the datatype. If a datatype has a fixed scale, then `MINIMUM_SCALE` holds the same value. NULL (`undef`) is returned for datatypes for which this is not applicable.

SQL_DATA_TYPE (integer)

This column is the same as the `DATA_TYPE` column, except for interval and datetime datatypes. For interval and datetime datatypes, the `SQL_DATA_TYPE` field will return `SQL_INTERVAL` or `SQL_DATETIME`, and the `SQL_DATETIME_SUB` field below will return the subcode for the specific interval or datetime datatype. If this field is NULL, then the driver does not support or report on interval or date subtypes.

SQL_DATETIME_SUB (integer)

For interval or datetime datatypes, where the `SQL_DATA_TYPE` field above is `SQL_INTERVAL` or `SQL_DATETIME`, this field will hold the subcode for the specific interval or datetime datatype. Otherwise it will be NULL (`undef`).

NUM_PREC_RADIX (integer)

The radix value of the datatype. For approximate numeric types, `NUM_PREC_RADIX` contains the value 2 and `COLUMN_SIZE` holds the number of bits. For exact numeric types, `NUM_PREC_RADIX` contains the value 10 and `COLUMN_SIZE` holds the number of decimal digits. NULL (`undef`) is returned either for datatypes for which this is not applicable or if the driver cannot report this information.

INTERVAL_PRECISION (integer)

The interval leading precision for interval types. NULL is returned either for datatypes for which this is not applicable or if the driver cannot report this information.

Since DBI and ODBC drivers vary in how they map their types into the ISO standard types, you may need to search for more than one type. Here's an example looking for a usable type to store a date:

```
$my_date_type = $dbh->type_info( [ SQL_DATE, SQL_TIMESTAMP ] );
```

Similarly, to more reliably find a type to store small integers, you could use a list starting with SQL_SMALLINT, SQL_INTEGER, SQL_DECIMAL, etc.

For more detailed information about these fields and their meanings, refer to:

http://msdn.microsoft.com/library/psdk/dasdk/odch6yy7.htm

If that URL ceases to work, then use the MSDN search facility at:

http://search.microsoft.com/us/dev/

and search the MSDN library for SQLGetTypeInfo returns using the exact phrase option. The link you want will probably just be called SQLGetTypeInfo (there may be more than one).

The individual datatypes are currently described here:

http://msdn.microsoft.com/library/psdk/dasdk/odap8fcj.htm

If that URL ceases to work, or to get more general information, use the MSDN search facility as described above, and search for SQL Data Types.

quote

```
$sql = $dbh->quote($value);
$sql = $dbh->quote($value, $data_type);
```

Quotes a string literal for use as a literal value in an SQL statement, by escaping any special characters (such as quotation marks) contained within the string and adding the required type of outer quotation marks.

```
$sql = sprintf "SELECT foo FROM bar WHERE baz = %s",
               $dbh->quote("Don't");
```

For most database types, quote would return 'Don''t' (including the outer quotation marks).

An undefined $value value will be returned as the string NULL (without quotation marks) to match how NULLs are represented in SQL.

If $data_type is supplied, it is used to try to determine the required quoting behavior by using the information returned by type_info. As a special case, the standard numeric types are optimized to return $value without calling type_info.

quote will probably *not* be able to deal with all possible input (such as binary data or data containing newlines), and is not related in any way with escaping or quoting shell meta-characters. There is no need to quote values being used with placeholders and bind values.

Database Handle Attributes

This section describes attributes specific to database handles.

Changes to these database handle attributes do not affect any other existing or future database handles.

Attempting to set or get the value of an unknown attribute is fatal, except for private driver-specific attributes (which all have names starting with a lowercase letter).

For example:

```
$h->{AutoCommit} = ...;        # set/write
... = $h->{AutoCommit};        # get/read
```

AutoCommit (boolean)

If true, then database changes cannot be rolled back (undone). If false, then database changes automatically occur within a "transaction," which must either be committed or rolled back using the commit or rollback methods.

Drivers should always default to AutoCommit mode (an unfortunate choice largely forced on the DBI by ODBC and JDBC conventions.)

Attempting to set AutoCommit to an unsupported value is a fatal error. This is an important feature of the DBI. Applications that need full transaction behavior can set $dbh->{AutoCommit} = 0 (or set AutoCommit to 0 via connect) without having to check that the value was assigned successfully.

For the purposes of this description, we can divide databases into three categories:

Databases that don't support transactions at all.
Databases in which a transaction is always active.
Databases in which a transaction must be explicitly started ('BEGIN WORK').

Databases that don't support transactions at all

For these databases, attempting to turn `AutoCommit` off is a fatal error. `commit` and `rollback` both issue warnings about being ineffective while `AutoCommit` is in effect.

Databases in which a transaction is always active

These are typically mainstream commercial relational databases with "ANSI standard" transaction behavior. If `AutoCommit` is off, then changes to the database won't have any lasting effect unless `commit` is called (but see also `disconnect`). If `rollback` is called, then any changes since the last `commit` are undone.

If `AutoCommit` is on, then the effect is the same as if the DBI called `commit` automatically after every successful database operation. In other words, calling `commit` or `rollback` explicitly while `AutoCommit` is on would be ineffective because the changes would have already been commited.

Changing `AutoCommit` from off to on should issue a `commit` in most drivers.

Changing `AutoCommit` from on to off should have no immediate effect.

For databases that don't support a specific autocommit mode, the driver has to commit each statement automatically using an explicit `COMMIT` after it completes successfully (and roll it back using an explicit `rollback` if it fails). The error information reported to the application will correspond to the statement that was executed, unless it succeeded and the `commit` or `rollback` failed.

Databases in which a transaction must be explicitly started

For these databases, the intention is to have them act like databases in which a transaction is always active (as described earlier).

To do this, the DBI driver will automatically begin a transaction when `Auto-Commit` is turned off (from the default "on" state) and will automatically begin another transaction after a `commit` or `rollback`. In this way, the application does not have to treat these databases as a special case.

See `disconnect` for other important notes about transactions.

Driver (handle)

Holds the handle of the parent driver. The only recommended use for this attribute is to find the name of the driver using:

```
$dbh->{Driver}->{Name}
```

Name (string)

Holds the "name" of the database. Usually (and recommended to be) the same as the "dbi:DriverName:..." string used to connect to the database, but with the leading dbi:DriverName: removed.

RowCacheSize (integer) (NEW)

A hint to the driver indicating the size of the local row cache that the application would like the driver to use for future SELECT statements. If a row cache is not implemented, then setting RowCacheSize is ignored and getting the value returns undef.

Some RowCacheSize values have special meaning, as follows:

0 Automatically determine a reasonable cache size for each SELECT.

1 Disable the local row cache.

>1 Cache this many rows.

<0 Cache as many rows that will fit into this much memory for each SELECT.

Note that large cache sizes may require a very large amount of memory (cached rows × maximum size of row). Also, a large cache will cause a longer delay not only for the first fetch, but also whenever the cache needs refilling.

See also the RowsInCache statement handle attribute.

DBI Statement Handle Objects

This section lists the methods and attributes associated with DBI statement handles.

Statement Handle Methods

The DBI defines the following methods for use on DBI statement handles:

bind_param

```
$rc = $sth->bind_param($p_num, $bind_value)    || die $sth->errstr;
$rv = $sth->bind_param($p_num, $bind_value, \%attr)    || ...
$rv = $sth->bind_param($p_num, $bind_value, $bind_type) || ...
```

The bind_param method can be used to bind a value with a placeholder embedded in the prepared statement. Placeholders are indicated with the question mark character (?). For example:

```
$dbh->{RaiseError} = 1;        # save having to check each method call
$sth = $dbh->prepare("SELECT name, age FROM people WHERE name LIKE ?");
```

```
$sth->bind_param(1, "John%");  # placeholders are numbered from 1
$sth->execute;
DBI::dump_results($sth);
```

Note that the ? is not enclosed in quotation marks, even when the placeholder represents a string. Some drivers also allow placeholders like :*name* and :*n* (e.g., :1, :?, and so on) in addition to ?, but their use is not portable. Undefined bind values or **undef** can be used to indicate null values.

Some drivers do not support placeholders.

With most drivers, placeholders can't be used for any element of a statement that would prevent the database server from validating the statement and creating a query execution plan for it. For example:

```
"SELECT name, age FROM ?"    # wrong (will probably fail)
"SELECT name, ?   FROM people"   # wrong (but may not 'fail')
```

Also, placeholders can only represent single scalar values. For example, the following statement won't work as expected for more than one value:

```
"SELECT name, age FROM people WHERE name IN (?)"    # wrong
```

Datatypes for placeholders

The **\%attr** parameter can be used to hint at which datatype the placeholder should have. Typically, the driver is interested in knowing only if the placeholder should be bound as a number or a string. For example:

```
$sth->bind_param(1, $value, { TYPE => SQL_INTEGER });
```

As a shortcut for this common case, the datatype can be passed directly, in place of the **\%attr** hash reference. This example is equivalent to the one above:

```
$sth->bind_param(1, $value, SQL_INTEGER);
```

The **TYPE** value indicates the standard (non-driver-specific) type for this parameter. To specify the driver-specific type, the driver may support a driver-specific attribute, such as { ora_type => 97 }. The datatype for a placeholder cannot be changed after the first **bind_param** call. However, it can be left unspecified, in which case it defaults to the previous value.

Perl only has string and number scalar datatypes. All database types that aren't numbers are bound as strings and must be in a format the database will understand.

As an alternative to specifying the datatype in the **bind_param** call, you can let the driver pass the value as the default type (**VARCHAR**). You can then use an SQL function to convert the type within the statement. For example:

```
INSERT INTO price(code, price) VALUES (?, CONVERT(MONEY,?))
```

The CONVERT function used here is just an example. The actual function and syntax will vary between different databases and is non-portable.

See also "Placeholders and Bind Values" for more information.

bind_param_inout

```
$rc = $sth->bind_param_inout($p_num, \$bind_value, $max_len)   || die $sth->errstr;
$rv = $sth->bind_param_inout($p_num, \$bind_value, $max_len, \%attr)     || ...
$rv = $sth->bind_param_inout($p_num, \$bind_value, $max_len, $bind_type) || ...
```

This method acts like bind_param, but also enables values to be updated by the statement. The statement is typically a call to a stored procedure. The $bind_value must be passed as a reference to the actual value to be used.

Note that unlike bind_param, the $bind_value variable is not read when bind_param_inout is called. Instead, the value in the variable is read at the time execute is called.

The additional $max_len parameter specifies the minimum amount of memory to allocate to $bind_value for the new value. If the value returned from the database is too big to fit, then the execution should fail. If unsure what value to use, pick a generous length, i.e., a length larger than the longest value that would ever be returned. The only cost of using a larger value than needed is wasted memory.

It is expected that few drivers will support this method. The only driver currently known to do so is DBD::Oracle (DBD::ODBC may support it in a future release). Therefore, it should not be used for database-independent applications.

Undefined values or undef are used to indicate null values. See also "Placeholders and Bind Values" for more information.

execute

```
$rv = $sth->execute                || die $sth->errstr;
$rv = $sth->execute(@bind_values)  || die $sth->errstr;
```

Performs whatever processing is necessary to execute the prepared statement. An undef is returned if an error occurs. A successful execute always returns true regardless of the number of rows affected, even if it's zero (see below). It is always important to check the return status of execute (and most other DBI methods) for errors.

For a *non*-SELECT statement, execute returns the number of rows affected, if known. If no rows were affected, then execute returns 0E0, which Perl will treat as 0 but will regard as true. Note that it is *not* an error for no rows to be affected by a statement. If the number of rows affected is not known, then execute returns −1.

For SELECT statements, execute simply "starts" the query within the database engine. Use one of the fetch methods to retrieve the data after calling execute. The execute method does *not* return the number of rows that will be returned by the query (because most databases can't tell in advance), it simply returns a true value.

If any arguments are given, then execute will effectively call bind_param for each value before executing the statement. Values bound in this way are usually treated as SQL_VARCHAR types unless the driver can determine the correct type (which is rare), or unless bind_param (or bind_param_inout) has already been used to specify the type.

fetchrow_arrayref

```
$ary_ref = $sth->fetchrow_arrayref;
$ary_ref = $sth->fetch;     # alias
```

Fetches the next row of data and returns a reference to an array holding the field values. Null fields are returned as undef values in the array. This is the fastest way to fetch data, particularly if used with $sth->bind_columns.

If there are no more rows, or if an error occurs, then fetchrow_arrayref returns an undef. You should check $sth->err afterwards (or use the RaiseError attribute) to discover if the undef returned was due to an error.

Note that the same array reference will currently be returned for each fetch, so don't store the reference and then use it after a later fetch.

fetchrow_array

```
 @ary = $sth->fetchrow_array;
```

An alternative to fetchrow_arrayref. Fetches the next row of data and returns it as a list containing the field values. Null fields are returned as undef values in the list.

If there are no more rows, or if an error occurs, then fetchrow_array returns an empty list. You should check $sth->err afterwards (or use the RaiseError attribute) to discover if the empty list returned was due to an error.

In a scalar context, fetchrow_array returns the value of the first field. An undef is returned if there are no more rows or if an error occurred. Since that undef can't be distinguished from an undef returned because the first field value was NULL, you should exercise some caution if you use fetchrow_array in a scalar context.

fetchrow_hashref

```
$hash_ref = $sth->fetchrow_hashref;
$hash_ref = $sth->fetchrow_hashref($name);
```

An alternative to `fetchrow_arrayref`. Fetches the next row of data and returns it as a reference to a hash containing field name and field value pairs. Null fields are returned as `undef` values in the hash.

If there are no more rows, or if an error occurs, then `fetchrow_hashref` returns an `undef`. You should check `$sth->err` afterwards (or use the `RaiseError` attribute) to discover if the `undef` returned was due to an error.

The optional `$name` parameter specifies the name of the statement handle attribute. For historical reasons it defaults to `NAME`; however, using either `NAME_lc` or `NAME_uc` is recommended for portability.

The keys of the hash are the same names returned by `$sth->{$name}`. If more than one field has the same name, there will only be one entry in the returned hash for those fields.

Because of the extra work `fetchrow_hashref` and Perl have to perform, this attribute is not as efficient as `fetchrow_arrayref` or `fetchrow_array`.

Currently, a new hash reference is returned for each row. *This will change* in the future to return the same hash ref each time, so don't rely on the current behavior.

fetchall_arrayref

```
$tbl_ary_ref = $sth->fetchall_arrayref;
$tbl_ary_ref = $sth->fetchall_arrayref( $slice_array_ref );
$tbl_ary_ref = $sth->fetchall_arrayref( $slice_hash_ref );
```

The `fetchall_arrayref` method can be used to fetch all the data to be returned from a prepared and executed statement handle. It returns a reference to an array that contains one reference per row.

If there are no rows to return, `fetchall_arrayref` returns a reference to an empty array. If an error occurs, `fetchall_arrayref` returns the data fetched thus far, which may be none. You should check `$sth->err` afterwards (or use the `RaiseError` attribute) to discover if the data is complete or was truncated due to an error.

When passed an array reference, `fetchall_arrayref` uses `fetchrow_arrayref` to fetch each row as an array ref. If the parameter array is not empty, then it is used as a slice to select individual columns by index number.

With no parameters, `fetchall_arrayref` acts as if passed an empty array ref.

When passed a hash reference, `fetchall_arrayref` uses `fetchrow_hashref` to fetch each row as a hash reference. If the parameter hash is not empty, then it is used as a slice to select individual columns by name. The names should be lower case regardless of the letter case in `$sth->{NAME}`. The values of the hash should be set to 1.

For example, to fetch just the first column of every row:

```
$tbl_ary_ref = $sth->fetchall_arrayref([0]);
```

To fetch the second to last and last column of every row:

```
$tbl_ary_ref = $sth->fetchall_arrayref([-2,-1]);
```

To fetch only the fields called "foo" and "bar" of every row:

```
$tbl_ary_ref = $sth->fetchall_arrayref({ foo=>1, bar=>1 });
```

The first two examples return a reference to an array of array refs. The last returns a reference to an array of hash refs.

finish

```
$rc = $sth->finish;
```

Indicates that no more data will be fetched from this statement handle before it is either executed again or destroyed. The `finish` method is rarely needed, but can sometimes be helpful in very specific situations to allow the server to free up resources (such as sort buffers).

When all the data has been fetched from a SELECT statement, the driver should automatically call `finish` for you. So you should not normally need to call it explicitly.

Consider a query like:

```
SELECT foo FROM table WHERE bar=? ORDER BY foo
```

where you want to select just the first (smallest) "foo" value from a very large table. When executed, the database server will have to use temporary buffer space to store the sorted rows. If, after executing the handle and selecting one row, the handle won't be re-executed for some time and won't be destroyed, the `finish` method can be used to tell the server that the buffer space can be freed.

Calling `finish` resets the Active attribute for the statement. It may also make some statement handle attributes (such as NAME and TYPE) unavailable if they have not already been accessed (and thus cached).

The `finish` method does not affect the transaction status of the database connection. It has nothing to do with transactions. It's mostly an internal "housekeeping" method that is rarely needed. There's no need to call `finish` if you're about to destroy or re-execute the statement handle. See also **disconnect** and the **Active** attribute.

rows

```
$rv = $sth->rows;
```

Returns the number of rows affected by the last row-affecting command, or −1 if the number of rows is not known or not available.

Generally, you can only rely on a row count after a *non-***SELECT execute** (for some specific operations like **UPDATE** and **DELETE**), or after fetching all the rows of a **SELECT** statement.

For **SELECT** statements, it is generally not possible to know how many rows will be returned except by fetching them all. Some drivers will return the number of rows the application has fetched so far, but others may return −1 until all rows have been fetched. So use of the **rows** method or **$DBI::rows** with **SELECT** statements is not recommended.

One alternative method to get a row count for a **SELECT** is to execute a "**SELECT COUNT(*) FROM ...**" SQL statement with the same "**...**" as your query, and then fetch the row count from that.

bind_col

```
$rc = $sth->bind_col($column_number, \$var_to_bind);
```

Binds an output column (field) of a **SELECT** statement to a Perl variable. See **bind_columns** for an example. Note that column numbers count up from 1.

Whenever a row is fetched from the database, the corresponding Perl variable is automatically updated. There is no need to fetch and assign the values manually. The binding is performed at a very low level using Perl aliasing, so there is no extra copying taking place. This makes using bound variables very efficient.

For maximum portability between drivers, **bind_col** should be called after **execute**. This restriction may be removed in a later version of the DBI.

You do not need to bind output columns in order to fetch data, but it can be useful for some applications that need either maximum performance or greater clarity of code. The **bind_param** method performs a similar but opposite function for input variables.

bind_columns

```
$rc = $sth->bind_columns(@list_of_refs_to_vars_to_bind);
```

Calls `bind_col` for each column of the `SELECT` statement. The `bind_columns` method will die if the number of references does not match the number of fields.

For maximum portability between drivers, `bind_columns` should be called after `execute`.

For example:

```
$dbh->{RaiseError} = 1; # Do this, or check every call for errors
$sth = $dbh->prepare(q{ SELECT region, sales FROM sales_by_region });
$sth->execute;
my ($region, $sales);

# Bind Perl variables to columns:
$rv = $sth->bind_columns(\$region, \$sales);

# You can also use Perl's \(...) syntax (see perlref docs):
#       $sth->bind_columns(\($region, $sales));

# Column binding is the most efficient way to fetch data
while ($sth->fetch) {
    print "$region: $sales\n";
}
```

For compatibility with old scripts, the first parameter will be ignored if it is **undef** or a hash reference.

dump_results

```
$rows = $sth->dump_results($maxlen, $lsep, $fsep, $fh);
```

Fetches all the rows from `$sth`, calls `DBI::neat_list` for each row, and prints the results to `$fh` (defaults to `STDOUT`) separated by `$lsep` (default `"\n"`). `$fsep` defaults to `", "` and `$maxlen` defaults to 35.

This method is designed as a handy utility for prototyping and testing queries. Since it uses `neat_list` to format and edit the string for reading by humans, it is not recommended for data transfer applications.

Statement Handle Attributes

This section describes attributes specific to statement handles. Most of these attributes are read-only.

Changes to these statement handle attributes do not affect any other existing or future statement handles.

Attempting to set or get the value of an unknown attribute is fatal, except for private driver-specific attributes (which all have names starting with a lowercase letter).

For example:

```
... = $h->{NUM_OF_FIELDS};    # get/read
```

Note that some drivers cannot provide valid values for some or all of these attributes until after $sth->execute has been called.

See also finish to learn more about the effect it may have on some attributes.

NUM_OF_FIELDS (integer, read-only)

Number of fields (columns) the prepared statement will return. *Non*-SELECT statements will have NUM_OF_FIELDS == 0.

NUM_OF_PARAMS (integer, read-only)

The number of parameters (placeholders) in the prepared statement. See "Substitution Variables" later in this appendix for more details.

NAME (array-ref, read-only)

Returns a reference to an array of field names for each column. The names may contain spaces but should not be truncated or have any trailing space. Note that the names have the letter case (upper, lower, or mixed) as returned by the driver being used. Portable applications should use NAME_lc or NAME_uc. For example:

```
print "First column name: $sth->{NAME}->[0]\n";
```

NAME_lc (array-ref, read-only)

Like NAME but always returns lowercase names.

NAME_uc (array-ref, read-only)

Like NAME but always returns uppercase names.

TYPE (array-ref, read-only) (NEW)

Returns a reference to an array of integer values for each column. The value indicates the datatype of the corresponding column.

The values correspond to the international standards (ANSI X3.135 and ISO/IEC 9075), which, in general terms, means ODBC. Driver-specific types that don't exactly match standard types should generally return the same values as an ODBC driver supplied by the makers of the database. That might include private type numbers in ranges the vendor has officially registered.

For more information, see:

> *ftp://jerry.ece.umassd.edu/isowg3/dbl/SQL_Registry*

Where there's no vendor-supplied ODBC driver to be compatible with, the DBI driver can use type numbers in the range that is now officially reserved for use by the DBI: –9999 to –9000.

All possible values for TYPE should have at least one entry in the output of the type_info_all method (see type_info_all).

PRECISION *(array-ref, read-only) (NEW)*

Returns a reference to an array of integer values for each column. For non-numeric columns, the value generally refers to either the maximum length or the defined length of the column. For numeric columns, the value refers to the maximum number of significant digits used by the datatype (without considering a sign character or decimal point). Note that for floating-point types (REAL, FLOAT, DOUBLE), the "display size" can be up to seven characters greater than the precision. (for the sign + decimal point + the letter E + a sign + two or three digits).

SCALE *(array-ref, read-only) (NEW)*

Returns a reference to an array of integer values for each column. NULL (undef) values indicate columns where scale is not applicable.

NULLABLE *(array-ref, read-only)*

Returns a reference to an array indicating the possibility of each column returning a NULL. Possible values are 0 = no, 1 = yes, 2 = unknown. For example:

```
print "First column may return NULL\n" if $sth->{NULLABLE}->[0];
```

CursorName *(string, read-only)*

Returns the name of the cursor associated with the statement handle, if available. If not available, or if the database driver does not support the "where current of ..." SQL syntax, then it returns undef.

Statement *(string, read-only) (NEW)*

Returns the statement string passed to the prepare method.

RowsInCache (integer, read-only)

If the driver supports a local row cache for SELECT statements, then this attribute holds the number of unfetched rows in the cache. If the driver doesn't, then it returns undef. Note that some drivers pre-fetch rows on execute, whereas others wait till the first fetch.

See also the RowCacheSize database handle attribute.

Further Information

Threads and Thread Safety

Perl versions 5.004_50 and later include optional experimental support for multiple threads on many platforms. If the DBI is built using a Perl that has threads enabled, then it will use a per-driver mutex to ensure that only one thread is with a driver at any one time. Please note that support for threads in Perl is still experimental and is known to have some significant problems. It's use is not recommended.

Signal Handling and Canceling Operations

The first thing to say is that signal handling in Perl is currently *not* safe. There is always a small risk of Perl crashing and/or core dumping during or after handling a signal. (The risk was reduced with 5.004_04 but is still present.)

The two most common uses of signals in relation to the DBI are for canceling operations when the user types Ctrl-C (interrupt), and for implementing a timeout using alarm() and $SIG{ALRM}.

To assist in implementing these operations, the DBI provides a cancel method for statement handles. The cancel method should abort the current operation and is designed to be called from a signal handler.

However, it must be stressed that: a) few drivers implement this functionality at the moment (the DBI provides a default method that just returns undef); and b) even if implemented, there is still a possibility that the statement handle, and possibly the parent database handle, will not be usable afterwards.

If cancel returns true, then it has successfully invoked the database engine's own cancel function. If it returns false, then cancel failed. If it returns undef, then the database engine does not have cancel implemented.

See Also

Driver and Database Documentation

Refer to the documentation for the DBD driver you are using.

Refer to the SQL language reference manual for the database engine you are using.

Books and Journals

Programming the Perl DBI, by Alligator Descartes and Tim Bunce
Programming Perl, 2nd Ed, by Larry Wall, Tom Christiansen, and Randal Schwartz
Learning Perl, by Randal Schwartz
Dr Dobb's Journal, November 1996
The Perl Journal, April 1997

Manual Pages

Consult the *perl* manpage, the *perlmod* manpage, and the *perlbook* manpage.

Mailing List

The *dbi-users* mailing list is the primary means of communication among users of the DBI and its related modules. Subscribe and unsubscribe via:

http://www.isc.org/dbi-lists.html

There are typically between 700 and 900 messages per month. You have to subscribe in order to be able to post. However, you can opt for a "post-only" subscription.

Mailing list archives are held at:

http://www.xray.mpe.mpg.de/mailing-lists/dbi/
http://www.egroups.com/list/dbi-users/info.html
http://www.bitmechanic.com/mail-archives/dbi-users/

Assorted Related WWW Links

The DBI home page:

http://www.symbolstone.org/technology/perl/DBI

Other DBI-related links:

http://tegan.deltanet.com/~phlip/DBUIdoc.html
http://dc.pm.org/perl_db.html

http://wdvl.com/Authoring/DB/Intro/toc.html
http://www.hotwired.com/webmonkey/backend/tutorials/tutorial1.html

Other database-related links:

http://www.jcc.com/sql_stnd.html
http://cuiwww.unige.ch/OSG/info/FreeDB/FreeDB.home.html

Commercial and data warehouse links:

http://www.dwinfocenter.org
http://www.datawarehouse.com
http://www.datamining.org
http://www.olapcouncil.org
http://www.idwa.org
http://www.knowledgecenters.org/dwcenter.asp

Recommended Perl programming link:

http://language.perl.com/style/

FAQ

Please also read the DBI FAQ which is installed as a `DBI::FAQ` module. You can use `perldoc` to read it by executing the `perldoc DBI::FAQ` command.

Authors

DBI was created by Tim Bunce. This text by Tim Bunce, J. Douglas Dunlop, Jonathan Leffler, and others. Perl was created by Larry Wall and the `perl5-porters`.

Copyright

The DBI module is copyright © 1994–2000 Tim Bunce. England. All rights reserved.

You may distribute under the terms of either the GNU General Public License or the Artistic License, as specified in the Perl README file.

Acknowledgments

I would like to acknowledge the valuable contributions of the many people I have worked with on the DBI project, especially in the early years (1992–1994). In no particular order: Kevin Stock, Buzz Moschetti, Kurt Andersen, Ted Lemon, William

Hails, Garth Kennedy, Michael Peppler, Neil S. Briscoe, Jeff Urlwin, David J. Hughes, Jeff Stander, Forrest D. Whitcher, Larry Wall, Jeff Fried, Roy Johnson, Paul Hudson, Georg Rehfeld, Steve Sizemore, Ron Pool, Jon Meek, Tom Christiansen, Steve Baumgarten, Randal Schwartz, and a whole lot more.

Then, of course, there are the poor souls who have struggled through untold and undocumented obstacles to actually implement DBI drivers. Among their ranks are Jochen Wiedmann, Alligator Descartes, Jonathan Leffler, Jeff Urlwin, Michael Peppler, Henrik Tougaard, Edwin Pratomo, Davide Migliavacca, Jan Pazdziora, Peter Haworth, Edmund Mergl, Steve Williams, Thomas Lowery, and Phlip Plumlee. Without them, the DBI would not be the practical reality it is today. I'm also especially grateful to Alligator Descartes for starting work on the *Programming the Perl DBI* book and letting me jump on board.

Translations

A German translation of this text and other Perl module documentation (all probably slightly out-of-date) is available, thanks to O'Reilly, at:

> *http://www.oreilly.de/catalog/perlmodger*

Some other translations:

> *Spanish—http://cronopio.net/perl/*
> *Japanese—http://member.nifty.ne.jp/hippo2000/dbimemo.htm*

Support/Warranty

The DBI is free software. *It comes without warranty of any kind.*

Commercial support for Perl and the DBI, `DBD::Oracle`, and Oraperl modules can be arranged via The Perl Clinic. For more details, visit:

> *http://www.perlclinic.com*

Training

Here are some references to DBI-related training resources (no recommendation implied):

> *http://www.treepax.co.uk/*
> *http://www.keller.com/dbweb/*

B

Driver and Database Characteristics

In this appendix, we hope to give you a flavor of the functionality and quirks of different DBI drivers and their databases.

The line between the functionality and quirks of a given driver and the functionality and quirks of its corresponding database is rather blurred. In some cases, the database has functionality that the driver can't or doesn't access; in others, the driver may emulate functionality that the database doesn't support, such as placeholders. So when you see the terms *driver* or *database* below, take them with a pinch of salt.

Our primary goals are:

- to provide a simple overview of each driver and database.
- to help you initially select a suitable DBI driver and database for your new applications.
- to help you identify potential issues if you need to port an existing application from one driver and database combination to another.

We don't attempt to describe the drivers and databases in detail here, and we're not reproducing their documentation. We're only interested in the key features that are most commonly used or relevant to our goals. And for those features, we're just providing an outline guide, sometimes little more than signposts. Consult the database and driver documentation for full details.

With the cooperation of the driver authors, we have produced descriptions for the following drivers and databases:

DBD::ADO
    Microsoft "Active Data Objects"

DBD::CSV
> General "Comma Separated Value" ASCII files

DBD::DB2
> IBM DB2

DBD::Empress
> Empress

DBD::Informix
> Informix

DBD::Ingres
> Ingres

DBD::InterBase
> InterBase

DBD::mysql & DBD::mSQL
> MySQL and mSQL database

DBD::ODBC
> For any ODBC data source

DBD::Oracle
> Oracle

DBD::Pg
> PostgreSQL

DBD::SearchServer
> Fulcrum Search Server

DBD::Sybase
> For Sybase and Microsoft SQL Server

DBD::XBase
> For XBase files (dBase, etc.)

For each of these drivers, we've tried to cover the same range of topics in the same order.

The topics include:

- Driver summary information
- How to connect
- Supported datatypes, their ranges and functionality
- Variations in SQL dialect and default behaviors
- Advanced database features
- How to access database metadata

Reading straight through is not for the faint-hearted. We recommend dipping in on an as-needed basis.

Acquiring the DBI and Drivers

Before you can use a DBI driver module, you obviously need to get it from somewhere and install it on your system.

If you're on a Microsoft Windows system and using the ActiveState version of Perl, then the first thing to try is their *Perl Package Manager,* or *PPM* for short. The PPM utility is installed with ActiveState Perl and greatly simplifies downloading and installing pre-compiled modules. Installing a DBI driver using PPM also automatically installs the DBI if it's not already installed. For more information refer to:

> *http://www.activestate.com/PPM/*

That simple solution won't work for everyone. If you're not using ActiveState Perl on Microsoft Windows, or the driver you want isn't one that they have pre-compiled for downloading via PPM, then you'll have to travel the longer road: download the source code for the driver and build it yourself. It's usually not as hard as it may sound.

The source code for DBI drivers can be downloaded from any site that is part of the *Comprehensive Perl Archive Network* (CPAN). Here are a few handy URLs to get you started:

> *http://www.perl.com/CPAN/modules/by-module/DBD/*
> *http://www.perl.org/CPAN/modules/by-module/DBD/*
> *http://search.cpan.org/search?mode=module&query=DBD*

If you've not already installed the DBI, then you'll need to do that first. Simply substituting DBI for DBD in the URLs above will take you to the source code for the DBI module.

Remember that many drivers for database systems require some database-specific client software to be installed on the machine in order to be able to build the driver. The driver documentation should explain what's needed.

DBD::ADO

General Information

Driver version

DBD::ADO version 0.03.

At the time of this writing, the DBD::ADO driver, and even ADO itself, are relatively new. Things are bound to change, so be sure to read the latest documentation.

Feature summary

Because DBD::ADO acts as an interface to other lower-level database drivers within Windows, much of its behavior is governed by those drivers.

Transactions	Dependent on connected data source
Locking	Dependent on connected data source
Table joins	Dependent on connected data source
LONG/LOB datatypes	Dependent on connected data source
Statement handle attributes available	After execute()
Placeholders	No, not yet
Stored procedures	Limited support, no parameters
Bind output values	No
Table name letter case	Dependent on connected data source
Field name letter case	Dependent on connected data source
Quoting of otherwise invalid names	Dependent on connected data source
Case-insensitive "LIKE" operator	Dependent on connected data source
Server table ROW ID pseudocolumn	Dependent on connected data source
Positioned update/delete	No
Concurrent use of multiple handles	Dependent on connected data source

Author and contact details

The driver is maintained by Thomas Lowery and Phlip Plumlee. They can be contacted via the *dbi-users* mailing list.

Supported database versions and options

The DBD::ADO module requires Microsoft ADO version 2.1 or later to work reliably. Using NT with Service Pack 4 is recommended. The module is pure Perl, making use of the Win32::OLE module to handle the ADO requests.

The DBD::ADO module supports the use of SQL statements to query any data source your raw ADO supports. This can include the Jet data drivers for the various Microsoft Office file formats, any number of ODBC data drivers, or experimental data providers that expose file system folder hierarchies or Internet directory services as data sources.

Each provider system supports SQL in some format, either in a native format like MS-SQL Server's Transact SQL or as an emulation layer in the data provider, such as a Jet data driver reading an Excel spreadsheet.

Information about ADO can be found at *http://www.microsoft.com/data/ado/*.

Differences from the DBI specification

DBD::ADO is a very new and currently incomplete driver. It is evolving rapidly though, and since it's written in pure Perl using Win32::OLE, it's easy for people to enhance.

Connect Syntax

The `DBI->connect()` Data Source Name, or *DSN*, has the following format:

```
dbi:ADO:DSN
```

DSN must be an ODBC Data Source Name registered with the Control Panel ODBC Data Sources applet. If your DBI application runs as a service or daemon, such as a CGI script, the DSN must appear on the "System DSN" tab.

There are no driver-specific attributes for the `DBI->connect()` method. `DBD::ADO` supports an unlimited number of concurrent data source connections to one or more data sources, subject to the limitations of those data sources.

Datatypes

The numeric, string, date, and LONG/LOB datatypes depend on the interaction of four forces: what a Perl "scalar" supports, how the `Win32::OLE` layer translates VARIANTs into scalars, the types that VARIANT itself permits, and the types your target provider emits.

A user/programmer must research those forces in his or her relevant documentation. Rest assured that `DBD::ADO` will then transmit the type correctly.

Transactions, Isolation, and Locking

`DBD::ADO` reflects the capabilities of the native *connection* to the user. Transactions, if a provider supports them, are per connection—all statements derived from one connection will "see" updates to the data that awaits a `COMMIT` statement. Other connections to that data source will not see these pending updates.

SQL Dialect

Because `DBD::ADO` acts as an interface to other database drivers, the following issues are governed by those drivers and the databases they connect to:

- Case-sensitivity of LIKE operator
- Table join syntax
- Table and column names
- Row ID
- Automatic key or sequence generation
- Automatic row numbering and row count limiting

For more information, refer to the documentation for the drivers and the database being used.

The `DBD::ADO` driver does not support positioned updates and deletes.

Parameter Binding

Parameter binding is not yet supported by DBD::ADO.

Stored Procedures

Calling stored procedures is supported by DBD::ADO using the ODBC style {call procedure_name()} syntax.

Table Metadata

DBD::ADO does not currently support the table_info() method. It awaits the needed slack time and/or other volunteers.

Driver-Specific Attributes and Methods

The ADO *connection* object can be accessed from database and statement handles via the ado_conn attribute.

The ADO *RecordSet* object can be accessed from statement handles via the ado_rs attribute.

DBD::CSV

General Information

Driver version

DBD::CSV version 0.1019

Feature summary

Transactions	No
Locking	Implicit, per-statement only
Table joins	No
LONG/LOB datatypes	Yes, up to 4 GB
Statement handle attributes available	After execute()
Placeholders	Yes, "?" style
Stored procedures	No
Bind output values	No
Table name letter case	Sensitive, partly depends on filesystem
Field name letter case	Sensitive, stored with original letter case
Quoting of otherwise invalid names	No
Case-insensitive "LIKE" operator	Yes, "CLIKE"
Server table ROW ID pseudocolumn	No
Positioned update/delete	No
Concurrent use of multiple handles	Unrestricted

Author and contact details

The driver author is Jochen Wiedmann. He can be contacted via the *dbi-users* mailing list.

Supported database versions and options

The `DBD::CSV` driver is built upon the services of several other related modules. The `Text::CSV_XS` module is used for reading and writing CSV files. The abstract generic `DBD::File` class provides the driver framework for handling *flat files*. That, in turn, uses the `SQL::Statement` module to parse and evaluate simple SQL statements.

It's important to note that while just about everyone thinks they know what the CSV file format is, there is actually no formal definition of the format, and there are many subtle differences.

Here's one description of a CSV file:

> *http://www.whatis.com/csvfile.htm*

Differences from the DBI specification

`DBD::CSV` does not fully parse the statement until it's executed. Thus, attributes like `$sth->{NUM_OF_FIELDS}` are not available until after `$sth->execute()` has been called. This is valid behavior but is important to note when porting applications originally written for other drivers.

The statement handle attributes `PRECISION`, `SCALE`, and `TYPE` are not supported. Also note that many statement attributes cease to be available after fetching all the result rows or calling the `finish()` method.

Connect Syntax

The `DBI->connect()` Data Source Name, or DSN, can be one of the following:

```
dbi:CSV:
dbi:CSV:attrs
```

where `attrs` is an optional semicolon-separated list of *key=value* pairs.

The number of database handles is limited by memory only. It is recommended to use multiple database handles for different table formats.

Commonly used attributes include:

`f_dir=directory`

> By default, files in the current directory are treated as tables. The attribute `f_dir` makes the module open files in the given directory.

```
csv_eol
csv_sep_char
csv_quote_char
csv_escape_char
```

These attributes are used for describing the CSV file format in use. For example, to open */etc/passwd*, which is colon-separated and line-feed terminated, as a table, one would use:

```
csv_eol=\n;csv_sep_char=:
```

The defaults are `\r\n`, comma (`,`), double quote (`"`), and double quote (`"`) respectively. All of these attributes and defaults are inherited from the `Text::CSV_XS` module.

Datatypes

Numeric data handling

Without question, the main disadvantage of the `DBD::CSV` module is the lack of appropriate type handling. While reading a CSV table, you have no way to reliably determine the correct datatype of the fields. All fields look like strings and are treated as such by default.

The `SQL::Statement` module, and hence the `DBD::CSV` driver, accepts the numeric types `INTEGER` and `REAL` in `CREATE TABLE` statements, but they are always stored as strings and, by default, retrieved as strings.

It is possible to read individual columns as integers or doubles, in which case they are converted to Perl's internal datatypes IV and NV—integer and numeric value respectively. Unsigned values are not supported.

To assign certain datatypes to columns, you have to create *metadata definitions*. The following example reads a table *table_name* with columns I, N, and P of type `INTEGER`, `DOUBLE`, and `STRING`, respectively:

```
my $dbh = DBI->connect("DBI:CSV:", '', '');
$dbh->{csv_tables}->{table_name}->{types} = [
    Text::CSV_XS::IV(), Text::CSV_XS::NV(), Text::CSV_XS::PV()
];
my $sth = $dbh->prepare("SELECT id, sales, description FROM table_name");
```

String data handling

Similar to numeric values, `DBD::CSV` accepts more datatypes in `CREATE TABLE` statements than it really supports. You can use `CHAR(n)` and `VARCHAR(n)` with arbitrary numbers n, `BLOB`, or `TEXT`, but in fact these are always `BLOB`s, in a loose kind of way.

The one underlying string type can store any binary data including embedded NUL characters. However, many other CSV tools may choke if given such data.

Date data handling

No date or time types are directly supported.

LONG/BLOB data handling

BLOBs are equivalent to strings. They are only limited in size by available memory.

Other data handling issues

The `type_info()` method is supported.

Transactions, Isolation, and Locking

The driver doesn't support transactions.

No explicit locks are supported. Tables are locked while statements are executed, but the lock is immediately released once the statement is completed.

SQL Dialect

Case sensitivity of LIKE operator

Two different `LIKE` operators are supported. `LIKE` is case-sensitive, whereas `CLIKE` is not.

Table join syntax

Table joins are not supported.

Table and column names

Table and column names are case-sensitive. However, you should consider that table names are in fact filenames, so tables *Foo* and *foo* may both be present with the same data. However, they may be subject to different metadata definitions in `$dbh->{csv_tables}`.

See "Table Metadata" for more details on table and column names.

Row ID

Row IDs are not supported.

Automatic key or sequence generation

Neither automatic keys nor sequences are supported.

Automatic row numbering and row count limiting

Neither automatic row numbering nor row count limitations are supported.

Positioned updates and deletes

Positioned updates and deletes are not supported.

Parameter Binding

Question marks are supported as placeholders, as in:

```
$dbh->do("INSERT INTO A VALUES (?, ?)", undef, $id, $name);
```

The :1 placeholder style is not supported.

Stored Procedures

Stored procedures are not supported.

Table Metadata

By default, the driver expects the column names to be stored in the table's first row, as in:

```
login:password:uid:gid:comment:shell:homedir
root:s34hj34n34jh:0:0:Superuser:/bin/bash:/root
```

If column names are not present, you may specify column names via:

```
$dbh->{csv_tables}->{$table}->{skip_rows} = 0;
$dbh->{csv_tables}->{$table}->{col_names} =
    [qw(login password uid gid comment shell homedir)];
```

in which case the first row is treated as a data row.

If column names are not supplied and not read from the first row, the names *col0*, *col1*, etc. are generated automatically.

Column names can be retrieved via the standard $sth->{NAME} attribute. The NULLABLE attribute returns an array of all ones. Other metadata attributes are not supported.

The table names, or filenames, can be read via $dbh->table_info() or $dbh-> tables() as usual.

Driver-Specific Attributes and Methods

Besides the attributes f_dir, csv_eol, csv_sep_char, csv_quote_char, and csv_sep_char that have already been discussed above, the most important database handle attribute is:

```
$dbh->{csv_tables}
```

`csv_tables` is used for specifying table metadata. It is a hash ref with table names as keys, the values being hash refs with the following attributes:

`file`
> The filename being associated with the table. By default, the file name is `$dbh->{f_dir}/$table`.

`col_names`
> An array ref of column names.

`skip_rows`
> This number of rows will be read from the top of the file before reading the table data, and the first of those will be treated as an array of column names. However, the `col_names` attribute takes precedence.

`types`
> This is an array ref of the `Text::CSV_XS` type values for the corresponding columns. Three types are supported and their values are defined by the `IV()`, `NV()`, and `PV()` functions in the `Text::CSV_XS` package.

There are no driver-specific statement handle attributes and no private methods for either type of handle.

DBD::DB2

General Information

Driver version

`DBD::DB2` version 0.71

Feature summary

Transactions	Yes
Locking	Yes, implicit and explicit
Table joins	Yes, inner and outer
LONG/LOB datatypes	Yes, up to 2 GB
Statement handle attributes available	After prepare()
Placeholders	Yes, "?" (native)
Stored procedures	Yes
Bind output values	No
Table name letter case	Insensitive, stored as uppercase
Field name letter case	Insensitive, stored as uppercase
Quoting of otherwise invalid names	Yes, via double quotes
Case-insensitive "LIKE" operator	No
Server table ROW ID pseudocolumn	No
Positioned update/delete	Yes
Concurrent use of multiple handles	Unrestricted

Author and contact details

Support for the DBD::DB2 driver is provided by IBM through its service agreements for DB2 UDB. Any comments, suggestions, or enhancement requests can be sent via email to *db2perl@ca.ibm.com*. Please see the web site at:

> *http://www.ibm.com/data/db2/perl*

for more information.

Supported database versions and options

The DBD::DB2 driver supports DB2 UDB V5.2 and later.

Here are some URLs to more database/driver-specific information:

> *http://www.software.ibm.com/data/db2/perl*
> *http://www.software.ibm.com/data/db2*
> *http://www.software.ibm.com/data/db2/library*
> *http://www.software.ibm.com/data/db2/udb/ad*

Differences from the DBI specification

The only significant difference in behavior from the current DBI specification is the way in which datatypes are specified in the bind_param() method. Please see the information later in this section of the document about using the bind_param() method with the DBD::DB2 driver.

Connect Syntax

The DBI->connect() Data Source Name, or DSN, is specified as follows:

```
dbi:DB2:database_name
```

There are no driver-specific attributes for the DBI->connect() method.

DBD::DB2 supports concurrent database connections to one or more databases

Datatypes

Numeric data handling

DB2 UDB supports the following numeric datatypes:

```
SMALLINT
INTEGER
BIGINT
REAL
DOUBLE
FLOAT
DECIMAL or NUMERIC
```

A `SMALLINT` is a two-byte integer than can range from –32768 to +32767. The maximum precision is 5. Scale is not applicable.

An `INTEGER` is a four-byte integer that can range from –2147483648 to +2147483647. The maximum precision is 10. Scale is not applicable.

A `BIGINT` is an eight-byte integer that can range from –9223372036854775808 to +9223372036854775807. The maximum precision is 19. Scale is not applicable.

A `REAL` is a 32-bit approximation of a real number. The number can be 0 or can range from –3.402e+38 to –1.175e–37, or from +1.175e–37 to +3.402e+38. The maximum precision is 7. Scale is not applicable.

A `DOUBLE` or `FLOAT` is a 64-bit approximation of a real number. The number can be 0 or can range from –1.79769e+308 to –2.225e–307, or from 2.225e–307 to 1.79769e+308. The maximum precision is 15. Scale is not applicable.

A `DECIMAL` or `NUMERIC` value is a packed decimal number with an implicit decimal point that can range from –10**31+1 to +10**31–1. The maximum precision is 31 digits. The scale cannot be negative or greater than the precision.

Notice that DB2 supports numbers outside the typical valid range for Perl numbers. This isn't a major problem because `DBD::DB2` always returns all numbers as strings.

String data handling

DB2 UDB supports the following string datatypes:

```
CHAR
CHAR FOR BIT DATA
VARCHAR
VARCHAR FOR BIT DATA
GRAPHIC
VARGRAPHIC
```

`CHAR` is a fixed-length character string that can be up to 254 bytes long. `VARCHAR` is a variable-length character string that can be up to 32672 bytes. The `FOR BIT DATA` variants are used for data not associated with a particular coded character set.

`GRAPHIC` is a fixed-length string of double-byte characters that can be up to 127 characters long.

`VARGRAPHIC` is a variable-length string of double-byte characters that can be up to 16336 characters long.

The `CHAR` and `GRAPHIC` types are fixed-length strings, padded with blanks.

For DB2 UDB, `CHAR` fields can be in mixed codesets (national character sets). The non-ASCII characters are handled according to the mixed code page definition. For example, Shift-JIS characters in the range 0x81 to 0x9F and 0xE0 to 0xFC are DBCS introducer bytes, and characters in the range 0xA0 to 0xDF are single-byte Katakana characters. Blank padding for CHAR fields is always with ASCII blank (single-byte blank). For UTF-8, characters with the sign bit set are interpreted according to the UTF-8 definition.

GRAPHIC datatypes are stored as pure double-byte in the default code page of the database, or in UCS-2 in the case of a Unicode database. Blank padding for GRAPHIC fields is always with the DBCS blank of the corresponding code page, or with the UCS-2 blank (U+0020) in the case of a Unicode database.

Code page conversions between the client code page and the database code page are automatically performed by DB2 UDB.

Unicode support is provided with DB2 UDB Version 5 + FixPak 7 (DB2 UDB V5.2 is actually DB2 UDB V5 + FixPak 6). In a Unicode database, CHAR datatypes are stored in UTF-8 format and GRAPHIC datatypes are stored in UCS-2 format.

With DB2 UDB Version 6.1, the VARCHAR() function has been extended to convert graphic string datatypes to a VARCHAR, with the exception of LONG VARGRAPHIC and DBCLOB. This function is valid for UCS-2 databases only. For non-Unicode databases, this is not allowed.

All character types can store strings with embedded nul("\0") bytes.

Strings can be concatenated using the || operator or the CONCAT(s1,s2) SQL function.

Date data handling

DB2 UDB supports the following date, time, and date/time datatypes:

```
DATE
TIME
TIMESTAMP
```

DATE is a three-part value consisting of year, month, and day. The range of the year part is 0001 to 9999. Two-digit years cannot be used with DB2 UDB. Years must be specified with all four digits.

TIME is a three-part value consisting of hour, minute, and second designates a time of day under a 24-hour clock.

TIMESTAMP is a seven-part value, consisting of year, month, day, hour, minute, second, and microsecond, that designates a date and time as defined above, except that the time includes a fractional specification of microseconds. If you specify a TIMESTAMP value without a time component, the default time is 00:00:00 (midnight).

The current date, time, and date/time can be retrieved using the CURRENT DATE, CURRENT TIME, and CURRENT TIMESTAMP special registers.

DB2 UDB supports the following date, time, and date/time formats:

```
ISO    (International Standards Organization)
USA    (IBM USA standard)
EUR    (IBM European standard)
JIS    (Japanese Industrial Standard Christian era)
LOC    (site-defined, depends on database country code)
```

You can input date and date/time values in any supported format. For example:

```
create table datetest(dt date);
insert into datetest('1991-10-27');
insert into datetest('10/27/1991');
```

The default output format for DATE, TIME, and TIMESTAMP is that format that is associated with the country code of the database (LOC format above). You can use the CHAR() function and specify an alternate format.

Datetime values can be incremented, decremented, and subtracted. DB2 UDB provides a wide range of date functions including DAY(), DAYOFWEEK(), DAYOFYEAR(), MONTHNAME(), and TIMESTAMPDIFF(). See the DB2 UDB documentation for additional functions.

The following SQL expression can be used to convert an integer "seconds since 1-jan-1970" value to the corresponding database date/time (local time not GMT):

```
TIMESTAMP('1970-01-01','00:00') + seconds_since_epoch
```

There is no simple expression that will do the reverse. Subtracting time-stamp('1970-01-01','00:00') from another timestamp gives a timestamp duration which is a DECIMAL(20,6) value with format yyyymmddhhmmss.zzzzzz.

DB2 does no automatic time zone adjustments.

LONG/BLOB data handling

DB2 UDB supports the following LONG/BLOB datatypes:

```
BLOB
CLOB
DBCLOB
LONG VARCHAR
LONG VARCHAR FOR BIT DATA
LONG VARGRAPHIC
```

BLOB (binary large object) is a variable-length string measured in bytes that can be up to 2 GB long. A BLOB is primarily intended to hold non-traditional data such as pictures, voice, and mixed media. BLOBs are not associated with a coded character set (similar to FOR BIT DATA character strings; see below).

CLOB (character large object) is a variable-length string measured in bytes that can be up to 2 GB long. A CLOB is used to store large character-based data.

DBCLOB (double-byte character large object) is a variable-length string of double-byte characters that can be up to 1,073,741,823 characters long. A DBCLOB is used to store large DBCS character based data.

LONG VARCHAR is a variable-length character string that can be up to 32,700 bytes long. LONG VARCHAR FOR BIT DATA is used for data not associated with a coded character set.

LONG VARGRAPHIC is a variable-length string of double-byte characters that can be up to 16,350 characters long.

None of these types need to be passed to and from the database as pairs of hex digits.

Sadly, the DBD::DB2 driver does not yet support the LongReadLen and Long-TruncOk attributes. Values of any length can be inserted and fetched up to the maximum size of the corresponding datatype although system resources may be a constraint.

The DBD::DB2 driver is unusual in that it requires heavy use of bind parameter attributes both for ordinary types and for LONG/BLOB types. (See the "Parameter Binding" section for discussion on attribute hashes.) For example, here's an attribute hash for a CLOB, which will have a maximum length of 100K in this particular application:

```
$attrib_clob = {
  ParamT => SQL_PARAM_INPUT,
  Ctype  => SQL_C_CHAR,
  Stype  => SQL_CLOB,
  Prec   => 100000
  Scale  => 0,
};
```

Other data handling issues

The DBD::DB2 driver does not yet support the type_info() method.

DB2 UDB does not automatically convert strings to numbers or numbers to strings.

Transactions, Isolation, and Locking

DB2 UDB supports transactions and four transaction isolation levels: Repeatable Read, Read Stability, Cursor Stability, Uncommited Read. The default transaction isolation level is Cursor Stability.

For the DBD::DB2 driver, the isolation level can be changed by setting the TXNISOLATION keyword in the *db2cli.ini* file to the desired value. This keyword is set in a database-specific section, meaning that it will affect all applications that connect to that particular database. There is no way to change the isolation level from SQL.

The default behavior for reading and writing is based on the isolation level. Rows returned by a `SELECT` statement can be explicitly locked by appending `FOR UPDATE` and a list of field names to the `SELECT` statement. For example:

```
SELECT colname1, colname2
FROM tablename
WHERE colname1 = 'testvalue'
FOR UPDATE OF colname1, colname2
```

The `LOCK TABLE table_name IN lock_mode` statement can be used to apply an explicit lock on an entire table.

SQL Dialect

Case sensitivity of LIKE operator

The `LIKE` operator is case-sensitive.

Table join syntax

You can perform an equi-join, or inner join, using the standard `WHERE a.field = b.field` syntax. You can also use the following syntax:

```
SELECT tablea.col1, tableb.col1
FROM tablea INNER JOIN tableb
ON tableb.name = tablea.name
```

DB2 UDB supports left outer joins, right outer joins, and full outer joins. For example, to perform a left outer join, you can use the following statement:

```
SELECT tablea.col1, tablea.col2, tableb.col1, tableb.col2
FROM tablea LEFT OUTER JOIN tableb
ON tableb.name = tablea.name
```

Changing "LEFT" to "RIGHT" or "FULL" gives you the other forms of outer join.

Table and column names

In DB2 UDB Version 5.2, the maximum length of table names and column names is 18. In DB2 UDB Version 6.1, the maximum length of table names will be increased to 128 and the maximum length of column names will be increased to 30.

The first character must be a letter, but the rest can be any combination of upper-case letters, digits, and underscores.

Table and field names can be delimited by double quotes (") and can contain the same characters as described above plus lowercase letters.

Table and column names are stored as uppercase in the catalogs unless delimited. Delimited identifiers preserve the case. Two consecutive quotation marks are used to represent one quotation mark within the delimited identifier.

National characters can be used in table and column names.

Row ID

DB2 UDB does not support a "table row ID" pseudocolumn.

Automatic key or sequence generation

The GENERATE_UNIQUE function can be used to provide unique values (keys) in a table. For example:

```
CREATE TABLE EMP_UPDATE (
   UNIQUE_ID CHAR(13) FOR BIT DATA,  -- note the "FOR BIT DATA"
   EMPNO CHAR(6),
   TEXT VARCHAR(1000)
)
INSERT INTO EMP_UPDATE VALUES
   (GENERATE_UNIQUE(), '000020', 'Update entry...'),
   (GENERATE_UNIQUE(), '000050', 'Update entry...')
```

Sadly, DB2 does not provide any way to discover the most recent value generated by GENERATE_UNIQUE.

DB2 UDB does not support named sequence generators.

Automatic row numbering and row count limiting

There is no pseudocolumn that can be used to sequentially number the rows fetched by a SELECT statement. However, you can number the rows of a result set using the OLAP function ROWNUMBER. For example:

```
SELECT ROWNUMBER() OVER (order by lastname) AS number, lastname, salary
FROM employee ORDER BY number;
```

This returns the rows of the employee table with numbers assigned according to the ascending order of last names, ordered by the row numbers.

A cursor can be declared with the FETCH FIRST n ROWS ONLY clause to limit the number of rows returned.

Positioned updates and deletes

DB2 UDB supports positioned updates and deletes. Since specific testing of this functionality has not been done with the DBD::DB2 driver, it's not officially supported; however, no problems are anticipated.

The syntax for a positioned update is as follows. DELETE has a similar syntax.

```
"UPDATE ... WHERE CURRENT OF $sth->{CursorName}"
```

Parameter Binding

Parameter binding is directly supported by DB2 UDB. Only the standard ? style of placeholders is supported.

The DBD::DB2 driver does not support the TYPE attribute exactly as described in the DBI documentation. Attribute hashes are used to pass type information to the bind_param() method. An attribute hash is simply a collection of information about a particular type of data. (See the DBD::DB2 documentation for a list of pre-defined attribute hashes).

The following is an example of how a complete new attribute hash can be created:

```
$attrib_char = {
  ParamT => SQL_PARAM_INPUT,
  Ctype  => SQL_C_CHAR,
  Stype  => SQL_CHAR,
  Prec   => 254,
  Scale  => 0,
};
```

Stored Procedures

Stored procedures are invoked by using the following SQL syntax:

```
CALL procedure-name(argument, ...)
```

Table Metadata

DBD::DB2 does not yet support the table_info() method.

The SYSCAT.COLUMNS view contains one row for each column that is defined for all tables and views in the database.

The SYSCAT.INDEXES view contains one row for each index that is defined for all tables in a database. Primary keys are implemented as unique indexes.

Driver-Specific Attributes and Methods

DBD::DB2 has no driver-specific attributes or methods.

DBD::Empress and DBD::EmpressNet

General Information

Driver version

DBD::Empress version 0.51.

Feature summary

Transactions	Yes
Locking	Yes, implicit and explicit
Table joins	Yes, inner and outer
LONG/LOB datatypes	Yes, up to 2 GB
Statement handle attributes available	After prepare()
Placeholders	Yes, "?" (native)
Stored procedures	Yes
Bind output values	No
Table name letter case	Sensitive, stored as defined
Field name letter case	Sensitive, stored as defined
Quoting of otherwise invalid names	Yes, via double quotes
Case-insensitive "LIKE" operator	Yes, "MATCH"
Server table ROW ID pseudocolumn	Yes, "MS_RECORD_NUMBER"
Positioned update/delete	No
Concurrent use of multiple handles	Yes, with some restrictions

Author and contact details

The driver was written by Steve Williams. He can be contacted at *swilliam@ empress.com*.

Supported database versions and options

`DBD::Empress` supports Empress V6.10 and later. For further information refer to:

http://www.empress.com

These drivers use the same Perl interface but use a different underlying database interface. `DBD::Empress` is for direct access of databases, while `DBD::Empress-Net` is for distibuted database connected via the Empress Connectivity Server (referred to in Empress v8.10 and earlier as the Empress ODBC server).

Differences from the DBI specification

There are no significant differences.

Connect Syntax

The `DBI->connect()` Data Source Name, or DSN, can be one of the following:

```
dbi:Empress:physical_database
dbi:EmpressNet:logical_database
dbi:EmpressNet:SERVER=server_name;DATABASE=physical_database;PORT=port_number
```

There are no driver-specific attributes for the `DBI->connect()` method.

`DBD::EmpressNet` supports an unlimited number of concurrent database connections to one or more databases.

`DBD::Empress` also supports multiple concurrent database connections to one or more databases. However, these connections are simulated, and there are therefore a number of limitations. Most of these limitations are associated with transaction processing: 1) `AutoCommit` must be on or off for all connections; and 2) Switching processing from one database to another automatically commits any transactions on the first database.

Datatypes

Numeric data handling

Empress RDBMS supports the following numeric datatypes:

```
DECIMAL(p,s)      1 to 15 digits
DOLLAR(p,type)    1 to 13 digits
REAL              Typically 4-byte single precision float
FLOAT(p)          Typically 4 or 8-byte float as required
LONGFLOAT         Typically 8-byte double precision float
SHORTINTEGER            -127 to 127
INTEGER              -32767 to 32767
LONGINTEGER      -2147483647 to 2147483647
```

The DBD driver supports Empress Generic datatypes only. This means that all data for a specific group will be retrieved as the same datatype. For example, `SHORTINTEGER`, `INTEGER`, and `LONGINTEGER` will all be retrieved as `LONG-INTEGER`.

`DBD::Empress` always returns all numbers as strings.

String data handling

Empress RDBMS supports the following string datatypes:

```
CHAR (length, type)
NLSCHAR (length, type)
TEXT (display_length, primary, overflow, extent)
NLSTEXT (display_length, primary, overflow, extent)
```

All arguments have default values. See Empress SQL Reference (A4) for details. The maximum size for all string types is typically $2**31–1$ bytes (2 GB). None of the string types are blank padded.

`NLSCHAR` and `NLSTEXT` are can be used for storage of 8-bit and multibyte characters but UTF-8 is not currently supported.

Strings can be concatenated using the `s1 CONCAT(s2)` SQL function.

Date data handling

Empress RDBMS supports the following date/time datatypes:

```
DATE(t)             = 0000-01-01 to 9999-12-31 at 1 day resolution
TIME(t)             = 1970-01-01 to 2035-12-31 at 1 second resolution
MICROTIMESTAMP(t)   = 0000-01-01 to 9999-12-31 at 1 microsecond resolution
```

The (t) is the format type for default output. This is one of the nine types defined in the section on date/time formats.

Empress supports nine formats for date/time types:

Type	Date	Time	MicroTimestamp
0	yyyymmdd	yyyymmddhhmmss	yyyymmddhhmmssffffff
1	dd aaaaaaaaa yyyy	dd aaaaaaaaa yyyy hh:mm:ss	dd aaaaaaaaa yyyy hh:mm:ss. fffff
2	aaaaaaaaa dd, yyyy	aaaaaaaaa dd, yyyy hh:mm:ss	aaaaaaaaa dd, yyyy hh:mm: ss.fffff
3	mm/dd/yy	mm/dd/yy hh:mm:ss	mm/dd/yy hh:mm:ss.ffffff
4	dd/mm/yy	dd/mm/yy hh:mm:ss	dd/mm/yy hh:mm:ss.ffffff
5	dd aaa yy	dd aaa yy hh:mm:ss	dd aaa yy hh:mm:ss.ffffff
6	aaa dd, yy	aaa dd, yy hh:mm:ss	aaa dd, yy hh:mm:ss.fffff
7	mm/dd/yyyy	mm/dd/yyyy hh:mm:ss	mm/dd/yyyy hh:mm:ss.ffffff
8	dd/mm/yyyy	dd/mm/yyyy hh:mm:ss	dd/mm/yyyy hh:mm:ss.ffffff

The date part for all types is not optional. If you specify a value without a time component, the default time is 00:00:00 (midnight). If only two digits of the year are input, then the century pivots on the Empress variable MSDATELIMIT. For Empress v8.*xx* and above, the default for this is 1950. Earlier versions of Empress defaulted to 1900.

Empress accepts any of the nine specified types as input. The only limitation is that you cannot insert a four-digit year into a date type that uses a two-digit format. It always uses MSDATELIMIT for input dates.

For output, DBD::Empress uses just yyyymmddhhmmssffffff and DBD:: EmpressNet uses just yyyy-mm-dd hh:mm:ss.ffffff. Empress does not support changing of the default display formats. It is not possible to format a date/time value in other styles for output. The best approach is to select the components of the date/time, using SQL functions like DAYOF(d) and MONTHOF(d), and format them using Perl.

The current date/time at the server, can be obtained using the NOW or TODAY pseudo constants. NOW returns the current date and time. TODAY returns the date portion only.

Date and time arithmetic can be done using the Empress date/time operators. For example:

```
NOW + 2 MINUTES + 5 SECONDS
TODAY - 3 DAYS
```

Empress provides a wide range of date functions including DAYOF(), MONTHOF(), YEAROF(), HOUROF(), MINUTEOF(), SECONDOF(), WEEKOFYEAR(), DAYNAME(), DAYOFWEEK(), DAYOFYEAR(), and DATENEXT().

The following SQL expression:

```
'1 jan 1970' + unix_time_field SECONDS
```

would convert to a local time from 1 Jan 1970, but the GMT base cannot be generated directly.

The number of seconds since 1 Jan 1970 for date granularity can be obtained for the local time zone (not GMT) using:

```
(date_field - '1 jan 1970') * 86400
```

Empress does no automatic time zone adjustments.

LONG/BLOB data handling

Empress RDBMS supports the following LONG datatypes:

```
TEXT      Variable length 7-bit character data
NLSTEXT   As TEXT but allows 8-bit characters
BULK      User Interpreted (Byte Stream)
```

The maximum size for all these types is typically $2^{**}31-1$ bytes (2 GB).

LongReadLen works as defined for DBD::EmpressNet but is ignored for DBD::Empress. The maximum LongReadLen is limited to 2 GB typically. LongTruncOk is not implemented.

No special handling is required for binding LONG/BLOB datatypes. The TYPE attribute is currently not used when binding parameters. The maximum length of bind_param() parameters is limited by the capabilities of the OS or the size of the C int, whichever comes first.

Other data handling issues

The type_info() method is not supported.

Empress automatically converts strings to numbers and dates, and numbers and dates to strings, as needed.

Transactions, Isolation, and Locking

DBD::Empress supports transactions. The default isolation level is Serializable.

Other transaction isolation levels are not explicitly supported. However Read Uncommited is supported on a single query basis. This is activated by adding the BYPASS option into each SQL statement.

For example:

```
SELECT BYPASS * FROM table_name
```

Record level locking is the default. Read locks do not block other read locks, but read locks block write locks, and write locks block all other locks. Write locks can be bypassed for read using the BYPASS option.

When in transaction mode (AutoCommit off), selected rows are automatically locked against update unless the BYPASS option is used in the SELECT statement.

The LOCK TABLE table_name IN lock_mode statement can be used to apply an explicit lock on a table. Lock mode can be EXCLUSIVE or SHARE. SHARE requires the user to have SELECT or UPDATE privileges on the table. EXCLUSIVE requires the user to have UPDATE, INSERT, or DELETE privileges.

SQL Dialect

Case sensitivity of LIKE operator

The LIKE operator is case-sensitive. The MATCH operator is case-insensitive.

Table join syntax

For outer joins, the Empress keyword OUTER should be placed before the table(s) that should drive the outer join. For example:

```
SELECT customer_name, order_date
FROM OUTER customers, orders
WHERE customers.cust_id = orders.cust_id;
```

This returns all the rows in the customer's table that have no matching rows in the orders table. Empress returns NULL for any select list expressions containing columns from the orders table.

Table and Column Names

The names of Empress identifiers, such as tables and columns, cannot exceed 32 characters in length. The first character must be a letter, but the rest can be any combination of letters, numerals, and underscores (_). Empress table/column names are stored as defined. They are case-sensitive.

Empress tables and fields can contain most ASCII characters (except $ and ?) if they are quoted.

Any ISO-Latin characters can be used in the base product. Specific products for other languages, such as Japanese, can handle those character sets.

Row ID

A table row identifier can be referenced as MS_RECORD_NUMBER. It can be treated as a string during fetch; however, it must be treated as an integer when it is used in a WHERE clause. It is useful only for explicit fetch; inequalities are not allowed.

```
SELECT * FROM table_name WHERE MS_RECORD_NUMBER = ?
```

Automatic key or sequence generation

Empress has no "auto increment" or "system generated" key mechanism, and does not support sequence generators.

Automatic row numbering and row count limiting

Neither automatic row numbering nor row count limitations are supported.

Positioned updates and deletes

Positioned updates and deletes are not supported.

Parameter Binding

Parameter binding is directly supported by Empress. Only the standard ? style of placeholders is supported.

DBD::Empress recognizes the bind_param() TYPE attribute SQL_BINARY. All other types are automatically bound correctly without TYPE being used. Unsupported types are ignored without warning.

Stored Procedures

DBD::Empress does not explicitly support stored procedures. Implicit support is available for stored procedures in SQL statements. For example:

```
$sth->prepare("SELECT func(attribute) FROM table_name");
```

Table Metadata

DBD::Empress does not support the table_info() method.

The SYS_ATTRS and SYS_TABLES system tables can be used to obtain detailed information about the columns of a table. For example:

```
SELECT * FROM sys_attrs
WHERE attr_tabnum = (SELECT tab_number FROM sys_tables WHERE tab_name='x')
```

However, this requires SELECT privileges on these system tables.

Detailed information about indices or keys cannot currently be easily retrieved though DBD::Empress. It is possible, though difficult, to interpret the contents of the system tables to obtain this information.

Driver-Specific Attributes and Methods

DBD::Empress has no significant driver-specific handle attributes or private methods.

DBD::Informix

General Information

Driver version

DBD::Informix version 0.62.

Feature summary

Transactions	Yes, if enabled when database was created
Locking	Yes, implicit and explicit
Table joins	Yes, inner and outer
LONG/LOB datatypes	Yes, up to 2 GB
Statement handle attributes available	After prepare()
Placeholders	Yes, "?" (native)
Stored procedures	Yes
Bind output values	Yes
Table name letter case	Configurable
Field name letter case	Configurable
Quoting of otherwise invalid names	Yes, via double quotes
Case-insensitive "LIKE" operator	No
Server table ROW ID pseudocolumn	Yes, "ROWID"
Positioned update/delete	Yes
Concurrent use of multiple handles	Unrestricted

Author and contact details

The driver author is Jonathan Leffler. He can be contacted via the *dbi-users* mailing list.

Supported database versions and options

The DBD::Informix module supports Informix OnLine and SE from version 5.00 onwards. There are some restrictions in the support for IUS (a.k.a., IDS/UDO). It uses Informix-ESQL/C (a.k.a., Informix ClientSDK). You must have a development license for Informix-ESQL/C (or the C-code version of Informix-4GL) to be able to compile the DBD::Informix code.

For more information, refer to:

http://www.informix.com
http://www.iiug.org

Differences from the DBI Specification

If you change `AutoCommit` after preparing a statement, you will probably run into problems that you don't expect. So don't do that.

See the `DBD::Informix` documentation for more details on this and other assorted subtle compatibility issues.

Connect Syntax

The `DBI->connect()` Data Source Name, or DSN, has the following form:

```
dbi:Informix:connect_string
```

where `connect_string` is any valid string that can be passed to the Informix `CONNECT` statement (or to the `DATABASE` statement for version 5.*x* systems). The acceptable notations include:

```
dbase
dbase@server
@server
/path/to/dbase
//machine/path/to/dbase
```

There are no driver-specific attributes for the `DBI->connect()` method.

If you're using version 6.00 or later of ESQL/C, then the number of database handles is limited only by your imagination and the computer's physical constraints. If you're using 5.*x*, you're stuck with one connection at a time.

Datatypes

Numeric data handling

Informix supports these numeric datatypes:

```
INTEGER            - signed 32-bit integer, excluding -2**31
SERIAL             - synonym for INTEGER as far as scale is concerned
SMALLINT           - signed 16-bit integer, excluding -2**15
FLOAT              - Native C 'double'
SMALLFLOAT         - Native C 'float'
REAL               - Synonym for SMALLFLOAT
DOUBLE PRECISION   - Synonym for FLOAT
DECIMAL(s)         - s-digit floating point number (non-ANSI databases)
DECIMAL(s)         - s-digit integer (MODE ANSI databases)
DECIMAL(s,p)       - s-digit fixed-point number with p decimal places
MONEY(s)           - s-digit fixed-point number with 2 decimal places
MONEY(s,p)         - s-digit fixed-point number with p decimal places
NUMERIC(s)         - synonym for DECIMAL(s)
NUMERIC(s,p)       - synonym for DECIMAL(s,p)
INT8               - signed 64-bit integer, excluding -2**63 (IDS/UDO)
SERIAL8            - synonym for INT8 as far as scale is concerned
```

DBD::Informix always returns all numbers as strings. Thus the driver puts no restriction on size of PRECISION or SCALE.

String data handling

Informix supports the following string datatypes:

```
VARCHAR(size)
NVARCHAR(size)
CHAR
CHAR(size)
NCHAR
NCHAR(size)
CHARACTER VARYING(size)
NATIONAL CHARACTER VARYING(size)
NATIONAL CHARACTER(size)
CHARACTER(size)
VARCHAR(size,min)    -- and synonyms for this type
NVARCHAR(size,min)   -- and synonyms for this type
LVARCHAR             -- IDS/UDO only
```

Arguably, TEXT and BYTE blobs should also be listed here, as they are automatically converted from/to strings.

CHAR types have a limit of 32767 bytes in OnLine and IDS and a slightly smaller value (325*xx*) for SE. For VARCHAR types, the limit is 255. LVARCHAR columns are limited to 2 KB; when used to transfer other datatypes, up to 32 KB. DBD::Informix 0.61 doesn't have fully operational LVARCHAR support.

The CHAR and NCHAR types are fixed-length and blank-padded.

Handling of national character sets depends on the database version (and is different for versions 5, for versions 6 and 7.1*x*, and for versions 7.2*x* and later). Details for version 8.*x* vary depending on *x*. It depends on the locale, determined by a wide range of standard (e.g., LANG, LC_COLLATE) and non-standard (e.g., DBNLS, CLIENT_LOCALE) environment variables. For details, read the relevant manual. Unicode is not currently directly supported by Informix (as of 1999-02-28).

Strings can be concatenated using the || operator.

Date data handling

There are two basic date/time handling types: DATE and DATETIME. DATE supports dates in the range 01/01/0001 through 31/12/9999. It is fairly flexible in its input and output formats. Internally, it is represented by the number of days since December 31 1899, so January 1 1900 was day 1. It does not understand the calendric gyrations of 1752, 1582-4, or the early parts of the first millenium, and imposes the calendar as of 1970-01-01 on these earlier times.

DATETIME has to be qualified by two components from the set:

```
YEAR MONTH DAY HOUR MINUTE SECOND FRACTION FRACTION(n) for n = 1..5
```

These store a date using ISO 8601 format for the constants. For example, DATE("29/02/2000") is equivalent to:

```
DATETIME("2000-02-29") YEAR TO DAY,
```

and The Epoch for POSIX systems can be expressed as:

```
DATETIME(1970-01-01 00:00:00) YEAR TO SECOND
```

There is no direct support for time zones.

The default date/time format depends on the environment locale settings and the version and the datatype. The DATETIME types are rigidly ISO 8601 except for converting one-digit or two-digit years to a four-digit equivalent, subject to version and environment.

Handling of two-digit years depends on the version, the bugs fixed, and the environment. In general terms (for current software), if the environment variable DBCENTURY is unset or is set to 'R', then the current century is used. If DBCENTURY is 'F', the date will be in the future; if DBCENTURY is 'P', it will be in the past; if DBCENTURY is 'C', it will be the closest date (50-year window, based on current day, month and year, with the time of day untested).

The current datetime is returned by the CURRENT function, usually qualified as CURRENT YEAR TO SECOND.

Informix provides no simple way to input or output dates and times in other formats. Whole chapters can be written on this subject.

Informix supports a draft version of the SQL2 INTERVAL datatype:

```
INTERVAL start[(p1)] [TO end[(p2)]]
```

(Where [] indicates optional parts.)

The following interval qualifications are possible:

```
YEAR, YEAR TO MONTH,
MONTH,
DAY, DAY TO HOUR, DAY TO MINUTE, DAY TO SECOND,
HOUR, HOUR TO MINUTE, HOUR TO SECOND,
MINUTE, MINUTE TO SECOND,
SECOND, FRACTION
```

p1 specifies the number of digits specified in the most significant unit of the value, with a maximum of 9 and a default of 2 (except YEAR that defaults to 4). p2 specifies the number of digits in fractional seconds, with a maximum of 5 and a default of 3.

Literal interval values may be specified using the following syntax:

```
INTERVAL value start[(p1)] [TO end[(p2)]]
```

For example:

```
INTERVAL(2) DAY
INTERVAL(02:03) HOUR TO MINUTE
INTERVAL(12345:67.891) MINUTE(5) TO FRACTION(3)
```

The expression "2 UNITS DAY" is equivalent to the first of these, and similar expressions can be used for any of the basic types.

A full range of operations can be performed on dates and intervals, e.g., datetime-datetime=interval, datetime+interval=datetime, interval/number=interval.

The following SQL expression can be used to convert an integer "seconds since 1-jan-1970 GMT" value to the corresponding database date/time:

```
DATETIME(1970-01-01 00:00:00) YEAR TO SECOND + seconds_since_epoch UNITS SECOND
```

There is no simple expression for inline use that will do the reverse. Use a stored procedure; see the *comp.databases.informix* archives at DejaNews, or the Informix International Users Group (IIUG) web site at *http://www.iiug.org*.

Informix does not handle multiple time zones in a simple manner.

LONG/BLOB data handling

Informix supports the following large object types:

```
BYTE  - binary data     max 2 GB
TEXT  - text data       max 2 GB
BLOB  - binary data     max 2 GB (maybe bigger); IDS/UDO only
CLOB  - character data  max 2 GB (maybe bigger); IDS/UDO only
```

DBD::Informix does not currently have support for BLOB and CLOB datatypes, but does support the BYTE and TEXT types.

The DBI LongReadLen and LongTruncOk attributes are not implemented. If the data selected is a BYTE or TEXT type, then the data is stored in the relevant Perl variable, unconstrained by anything except memory up to a limit of 2 GB.

The maximum length of bind_param() parameter value that can be used to insert BYTE or TEXT data is 2 GB. No specialized treatment is necessary for fetch or insert. UPDATE simply doesn't work.

The bind_param() method doesn't pay attention to the TYPE attribute. Instead, the string presented will be converted automatically to the required type. If it isn't a string type, it needs to be convertible by whichever bit of the system ends up doing the conversion. UPDATE can't be used with these types in DBD::Informix; only version 7.30 IDS provides the data necessary to be able to handle blobs.

Other data handling issues

The `type_info()` method is not supported.

Non-BLOB types can be automatically converted to and from strings most of the time. Informix also supports automatic conversions between pure numeric datatypes whereever it is reasonable. Converting from `DATETIME` or `INTERVAL` to numeric datatypes is not automatic.

Transactions, Isolation, and Locking

Informix databases can be created with or without transaction support.

Informix supports several transaction isolation levels: REPEATABLE READ, CURSOR STABILITY, COMMITTED READ, and DIRTY READ. Refer to the Informix documentation for their exact meaning. Isolation levels apply only to ONLINE and IDS and relatives; SE supports only a level somewhere in between COMMITTED READ and DIRTY READ.

The default isolation level depends on the type of database to which you're connected. You can use `SET ISOLATION TO level` to change the isolation level. If the database is unlogged (that is, it has no transaction support), you can't set the isolation level. In some more recent versions, you can also set a transaction to `READ ONLY`.

The default locking behavior for reading and writing depends on the isolation level, the way the table was defined, and on whether or not the database was created with transactions enabled.

Rows returned by a `SELECT` statement can be locked to prevent them being changed by another transaction, by appending `FOR UPDATE` to the select statement. Optionally, you can specify a column list in parentheses after the `FOR UPDATE` clause.

The `LOCK TABLE table_name IN lock_mode` statement can be used to apply an explicit lock on a table. The lock mode can be `SHARED` or `EXCLUSIVE`. There are constraints on when tables can be unlocked, and when locks can be applied. Row/page locking occurs with cursors `FOR UPDATE`. In some types of database, some cursors are implicitly created `FOR UPDATE`.

SQL Dialect

Case sensitivity of LIKE operator

The `LIKE` operator is case-sensitive.

Table join syntax

All Informix versions support the basic `WHERE a.field = b.field` style join notation. Support for SQL-92 join notation depends on DBMS version; most do not.

Outer joins are supported. The basic version is:

```
SELECT * FROM A, OUTER B WHERE a.col1 = b.col2
```

All rows from `A` will be selected. Where there is one or more rows in `B` matching the row in `A` according to the join condition, the corresponding rows will be returned. Where there is no matching row in `B`, NULL will be returned in the *B*-columns in the `SELECT` list. There are all sorts of other contortions, such as complications with criteria in the `WHERE` clause, or nested outer joins.

Table and column names

For most versions, the maximum size of a table name or column name is 18 characters, as required by SQL-86. For the latest versions (Centaur, provisionally 9.2 or 7.4), the answer will be 128, as required by SQL-92. Owner (schema) names can be eight characters in the older versions and 32 in the versions with long table/column names.

The first character must be a letter, but the rest can be any combination of letters, numerals, and underscores (_).

If the `DELIMIDENT` environment variable is set, then table and column and owner names can be quoted inside double quotes, and any characters become valid. To embed a double quote in the name, use two adjacent double quotes, such as `"I said, ""Don't"""`. (Normally, Informix is very relaxed about treating double quotes and single quotes as equivalent, so often you could write `'I said, "Don''t"'` as the equivalent of the previous example. With `DELIMIDENT` set, you have to be more careful.) Owner names are delimited identifiers and should be embedded in double quotes for maximum safety.

The case-preserving and case-sensitive behavior of table and column names depends on the environment and the quoting mechanisms used.

Support for using national character sets in names depends on the version and the environment (locale).

Row ID

Most tables have a virtual ROWID column which can be selected. Fragmented tables do not have one unless it is specified in the `WITH ROWIDS` clause when the table is created or altered. In that case, it is a physical ROWID column that otherwise appears as a virtual column (meaning `SELECT *` does not select it).

As with any type except the BLOB types, a ROWID can be converted to a string and used as such. Note that ROWIDs need not be contiguous, nor start at either zero or one.

Automatic key or sequence generation

The SERIAL and SERIAL8 datatypes are "auto incrementing" keys. If you insert a zero into these columns, the next previously unused key number is *unrollbackably* allocated to that row. Note that NULL can't be used; you have to insert a zero. If you insert a non-zero value into the column, the specified value is used instead. Usually, there is a unique constraint on the column to prevent duplicate entries.

To get the value just inserted, you can use:

```
$sth->{ix_sqlerrd}[1]
```

Informix doesn't support sequence generators directly, but you can create your own with stored procedures.

Automatic row numbering and row count limiting

Informix does not support a way to automatically number returned rows.

Some recent versions of Informix support a FIRST row count limiting directive on SELECT statements:

```
SELECT FIRST num_of_rows ...
```

Positioned updates and deletes

Positioned updates and deletes are supported using the WHERE CURRENT OF syntax. For example:

```
$dbh->do("UPDATE ... WHERE CURRENT OF $sth->{CursorName}");
```

Parameter Binding

Parameter binding is directly supported by Informix. Only the standard ? style of placeholder is supported.

The TYPE attribute to bind_param() is not currently supported, but some support is expected in a future release.

Stored Procedures

Some stored procedures can be used as functions in ordinary SQL:

```
SELECT proc1(Col1) FROM SomeTable WHERE Col2 = proc2(Col3);
```

All stored procedures can be executed via the SQL EXECUTE PROCEDURE statement. If the procedure returns no values, it can just be executed. If the procedure does return values, even single values via a RETURN statement, then it can be treated like a SELECT statement. So after calling execute() you can fetch results from the statement handle as if a SELECT statement had been executed. For example:

```
$sth = $dbh->prepare("EXECUTE PROCEDURE CursoryProcedure(?,?)");
$sth->execute(1, 12);
$ref = $sth->fetchall_arrayref();
```

Table Metadata

The DBI table_info() method isn't currently supported. The private _tables() method can be used to get a list of all tables or a subset.

Details of the columns of a table can be fetched using the private _columns() method.

The keys/indexes of a table can be fetched by querying the system catalog.

Further information about these and other issues can be found via the *comp. databases.informix* newsgroup, and via the International Informix User Group (IIUG) at *http://www.iiug.org*.

Driver-Specific Attributes and Methods

Refer to the DBD::Informix documentation for details of driver-specific database and statement handle attributes.

Private _tables() and _columns() methods give easy access to table and column details.

Other Significant Database or Driver Features

Temporary tables can be created during a database session that are automatically dropped at the end of that session if they have not already been dropped explicitly. It's a very handy feature.

The latest versions of Informix (IDS/UDO, IUS) support user-defined routines and user-defined types, which can be implemented in the server in C or (shortly) Java.

The SQL-92 "CASE WHEN" syntax is supported by some versions of the Informix servers. That greatly simplifies some kinds of queries.

DBD::Ingres

General Information

Driver version

DBD::Ingres version 0.16 and, where noted, the 0.20 release

Feature summary

Transactions	Yes
Locking	Yes, implicit and explicit
Table joins	Yes, inner and outer
LONG/LOB datatypes	Yes, up to 2 GB
Statement handle attributes available	After prepare()
Placeholders	Yes, "?" and ":1" styles (native)
Stored procedures	Yes
Bind output values	Yes
Table name letter case	Insensitive, stored as uppercase
Field name letter case	Insensitive, stored as uppercase
Quoting of otherwise invalid names	Yes, via double quotes
Case-insensitive "LIKE" operator	No
Server table ROW ID pseudocolumn	Yes, "tid"
Positioned update/delete	No
Concurrent use of multiple handles	Unrestricted

Author and contact details

The driver author is Henrik Tougaard. He can be contacted via the *dbi-users* mailing list.

Supported database versions and options

The `DBD::Ingres` module supports both Ingres 6.4 and OpenIngres (1.*x* & II). For more information about Ingres, refer to:

> *http://www.cai.com/products/ingres.htm*

Differences from the DBI specification

Prepared statements do not work across transactions because commit/rollback and close/invalidate are all prepared statements. Work is underway to fix this deficiency.

Connect Syntax

The `DBI->connect()` Data Source Name, or DSN, can be one of the following:

```
dbi:Ingres:dbname
dbi:Ingres:vnode::dbname
dbi:Ingres:dbname;options
```

Where `options` are the SQL option flags as defined in the *CA-OpenIngres System Reference Guide.*

There are no driver-specific attributes for the `DBI->connect()` method.

`DBD::Ingres` supports an unlimited number of concurrent database connections to one or more databases.

Datatypes

Numeric data handling

The database and driver supports one-byte, two-byte and four-byte INTEGERs, four-byte and eight-byte FLOATS, and a currency type. The database and the driver (from version 0.20) supports the DECIMAL-number type.

Type	Description	Range
INTEGER1	1-byte integer	−128 to +127
SMALLINT	2-byte integer	−32,678 to +32,767
INTEGER	4-byte integer	−2,147,483,648 to +2,147,483,647
FLOAT4	4-byte floating	−1.0e+38 to 1.0e+38 (7 digits)
FLOAT	8-byte floating	−1.0e+38 to 1.0e+38 (16 digits)
MONEY	8-byte money	$−999,999,999,999.99 to $999,999,999,999.99
DECIMAL	fixed-point numeric	Depends on precision (max 31) and scale

DBD::Ingres always returns all numbers as Perl numbers—integers where possible, floating point otherwise. It is therefore possible that some precision may be lost when fetching DECIMAL types with a precision greater than Perl numbers (usually 16). If that's an issue, then convert the value to a string in the SELECT expression.

String data handling

Ingres and DBD::Ingres supports the following string datatypes:

```
VARCHAR(size)
CHAR(size)
TEXT(size)
C(size)
```

All string types have a limit of 2000 bytes. The CHAR, TEXT, and C types are fixed length and blank padded.

All string types can handle national character sets. The C type will accept only printing characters. CHAR and VARCHAR accept all character values including embedded nul characters ("\0"). Unicode is not formally supported yet.

Strings can be concatenated using the SQL + operator.

Date data handling

Ingres has just one date datatype: DATE. However, it can contain either an absolute date and time or a time interval. Dates and times are in second resolution between approximately 1-JAN-1581 and 31-DEC-2382. Intervals are stored to a one second resolution.

Ingres supports a variety of date formats, depending on the setting of the environment variable `II_DATE_FORMAT`. The default output format is `US: DD-MMM-YYYY HH:MM:SS`.

Many input formats are allowed. For the default format the following are accepted: `MM/DD/YYYY`, `DD-MMM-YYYY`, `MM-DD-YYYY`, `YYYY.MM.DD`, `YYYY_MM_DD`, `MMDDYY`, `MM-DD`, and `MM/DD`.

If you specify a `DATE` value without a time component, the default time is 00:00:00 (midnight). If you specify a `DATE` value without a date, the default date is the first day of the current month. If a date format that has a two-digit year, such as the `YY` in `DD-MON-YY` (a common default), then the date returned is always in the current century.

The following date-related functions are supported:

```
DATE(string)                - converts a string to a date
DATE_TRUNC(unit, date)      - date value truncated to the specified unit
DATE_PART(unit, date)       - integer containing the specified part
DATE_GMT(date)              - converts date to string "YYYY_MM_DD HH:MM:SS GMT"
INTERVAL(unit, interval)    - express interval as numeric count of units
```

The current date and time is returned by the `DATE('now')` function. The current date is returned by `DATE('today')`.

The following SQL expression can be used to convert an integer "seconds since 1-jan-1970 GMT" value to the corresponding database date/time:

```
DATE('01.01.1970 00:00 GMT')+DATE(CHAR(seconds_since_epoch)+' seconds')
```

And to do the reverse:

```
INT4(INTERVAL('seconds', DATE('now')-DATE('01.01.1970 00:00 GMT')))
```

A three-letter time zone name (from a limited set) can be appended to a date. If no time zone name is given, then the current *client* time zone is assumed. All datetimes are stored in the database as GMT and are converted back to the local time of the *client* fetching the data. All date comparisions in the server are done in GMT.

LONG/BLOB data handling

Ingres supports these `LONG` types:

```
LONG VARCHAR  - Character data of variable length up to 2 GB
LONG BYTE     - Raw binary data of variable length up to 2 GB
```

However, the `DBD::Ingres` driver does not yet support these types.

Other data handling issues

The `DBD::Ingres` driver supports the `type_info()` method.

Ingres supports automatic conversions between datatypes wherever it's reasonable.

Transactions, Isolation, and Locking

Ingres supports transactions. The default transaction isolation level is Serializable. OpenIngres II supports Repeatable Read, Read Commited, and Serializable.

The reading of a record sets a read-lock preventing writers from changing that record and, depending on lock granularity, possibly other records. Other readers are not hindered in their reading. Writing a record sets a lock that prevents other writers from writing, and readers from reading.

The `SET LOCKMODE` statement allows you to change the locking granularity. It can be set to:

```
ROW     - lock only the affected rows (OpenIngres II only)
PAGE    - lock the page that contains the affected row
TABLE   - lock the entire table
```

With the statement `SET LOCKMODE SESSION WHERE READLOCK=NOLOCK` it is possible, but definitely *not* recommended, to set the isolation level to Read Uncommited.

SQL Dialect

Case sensitivity of LIKE operator

The `LIKE` operator is case-sensitive.

Table join syntax

OpenIngres supports outer joins in ANSI SQL-92 syntax. Ingres 6.4 does not support outer joins.

Table and column names

The names of identifiers cannot exceed 32 characters. The first character must be a letter or an underscore (_), but the rest can be any combination of letters, numerals, dollar signs ($), pound signs (#), and at signs (@).

However, if an identifier is enclosed by double quotes ("), it can contain any combination of legal characters, including spaces but excluding quotation marks. This is not supported in Ingres 6.4.

Case significance is determined by the settings for the Ingres installation as set by the administrator when Ingres is installed.

National character sets can be used in identifiers, if enclosed in double quotes.

Row ID

The Ingres "row ID" pseudocolumn is called `tid`. It's an integer. It can be used without special handling. For example:

```
SELECT * FROM table WHERE tid=1029;
```

Automatic key or sequence generation

OpenIngres II supports "logical key" columns. They are defined by using a special datatype: `TABLE_KEY WITH SYSTEM MAINTAINED`. Ingres 6.4 required an extra-cost option to support that feature.

A column can be defined as either `TABLE_KEY` or `OBJECT_KEY`. Table_keys are unique in the table, whereas object_keys are unique in the entire database.

`DBD::Ingres` can't currently find the value of the last automatic key inserted, though it may do so in the future if enough people ask nicely, or someone contributes the code.

Automatic row numbering and row count limiting

Neither automatic row numbering nor row count limitations are supported.

Positioned updates and deletes

Positioned updates and deletes are supported in `DBD::Ingres` version 0.20 using the `WHERE CURRENT OF` syntax. For example:

```
$dbh->do("UPDATE ... WHERE CURRENT OF $sth->{CursorName}");
```

The `CursorName` is automatically defined by `DBD::Ingres` for each prepared statement.

Parameter Binding

Parameter binding is directly supported by Ingres. Only the standard ? placeholder style is supported.

When using the `bind_param()` method, the common integer, float, and char types can be defined using the `TYPE` attribute. Unsupported values of the `TYPE` attribute generate a warning.

Stored Procedures

Calling a stored procedure is done by the `execute procedure` statement. For example:

```
$dbh->do("execute procedure my_proc(param1='value')");
```

It is not yet possible to get results.

Table Metadata

DBD::Ingres version 0.20 supports the `table_info()` method.

The `IICOLUMNS` catalog contains information about all columns of a table.

The `IIINDEXES` catalog contains detailed information about all indexes in the database, one row per index. The `IIINDEX_COLUMNS` catalog contains information about the columns that make up each index.

Primary keys are indicated in the **key_sequence** field of the `IICOLUMNS` catalog.

Driver-Specific Attributes and Methods

DBD::Ingres has no driver-specific database handle attributes. However, it does support a number of statement handle attributes. Each returns a reference to an array of values, one for each column of the select results. These attributes are:

ing_type
:   'i' for integer columns, 'f' for float, and 's' for strings

ing_ingtype
:   The numeric Ingres type of the columns

ing_length
:   The Ingres length of the columns (as used in the database)

DBD::Ingres supports just one private method:

get_dbevent()
:   This private method calls GET DBEVENT and INQUIRE_INGRES to fetch a pending database event. If called without an argument, a blocking GET DBEVENT WITH WAIT is called. A numeric argument results in a call to GET DBEVENT WITH WAIT= :seconds.

DBD::InterBase

General Information

Driver version

DBD::InterBase version 0.021

This version of the DBD::InterBase driver is a pure Perl wrapper module around the IBPerl module. The author is working on a direct XS version, so be sure to read the latest documentation.

Feature summary

Transactions	Yes
Locking	Yes, implicit and explicit
Table joins	Yes, inner and outer
LONG/LOB datatypes	Yes, up to 4 GB
Statement handle attributes available	After first row fetched
Placeholders	Yes, "?" style (native)
Stored procedures	Yes
Bind output values	Yes
Table name letter case	Insensitive, stored as uppercase
Field name letter case	Insensitive, stored as uppercase
Quoting of otherwise invalid names	Yes, via double quotes
Case-insensitive "LIKE" operator	No
Server table ROW ID pseudocolumn	No
Positioned update/delete	No
Concurrent use of multiple handles	Unrestricted

Author and contact details

The driver author is Edwin Pratomo. He can be contacted via the *dbi-users* mailing list, or at *ed.pratomo@computer.org*.

Supported database versions and options

DBD::InterBase has been used to access InterBase 4.0 for Linux, and InterBase 5.5 for NT, and should also work with any version of InterBase above version 3.3 supported by IBPerl. DBD::InterBase also inherits all limitations applied to IBPerl 0.7, for instance, lack of metadata.

For further information about InterBase, refer to:

> *http://www.interbase.com*
> *http://www.interbase.com/products/dsqlsyntax.html*

Differences from the DBI specification

DBD::InterBase does not have access to statement metadata until after the statement has been executed *and the first row fetched.* Thus, attributes like $sth->{NUM_OF_FIELDS} are not available until after $sth->execute() and a fetch method has been called. Hopefully this will be fixed in a later version.

Connect Syntax

The DBI->connect() Data Source Name, or DSN, has the following format:

```
dbi:InterBase:attrs
```

where attrs is a semicolon-separated list of *key=value* pairs Valid attributes include:

database

Specifies the full path to the database within the server that should be made the default database.

host (optional)

Specify the host name of the InterBase server to connect to. Default to local-host.

role (optional)

Specify an SQL role name—supported only in InterBase 5.0 and later.

charset (optional)

Specify the client character set to use. Useful if the client's default character set is different from the server. Using this will enable automatic character conversion from one character set to the other. Default to NONE.

DBD::InterBase supports an unlimited number of concurrent database connections to one or more databases.

Datatypes

Numeric data handling

InterBase supports INTEGER, SMALLINT, FLOAT, DOUBLE PRECISION, NUMERIC (p,s), and DECIMAL(p,s).

FLOAT and INTEGER are always 32-bit, and SMALLINT is 16-bit. DOUBLE PRECISION is platform-dependent but generally 64-bit. Precision for NUMERIC/DECIMAL is from 1 to 15, and scale is from 1 to 15.

DBD::InterBase always returns all numbers as strings.

String data handling

InterBase supports the following string datatypes:

```
CHAR(size)      fixed length blank-padded
VARCHAR(size)   variable length with limit
```

Range of size is 1 to 32,767 bytes. The character set for each field may also be specified. For example:

```
CHAR(size) CHARACTER SET "ISO8859_1"
VARCHAR(size) CHARACTER SET "ISO8859_1"
```

InterBase also supports NCHAR(size) and NCHAR(size) VARYING as aliases for the CHARACTER SET "ISO8859_1" examples above.

Date data handling

InterBase supports one flexible date datatype: DATE, which includes either date, time, or date and time information. Data that will be stored as DATE datatype should be in format: DD MON YYYY HH:MM:SS, or DD-MON-YYYY HH:MM:SS. DD and MON parts must be supplied, other parts, if omitted, will be set to current year/time.

The DD MON YYYY parts can have any value from January 1, 100 AD to February 29, 32768 AD. HH:MM:SS ranges from 00:00:00 to 23:59:59.

The year part should be written in four digits, if it is only in two digits, then Inter-Base will infer the century number using a *sliding window* algorithm: subtracting the two-digit year number entered from the last two digits of the current year, if the absolute difference is greater than 50, then the century of the number entered is 20; otherwise, it is 19.

Fetched DATE values are formatted using a strftime() format string. This format string can be specified as DateFormat attribute when invoking prepare() method. If this attribute is left unspecified, then "%c" will be used as the format string. For example:

```
$stmt = "SELECT * FROM BDAY";
$opt = { 'DateFormat' => "%d %B %Y" };
$array_ref = $dbh->selectall_arrayref($stmt, $opt);
```

InterBase does not directly support SQL-92 DATE, TIME, and TIMESTAMP datatypes.

Date literals used by InterBase are: NOW, TODAY, YESTERDAY, and TOMORROW. For example:

```
CREATE TABLE SALES (
    ORDER_ID INTEGER NOT NULL,
    SHIP_DATE DATE DEFAULT "NOW" NOT NULL,
PRIMARY KEY(ORDER_ID));
```

LONG/BLOB data handling

InterBase supports a BLOB datatype. DBD::InterBase can handle BLOBs up to 4 GB, assuming you have that much memory in your system.

A BLOB column can be defined to hold either binary data or text data; if text, then a character set can also be specified. BLOB data is stored in *segments,* and the segment size (up to 64 KB) can also be specified for each BLOB column.

Other data handling issues

InterBase supports automatic conversions between datatypes wherever it is reasonable.

Transactions, Isolation, and Locking

InterBase supports transactions. Transaction isolation can be altered using the SET TRANSACTION ISOLATION LEVEL x statement. Refer to the InterBase DSQL manual for full details.

Rows returned by a `SELECT` statement can be locked to prevent them being changed by another transaction, by appending `FOR UPDATE` to the select statement. Optionally, you can specify a column list in parentheses after the `FOR UPDATE` clause.

There is no explicit `LOCK TABLE` statement.

SQL Dialect

Case sensitivity of LIKE operator

The `LIKE` operator is case-sensitive.

Table join syntax

Outer joins and inner joins are supported and are expressed using the ISO standard SQL syntax.

Table and column names

The maximum size of table and column names can't exceed 31 characters in length. Only alphanumeric characters can be used; the first character must be a letter.

InterBase converts all identifiers to uppercase.

Row ID

There is no "Row ID" concept.

Automatic key or sequence generation

A mechanism to create unique, sequential number that is automatically inserted at SQL operation such as `INSERT`, `UPDATE` is called `GENERATOR`. For example:

```
CREATE GENERATOR generator_name
SET GENERATOR generator_name TO integer_value
```

where `integer_value` is an integer value from $-2^{**}31$ to $2^{**}31 - 1$. The `SET GENERATOR` command sets the starting value of a newly created generator, or resets the value of an existing generator.

To use the generator, InterBase's `GEN_ID` function should be invoked. For example:

```
INSERT INTO SALES (PO_NUMBER) VALUES (GEN_ID(generator_name, step))
```

There's no `DROP GENERATOR` command; here is how to delete a `GENERATOR`:

```
DELETE FROM RDB$GENERATORS WHERE RDB$GENERATOR_NAME = 'generator_name'
```

Automatic row numbering and row count limiting

Neither automatic row numbering nor row count limitations are supported.

Positioned updates and deletes

InterBase does not support positioned updates or deletes.

Parameter Binding

Parameter binding is supported directly by InterBase. `DBD::InterBase` supports the ? placeholder style.

The TYPE attribute of the `bind_param()` as well as `type_info()` method are not yet supported.

Stored Procedures

InterBase does support stored procedures, but neither `DBD::InterBase` nor `IBPerl` has support for them that yet.

Table Metadata

`DBD::InterBase` hasn't yet supported the `table_info()` method.

Driver-Specific Attributes and Methods

There are no significant `DBD::InterBase` driver-specific database handle attributes.

DBD::mysql and DBD::mSQL

General Information

Driver version

`DBD::mysql` and `DBD::mSQL` versions 1.20*xx* and 1.21_*xx*

Version 1.20*xx* (even numbers) is the stable line, which is maintained for bug and portability fixes only. Version 1.21_*xx* (odd numbers) is used for development of the driver: all new features or interface modifications will be done in this line until it finally becomes 1.22*xx*.

Feature summary

```
Transactions                             No
Locking                                  Yes, explicit (MySQL only)
Table joins                              Yes, inner and outer (inner only for mSQL)
LONG/LOB datatypes                       Yes, up to 4 GB
Statement handle attributes available    After execute()
Placeholders                             Yes, "?" (emulated)
Stored procedures                        No
Bind output values                       No
Table name letter case                   Depends on filesystem, stored as defined
```

Field name letter case	Insensitive/Sensitive (MySQL/mSQL), stored as defined
Quoting of otherwise invalid names	No
Case-insensitive "LIKE" operator	Varies, see description below
Server table ROW ID pseudocolumn	Yes, "_rowid" (mSQL only)
Positioned update/delete	No
Concurrent use of multiple handles	Unrestricted

Author and contact details

The driver author is Jochen Wiedmann. He can be contacted via the mailing list *Msql-Mysql-modules@lists.mysql.com*.

Supported database versions and options

MySQL and mSQL are freely available, small, efficient database servers. MySQL has a rich feature set while mSQL is quite minimalist.

The `DBD::mysql` driver 1.20*xx* supports all MySQL versions since around 3.20. The `DBD::mysql` driver 1.21_*xx* supports MySQL 3.22 or later.

The `DBD::mSQL` drivers 1.20*xx* and 1.21_*xx* support all mSQL versions up to and including mSQL 2.0.*x*.

For further information about MySQL:

> *http://www.mysql.com/*

For further information about mSQL:

> *http://www.blnet.com/msqlpc*
> *http://www.hughes.com.au/*

Differences from the DBI specification

Both `DBD::mysql` and `DBD::mSQL` do not fully parse the statement until it's executed. Thus attributes like `$sth->{NUM_OF_FIELDS}` are not available until after `$sth->execute()` has been called. This is valid behavior, but is important to note when porting applications written originally for other drivers.

Also note that many statement attributes cease to be available after fetching all the result rows or calling the `finish()` method.

Connect Syntax

The `DBI->connect()` Data Source Name, or DSN, can be one of the following:

```
DBI:mysql:attrs
DBI:mSQL:attrs
```

where `attrs` is a semicolon-separated list of *key=value* pairs. Valid attributes include:

`database=$database`
    The database name you want to connect to.

`host=$host`
    The name of the machine running the server for the database you want to connect to, by default *localhost*.

`msql_configfile=$file`
    Load driver-specific settings from the given file, by default *InstDir/msql.conf*.

`mysql_compression=1`
    For slow connections, you may wish to compress the traffic between your client and the engine. If the MySQL engine supports it, this can be enabled by using this attribute. Default is off.

There are no driver-specific attributes applicable to the `connect()` method. The number of database and statement handles is limited by memory only. There are no restrictions on their concurrent use.

Datatypes

Numeric data handling

MySQL has five sizes of integer datatype, each of which can be signed (the default) or unsigned (by adding the word `UNSIGNED` after the type name).

Name	Bits	Signed Range	Unsigned Range
TINYINT	8	−128..127	0..255
SMALLINT	16	−32768..32767	0..65535
MEDIUMINT	24	−8388608..8388607	0..16777215
INTEGER	32	−2147483648..2147483647	0..4294967295
BIGINT	64	$-(2*63)..(2**63-1)$	$0..(2**64)$

The type `INT` can be used as an alias for `INTEGER`. Other aliases include `INT1=TINYINT`, `INT2=SMALLINT`, `INT3=MEDIUMINT`, `INT4=INT`, `INT8=BIGINT`, and `MIDDLEINT=MEDIUMINT`.

Note that all arithmetic is done using signed `BIGINT` or `DOUBLE` values, so you shouldn't use unsigned big integers larger than the largest signed big integer (except with bit functions). Note that −, +, and * will use `BIGINT` arithmetic when both arguments are `INTEGER` values. This means that if you multiply two big integers (or multiply the results from functions that return integers), you may get unexpected results if the result is bigger than 9223372036854775807.

MySQL has three main *non-integer* datatypes: FLOAT, DOUBLE, and DECIMAL. Aliases FLOAT4 for FLOAT and FLOAT8 for DOUBLE also work.

In what follows, the letter M is used for the *maximum display size* or *PRECISION* in ODBC and DBI terminology. The letter D is used for the number of digits that may follow the decimal point. (SCALE in ODBC and DBI terminology).

Maximum display size (PRECISION) and number of fraction digits (SCALE) are typically not required. For example, if you use just "DOUBLE," then default values will be silently inserted.

DOUBLE(M,D)

A normal-size (double-precision) floating-point number. Allowable values are −1.7976931348623157e+308 to −2.2250738585072014e−308, 0 and 2.225073858 5072014e−308 to 1.7976931348623157e+308.

REAL and DOUBLE PRECISION can be used as aliases for DOUBLE.

FLOAT(M,D)

A small (single-precision) floating-point number. Allowable values are −3. 402823466e+38 to −1.175494351e-38, 0 and −1.175494351e−38 to 3.40282346 6e+38.

FLOAT(M)

A floating-point number. Precision (M) can be 4 or 8. FLOAT(4) is a single-precision number and FLOAT(8) is a double-precision number. These types are like the FLOAT and DOUBLE types described above. FLOAT(4) and FLOAT(8) have the same ranges as the corresponding FLOAT and DOUBLE types, but their display size and number of decimals is undefined.

DECIMAL(M,D)

The DECIMAL type is an unpacked floating-point number type. NUMERIC is an alias for DECIMAL. It behaves like a CHAR column; "unpacked" means the number is stored as a string, using one character for each digit of the value, and the decimal point. If D is 0, values will have no decimal point or fractional part. The maximum range of DECIMAL values is the same as for DOUBLE, but the actual range for a given DECIMAL column may be constrained by the choice of M and D.

NUMERIC can be used as an alias for DECIMAL.

The numeric datatypes supported by mSQL are much more restricted:

INTEGER corresponds to MySQL's INTEGER type.
UINT corresponds to MySQL's INTEGER UNSIGNED type.
REAL corresponds to MySQL's REAL type.

The driver returns all datatypes, including numbers, as strings. It thus puts no restriction on size of PRECISION or SCALE.

String data handling

The following string types are supported by MySQL, quoted from *mysql.info* where *M* denotes the maximum display size or PRECISION:

CHAR(M)

> A fixed-length string that is always right-padded with spaces to the specified length. The range of M is 1 to 255 characters.

VARCHAR(M)

> A variable-length string. Note that trailing spaces are removed by the database when the value is stored (this differs from the ANSI SQL specification). The range of M is 1 to 255 characters.

ENUM('value1','value2',...)

> An enumeration. A string object that can have only one value, chosen from the specified list of values (or NULL). An ENUM can have a maxiumum of 65535 distinct values.

SET('value1','value2',...)

> A set. A string object that can have zero or more values, each of which must be chosen from the specified list of values. A SET can have a maximum of 64 members.

CHAR and VARCHAR types have a limit of 255 bytes. Binary characters, including the NUL byte, are supported by all string types. (Use the $dbh->quote() method for literal strings).

These aliases are also supported:

BINARY(num)	CHAR(num) BINARY
CHAR VARYING	VARCHAR
LONG VARBINARY	BLOB
LONG VARCHAR	TEXT
VARBINARY(num)	VARCHAR(num) BINARY

With DBD::mysql, the ChopBlanks attribute is always on. The MySQL engine itself removes spaces from the string's right end. Another "feature" is that CHAR and VARCHAR columns are always case-insensitive in comparisons and sort operations, unless you use the BINARY attribute, as in:

```
CREATE TABLE foo (A VARCHAR(10) BINARY)
```

With versions of MySQL after 3.23, you can perform a case-insensitve comparison of strings with the BINARY operator modifier:

```
SELECT * FROM table WHERE BINARY column = "A"
```

National language characters are handled in comparisons following the coding system that was specified at compile-time, by default ISO-8859-1. Non-ISO coding systems, and in particular UTF-16, are not supported.

Strings can be concatenated using the CONCAT(s1, s2, ...) SQL function.

The mSQL engine (and hence the DBD::mSQL driver) supports only the CHAR(M) string type, which corresponds to the MySQL's VARCHAR(M) type, and a TEXT(M) type, which is a cross between a CHAR and a BLOB. All string types have trailing spaces removed by mSQL. Also, mSQL has no way to concatenate strings.

Date data handling

The following date and time types are supported by MySQL, and quoted from *mysql.info*:

DATE

A date. The supported range is 0000-01-01 to 9999-12-31. MySQL displays DATE values in YYYY-MM-DD format, but allows you to assign values to DATE columns using these formats:

```
YYMMDD
YYYYMMDD
YY.MM.DD
YYYY.MM.DD
```

Where . may be any non-numerical separator, and a two-digit year is assumed to be 20YY if YY is less than 70.

DATETIME

A date and time combination. The supported range is 0000-01-01 00:00:00 to 9999-12-31 23:59:59. MySQL displays DATETIME values in YYYY-MM-DD HH:MM:SS format, but allows you to assign values to DATETIME columns using the formats shown for DATE above but with HH:MM:SS appended.

TIMESTAMP(M)

A timestamp. The range is 1970-01-01 00:00:00 to sometime in the year 2032 (or 2106, depending on the OS specific type time_t). MySQL displays TIMESTAMP values in YYYYMMDDHHMMSS, YYMMDDHHMMSS, YYYYMMDD, or YYMMDD format, depending on whether M is 14 (or missing), 12, 8, or 6, but allows you to assign values to TIMESTAMP columns using either strings or numbers. This output format behavior disagrees with the manual, so check your version because the behavior may change.

A TIMESTAMP column is useful for recording the time of an INSERT or UPDATE operation because it is automatically set to the time of the last operation if you don't give it a value yourself. You can also set it to the current time by giving it a NULL value.

TIME

A time. The range is -838:59:59 to 838:59:59. MySQL displays `TIME` values in `HH:MM:SS` format. You can assign values to `TIME` columns using these formats: `[[[DAYS] [H]H:]MM:]SS[.fraction]` or `[[[[H]H]H]H]MM]SS[.fraction]`.

YEAR

A year. The allowable values are 1901–2155, and 0000 in the four-digit year format, and 1970–2069 if you use the two-digit year format (70–69). On input, two-digit years in the range 00–69 are assumed to be 2000–2069. (`YEAR` is a new type for MySQL 3.22.)

If you are using two-digit years as in `YY-MM-DD` (dates) or `YY` (years), then they are converted into 2000–2069 and 1970–1999, repectively. Thus, MySQL has no Y2K problem, but a Y2070 problem!

In MySQL 3.23, this feature will be changed to 2000–2068 and 1969–1999, following the X/Open Unix standard.[*]

The `NOW()` function, and its alias `SYSDATE`, allow you to refer to the current date and time in SQL.

The `DATE_FORMAT(date, format)` function can be used to format date and time values using `printf`-like format strings.

MySQL has a rich set of functions operating on dates and times, including `DAYOFWEEK(date)` (1 = Sunday, ..., 7 = Saturday), `WEEKDAY(date)` (0 = Monday, ..., 6 = Sunday), `DAYOFMONTH(date)`, `DAYOFYEAR(date)`, `MONTH(date)`, `DAYNAME(date)`, `MONTHNAME(date)`, `WEEK(date)`, `YEAR(date)`, `HOUR(time)`, `MINUTE(time)`, `SECOND(time)`, `DATE_ADD(date, interval)` (`interval` being something like "2 HOURS"), and `DATE_SUB(date, interval)`.

The following SQL expression can be used to convert an integer "seconds since 1-jan-1970 GMT" value to the corresponding database date/time:

```
FROM_UNIXTIME(seconds_since_epoch)
```

and the reverse:

```
UNIX_TIMESTAMP(timestamp)
```

MySQL does no automatic time zone adjustments.

The mSQL database supports these date/time types:

```
DATE  - corresponds to MySQL's DATE type
TIME  - corresponds to MySQL's TIME type
```

---

[*] See *http://www.unix-systems.org/version2/whatsnew/year2000.html.*

The only date format supported by mSQL is DD-MMM-YYYY, where MMM is the three-character English abbreviation for the month name. The only time format supported by mSQL is HH:MM:SS.

LONG/BLOB data handling

These are MySQL's BLOB types, quoted from *mysql.info*:

```
TINYBLOB   / TINYTEXT    maximum length of 255 (2**8 - 1)
BLOB       / TEXT        maximum length of 65535 (2**16 - 1)
MEDIUMBLOB / MEDIUMTEXT  maximum length of 16777215 (2**24 - 1)
LONGBLOB   / LONGTEXT    maximum length of 4294967295 (2**32 - 1)
```

Binary characters in all BLOB types are allowed. The LongReadLen and Long-TruncOk types are not supported.

The maximum length of bind_param() parameter values is only limited by the maximum length of an SQL statement. By default that's 1MB but can be extended to just under 24 MB by changing the *mysqld* variable max_allowed_packet.

No TYPE or other attributes need to be given to bind_param() when binding these types.

The only BLOB type supported by mSQL is TEXT. This is a cross between a traditional VARCHAR type and a BLOB. An *average* width is specified, and data longer than *average* is automatically stored in an overflow area in the table.

Other data handling issues

The driver versions 1.21_*xx* and above do support the type_info() method.

MySQL supports automatic conversions between datatypes wherever it's reasonable. mSQL, on the other hand, supports none.

Transactions, Isolation, and Locking

Both mSQL and MySQL do *not* support transactions.

Since both mSQL and MySQL currently execute statements from multiple clients one at a time (atomic), and don't support transactions, there's no need for a default locking behavior to protect transaction isolation.

With MySQL, locks can be explicitly obtained on tables. For example:

```
LOCK TABLES table1 READ, table2 WRITE
```

Locks are released with any subsequent LOCK TABLES statement, by dropping a connection or with an explicit command:

```
UNLOCK TABLES
```

There are also user-defined locks that can be manipulated with the GET_LOCK() and RELEASE_LOCK() SQL functions. You can't automatically lock rows or tables during SELECT statements; you have to do it explicitly.

And, as you might guess, mSQL doesn't support any kind of locking at the moment.

SQL Dialect

Case sensitivity of LIKE operator

With MySQL, case-sensitivity of *all* character comparison operators, including LIKE, requires on the presence of the BINARY attribute on at least one of the fields—either on the field type in the CREATE TABLE statement or on the field name in the comparison operator. However, you can always force case-insensitivity using the TOLOWER function.

mSQL has three LIKE operators: LIKE is case-sensitive, CLIKE is case-insensitive, and RLIKE uses Unix style regular expressions.

Table join syntax

Joins are supported with the usual syntax:

```
SELECT * FROM a,b WHERE a.field = b.field
```

or, alternatively:

```
SELECT * FROM a JOIN b USING field
```

Outer joins are supported by MySQL, not mSQL, with:

```
SELECT * FROM a LEFT OUTER JOIN b ON condition
```

Outer joins in MySQL are always left outer joins.

Table and column names

MySQL table and column names may have at most 64 characters. mSQL table and column names are limited to 35 characters.

With MySQL, you can put single quotes around table or column names (you can use the standard double quotes if the database is started with the --ansi-mode option). You need to do that if the name contains special characters or matches a reserved word. Quoting identifiers isn't supported by mSQL.

Table names are limited by the fact that tables are stored in files and the table names are really file names. In particular, the case-sensitivity of table names depends on the underlying file system and some characters like . and / are not allowed.

Column names are case-insensitive with MySQL and case-sensitive with mSQL, but both engines store them without case conversions.

Names can include national character set characters (with the eighth bit set) in MySQL but not mSQL.

Row ID

MySQL doesn't have row IDs. mSQL has a pseudocolumn _rowid.

The mSQL _rowid column value is numeric and, since mSQL doesn't automatically convert strings to numbers, you must take care not to quote the value when using it in later SELECT statements.

Note that because transactions and locking aren't supported, there's a greater risk that the row identified by a _rowid value you just fetched may have been deleted and possibly replaced by a different row by the time you use the row ID value moments later.

Automatic key or sequence generation

All MySQL integer table fields can have an AUTO_INCREMENT attribute. That is, given a table:

```
CREATE TABLE a (
    id INTEGER AUTO_INCREMENT NOT NULL PRIMARY KEY,
    ...)
```

and a statement:

```
INSERT INTO a (id, ...) VALUES (NULL, ...)
```

a unique ID will be generated automatically (similarly, if the ID field had not been mentioned in the insert statement at all). The generated ID can later be retrieved with:

```
$sth->{mysql_insertid}          (1.21_xx)
$sth->{insertid}                (1.20_xx)
```

or, if you've used $dbh->do and not prepare/execute, then use:

```
$dbh->{mysql_insertid}                      (1.21_xx)
$dbh->do("SELECT LAST_INSERT_ID()");        (1.20_xx)
```

MySQL does not support sequence generators directly, but they can be emulated with a little care (refer to the MySQL manual for details). For example:

```
UPDATE seq SET id=last_insert_id(id+1)
```

The mSQL database supports sequence generators, but just one per table. After executing:

```
CREATE SEQUENCE on A
```

you can later do:

```
SELECT _seq FROM A
```

to fetch the value. You can't refer directly to the sequence from an insert statement; instead, you have to fetch the sequence value and then execute an insert with that value.

Automatic row numbering and row count limiting

Neither engine supports automatic row numbering of **SELECT** statement results.

Both mSQL and MySQL support row count limiting with:

```
SELECT * FROM A LIMIT 10
```

to retrieve the first 10 rows only, but only MySQL supports:

```
SELECT * FROM A LIMIT 20, 10
```

to retrieve rows 20–29, with the count starting at 0.

Positioned updates and deletes

Neither positioned updates nor deletes are supported by MySQL or mSQL.

Parameter Binding

Neither engine supports placeholders, but the **DBD::mysql** and **DBD::mSQL** drivers provide full emulation. Question marks are used as placeholders, as in:

```
$dbh->do("INSERT INTO table VALUES (?, ?)", undef, $id, $name);
```

The **:1** placeholder style is not supported.

In the above example, the driver attempts to guess the datatype of the inserted values by looking at Perl's own internal string versus number datatype hints. This is fine with MySQL, because MySQL can deal with expressions like:

```
INSERT INTO table (id_number) VALUES ('2')
```

where **id_number** is a numeric column. But this doesn't apply to mSQL, which would treat that as an error. So you sometimes need to force a datatype, either by using:

```
$dbh->do("INSERT INTO table VALUES (?, ?)", undef, int($id), "$name");
```

or by using the **TYPE** attribute of the **bind_param()** method:

```
use DBI qw(:sql_types);
$sth = $dbh->prepare("INSERT INTO table VALUES (?, ?)");
$sth->bind_param(1, $id,   SQL_INTEGER);
$sth->bind_param(2, $name, SQL_VARCHAR);
$sth->execute();
```

Unsupported values of the TYPE attribute do not currently generate a warning.

Stored Procedures

Neither mSQL nor MySQL have a concept of stored procedures, although there are plans to add some stored procedure features to MySQL.

Table Metadata

The 1.21_*xx* version of the drivers was the first to support the table_info() method.

To obtain information on a generic table, you can use the query:

```
LISTFIELDS $table
```

This will return a statement handle without result rows. The TYPE, NAME, ... attributes are describing the table.

With MySQL you can use:

```
SHOW INDEX FROM $table
```

to retrieve information on a table's indexes, in particular a primary key. The information will be returned in rows. The DBD::mSQL driver does support a similar thing using:

```
LISTINDEX $table $index
```

with $index being the name of a given index.

Driver-Specific Attributes and Methods

The following driver specific database handle attributes are supported:

mysql_info
mysql_thread_id
mysql_insertid

> These attributes correspond to the C calls mysql_info(), mysql_thread_id(), and mysql_insertid(), respectively.

The following driver-specific statement handle attributes are supported:

mysql_use_result
mysql_store_result

> With DBD::mysql, there are two different ways the driver fetches results from the server. With mysql_store_result enabled, it fetches all rows at once, creating a result table in memory and returns it to the caller (a 100% row cache).

With `mysql_use_result`, it returns rows to the application as they are fetched. This is less memory-consuming on the client side, but should not be used in situations where multiple people can query the database, because it can block other applications. (Don't confuse that with locking!)

`mysql_insertid`

A previously generated `auto_increment` column value, if any.

`mysql_is_blob`

`mysql_is_key`

`msql_is_num`

`mysql_is_num`

`msql_is_pri_key`

`mysql_is_pri_key`

These attributes return an array ref with the given flags set for any column of the result set. Note you may use these with the `LISTFIELDS` query to obtain information about the columns of a table.

`mysql_max_length`

Unlike the `PRECISION` attribute, this returns the true actual maximum length of the particular data in the current result set. This can be helpful, for example, when displaying ASCII tables.

This attribute doesn't work with `mysql_use_result` enabled, since it needs to look at all the data.

`msql_table`

`mysql_table`

Similar to `NAME`, but the table names and not the column names are returned.

`msql_type`

`mysql_type`

Similar to `TYPE`, but they return the respective engine's native type.

`msql_type_name`

`mysql_type_name`

Similar to `msql_type` and `mysql_type`, but column names are returned, that you can use in a `CREATE TABLE` statement.

A single private method called `admin()` is supported. It provides a range of administration functions:

```
$rc = $drh->func('createdb', $db, $host, $user, $password, 'admin');
$rc = $drh->func('dropdb',   $db, $host, $user, $password, 'admin');
$rc = $drh->func('shutdown',      $host, $user, $password, 'admin');
$rc = $drh->func('reload',        $host, $user, $password, 'admin');

$rc = $dbh->func('createdb', $database, 'admin');
$rc = $dbh->func('dropdb',   $database, 'admin');
```

```
$rc = $dbh->func('shutdown',        'admin');
$rc = $dbh->func('reload',          'admin');
```

These correspond to the respective commands of mysqladmin and msqladmin.

DBD::ODBC

General Information

Driver version

DBD::ODBC version 0.20

Feature summary

Because DBD::ODBC acts as an interface to other database drivers, much of its behavior is governed by those drivers.

Transactions	Dependent on connected data source
Locking	Dependent on connected data source
Table joins	Dependent on connected data source
LONG/LOB datatypes	Dependent on connected data source
Statement handle attributes available	After prepare()
Placeholders	Yes
Stored procedures	Yes
Bind output values	No
Table name letter case	Dependent on connected data source
Field name letter case	Dependent on connected data source
Quoting of otherwise invalid names	Dependent on connected data source
Case-insensitive "LIKE" operator	Dependent on connected data source
Server table ROW ID pseudocolumn	Dependent on connected data source
Positioned update/delete	Yes
Concurrent use of multiple handles	Dependent on connected data source

Author and contact details

The driver authors are Jeff Urlwin and Tim Bunce. The original work was based upon an early version of Thomas Wenrich's DBD::Solid. The authors can be contacted via the *dbi-users* mailing list.

Supported database versions and options

The DBD::ODBC module supports ODBC Version 2.*x* and 3.*x* on Unix and Win32. For all platforms, both an ODBC driver manager *and* an ODBC driver are required *in addition* to the DBD::ODBC module.

For Win32, the driver manager is included with the operating system. For Unix and variants, the iODBC driver manager source is included in the iodbcsrc directory. While iODBC acts as the driver *manager*, you still have to find an actual driver for your platform and database.

Driver providers include:

> Intersolv: *http://www.intersolv.com*
>
> OpenLink: *http://www.openlinksw.com*

There are other vendors; this is not an exhaustive list. Other related ODBC links include:

> *http://www.genix.net/unixODBC*
>
> *http://www.openlinksw.com/iodbc*
>
> *http://www.microsoft.com/data/odbc*

To subscribe to the *freeodbc* development mailing list, send a message to *freeodbc-request@as220.org* with just the word `subscribe` in the body of the message.

Differences from the DBI specification

`DBD::ODBC` does not currently support "out" parameter binding. That should be fixed in a later release.

Connect Syntax

The `DBI->connect()` Data Source Name, or DSN, has the following forms:

```
dbi:ODBC:odbc_dsn
dbi:ODBC:driver=Microsoft Access Driver (*.mdb);dbq=\\server\share\access.mdb
```

In the first example above, **odbc_dsn** is an ODBC Data Source Name (DSN). An ODBC DSN is simply a name you use to refer to a set of driver-specific connection parameters defined elsewhere. Connection parameters typically include the name of the ODBC driver to use, the database name, and any required connection details.

Under Win32, the best method of creating an ODBC DSN is by using the ODBC32 applet on the Windows Control Panel. Under Unix variants, you typically need to edit a text file called *.odbc.ini* in your home directory. Refer to your driver manager documentation for more details.

The second connection example above uses the driver-specific connection string. By specifying all the required information, you can bypass the need to use a previously defined DSN. In our example we're using the "`Microsoft Access Driver (*.mdb)`" driver to reach the data in the *\\server\share\access.mdb* Access database file.

There are currently no driver-specific attributes for the `DBI->connect()` method.

Most ODBC drivers and databases let you make multiple concurrent database connections to the same database. A few do not.

Some ODBC drivers and databases, most notably Sybase and SQL Server, do not let you prepare and execute a new statement handle while still fetching data from another statement handle associated with the same database handle.

Datatypes

Numeric data handling

The numeric data handling for ODBC is dependent upon a variety of factors. One of those critical factors is the end database. For example, Oracle supports different numeric types than Sybase which, in turn, supports different numeric types than a CSV file. You will need to read your database documentation for more information.

Unfortunately, the second critical set of factors are the ODBC driver manufacturer and version of the driver. For example, I have seen a great variety in the handling of numeric values between versions of Oracle's ODBC drivers. What works with one version, sadly, may not work with even a later version of Oracle's drivers. You will need to read your ODBC driver documentation for more information.

The DBI `type_info()` and `type_info_all()` methods provide information about the datatypes supported by the database and driver being used.

String data handling

As with numeric handling, string data handling is dependent upon the database and driver. Please see "Numeric Data Handling" above for more information.

Strings can be concatenated using the `CONCAT(s1,s2)` SQL function.

Date data handling

As with numeric handling, date data handling is dependent upon the database and driver. Please see "Numeric Data Handling" above for more information.

You can use ODBC escape sequences to define a date in a database-independent way. For example, to insert a date of Jan 21, 1998 into a table, you could use:

```
INSERT INTO table_name (date_field) VALUES ({d '1998-01-21'});
```

You can use placeholders within escape sequences instead of literal values. For example:

```
INSERT INTO table_name (date_field) VALUES ({d ?});
```

Similar escape sequences are defined for other date/time types. Here's the full set:

```
{d 'YYYY-MM-DD'}                    – date
{t 'HH:MM:SS'}                      – time
{ts 'YYYY-MM-DD HH:MM:SS'}          – timestamp
{ts 'YYYY-MM-DD HH:MM:SS.FFFFFFF'}  – timestamp
```

If you specify a DATE value without a time component, the default time is 00:00:00 (midnight). There is also an interval escape clause which is constructed like this:

```
{interval [+|-] 'value' [interval_qualifier]}
```

For example:

```
{interval '200-11' YEAR(3) TO MONTH}
```

Please see an ODBC reference guide for more information.

The current date and time on the server can be found by using an ODBC scalar function escape sequence to call the appropriate function. For example:

```
INSERT INTO table_name (date_field) VALUES ({fn CURDATE});
```

The {fn ...} escape sequence isn't required if the entire SQL statement conforms to the level of SQL-92 grammar supported by your ODBC driver.

Other related functions include CURTIME(), NOW(), CURRENT_DATE(), CURRENT_TIME(), and CURRENT_TIMESTAMP(). The last three require an ODBC v3 driver.

Other date/time related functions include: DAYNAME(), DAYOFMONTH(), DAYOFWEEK(), DAYOFYEAR(), EXTRACT(), HOUR(), MINUTE(), MONTH(), MONTHNAME(), SECOND(), WEEK(), and YEAR().

Basic date/time arithmetic can be performed using the TIMESTAMPADD() and TIMESTAMPDIFF() functions.

The following SQL expression can be used to convert an integer "seconds since 1-jan-1970" value to the corresponding database date/time:

```
TIMESTAMPADD(SQL_TSI_SECOND, seconds_since_epoch, {d '1970-01-01'})
```

to do the reverse you can use:

```
TIMESTAMPDIFF(SQL_TSI_SECOND, {d '1970-01-01'}, date_field)
```

ODBC itself does not have any support for time zones, though the database to which you are connected may.

LONG/BLOB data handling

Support for LONG/BLOB datatypes and their maximum lengths are very dependent on the database to which you are connected.

The LongReadLen and LongTruncOk attributes work as defined. However, the driver implementations do affect this. Some drivers do not properly indicate that they have truncated the data, or they have more data available than was actually returned. The DBD::ODBC tests attempt to determine correct support for this.

No special handling is required for LONG/BLOB datatypes. They can be treated just like any other field when fetching or inserting, etc.

Other data handling issues

The DBD::ODBC driver supports the type_info() method.

Transactions, Isolation, and Locking

DBD::ODBC supports transactions if the databases you are connected to supports them.

Supported isolation levels, the default isolation level, and locking behavior are all dependent on the database to which you are connected.

SQL Dialect

Because DBD::ODBC acts as an interface to other database drivers, the following issues are governed by those drivers and the databases they connect to:

- Case-sensitivity of LIKE operator
- Table and column names
- Row ID
- Automatic key or sequence generation
- Automatic row numbering and row count limiting

For more information, refer to the documentation for the drivers and the database being used.

Table join syntax

Table join syntax is partly dependent on the database to which you are connected and the ODBC driver you are using. The ODBC standard SQL defines the standard syntax for inner joins and an escape sequence to use for outer joins:

```
{oj outer_join}
```

where outer_join is defined as:

```
table_name [LEFT | RIGHT | FULL]
    OUTER JOIN [ table_name | outer_join] ON condition
```

An outer join request must appear after the FROM clause of a SELECT but before a WHERE clause, if one exists.

Positioned updates and deletes

This is dependent on the database to which you are connected. Positioned updates and deletes are supported in ODBC SQL using the WHERE CURRENT OF syntax.

For example:

```
$dbh->do("UPDATE ... WHERE CURRENT OF $sth->{CursorName}");
```

Parameter Binding

Parameter binding is supported by DBD::ODBC if the underlying ODBC driver driver supports it. Only the standard ? style of placeholders is supported.

The TYPE attribute to the bind_param() method is supported.

Stored Procedures

Stored procedures can be called using the following ODBC escape sequence:

```
{call procedure1_name}
{call procedure2_name(?, ?)}
{?= call procedure3_name(?, ?)}
```

The last form would be used to return values from the procedure, but DBD::ODBC currently does not support output parameters.

Table Metadata

DBD::ODBC supports the table_info() method.

DBD::ODBC also supports many of the ODBC *metadata* functions that can be used to discover information about the tables within a database. These can be accessed as driver-specific private methods:

```
SQLGetTypeInfo    --  $dbh->func(xxx,           'GetTypeInfo')
SQLDescribeCol    --  $sth->func(colno,         'DescribeCol')
SQLColAttributes  --  $sth->func(xxx, colno, 'ColAttributes')
SQLGetFunctions   --  $dbh->func(xxx,           'GetFunctions')
SQLColumns        --  $dbh->func(catalog, schema, table, column, 'columns')
SQLStatistics     --  $dbh->func(catalog, schema, table, unique, 'Statistics')
SQLPrimaryKeys    --  $dbh->func(catalog, schema, table, 'PrimaryKeys')
SQLForeignKeys    --  $dbh->func(pkc, pks, pkt, fkc, fks, fkt, 'ForeignKeys')
```

The DBI will provide standard methods for these soon, possibly by the time you read this book.

Driver-Specific Attributes and Methods

DBD::ODBC has no driver-specific handle attributes.

In addition to the private methods described in "Table Metadata" above, the GetInfo() private method can be used to discover many details about the driver and database you are using.

DBD::Oracle

General Information

Driver version

DBD::Oracle version 1.03

Feature summary

Transactions	Yes
Locking	Yes, implicit and explicit
Table joins	Yes, inner and outer
LONG/LOB datatypes	Yes, up to 4 GB
Statement handle attributes available	After prepare()
Placeholders	Yes, "?" and ":1" styles (native)
Stored procedures	Yes
Bind output values	Yes
Table name letter case	Insensitive, stored as uppercase
Field name letter case	Insensitive, stored as uppercase
Quoting of otherwise invalid names	Yes, via double quotes
Case-insensitive "LIKE" operator	No
Server table ROW ID pseudocolumn	Yes, "ROWID"
Positioned update/delete	No
Concurrent use of multiple handles	Unrestricted

Author and contact details

The driver author is Tim Bunce. He can be contacted via the *dbi-users* mailing list.

Supported database versions and options

The DBD::Oracle module supports both Oracle 7 and Oracle 8.

Building for Oracle 8 defaults to use the new Oracle 8 OCI interface, which enables use of some Oracle 8 features including LOBs and "INSERT ... RETURNING ...".

An emulation module for the old Perl4 oraperl software is supplied with DBD::Oracle, making it very easy to upgrade oraperl scripts to Perl5.

For further information about Oracle, refer to:

http://www.oracle.com
http://technet.oracle.com

Differences from the DBI specification

DBD::Oracle has no known significant differences in behavior from the current DBI specification.

Connect Syntax

The `DBI->connect()` Data Source Name, or DSN, can be one of the following:

```
dbi:Oracle:tnsname
dbi:Oracle:sidname
dbi:Oracle:host=hostname;sid=sid
```

Some other less common formats also work if supported by the Oracle client version being used.

There are no significant driver-specific attributes for the `DBI->connect()` method.

`DBD::Oracle` supports an unlimited number of concurrent database connections to one or more databases.

Datatypes

Numeric data handling

Oracle has only one flexible underlying numeric type, NUMBER. But Oracle does support several ANSI standard and IBM datatype names as aliases, including:

```
INTEGER       = NUMBER(38)
INT           = NUMBER(38)
SMALLINT      = NUMBER(38)
DECIMAL(p,s)  = NUMBER(p,s)
NUMERIC(p,s)  = NUMBER(p,s)
FLOAT         = NUMBER
FLOAT(b)      = NUMBER(p)    where b is the binary precision, 1 to 126
REAL          = NUMBER(18)
```

The NUMBER datatype stores positive and negative fixed and floating-point numbers with magnitudes between $1.0 \times 10\text{-}130$ and $9.9...9 \times 10125$ (38 nines followed by 88 zeroes), with 38 digits of precision.

You can specify a fixed-point number using the following form: `NUMBER(p,s)` where `s` is the scale, or the number of digits to the right of the decimal point. The scale can range from −84 to 127.

You can specify an integer using `NUMBER(p)`. This is a fixed-point number with precision `p` and scale 0. This is equivalent to `NUMBER(p,0)`.

You can specify a floating-point number using `NUMBER`. This is a floating-point number with decimal precision 38. A scale value is not applicable for floating-point numbers.

`DBD::Oracle` always returns all numbers as strings. Thus the driver puts no restriction on size of `PRECISION` or `SCALE`.

String data handling

Oracle supports the following string datatypes:

```
VARCHAR2(size)
NVARCHAR2(size)
CHAR
CHAR(size)
NCHAR
NCHAR(size)
RAW(size)
```

The RAW type is presented as hexadecimal characters. The contents are treated as non-character binary data and thus are never "translated" by character set conversions or gateway interfaces.

CHAR types and the RAW type have a limit of 2000 bytes. For VARCHAR types the limit is 2000 bytes in Oracle 7 and 4000 in Oracle 8.

The NVARCHAR2 and NCHAR variants hold string values of a defined national character set (Oracle 8 only). For those types the maximum number of characters stored may be lower when using multibyte character sets.

The CHAR and NCHAR types are fixed length and blank padded.

Oracle automatically converts character data between the character set of the database defined when the database was created and the character set of the client, defined by the NLS_LANG parameter for the CHAR and VARCHAR2 types or the NLS_NCHAR parameter for the NCHAR and NVARCHAR2 types.

CONVERT(string, dest_char_set, source_char_set) can be used to convert strings between character sets. Oracle 8 supports 180 storage character sets. UTF-8 is supported. See the "National Language Support" section of the Oracle Reference manual for more details on character set issues.

Strings can be concatenated using either the CONCAT(s1,s2,...) SQL function or the || operator.

Date data handling

Oracle supports one flexible date/time datatype: DATE. A DATE can have any value from January 1, 4712 BC to December 31, 4712 AD with a one second resolution.

Oracle supports a very wide range of date formats and can use one of several calendars (Arabic Hijrah, English Hijrah, Gregorian, Japanese Imperial, Persian, ROC Official (Republic of China), and Thai Buddha). We'll only consider the Gregorian calendar here.

The default output format for the DATE type is defined by the NLS_DATE_FORMAT configuration parameter, but it's typically DD-MON-YY, e.g., 20-FEB-99 in most western installations. The default input format for the DATE type is the same as the output format. Only that one format is recognized.

If you specify a DATE value without a time component, the default time is 00:00:00 (midnight). If you specify a DATE value without a date, the default date is the first day of the current month. If a date format that has a two-digit year, such as the YY in DD-MON-YY (a common default) then the date returned is always in the current century. The RR format can be used instead to provide a fifty-year pivot.

The default date format is specified either explicitly with the initialization parameter NLS_DATE_FORMAT or implicitly with the initialization parameter NLS_TERRITORY. For information on these parameters, see Oracle8 Reference.

You can change the default date format for your session with the ALTER SESSION command. For example:

```
ALTER SESSION SET NLS_DATE_FORMAT = 'MM/DD/YYYY'
```

The TO_DATE() function can be used to parse a character string containing a date in a known format. For example:

```
UPDATE table SET date_field = TO_DATE('1999-02-21', 'YYYY-MM-DD')
```

The TO_CHAR() function can be used to format a date. For example:

```
SELECT TO_CHAR(SYSDATE, 'YYYY-MM-DD') FROM DUAL
```

The current date/time is returned by the SYSDATE() function.

You can add numbers to DATE values. The number is interpreted as numbers of days; for example, SYSDATE + 1 is this time tomorrow, and SYSDATE - (3/1440) is three minutes ago. You can subtract two dates to find the difference, in days, between them.

Oracle provides a wide range of date functions including ROUND(), TRUNC(), NEXT_DAY(), ADD_MONTHS(), LAST_DAY() (of the month), and MONTHS_BETWEEN().

The following SQL expression can be used to convert an integer "seconds since 1-jan-1970" value to the corresponding database date/time:

```
to_date(trunc(:unixtime/86400, 0) + 2440588, 'J') -- date part
+(mod(:unixtime,86400))/86400                       -- time part
```

To do the reverse you can use:

```
(date_time_field - TO_DATE('01-01-1970','DD-MM-YYYY')) * 86400
```

Oracle does no automatic time zone adjustments. However it does provide a NEW_TIME() function that calculates time zone adjustments for a range of time zones. NEW_TIME(d, z1, z2) returns the date and time in time zone z2 when the date and time in time zone z1 are represented by d.

LONG/BLOB data handling

Oracle supports these LONG/BLOB datatypes:

```
LONG        - Character data of variable length
LONG RAW    - Raw binary data of variable length
CLOB        - A large object containing single-byte characters
NCLOB       - A large object containing national character set data
BLOB        - Binary large object
BFILE       - Locator for external large binary file
```

The LONG types can hold up to 2 GB. The other types (LOB and FILE) can hold up to 4 GB. The LOB and FILE types are only available when using Oracle 8 OCI.

The LONG RAW and RAW types are passed to and from the database as strings consisting of pairs of hex digits.

The LongReadLen and LongTruncOk attributes work as defined. However, the LongReadLen attribute seems to be limited to 65535 bytes on most platforms when using Oracle 7. Building DBD::Oracle with Oracle 8 OCI raises that limit to 4 GB.

The maximum length of bind_param() parameter value that can be used to insert LONG data seems to be limited to 65535 bytes on most platforms when using Oracle 7. Building DBD::Oracle with Oracle 8 OCI raises that limit to 4 GB.

The TYPE attribute value SQL_LONGVARCHAR indicates an Oracle LONG type. The value SQL_LONGVARBINARY indicates an Oracle LONG RAW type. These values are not always required but their use is strongly recommended.

No other special handling is required for LONG/BLOB datatypes. They can be treated just like any other field when fetching or inserting, etc.

Other data handling issues

The DBD::Oracle driver supports the type_info() method.

Oracle supports automatic conversions between datatypes wherever it's reasonable.

Transactions, Isolation, and Locking

DBD::Oracle supports transactions. The default transaction isolation level is READ COMMITED.

Oracle supports READ COMMITED and SERIALIZABLE isolation levels. The level may be changed once per-transaction by executing a SET TRANSACTION ISOLATION LEVEL x statement (where x is the name of the isolation level required).

Oracle also supports transaction-level read consistency. This can be enabled by issuing a SET TRANSACTION statement with the READ ONLY option.

In Oracle, the default behavior is that a lock never prevents other users from querying the table. A query never places a lock on a table. Readers never block writers, and writers never block readers.

Rows returned by a `SELECT` statement can be locked to prevent them from being changed by another transaction by appending `FOR UPDATE` to the `SELECT` statement. Optionally, you can specify a column list in parentheses after the `FOR UPDATE` clause.

The `LOCK TABLE table_name IN lock_mode` statement can be used to apply an explicit lock on an entire table. A range of row and table locks are supported.

SQL Dialect

Case sensitivity of LIKE operator

The `LIKE` operator is case-sensitive.

Table join syntax

Oracle supports inner joins with the usual syntax:

```
SELECT * FROM a, b WHERE a.field = b.field
```

To write a query that performs an outer join of tables A and B and returns all rows from A, the Oracle outer join operator (+) must be applied to all column names of B that appear in the join condition. For example:

```
SELECT customer_name, order_date
FROM customers, orders
WHERE customers.cust_id = orders.cust_id (+);
```

For all rows in the customer's table that have no matching rows in the orders table, Oracle returns NULL for any select list expressions containing columns from the orders table.

Table and column names

The names of Oracle identifiers, such as tables and columns, cannot exceed thirty characters in length.

The first character must be a letter, but the rest can be any combination of letters, numerals, dollar signs ($), pound signs (#), and underscores (_).

However, if an Oracle identifier is enclosed by double quotes ("), it can contain any combination of legal characters including spaces but excluding quotation marks.

Oracle converts all identifiers to uppercase unless enclosed in double quotes. National characters can also be used when identifiers are quoted.

Row ID

The Oracle "row id" pseudocolumn is called ROWID. Oracle ROWIDs are alphanumeric case-sensitive strings. They can be treated as ordinary strings and used to rapidly (re)select rows.

Automatic key or sequence generation

Oracle supports "sequence generators". Any number of named sequence generators can be created in a database using the CREATE SEQUENCE seq_name SQL command. Each has pseudocolumns called NEXTVAL and CURRVAL. The typical usage is:

```
INSERT INTO table (k, v) VALUES (seq_name.nextval, ?)
```

To get the value just inserted you can use:

```
SELECT seq_name.currval FROM DUAL
```

Oracle does not support automatic key generation such as "auto increment" or "system generated" keys. However they can be emulated using triggers and sequence generators.

For example:

```
CREATE TRIGGER trigger_name
   BEFORE INSERT ON table_name FOR EACH ROW
   DECLARE newid integer;
BEGIN
   IF (:NEW.key_field_name IS NULL)
   THEN
      SELECT sequence_name.NextVal INTO newid FROM DUAL;
      :NEW.key_field_name := newid;
   END IF;
```

Oracle8i (8.1.0 and above) supports Universal Unique ID number generation, per the IETF Internet-Draft, using the new SYS_GUID() function. GUIDs are more useful than sequence generators in a distributed database since no two hosts will generate the same GUID.

Automatic row numbering and row count limiting

The ROWNUM pseudocolumn can be used to sequentially number selected rows (starting at 1). Sadly, however, Oracle's ROWNUM has some frustrating limitations. Refer to the Oracle SQL documentation.

Positioned updates and deletes

Oracle does not support positioned updates or deletes.

Parameter Binding

Parameter binding is directly supported by Oracle. Both the ? and :1 style of placeholders are supported. The :name style is also supported, but is not portable.

The bind_param() method TYPE attribute can be used to indicate the type a parameter should be bound as. These SQL types are bound as VARCHAR2: SQL_ NUMERIC, SQL_DECIMAL, SQL_INTEGER, SQL_SMALLINT, SQL_FLOAT, SQL_REAL, SQL_DOUBLE, and SQL_VARCHAR. Oracle will automatically convert from VARCHAR2 to the required type.[*]

The SQL_CHAR type is bound as a CHAR, thus enabling fixed-width, blank-padded comparison semantics.

The SQL_BINARY and SQL_VARBINARY types are bound as RAW. SQL_LONGVAR-BINARY is bound as LONG RAW and SQL_LONGVARCHAR as LONG.

Unsupported values of the TYPE attribute generate a warning.

Refer to the DBD::Oracle documentation for details of how to bind LOBs and CURSORs.

Stored Procedures

Oracle stored procedures are implemented in the Oracle PL/SQL language.[†]

The DBD::Oracle module can be used to execute a block of PL/SQL code by starting it with a BEGIN and ending it with an END;. PL/SQL blocks are used to call stored procedures. Here's a simple example that calls a stored procedure called "foo" and passes it two parameters:

```
$sth = $dbh->prepare("BEGIN foo(:1, :2) END;");
$sth->execute("Baz", 24);
```

Here's a more complex example that shows a stored procedure being called with two parameters and returning the return value of the procedure. The second parameter of the procedure is defined as IN OUT so we bind that using bind_ param_inout() to enable it to update the Perl variable:

```
$sth = $dbh->prepare("BEGIN :result = func_name(:id, :changeme) END;");
$sth->bind_param(":id", "FooBar");
my ($result, $changeme) = (41, 42);
$sth->bind_param_inout(":result",  \$result,  100);
$sth->bind_param_inout(":changeme", \$changeme, 100);
```

---

[*] Working with strings and letting Oracle handle the conversions actually has many benefits. Oracle's packed decimal numeric format is compact, fast, and has far larger scale and precision than Perl's own numeric values.

[†] A procedural extension to SQL that supports variables, control flow, packages, exceptions, etc. With Oracle8i, stored procedures can also be implemented in Java.

```
$sth->execute();
print "func_name returned '$result' and updated changeme to '$changeme'\n";
```

Table Metadata

DBD::Oracle supports the table_info() method.

The ALL_TABLES view contains detailed information about all tables in the database, one row per table.

The ALL_TAB_COLUMNS view contains detailed information about all columns of all the tables in the database, one row per table.

The ALL_INDEXES view contains detailed information about all indexes in the database, including primary keys, one row per index.

The ALL_IND_COLUMNS view contains information about the columns that make up each index.

(Note that for all these views, fields containing statistics derived from the actual data in the corresponding table are updated only when the SQL ANALYSE command is executed for that table.)

Driver-Specific Attributes and Methods

DBD::Oracle has no significant driver-specific database or statement handle attributes.

The following private methods are supported:

plsql_errstr

```
$plsql_errstr = $dbh->func('plsql_errstr');
```

Returns error text from the USER_ERRORS table.

dbms_output_enable

```
$dbh->func('dbms_output_enable');
```

Enables the DBMS_OUTPUT package. The DBMS_OUTPUT package is typically used to receive trace and informational messages from stored procedures.

dbms_output_get

```
$msg  = $dbh->func('dbms_output_get');
@msgs = $dbh->func('dbms_output_get');
```

Gets a single line or all available lines using DBMS_OUTPUT.GET_LINE.

dbms_output_put

```
$msg  = $dbh->func('dbms_output_put', @msgs);
```

Puts messages using DBMS_OUTPUT.PUT_LINE.

DBD::Pg

General Information

Driver version

DBD::Pg version 0.91

Feature summary

Transactions	Yes
Locking	Yes, implicit and explicit
Table joins	Yes, inner only
LONG/LOB datatypes	Yes, max size depends on filesystem
Statement handle attributes available	After execute()
Placeholders	Yes, "?" and ":1" styles (native)
Stored procedures	No
Bind output values	No
Table name letter case	Insensitive, stored as lowercase
Field name letter case	Insensitive, stored as lowercase
Quoting of otherwise invalid names	Yes, via double quotes
Case-insensitive "LIKE" operator	No, but has "~*" case-insensitive regex match
Server table ROW ID pseudocolumn	Yes, "oid"
Positioned update/delete	No
Concurrent use of multiple handles	Unrestricted

Author and contact details

The driver author is Edmund Mergl. He can be contacted via the *dbi-users* mailing list.

Supported database versions and options

The DBD-Pg-0.91 module supports PostgreSQL 6.4. For futher information please refer to:

> *http://www.postgresql.org*

Differences from the DBI Specification

DBD::Pg does not fully parse the statement until it's executed. Thus, attributes like $sth->{NUM_OF_FIELDS} are not available until after $sth->execute() has been called. This is valid behavior, but it is important to note when porting applications originally written for other drivers.

Connect Syntax

The DBI->connect() Data Source Name, or DSN, can be one of the following:

```
dbi:Pg:dbname=$dbname
dbi:Pg:dbname=$dbname;host=$host;port=$port;options=$options;tty=$tty
```

All parameters, including the userid and password parameter of the **connect** command, have a hard-coded default that can be overridden by setting appropriate environment variables.

There are no driver-specific attributes for the **DBI->connect()** method.

DBD::Pg supports an unlimited number of concurrent database connections to one or more databases.

Datatypes

Numeric data handling

PostgreSQL supports the following numeric types:

PostgreSQL	Range
int2	–32768 to +32767
int4	–2147483648 to +2147483647
float4	6 decimal places
float8	15 decimal places

Some platforms also support the int8 type. **DBD::Pg** always returns all numbers as strings.

String data handling

PostgreSQL supports the following string datatypes:

```
CHAR            single character
CHAR(size)      fixed length blank-padded
VARCHAR(size)   variable length with limit
TEXT            variable length
```

All string datatypes have a limit of 4096 bytes. The **CHAR** type is fixed length and blank padded.

There is no special handling for data with the eighth bit set. They are stored unchanged in the database. None of the character types can store embedded nulls and Unicode is not formally supported.

Strings can be concatenated using the || operator.

Date data handling

PostgreSQL supports the following date/time datatypes:

Datatype	Storage	Recommendation	Description
abstime	4 bytes	original date and time	limited range
date	4 bytes	SQL92 type	wide range
datetime	8 bytes	best general date and time	wide range, high precision
interval	12 bytes	SQL92 type	equivalent to timespan
reltime	4 bytes	original time interval	limited range, low precision
time	4 bytes	SQL92 type	wide range
timespan	12 bytes	best general time interval	wide range, high precision
timestamp	4 bytes	SQL92 type	limited range

Datatype	Range		Resolution
abstime	1901-12-14	2038-01-19	1 sec
date	4713 B.C.	32767 A.D.	1 day
datetime	4713 B.C.	1465001 A.D.	1 microsec
interval	−178000000 years	+178000000 years	1 microsec
reltime	−68 years	+68 years	1 sec
time	00:00:00:00	23:59:59:99	1 microsec
timespan	−178000000 years	178000000 years	1 microsec
timestamp	1901-12-14	2038-01-19	1 sec

PostgreSQL supports a range of date formats:

Name	Example
ISO	1997-12-17 0:37:16-08
SQL	12/17/1997 07:37:16.00 PST
Postgres	Wed Dec 17 07:37:16 1997 PST
European	17/12/1997 15:37:16.00 MET
NonEuropean	12/17/1997 15:37:16.00 MET
US	12/17/1997 07:37:16.00 MET

The default output format does not depend on the client/server locale. It depends on, in increasing priority: the PGDATESTYLE environment variable at the server, the PGDATESTYLE environment variable at the client, and the SET DATESTYLE SQL command.

All of the formats described above can be used for input. A great many others can also be used. There is no specific default input format. If the format of a date input is ambiguous then the current DATESTYLE is used to help disambiguate.

If you specify a date/time value without a time component, the default time is 00:00:00 (midnight). To specify a date/time value without a date is not allowed. If a date with a two-digit year is input, then if the year was less than 70, add 2000; otherwise, add 1900.

The current date/time is returned by the keyword 'now' or 'current' , which has to be cast to a valid datatype. For example:

```
SELECT 'now'::datetime
```

PostgreSQL supports a range of date/time functions for converting between types, extracting parts of a date/time value, truncating to a given unit, etc. The usual arithmetic can be performed on date and interval values, e.g., date-date=interval, etc.

The following SQL expression can be used to convert an integer "seconds since 1-jan-1970 GMT" value to the corresponding database date/time:

```
DATETIME(unixtime_field)
```

and to do the reverse:

```
DATE_PART('epoch', datetime_field)
```

The server stores all dates internally in GMT. Times are converted to local time on the database server before being sent to the client frontend, hence by default are in the server time zone.

The TZ environment variable is used by the server as default time zone. The PGTZ environment variable on the client side is used to send the time zone information to the backend upon connection. The SQL SET TIME ZONE command can set the time zone for the current session.

LONG/BLOB data handling

PostgreSQL handles BLOBs using a so-called "large objects" type. The handling of this type differs from all other datatypes. The data are broken into chunks, which are stored in tuples in the database. Access to large objects is given by an interface which is modelled closely after the Unix file system. The maximum size is limited by the file size of the operating system.

If you just select the field, you get a "large object identifier" and not the data itself. The LongReadLen and LongTruncOk attributes are not implemented because they don't make sense in this case. The only method implemented by the driver is the undocumented DBI method blob_read().

Other data handling issues

The DBD::Pg driver supports the type_info() method.

PostgreSQL supports automatic conversions between datatypes wherever it's reasonable.

Transactions, Isolation, and Locking

PostgreSQL supports transactions. The current default isolation transaction level is Serializable and is currently implemented using table-level locks. Both may change. No other isolation levels for transactions are supported.

With AutoCommit on, a query never places a lock on a table. Readers never block writers, and writers never block readers. This behavior changes whenever a transaction is started (with AutoCommit off). Then a query induces a shared lock on a table and blocks anyone else until the transaction has been finished.

The LOCK TABLE table_name statement can be used to apply an explicit lock on a table. This works only inside a transaction (with AutoCommit off).

To ensure that a table being selected does not change before you make an update later in the transaction, you must explicitly lock it with a LOCK TABLE statement before executing the select.

SQL Dialect

Case sensitivity of LIKE operator

PostgreSQL has the following string matching operators:

Glyph	Description	Example
~~	Same as SQL "LIKE" operator	`'scrappy,marc' ~~ '%scrappy%'`
!~~	Same as SQL "NOT LIKE" operator	`'bruce' !~~ '%al%'`
~	Match (regex), case-sensitive	`'thomas' ~ '.*thomas.*'`
~*	Match (regex), case-insensitive	`'thomas' ~* '.*Thomas.*'`
!~	Doesn't match (regex), case-sensitive	`'thomas' !~ '.*Thomas.*'`
!~*	Doesn't match (regex), case-insensitive	`'thomas' !~ '.*vadim.*'`

Table join syntax

Outer joins are not supported. Inner joins use the traditional syntax.

Table and column names

The maximum size of table and column names cannot exceed 31 charaters in length. Only alphanumeric characters can be used; the first character must be a letter.

If an identifier is enclosed by double quotes ("), it can contain any combination of characters except double quotes.

PostgreSQL converts all identifiers to lowercase unless enclosed in double quotes. National character set characters can be used, if enclosed in quotation marks.

Row ID

The PostgreSQL "row id" pseudocolumn is called *oid*, object identifier. It can be treated as a string and used to rapidly (re)select rows.

Automatic key or sequence generation

PostgreSQL does not support automatic key generation such as "auto increment" or "system generated" keys.

However, PostgreSQL does support "sequence generators." Any number of named sequence generators can be created in a database. Sequences are used via functions called NEXTVAL and CURRVAL. The typical usage is:

```
INSERT INTO table (k, v) VALUES (NEXTVAL('seq_name'), ?);
```

To get the value just inserted, you can use the corresponding currval() SQL function in the same session, or:

```
SELECT last_value FROM seq_name
```

Automatic row numbering and row count limiting

Neither automatic row numbering nor row count limitations are supported.

Positioned updates and deletes

PostgreSQL does not support positioned updates or deletes.

Parameter Binding

Parameter binding is emulated by the driver. Both the ? and :1 style of placeholders are supported.

The TYPE attribute of the bind_param() method may be used to influence how parameters are treated. These SQL types are bound as VARCHAR: SQL_NUMERIC, SQL_DECIMAL, SQL_INTEGER, SQL_SMALLINT, SQL_FLOAT, SQL_REAL, SQL_DOUBLE, and SQL_VARCHAR.

The SQL_CHAR type is bound as a CHAR, thus enabling fixed-width, blank-padded comparison semantics.

Unsupported values of the TYPE attribute generate a warning.

Stored Procedures

DBD::Pg does not support stored procedures.

Table Metadata

DBD::Pg supports the `table_info()` method.

The `pg_attribute` table contains detailed information about all columns of all the tables in the database, one row per table.

The `pg_index` table contains detailed information about all indexes in the database, including primary keys, one row per index.

Driver-Specific Attributes and Methods

There are no significant DBD::Pg driver-specific database handle attributes.

DBD::Pg has the following driver-specific statement handle attributes:

`pg_size`

> Returns a reference to an array of integer values for each column. The integer shows the storage (not display) size of the column in bytes. Variable length columns are indicated by –1.

`pg_type`

> Returns a reference to an array of strings for each column. The string shows the name of the datatype.

`pg_oid_status`

> Returns the OID of the last `INSERT` command.

`pg_cmd_status`

> Returns the name of the last command type. Possible types are: `INSERT`, `DELETE`, `UPDATE`, and `SELECT`.

DBD::Pg has no private methods.

Other Significant Database or Driver Features

PostgreSQL offers substantial additional power by incorporating the following four additional basic concepts in such a way that users can easily extend the system: classes, inheritance, types, and functions.

Other features provide additional power and flexibility: constraints, triggers, rules, transaction integrity, procedural languages, and large objects.

It's also free Open Source Software with an active community of developers.

DBD::SearchServer

General Information

Driver version

DBD::SearchServer version 0.20

This driver was previously known as DBD::Fulcrum.

Feature summary

Transactions	No
Locking	Yes, implicit and explicit
Table joins	No, but see description below
LONG/LOB datatypes	Yes, up to 2 GB
Statement handle attributes available	After execute()
Placeholders	Yes, "?" and ":1" styles (emulated)
Stored procedures	No
Bind output values	No
Table name letter case	Insensitive, stored as uppercase
Field name letter case	Insensitive, stored as uppercase
Quoting of otherwise invalid names	Yes, via double quotes
Case-insensitive "LIKE" operator	Yes, "LIKE"
Server table ROW ID pseudocolumn	Yes, "FT_CID"
Positioned update/delete	Yes
Concurrent use of multiple handles	Unrestricted

Author and contact details

The driver author is Davide Migliavacca. He can be contacted via the *dbi-users* mailing list. Davide Migliavacca has no relationship with PCDOCS/Fulcrum, the maker of SearchServer, and particularly no contact with product support for PCDOCS/Fulcrum customers.

Supported database versions and options

The DBD::SearchServer module supports PCDOCS/Fulcrum SearchServer, versions 2.*x* thru 3.5.

Fulcrum SearchServer is a very powerful text-retrieval system with a SQL interface. You should not expect to find a full-fledged SQL RDBMS here. Refer to the product documentation for details about the query language.

For further information about SearchServer, refer to:

http://www.pcdocs.com

Differences from the DBI specification

DBD::SearchServer doesn't fully parse the statement until it's executed. Attributes like $sth->{NUM_OF_FIELDS} aren't available until after $sth->execute() has been called. This is valid behavior but is important to note when porting applications originally written for other drivers.

Connect Syntax

Under Unix, you may specify where SearchServer will find the database tables by using a set of environment variables: FULSEARCH, FULCREATE, and FULTEMP. So the connect string is always just:

```
dbi:SearchServer:
```

Under WIN32, you may use the fully qualified DSN syntax using the ODBC data source name as the third component of the connect string:

```
dbi:SearchServer:DSN
```

There are no driver-specific attributes for the DBI->connect() method.

DBD::SearchServer supports an unlimited number of concurrent database connections to the same server.

Datatypes

Numeric data handling

SearchServer has two numeric datatypes: INTEGER and SMALLINT. INTEGER (or INT) is an unsigned 32-bit binary integer with 10 digits of precision. SMALLINT is a signed 16-bit binary integer with 5 digits of precision.

String data handling

SearchServer supports the following string datatypes:

```
CHAR(size)
VARCHAR(size)
APVARCHAR(size)
```

A CHAR column is of fixed size, whereas a VARCHAR column can be of varying length up to the specified maximum size. If the size is not specified, it defaults to 1. The maximum size for a CHAR or VARCHAR column is 32,767.

APVARCHAR is a special datatype. You can have at most one APVARCHAR column per table; it is designed to contain the full text of the document to be indexed and it is used in queries to retrieve the text. It is eventually modified to identify spots where the query matched. The maximum length of the APVARCHAR column is 2,147,483,647.

The CHAR type is fixed-length and blank-padded to the right.

SearchServer has its own conversion functionality for national language character sets. Basically, it treats all text as being specified in one of three internal character sets (FTICS). It is up to the application to use character sets consistently. The document readers (software that is used by SearchServer to actually access documents when indexing) are responsible for translating from other characters sets to FTICS. A number of "translation" filters are distributed with the product.

ISO Latin 1 (8859-1) is supported. See the "Character Sets" section of the Search-SQL Reference Manual for more details on character set issues.

Date data handling

SearchServer supports only a `DATE` datatype. A `DATE` can have any value from January 1, 100 AD to December 31, 2047 AD with one-day resolution. Rows in tables have an automatic read-only `FT_TIMESTAMP` column with a better resolution, but it is not of a `DATE` type (it is an `INTEGER`). Also, only date literals can be used with `DATE` columns.

The date format is `YYYY-MM-DD` (ISO standard). There are provisions for other formats, but their use is discouraged.

Only the ISO date format is recognized for input.

If a two-digit year value is entered, then 1900 is added to the value. However, this isn't supported functionality, for good reason.

No date/time arithmetic or functions are provided, and there is no support for time zones.

LONG/BLOB data handling

The `APVARCHAR` type can hold up to 2 GB.

`LongReadLen` and `LongTruncOk` are ignored due to very different semantics of the `APVARCHAR` type.

You need to use the undocumented `blob_read()` method to fetch data from an `APVARCHAR` column. Inserting an `APVARCHAR` column happens indirectly by specifying an external document in the `FT_SFNAME` reserved column. Document data is not really inserted into the tables, it is indexed. Later, however, you can fetch the document selecting the `APVARCHAR` column.

Other data handling issues

The `DBD::SearchServer` driver does not support the `type_info()` method.

Transactions, Isolation, and Locking

`DBD::SearchServer` does not support transactions.

Locking is performed based on the characteristics of the table, set at creation time or modified later with an external utility, `ftlock`.

By default, `ROWLOCKING` is applied, which applies "transient" locks during normal operations including select, searched update, and delete. These locks should not prevent reading the affected rows, but will block additional concurrent modifications, and prevent reindexing of the locked rows.

If set to `NOLOCKING`, no locking will be performed on that table by the engine, meaning that data integrity is left for the application to manage. Please read the documentation carefully before playing with these parameters; there is additional feedback with the `PERIODIC` or `IMMEDIATE` indexing mode.

Rows returned by a `SELECT` statement can be locked to prevent them from being changed by another transaction, by appending `FOR UPDATE` to the select statement.

There is no explicit table lock facility. You can prevent a table *schema* being modified, dropped, or even reindexed using `PROTECT TABLE`, but this does not include row-level modifications, which are still allowed. `UNPROTECT TABLE` restores normal behavior.

SQL Dialect

Case sensitivity of LIKE operator

The `LIKE` operator is *not* case-sensitive.

Table join syntax

SearchServer does not really supports joins, however it does support a kind of *view* mechanism.

With views, tables must be located on the same node and have the same schema. Only read-only access is granted with views, and they have to be described using a special syntax file. Please refer to the "Data Administration and Preparation" manual for more information on views.

Table and column names

Letters, numbers, and underscores (_) are valid characters in identifiers. The maximum size of table and column names is not known at this time.

SearchServer converts all identifiers to uppercase. Table and column names are not case-sensitive. National characters can be used in identifier names.

Row ID

The SearchServer "row id" pseudocolumn is called `FT_CID` and is of the `INTEGER` datatype. `FT_CID` can be used in a WHERE clause, but only with the = operator.

Automatic key or sequence generation

SearchServer does not support automatic key generation such as "auto increment" or "system generated" keys. However, the integer FT_CID pseudocolumn is not reissued when rows are deleted.

There is no support for sequence generators.

Automatic row numbering and row count limiting

Neither automatic row numbering nor row count limitations are supported.

Positioned updates and deletes

Positioned updates and deletes are supported using the WHERE CURRENT OF syntax. For example:

```
$dbh->do("UPDATE ... WHERE CURRENT OF $sth->{CursorName}");
```

Parameter Binding

Both the ? and :1 style of placeholders are supported by driver emulation.

The TYPE attribute to bind_param() is ignored, so no warning is generated for unsupported values.

Stored Procedures

There are no stored procedures or functions in SearchServer.

Table Metadata

DBD::SearchServer supports the table_info() method.

The COLUMNS system table contains detailed information about all columns of all the tables in the database, one row per column. The COLUMNS system table uses the INDEX_MODE column to identify indexed columns and which indexing mode is used for them.

Driver-Specific Attributes and Methods

DBD::SearchServer has no driver-specific database handle attributes. It does have one driver-specific statement handle attribute:

ss_last_row_id

> This attribute is read-only and is valid after an INSERT, DELETE, or UPDATE statement. It will report the FT_CID (row ID) of the last affected row in the statement. You'll have to prepare/execute the statement (as opposed to simply do()-ing it) in order to fetch the attribute.

There are no private methods.

DBD::Sybase—For Sybase and Microsoft SQL Server

General Information

Driver version

DBD::Sybase version 0.14

Feature summary

Transactions	Yes
Locking	Yes, implicit and explicit
Table joins	Yes, inner and outer
LONG/LOB datatypes	Yes, up to 2 GB
Statement handle attributes available	After execute()
Placeholders	Yes, "?" style (native), see text below
Stored procedures	Yes
Bind output values	No, all values returned via fetch methods
Table name letter case	Sensitive, stored as defined, configurable
Field name letter case	Sensitive, stored as defined, configurable
Quoting of otherwise invalid names	Yes, via double quotes
Case-insensitive "LIKE" operator	No
Server table ROW ID pseudocolumn	No
Positioned update/delete	No
Concurrent use of multiple handles	Statement handles restricted, see below

Author and contact details

The driver author is Michael Peppler. He can be contacted via the *dbi-users* mailing list, or at *mpeppler@peppler.org*.

Supported database versions and options

The DBD::Sybase module supports Sybase 10.*x* and 11.*x*, and offers limited support for accessing Sybase 4.*x* and Microsoft MS-SQL servers, assuming availability of Sybase OpenClient, or the FreeTDS libraries.

The standard release of MS-SQL 7 can not be accessed using the Sybase libraries, but can be used using the FreeTDS libraries. There is a patch for MS-SQL 7 to allow Sybase clients to connect:

> *http://support.microsoft.com/support/kb/articles/q239/8/83.asp*

The FreeTDS libraries (*www.freetds.org*) is an Open Source effort to reverse engineer the TDS (Tabular Data Stream) protocol that both Sybase and Microsoft use. FreeTDS is still in alpha, but DBD::Sybase builds cleanly against the latest release and suppports most functions (apart from ?-style placeholders).

Here are some URLs to more database/driver specific information:

http://www.sybase.com
http://techinfo.sybase.com
http://sybooks.sybase.com
http://www.microsoft.com/sql
http://www.freetds.org

Differences from the DBI specification

The `LongReadLen` and `LongTruncOk` attributes are not supported.

Note that `DBD::Sybase` does not fully parse the statement until it's executed. Thus, attributes like `$sth->{NUM_OF_FIELDS}` are not available until after `$sth->execute()` has been called. This is valid behavior but is important to note when porting applications originally written for other drivers.

Connect Syntax

The `DBI->connect()` Data Source Name, or DSN, has the following format:

```
dbi:Sybase:attrs
```

where `attrs` is a semicolon-separated list of *key=value* pairs. Valid attributes include:

server
> Specifies the Sybase server to connect to.

database
> Specifies the database within the server that should be made the default database for this session (via `USE database`).

charset
> Specifies the client character set to use. Useful if the client's default character set is different from the server. Using this will enable automatic character conversion from one character set to the other.

`DBD::Sybase` supports an unlimited number of concurrent database connections to one or more databases.

It is not normally possible for Sybase clients to prepare/execute a new statement handle while still fetching data from another statement handle that is associated with the same database handle. However, `DBD::Sybase` emulates this process by opening a new connection that will automatically be closed when the new statement handle is destroyed. You should be aware that there are some subtle but significant transaction issues with this approach.

Datatypes

Numeric data handling

The driver supports INTEGER, SMALLINT, TINYINT, MONEY, SMALLMONEY, FLOAT, REAL, DOUBLE, NUMERIC(p,s), and DECIMAL(p,s).

INTEGER is always a 32-bit int, SMALLINT is 16-bit, and TINYINT is 8-bit. All others except the NUMERIC/DECIMAL datatypes are hardware specific. Precision for NUMERIC/DECIMAL is from 1 to 38, and scale is from 0 to 38.

NUMERIC/DECIMAL values are returned as Perl strings by default, even if the scale is 0 and the precision is small enough to fit in an integer value. All other numbers are returned in native format.

String data handling

DBD::Sybase supports CHAR, VARCHAR, BINARY, and VARBINARY, all limited to 255 characters in length. The CHAR type is fixed-length and blank-padded.

Sybase automatically converts CHAR and VARCHAR data between the character set of the server (see the syscharset system table) and the character set of the client, defined by the locale setting of the client. The BINARY and VARBINARY types are not converted. UTF-8 is supported.

See the "OpenClient International Developer's Guide" in the Sybase OpenClient manuals for more on character set issues.

Strings can be concatenated using the SQL + operator.

Date data handling

Sybase supports the DATETIME and SMALLDATETIME values. A DATETIME can have a value from Jan 1 1753 to Dec 31, 9999 with a 300th of a second resolution. A SMALLDATETIME has a range of Jan 1 1900 to Jun 6 2079 with a one-minute resolution.

The current date on the server is obtained with the GETDATE() SQL function.

The Sybase date format depends on the locale settings for the client. The default date format is based on the "C" locale:

```
Feb 16 1999 12:07PM
```

In this same locale, Sybase understands several input formats in addition to the one above:

```
2/16/1998 12:07PM
1998/02/16 12:07
1998-02-16 12:07
19980216 12:07
```

If the time portion is omitted, it is set to 00:00. If the date portion is omitted, it is set to Jan 1 1900. If the century is omitted, it is assumed to be 2000 if year < 50, and 1900 if year >= 50.

You can use the special `_date_fmt()` private method (accessed via `$dbh->func()`) to change the date input and output format. The formats are based on Sybase's standard conversion routines. The following subset of available formats has been implemented:

```
LONG          - Nov 15 1998 11:30:11:496AM
SHORT         - Nov 15 1998 11:30AM
DMY4_YYYY     - 15 Nov 1998
MDY1_YYYY     - 11/15/1998
DMY1_YYYY     - 15/11/1998
HMS           - 11:30:11
```

Use the **CONVERT()** SQL function to convert date and time values from other formats. For example:

```
UPDATE a_table
    SET date_field = CONVERT(datetime_field, '1999-02-21', 105)
```

CONVERT() is a generic conversion function that can convert to and from most datatypes. See the **CONVERT()** function in Chapter 2 of the *Sybase Reference Manual*.

Arithmetic on date/time types is done on dates via the **DATEADD()**, **DATEPART()**, and **DATEDIFF()** Transact SQL functions. For example:

```
SELECT DATEDIFF(ss, date1, date2)
```

returns the difference in seconds between **date1** and **date2**.

Sybase does not understand time zones at all, except that the **GETDATE()** SQL function returns the date in the time zone that the server is running in (via `localtime`).

The following SQL expression can be used to convert an integer "seconds since 1-jan-1970" value ("Unix time") to the corresponding database date/time:

```
DATEADD(ss, unixtime_field, 'Jan 1 1970')
```

Note however that the server does not understand time zones, and will therefore give the local Unix time on the server, and not the correct value for the GMT time zone.

If you know that the server runs in the same time zone as the client, you can use:

```
use Time::Local;
$time_to_database = timegm(localtime($unixtime));
```

to convert the Unix time value before sending it to Sybase.

To do the reverse, converting from a database date/time value to Unix time, you can use:

```
DATEDIFF(ss, 'Jan 1 1970', datetime_field)
```

The same GMT versus localtime caveat applies in this case. If you know that the server runs in the same time zone as the client, you can convert the returned value to the correct GMT-based value with this Perl expression:

```
use Time::Local;
$time = timelocal(gmtime($time_from_database));
```

LONG/BLOB data handling

Sybase supports an IMAGE and a TEXT type for LONG/BLOB data. Each type can hold up to 2 GB of binary data, including nul characters. The main difference between an IMAGE and a TEXT column lies in how the client libraries treat the data on input and output. TEXT data is entered and returned "as is." IMAGE data is returned as a long hex string, and should be entered in the same way.

LongReadLen and LongTrunkOk attributes have no effect. The default limit for TEXT/IMAGE data is 32 KB, but this can be changed by the SET TEXTSIZE Transact-SQL command.

Bind parameters can *not* be used to insert TEXT or IMAGE data to Sybase.

Other data handling issues

The DBD::Sybase driver does not support the type_info() method yet.

Sybase does not automatically convert numbers to strings or strings to numbers. You need to explicitly call the CONVERT SQL function. However, placeholders don't need special handling because DBD::Sybase knows what type each placeholder needs to be.

Transactions, Isolation, and Locking

DBD::Sybase supports transactions. The default transaction isolation level is READ COMMITTED.

Sybase supports READ COMMITED, READ UNCOMMITED, and SERIALIZABLE isolation levels. The level be changed per-connection or per-statement by executing SET TRANSACTION_ISOLATION LEVEL x, where x is 0 for READ UNCOMMITED, 1 for READ COMMITED, and 3 for SERIALIZABLE.

By default, a READ query will acquire a shared lock on each page that it reads. This will allow any other process to read from the table, but will block any process trying to obtain an exclusive lock (for update). The shared lock is only maintained for the time the server needs to actually read the page, not for the entire length of the `SELECT` operation. (11.9.2 and later servers have various additional locking mechanisms.)

There is no explicit `LOCK TABLE` statement. Appending `WITH HOLDLOCK` to a `SELECT` statement can be used to force an exclusive lock to be acquired on a table, but is rarely needed.

The correct way to do a multi-table update with Sybase is to wrap the entire operation in a transaction. This will ensure that locks will be acquired in the correct order, and that no intervening action from another process will modify any rows that your operation is currently modifying.

SQL Dialect

Case sensitivity of LIKE operator

The `LIKE` operator is case-sensitive.

Table join syntax

Outer joins are supported using the `=*` (right outer join) and `*=` (left outer join) operators:

```
SELECT customers.customer_name, orders.order_date
FROM customers, orders
WHERE customers.cust_id =* orders.cust_id
```

For all rows in the customer's table that have no matching rows in the orders table, Sybase returns NULL for any select list expressions containing columns from the orders table.

Table and column names

The names of identifiers, such as tables and columns, cannot exceed thirty characters in length.

The first character must be an alphabetic character (as defined by the current server character set) or an underscore (_). Subsequent characters can be alphabetic, and may include currency symbols, @, #, and _. Identifiers can't include embedded spaces or the %, !, ^, *, or . symbols. In addition, identifiers must not be on the "reserved word" list (see the Sybase documentation for a complete list).

Table names or column names *may* be quoted if the `set quoted_identifier` option is turned on. This allows the user to get around the reserved word limitation. When this option is set, character strings enclosed in double quotes are treated as identifiers, and strings enclosed in single quotes are treated as literal strings.

By default identifiers are case-sensitive. This can be turned off by changing the default sort order for the server.

National characters can be used in identifier names without quoting.

Row ID

Sybase does not support a pseudo "row ID" column.

Automatic key or sequence generation

Sybase supports an `IDENTITY` feature for automatic key generation. Declaring a table with an `IDENTITY` column will generate a new value for each insert. The values assigned always increase but are not guaranteed to be sequential.

To fetch the value generated and used by the last insert, you can:

```
SELECT @@IDENTITY
```

Sybase does not support sequence generators, although ad hoc stored procedures to generate sequence numbers are quite easy to write.[*]

Automatic row numbering and row count limiting

Neither automatic row numbering nor row count limitations are supported.

Positioned updates and deletes

Sybase does not support positioned updates or deletes.

Parameter Binding

Parameter binding is directly suported by Sybase. However, there are two downsides that you should be aware of.

Firstly, `DBD::Sybase` creates an internal stored procedure for each **prepare()** call that includes ? style parameters. These stored procedures live in the *tempdb* database, and are only destroyed when the connection is closed. It is quite possible to run out of *tempdb* space if a lot of **prepare()** calls with placeholders are being made in a script.

Secondly, because all the temporary stored procedures are created in *tempdb*, this causes a potential hot spot due to the locking of system tables in *tempdb*. This performance problem may be removed in an upcoming release of Sybase (possibly 11.9.4 or 12.0).

---

[*] See *http://techinfo.sybase.com/css/techinfo.nsf/DocID/ID=860* for a complete explanation of the various possibilities.

The :1 placeholder style is not supported and the TYPE attribute to bind_ param() is currently ignored, so unsupported values don't generate a warning. Finally, trying to bind a TEXT or IMAGE datatype will fail.

Stored Procedures

Sybase stored procedures are written in Transact-SQL, which is Sybase's procedural extension to SQL.

Stored procedures are called exactly the same way as regular SQL, and can return the same types of results (i.e., a SELECT in the stored procedure can be retrieved with $sth->fetch()).

If the stored procedure returns data via OUTPUT parameters, then these must be declared first:

```
$sth = $dbh->prepare(qq[
    declare \@name varchar(50)
    exec getName 1234, \@name output
]);
```

Stored procedures can't be called with bind (?) parameters. So the following code would be illegal:

```
$sth = $dbh->prepare("exec my_proc ?");  # illegal
$sth->execute($foo);
```

Use this code instead:

```
$sth = $dbh->prepare("exec my_proc '$foo'");
$sth->execute();
```

Because Sybase stored procedures almost always return more than one result set, you should always make sure to use a loop until syb_more_results is 0:

```
do {
  while($data = $sth->fetch) {
    ...
  }
} while($sth->{syb_more_results});
```

Table Metadata

DBD::Sybase supports the table_info() method.

The syscolumns table has one row per column per table. See the definitions of the Sybase system tables for details. However, the easiest method to obtain table metadata is to use the sp_help stored procedure.

The easiest way to get detailed information about the indexes of a table is to use the sp_helpindex (or sp_helpkey) stored procedure.

Driver-Specific Attributes and Methods

DBD::Sybase has the following driver-specific database handle attributes:

syb_show_sql

> If set, then the current statement is included in the string returned by $dbh->errstr.

syb_show_eed

> If set, then extended error information is included in the string returned by $dbh->errstr. Extended error information includes the index causing a duplicate insert to fail, for example.

DBD::Sybase has the following driver-specific statement handle attributes:

syb_more_results

> Described elsewhere in this document.

syb_result_type

> Returns the numeric result type of the current result set. Useful when executing stored procedures to determine what type of information is currently fetchable (normal select rows, output parameters, status results, etc.).

One private method is provided:

_date_fmt

> Sets the default date conversion and display formats. See the description elsewhere in this document.

Other Significant Database or Driver Features

Sybase and DBD::Sybase allow multiple statements to be prepared with one call and then executed with one call. The results are fed back to the client as a stream of tabular data. Stored procedures can also return a stream of multiple data sets. Each distinct set of results is treated as a normal single result set, so fetch() returns undef at the end of each set. To see if there are more data sets to follow, the syb_more_results attribute can be checked. Here is a typical loop making use of this Sybase-specific feature:

```
do {
  while($d = $sth->fetch) {
    ... do something with the data
  }
} while($sth->{syb_more_results});
```

Sybase also has rich and powerful stored procedure and trigger functionality and encourages you to use them.

DBD::XBase

General Information

Driver version

DBD::XBase version 0.145

Feature summary

Transactions	No
Locking	No
Table joins	No
LONG/LOB datatypes	Yes, up to 2 GB
Statement handle attributes available	After execute()
Placeholders	Yes, "?" and ":1" styles (emulated)
Stored procedures	No
Bind output values	No
Table name letter case	Sensitive, stored as defined
Field name letter case	Insensitive, stored as uppercase
Quoting of otherwise invalid names	No
Case-insensitive "LIKE" operator	Yes, "LIKE"
Server table ROW ID pseudocolumn	No
Positioned update/delete	No
Concurrent use of multiple handles	Unrestricted

Author and contact details

The driver author is Jan Pazdziora. He can be contacted at *adelton@fi.muni.cz* or *via* the *dbi-users* mailing list.

Supported database versions and options

The DBD::XBase module supports dBaseIII and IV and Fox* flavors of *dbf* files, including their *dbt* and *fpt* memo files.

Very comprehensive information about the XBase format, along with many references, can be found at:

> *http://www.e-bachmann.dk/docs/xbase.htm*

Differences from the DBI specification

DBD::XBase does not fully parse the statement until it is executed. Thus attributes like $sth->{NUM_OF_FIELDS} are not available until after $sth->execute() has been called. This is valid behavior but is important to note when porting applications written originally for other drivers.

Connect Syntax

The `DBI->connect()` Data Source Name, or DSN, should include the directory where the *dbf* files are located as the third part:

```
dbi:XBase:/path/to/directory
```

It defaults to the current directory.

There are no driver-specific attributes for the `DBI->connect()` method.

`DBD::XBase` supports an unlimited number of concurrent database connections to one or more databases.

Datatypes

Numeric data handling

`DBD::XBase` supports generic `NUMBER(p,s)`, `FLOAT(p,s)`, and `INTEGER(l)` types. The maximum scale and precision is limited by Perl's handling of numbers. In the *dbf* files, the numbers are stored as ASCII strings, binary integers, or floats.

Existing *dbf* files come with the field types defined in the *dbf* file header. Numeric types can be either stored as ASCII string or in some binary format. `DBD::XBase` (via `XBase.pm`) parses this information and reads and writes the fields in that format.

When you create a new *dbf* file via `CREATE TABLE`, the numeric fields are always created in the traditional XBase way, as an ASCII string. (The `XBase.pm` module offers more control over this process.)

Numeric fields are always returned as Perl numeric values, not strings. Consequently, numbers outside of Perl's valid range are not possible. This restriction might be withdrawn in the future.

String data handling

`DBD::XBase` has `CHAR(length)` and `VARCHAR(length)` datatypes.

The maximum length is 65535 characters for both types.[*]

Both `CHAR` *and* `VARCHAR` are blank-padded, so `ChopBlanks` applies to both.

Data with the eighth bit set are handled transparently. No national language character set conversions are done. Since the string types can store binary data, Unicode strings can be stored.

---

[*] This limit is effective even though the older dBases allowed only 254 characters. Therefore, newly created *dbf* files might not be portable to older XBase-compatible software.

Date data handling

DBD::XBase supports these date and time types:

```
DATE
DATETIME
TIME
```

The DATE type holds an eight-character string in the format YYYYMMDD. Only that format can be used for input and output. DBD::XBase doesn't check for validity of the values.

The DATETIME and TIME types internally store a four-byte integer day value and a four-byte integer seconds value (counting 1/1000's of a second). DBD::XBase inputs and outputs these types using a floating-point Unix-style "seconds-since-epoch" value (possibly with decimal part). This might change in the future.

There is no way to get the current date/time, and no SQL date/time functions are supported. There is also no concept of time zones.

LONG/BLOB data handling

DBD::XBase supports a MEMO datatype. BLOB can be used as an alias for MEMO. Strings up to 2 GB can be stored in MEMO fields (for all types of XBase memo files).

With dBaseIII *dbt* files, the memo field cannot contain a 0x1A byte. With dBaseIV and Fox* dbt/fpts, any character values can be stored.

No special handling is required for fetching or inserting MEMO fields. The LongReadLen and LongTruncOk attributes are currently ignored.

Other data handling issues

The DBD::XBase driver supports the type_info() method.

DBD::XBase supports automatic conversions between datatypes wherever it's reasonable.

Transactions, Isolation, and Locking

DBD::XBase does not support transactions and does *not* lock the tables it is working on.

SQL Dialect

Case sensitivity of LIKE operator

The LIKE operator is *not* case-sensitive.

Table join syntax

DBD::XBase does not support table joins.

Table and column names

The XBase format stores each table as a distinct file. Memo fields are stored in an additional file. The table names are limited by the filesystem's maximum filename length. They are stored and treated as entered. The case-sensitivity depends on the filesystem that the file is stored on.

Column names are limited to eleven characters. They are stored as uppercase, but are not case-sensitive.

Table and field names have to start with letter. Any combination of letters, digits, and underscores may follow. National character sets can be used.

DBD::XBase does not support putting quotes around table or column names.

Row ID

DBD::XBase does not support a "row ID" pseudocolumn.

Automatic key or sequence generation

DBD::XBase does not support automatic key generation or sequence generators owing to the limitations of the XBase format.

Automatic row numbering and row count limiting

Neither automatic row numbering nor row count limitations are supported.

Positioned updates and deletes

DBD::XBase does not support positioned updates or deletes.

Parameter Binding

Parameter binding is implemented in the driver and supports the ?, :1, and :name placeholder styles.

The TYPE attribute to bind_param() is ignored. Consequently, unsupported values of the TYPE attribute do not currently generate a warning.

Stored Procedures

Stored procedures are not applicable in the XBase format.

Table Metadata

DBD::XBase supports the `table_info` method.

There is no way to get detailed information about the columns of a table (at the moment) other than by doing a SELECT * FROM table and using the NAME and TYPE attributes of the statement handle.

Keys and indexes are not currently supported.

Driver-Specific Attributes and Methods

DBD::XBase has just one driver-specific attribute and that is valid for both database and statement handles:

xbase_ignorememo

> Ignore memo files and thus don't fail to read a table where the memo file is missing or corrupt.

DBD::XBase has no generally useful private methods.

C

ASLaN Sacred Site Charter

If this book has piqued your interest in megalithic sites, please read the following charter outlining what is, and what isn't, respectable behavior at these sites. Many sites have been lost over the centuries due to vandalism and willful destruction. We would like to ensure that no more are lost for the same reasons.

In an effort to preserve our dwindling megalithic sites, the following requests are commonly included in literature that discusses megaliths. While a simple plea such as "Please don't trash megalithic sites" might be more appropriate for a book of this type, such a plea is, sadly, often ignored. We are including this document in the hopes that it will have more impact and impart a greater understanding of the issues involved.

We'd also like to draw your attention to the fact that many sites are in government care and, as such, any destructive behavior is *illegal*.

Doom and gloom aside, the sites are there to be enjoyed and have different meanings for different people. Enjoy!

- Please take care when visiting sacred sites to leave them as the next visitor would like to find them. Respect the land and all its inhabitants—people, animals, and plants.

- Digging holes for any purpose will damage plants and probably insects and archaeological remains. Damaging archaeology makes it harder for us, and future generations, to understand the history of the site. Damaging any aspect of the site will damage the spirit of the place.

- Lighting fires can cause similar damage to digging. A fire can damage standing stones—if they get too hot, they split. Fires can spread quickly in summer, killing wildlife, and it can be very difficult to make sure a fire is truly out. Fires also cause archaeological damage by preventing geophysical surveys and contaminating archaeological layers with ash and charcoal. Heat, candle wax, and graffiti damage moss and lichens, which can take decades to recover. Damage caused by fires will damage the spirit of the place.

- If an offering seems appropriate, please think about all its effects. Don't leave artificial materials. Choose your offerings carefully so that they can't be mistaken for litter. Please don't bury things. Biodegradable offerings decay— please bear this in mind if you leave them. If there are already offerings at the site, consider the effects of adding more.

- Please don't take anything, except litter, from a site. Much of the vegetation around sacred sites is unusual or rare, so don't pick flowers. Don't take stones —they may be an important part of the site in ways that aren't obvious.

- In times past, it was traditional to leave no traces of any ritual because of persecution. This tradition is worth reviving because it shows reverence to nature and the spirit of the place.

- Don't change the site; let the site change you.

ASLaN is the Ancient Sacred Landscape Network, formed to be a national focus for the preservation and protection of sacred sites and their settings, and maintenance of and access to them. More information on ASLaN can be found at:

> *http://www.symbolstone.org/archaeology/aslan*

Index

About the Authors

Alligator Descartes has been an itinerant fiddler with computers from a very early age, ruined only by obtaining a BSc in Computer Science from the University of Strathclyde, Glasgow. His computing credits include several years of Oracle DBA work, multi-user Virtual Reality servers, high-performance 3D graphics programming, and several Perl modules. His spare time is spent trudging around Scotland looking for stone circles and Pictish symbol stones to photograph.

Alligator Descartes is not his real name.

Tim Bunce developed and released the first version of the DBI and DBD::Oracle modules in 1994, just as Perl 5.000 was released. Since then, he has developed the DBI into the most popular database access technology for Perl.

Tim has been an active perl5-porter since 1994, contributing to the development of the Perl language and to many of its core modules such as DynaLoader, Make-Maker, and Exporter. He was responsible for building and releasing maintenance versions of Perl from 5.004_01 through to 5.004_04. He is also the author and co-maintainer of the Perl Module List.

Tim is the Technical Director of the Ingram Group, where he designs and develops large scale data processing, storage, and reporting applications in Perl. In 1998 he was recognized by British Telecom for his role in the launch of their Call Management Information service, a system implemented in Perl.

Colophon

Our look is the result of reader comments, our own experimentation, and feedback from distribution channels. Distinctive covers complement our distinctive approach to technical topics, breathing personality and life into potentially dry subjects.

The animal on the cover of *Programming the Perl DBI* is a cheetah (Acinonyx jubatus), one of the oldest big cats, dating back four million years.

The cheetah is the fastest land animal in the world, reaching speeds up to 70 miles per hour, powered by its long legs and lean body. Its body is tan with black spots, and, at a distance, it's hard to tell males from females. A cheetah grows to be approximately two and a half feet tall at the shoulder; it measures around four feet long, with a tail about two feet long. An adult weighs 90–130 pounds. The life span of the cheetah is about ten years.

A mother cheetah's litter includes four to five cubs, who stay with their mother for a year and a half. The young learn hunting and survival skills in that time. The cheetah hunts by stalking and chasing its prey, which includes antelope, gazelles, rabbits, and game birds.

The cheetah is now considered to be an endangered species, with only 10,000–12,000 alive today, living almost exclusively in the grasslands of Africa. That number is much lower than the estimated 100,000 in 1900. In fact, it is extinct in more than twenty of the countries it originally inhabited. The cheetah suffers from loss of both habitat and food, plus poaching. Conservation groups are working to help preserve the cheetah in its natural habitat and keep it from extinction.

Nicole Arigo was the production editor and copyeditor for this book. Madeleine Newell proofread the book. Melanie Wang, Sarah Jane Shangraw, and Jane Ellin provided quality control. Judy Hoer wrote the index.

Hanna Dyer designed the cover of this book, based on a series design by Edie Freedman. The cover image is a 19th-century engraving from the Dover Pictorial Archive. Kathleen Wilson produced the cover layout with QuarkXPress 4.04 using Adobe's ITC Garamond font. Alicia Cech designed the interior layout based on a series design by Nancy Priest. Mike Sierra implemented the design in FrameMaker 5.5. The text and heading fonts are ITC Garamond Light and Garamond Book. The illustrations that appear in the book were produced by Robert Romano using Macromedia FreeHand 8 and Adobe Photoshop 5. This colophon was written by Nicole Arigo.

Whenever possible, our books use RepKover™, a durable and flexible lay-flat binding. If the page count exceeds RepKover's limit, perfect binding is used.

Perl

Learning Perl, 2nd Edition

By Randal L. Schwartz & Tom Christiansen
Foreword by Larry Wall
2nd Edition July 1997
302 pages, ISBN 1-56592-284-0

In this update of a bestseller, two leading Perl trainers teach you to use the most universal scripting language in the age of the World Wide Web. Current for Perl version 5.004, this hands-on tutorial includes a lengthy chapter on CGI programming, while touching also on the use of library modules, references, and Perl's object-oriented constructs.

Learning Perl on Win32 Systems

By Randal L. Schwartz,
Erik Olson & Tom Christiansen
1st Edition August 1997
306 pages, ISBN 1-56592-324-3

In this carefully paced course, leading Perl trainers and a Windows NT practitioner teach you to program in the language that promises to emerge as the scripting language of choice on NT. Based on the "llama" book, this book features tips for PC users and new NT-specific examples, along with a foreword by Larry Wall, the creator of Perl, and Dick Hardt, the creator of Perl for Win32.

Learning Perl/Tk

By Nancy Walsh
1st Edition January 1999
376 pages, ISBN 1-56592-314-6

This tutorial for Perl/Tk, the extension to Perl for creating graphical user interfaces, shows how to use Perl/Tk to build graphical, event-driven applications for both Windows and UNIX. Rife with illustrations, it teaches how to implement and configure each Perl/Tk graphical element.

Mastering Regular Expressions

By Jeffrey E. F. Friedl
1st Edition January 1997
368 pages, ISBN 1-56592-257-3

Regular expressions, a powerful tool for manipulating text and data, are found in scripting languages, editors, programming environments, and specialized tools. In this book, author Jeffrey Friedl leads you through the steps of crafting a regular expression that gets the job done. He examines a variety of tools and uses them in an extensive array of examples, with a major focus on Perl.

Perl in a Nutshell

By Ellen Siever, Stephen Spainhour &
Nathan Patwardhan
1st Edition December 1998
674 pages, ISBN 1-56592-286-7

The perfect companion for working programmers, *Perl in a Nutshell* is a comprehensive reference guide to the world of Perl. It contains everything you need to know for all but the most obscure Perl questions. This wealth of information is packed into an efficient, extraordinarily usable format.

Perl Cookbook

By Tom Christiansen & Nathan Torkington
1st Edition August 1998
794 pages, ISBN 1-56592-243-3

The *Perl Cookbook* is a comprehensive collection of problems, solutions, and practical examples for anyone programming in Perl. You'll find hundreds of rigorously reviewed Perl "recipes" for manipulating strings, numbers, dates, arrays, and hashes; pattern matching and text substitutions; references, data structures, objects, and classes; signals and exceptions; and much more.

O'REILLY®

TO ORDER: **800-998-9938** • *order@oreilly.com* • *http://www.oreilly.com/*
OUR PRODUCTS ARE AVAILABLE AT A BOOKSTORE OR SOFTWARE STORE NEAR YOU.
FOR INFORMATION: **800-998-9938** • *707-829-0515* • *info@oreilly.com*

Perl

Mastering Algorithms with Perl

By Jon Orwant, Jarkko Hietaniemi &
John Macdonald
1st Edition August 1999
704 pages, ISBN 1-56592-398-7

There have been dozens of books on
programming algorithms, but never before
has there been one that uses Perl. Whether
you are an amateur programmer or know a
wide range of algorithms in other languages, this book will teach
you how to carry out traditional programming tasks in a high-
powered, efficient, easy-to-maintain manner with Perl. Topics range
in complexity from sorting and searching to statistical algorithms,
numerical analysis, and encryption.

Advanced Perl Programming

By Sriram Srinivasan
1st Edition August 1997
434 pages, ISBN 1-56592-220-4

This book covers complex techniques for
managing production-ready Perl programs
and explains methods for manipulating data
and objects that may have looked like magic
before. It gives you necessary background
for dealing with networks, databases, and GUIs, and includes a
discussion of internals to help you program more efficiently and
embed Perl within C or C within Perl.

The Perl CD Bookshelf

By O'Reilly & Associates, Inc.
1st Edition July 1999
ISBN 1-56592-462-2, Features CD-ROM

Perl programmer alert! Six bestselling
O'Reilly Animal Guides are now available
on CD-ROM, easily accessible with your
favorite Web browser: *Perl in a Nutshell;*
Programming Perl, 2nd Edition; Perl
Cookbook; Advanced Perl Programming;
Learning Perl; and *Learning Perl on Win32 Sytems*. As a bonus,
the new hard-copy version of *Perl in a Nutshell* is also included.

CGI Programming with Perl, 2nd Edition

By Shishir Gundavaram
2nd Edition June 2000 (est.)
450 pages (est.), ISBN 1-56592-419-3

Completely rewritten, this comprehensive
explanation of CGI for those who want to
provide their own Web servers features
Perl 5 techniques and shows how to use two
popular Perl modules, CGI.pm and CGI_lite.
It also covers speed-up techniques, such as FastCGI and mod_perl,
and new material on searching and indexing, security, generating
graphics through ImageMagick, database access through DBI,
Apache configuration, and combining CGI with JavaScript.

How to stay in touch with O'Reilly

1. Visit Our Award-Winning Web Site

http://www.oreilly.com/

★ "Top 100 Sites on the Web" —*PC Magazine*
★ "Top 5% Web sites" —*Point Communications*
★ "3-Star site" —*The McKinley Group*

Our web site contains a library of comprehensive product information (including book excerpts and tables of contents), downloadable software, background articles, interviews with technology leaders, links to relevant sites, book cover art, and more. File us in your Bookmarks or Hotlist!

2. Join Our Email Mailing Lists

New Product Releases

To receive automatic email with brief descriptions of all new O'Reilly products as they are released, send email to:
listproc@online.oreilly.com
Put the following information in the first line of your message (*not* in the Subject field):
subscribe oreilly-news

O'Reilly Events

If you'd also like us to send information about trade show events, special promotions, and other O'Reilly events, send email to:
listproc@online.oreilly.com
Put the following information in the first line of your message (*not* in the Subject field):
subscribe oreilly-events

3. Get Examples from Our Books via FTP

There are two ways to access an archive of example files from our books:

Regular FTP

* ftp to:
  ftp.oreilly.com
  (login: anonymous
  password: your email address)
* Point your web browser to:
  ftp://ftp.oreilly.com/

FTPMAIL

* Send an email message to:
  ftpmail@online.oreilly.com
  (Write "help" in the message body)

4. Contact Us via Email

order@oreilly.com
To place a book or software order online. Good for North American and international customers.

subscriptions@oreilly.com
To place an order for any of our newsletters or periodicals.

books@oreilly.com
General questions about any of our books.

software@oreilly.com
For general questions and product information about our software. Check out O'Reilly Software Online at **http://software.oreilly.com/** for software and technical support information. Registered O'Reilly software users send your questions to: **website-support@oreilly.com**

cs@oreilly.com
For answers to problems regarding your order or our products.

booktech@oreilly.com
For book content technical questions or corrections.

proposals@oreilly.com
To submit new book or software proposals to our editors and product managers.

international@oreilly.com
For information about our international distributors or translation queries. For a list of our distributors outside of North America check out:
http://www.oreilly.com/www/order/country.html

5. Work with Us

Check out our website for current employment opportunites:
www.jobs@oreilly.com
Click on "Work with Us"

O'Reilly & Associates, Inc.
101 Morris Street, Sebastopol, CA 95472 USA
TEL   707-829-0515 or 800-998-9938
          (6am to 5pm PST)
FAX   707-829-0104

International Distributors

UK, Europe, Middle East and Africa (except France, Germany, Austria, Switzerland, Luxembourg, Liechtenstein, and Eastern Europe)

INQUIRIES
O'Reilly UK Limited
4 Castle Street
Farnham
Surrey, GU9 7HS
United Kingdom
Telephone: 44-1252-711776
Fax: 44-1252-734211
Email: josette@oreilly.com

ORDERS
Wiley Distribution Services Ltd.
1 Oldlands Way
Bognor Regis
West Sussex PO22 9SA
United Kingdom
Telephone: 44-1243-779777
Fax: 44-1243-820250
Email: cs-books@wiley.co.uk

France

INQUIRIES
Éditions O'Reilly
18 rue Séguier
75006 Paris, France
Tel: 33-1-40-51-52-30
Fax: 33-1-40-51-52-31
Email: france@editions-oreilly.fr

ORDERS
GEODIF
61, Bd Saint-Germain
75240 Paris Cedex 05, France
Tel: 33-1-44-41-46-16 (French books)
Tel: 33-1-44-41-11-87 (English books)
Fax: 33-1-44-41-11-44
Email: distribution@eyrolles.com

Germany, Switzerland, Austria, Eastern Europe, Luxembourg, and Liechtenstein

INQUIRIES & ORDERS
O'Reilly Verlag
Balthasarstr. 81
D-50670 Köln
Germany
Telephone: 49-221-973160-91
Fax: 49-221-973160-8
Email: anfragen@oreilly.de (inquiries)
Email: order@oreilly.de (orders)

Canada (French language books)

Les Éditions Flammarion ltée
375, Avenue Laurier Ouest
Montréal (Québec) H2V 2K3
Tel: 00-1-514-277-8807
Fax: 00-1-514-278-2085
Email: info@flammarion.qc.ca

Hong Kong

City Discount Subscription Service, Ltd.
Unit D, 3rd Floor, Yan's Tower
27 Wong Chuk Hang Road
Aberdeen, Hong Kong
Tel: 852-2580-3539
Fax: 852-2580-6463
Email: citydis@ppn.com.hk

Korea

Hanbit Media, Inc.
Sonyoung Bldg. 202
Yeksam-dong 736-36
Kangnam-ku
Seoul, Korea
Tel: 822-554-9610
Fax: 822-556-0363
Email: hant93@chollian.dacom.co.kr

Philippines

Mutual Books, Inc.
429-D Shaw Boulevard
Mandaluyong City, Metro
Manila, Philippines
Tel: 632-725-7538
Fax: 632-721-3056
Email: mbikikog@mnl.sequel.net

Taiwan

O'Reilly Taiwan
No. 3, Lane 131
Hang-Chow South Road
Section 1, Taipei, Taiwan
Tel: 886-2-23968990
Fax: 886-2-23968916
Email: taiwan@oreilly.com

China

O'Reilly Beijing
Room 2410
160, FuXingMenNeiDaJie
XiCheng District
Beijing, China PR 100031
Tel: 86-10-66412305
Fax: 86-10-86631007
Email: beijing@oreilly.com

India

Computer Bookshop (India) Pvt. Ltd.
190 Dr. D.N. Road, Fort
Bombay 400 001 India
Tel: 91-22-207-0989
Fax: 91-22-262-3551
Email: cbsbom@giasbm01.vsnl.net.in

Japan

O'Reilly Japan, Inc.
Kiyoshige Building 2F
12-Bancho, Sanei-cho
Shinjuku-ku
Tokyo 160-0008 Japan
Tel: 81-3-3356-5227
Fax: 81-3-3356-5261
Email: japan@oreilly.com

All Other Asian Countries

O'Reilly & Associates, Inc.
101 Morris Street
Sebastopol, CA 95472 USA
Tel: 707-829-0515
Fax: 707-829-0104
Email: order@oreilly.com

Australia

WoodsLane Pty., Ltd.
7/5 Vuko Place
Warriewood NSW 2102
Australia
Tel: 61-2-9970-5111
Fax: 61-2-9970-5002
Email: info@woodslane.com.au

New Zealand

Woodslane New Zealand, Ltd.
21 Cooks Street (P.O. Box 575)
Waganui, New Zealand
Tel: 64-6-347-6543
Fax: 64-6-345-4840
Email: info@woodslane.com.au

Latin America

McGraw-Hill Interamericana
Editores, S.A. de C.V.
Cedro No. 512
Col. Atlampa
06450, Mexico, D.F.
Tel: 52-5-547-6777
Fax: 52-5-547-3336
Email: mcgraw-hill@infosel.net.mx